POLITICAL PHILOSOPHY

What is political philosophy? Ronald Beiner makes the case that it is centrally defined by supremely ambitious reflection on the ends of life. We pursue this reflection by exposing ourselves to, and participating in, a perennial dialogue among epic theorists who articulate grand visions of what constitutes the authentic good for human beings. Who are these epic theorists, and what are their strengths and weaknesses? Beiner selects a dozen leading candidates: Hannah Arendt, Michael Oakeshott, Leo Strauss, Karl Löwith, Eric Voegelin, Simone Weil, Hans-Georg Gadamer, Jürgen Habermas, Michel Foucault, Alasdair MacIntyre, John Rawls, and Richard Rorty. In each case, he shows both why the political philosophies continue to be intellectually compelling and why they are problematic or can be challenged in various ways. In this sense, *Political Philosophy: What It Is and Why It Matters* attempts to draw up a balance sheet of twentieth-century political philosophy by identifying a canon of towering contributions and reviewing the extent to which they fulfill their intellectual aspirations.

Ronald Beiner is a professor of political science at the University of Toronto and a Fellow of the Royal Society of Canada. He is the editor of Hannah Arendt's *Lectures on Kant's Political Philosophy* (1982) and the author of *Political Judgment* (1983); *What's the Matter with Liberalism?* (1992), which was awarded the Canadian Political Science Association's C. B. Macpherson Prize in 1994; *Philosophy in a Time of Lost Spirit* (1997); *Liberalism, Nationalism, Citizenship* (2003); and *Civil Religion* (Cambridge University Press, 2011).

Much of the best political philosophy in our time has been a running debate between critics of modernity and defenders of modernity. Charles Baudelaire, depicted in the sculpture by Raymond Duchamp-Villon on the cover, is generally credited with having coined the term modernity (*modernité*) in his famous essay, "The Painter of Modern Life."

POLITICAL PHILOSOPHY

What It Is and Why It Matters

RONALD BEINER
University of Toronto

CAMBRIDGE
UNIVERSITY PRESS

32 Avenue of the Americas, New York NY 10013-2473, USA

Cambridge University Press is part of the University of Cambridge.

It furthers the University's mission by disseminating knowledge in the pursuit of
education, learning and research at the highest international levels of excellence.

www.cambridge.org
Information on this title: www.cambridge.org/9781107680555

First published 2014

A catalogue record for this publication is available from the British Library

Library of Congress Cataloguing in Publication data
Beiner, Ronald, 1953–
Political philosophy : what it is and why it matters / Ronald Beiner.
pages   cm
Includes bibliographical references and index.
ISBN 978-1-107-06995-4 (hardback) – ISBN 978-1-107-68055-5 (paperback)
1. Political science – Philosophy.   I. Title.
JA71.B444   2014
320.01–dc23   2014002253

ISBN 978-1-107-06995-4 Hardback
ISBN 978-1-107-68055-5 Paperback

To Marcus, Mia, Zimra, and Gabriel

Contents

First Prologue: Horizons of Political Reflection

> We learn moral and political philosophy, and indeed any other part of philosophy, by studying the exemplars.
>
> John Rawls[1]

If John Rawls is right that "studying the exemplars" is essential to initiating ourselves into philosophy, including political philosophy, then we cannot avoid judgments about who the exemplars are. This book proposes twelve such exemplars; it tries to reflect on the state of political philosophy by testing the force of their respective philosophic visions and by pursuing a dialogue intended to encompass the author, the reader, and all twelve of these thinkers.[2] Machiavelli, in a famous letter, spoke of putting on "regal and courtly garments" and entering "the ancient courts of ancient men" in order to converse with privileged interlocutors.[3] Can we summon up a similar spirit in conversing with leading thinkers of the twentieth century?

As we discuss later, there is nothing neutral – nor could there be – about our selection of "classics." One could no doubt have a whole series of arguments about whether to add X or subtract Y, but all such (hypothetical) squabbles are more or less beside the point. For the time being, the reader will simply have to trust my judgment, pending my attempts in the following chapters to show why the twelve I have chosen are an interesting assemblage of thinkers, generating a worthwhile set of intramural debates and reciprocal challenges. Beyond the particular set of thinkers I have privileged,

---

[1] John Rawls, *Lectures on the History of Political Philosophy*, ed. Samuel Freeman (Cambridge, MA: Belknap Press, 2007), p. xiv.

[2] To quote Rawls again, "Political philosophy can only mean the tradition of political philosophy, and in a democracy this tradition is always the joint work of writers and of their readers. This work is joint, since it is writers and readers together who produce and cherish works of political philosophy over time" (ibid., p. 2).

[3] Niccolò Machiavelli, *The Prince*, trans. Harvey Mansfield, 2nd ed. (Chicago: University of Chicago Press, 1998), pp. 109–110.

ix

what matters is the idea of political philosophy as a dialogical enterprise conducted in relation to superlatively ambitious articulations of "the human good." Hence, even if other students of political philosophy would choose other exemplars, reconstructing a sustained dialogue among this particular group should serve to illustrate the intellectual potential of political philosophy conceived as such a dialogue, and help us begin the process of weighing to what extent political philosophy as it has been practiced over the last fifty or sixty years has fulfilled its aspirations or fallen short of them. Of course, it is not a tragedy if any particular political philosophy falls short of consummating its full aspirations, provided that the enterprise in general is and continues to be a meaningful and important one. My claim in this book is that it is.

As a means of initiation into the vocation of political philosophy, this book offers commentaries on twelve indispensable works of twentieth-century political philosophy: *The Human Condition* (1958) by Hannah Arendt (1906–1975); *On Human Conduct* (1975) by Michael Oakeshott (1901–1990); *Natural Right and History* (1953) by Leo Strauss (1899–1973); *Nature, History, and Existentialism* (1966) by Karl Löwith (1897–1973); *The New Science of Politics* (1952) by Eric Voegelin (1901–1985); *The Need for Roots* (1949) by Simone Weil (1909–1943); *Reason in the Age of Science* (1981) by Hans-Georg Gadamer (1900–2002); *The Philosophical Discourse of Modernity* (1985) by Jürgen Habermas (born 1929); *Discipline and Punish* (1975) by Michel Foucault (1926–1984); *After Virtue* (1981) by Alasdair MacIntyre (born 1929); *Political Liberalism* (1993) by John Rawls (1921–2002); and *Contingency, Irony, and Solidarity* (1989) by Richard Rorty (1931–2007).[4]

It goes without saying that our twelve authors wrote other famous books – and in some cases, books *more* famous than the ones I have selected. I do not proceed in every case by presenting a specific commentary on the chosen books. Rather, my idea is that each of these books articulates a distinct political philosophy, and my goal is to sketch an account of, *and offer critical engagement with*, each of these political philosophies (as well as,

---

[4] In each case (with the exception of the Gadamer book), I list dates for original publication in the languages in which these books were first published. *Reason in the Age of Science* is an exception because the English edition contains two essays beyond those published in the German book of the same title. All of these books were published during the authors' lifetimes, with the exception of *The Need for Roots*, which was published posthumously. If one looks more closely at the dates I have supplied, one can see that there was a brief period, extending roughly from 1967 (when Rorty published his first book) to 1973 (when Löwith and Strauss died), during which all of our theorists – with the obvious exception of Weil, who died very young – were simultaneously active on the intellectual scene.

to some extent, to sketch dialogue *between* these thinkers). I have sought to do this as efficiently as I can (subject to the space constraints that go with treating twelve ambitious thinkers within the compass of one book), whether by offering commentary on the books themselves or by drawing on other texts that help me encapsulate the political philosophies disclosed in these twelve books. Throughout, I have tried to put the toughest challenges to these thinkers that I can. My guiding philosophy has been that to do otherwise is a mode of condescending to these thinkers, which is the worst possible insult.

Just to underscore the "essential contestability" (to use a phrase from my intellectual youth) of political philosophy as an intellectual discipline, let me quote from one leading political philosopher, namely Brian Barry, as proof that there is no universal consensus on the part of theorists that all of these thinkers are practitioners of political philosophy in the proper sense. (The quotation is a lengthy one because, negatively, by providing a polemical foil, it defines the central purpose of this book in its entirety.) Barry starts by inserting himself into a debate between Iris Young and Bhikhu Parekh about "the history of political theory since 1945" and, in particular, about whether, during the 1950s and 1960s, political philosophy had fallen into a state of "decline or even death" from which it was rescued by the publication of John Rawls's *A Theory of Justice*, which, in one of these two competing views, brought the discipline back from the dead in 1971. Young and Barry endorse that narrative about death and rebirth; Parekh contests it. Here is Barry's account:

When Peter Laslett made the much-quoted assertion that "political philosophy is dead," he explained that what he had in mind was the absence of contributions to a line of thinkers in English that he took to run "from Hobbes to Bosanquet." Richard Tuck has recently written on similar lines of "the absence of major works of political philosophy, of a more or less familiar kind, between Sidgwick and Rawls." Whichever late Victorian we take as the last in the line, nothing that Parekh says seems to me to impugn the claim that nobody until Rawls produced anything that represented a continuation of the canon of political thought, as traditionally conceived. Parekh's description of the writers whose work he celebrates as gurus, and his remark that they generated disciples rather than critics, suggest that they might most aptly be thought of as the purveyors of secular religion. And, indeed, it might be said of their writings that [in Hobbes's words] "it is with the mysteries of our Religion, as with wholesome pills for the sick, which swallowed whole, have the virtue to cure; but chewed, are for the most part cast up again without effect." There was not much of a structure of argument to get your teeth stuck into. Either you found the vision of life attractive or not; either way there was little point in trying to take it apart. What Rawls reintroduced with *A Theory of Justice* was political philosophy that could be chewed in the same way as the canonical books could be (and continued to be throughout the ascendency of the gurus). Parekh notes the vitality of the subject today but attributes this simply to "changes in the intellectual climate." This misses the point that it is precisely the virtues of *A Theory of Justice* – above all its systematic argumentative quality – that created this climate. Perhaps in a counterfactual world in which *A Theory of Justice* did not exist, something else would have taken its place; but there is no doubt that in the actual world it is Rawls who deserves the credit. Parekh suggests that Rawls owed it to the gurus that he was able to put forward a theory that was "critical in nature, universal in scope, and quasi-foundational in orientation." I can see no basis for this claim. The index to *A Theory of Justice* does not contain entries for Arendt, Oakeshott, Popper, Strauss, or Voegelin.[5] The entries that are large enough to have subheads are for Aristotle, Bentham, Edgeworth, Hume, Kant, Mill, and Sidgwick. The obvious inference is that Rawls saw himself as engaged in the same kind of activity as them, and carried on where they left off. More specifically, Rawls orientated himself to the two major liberal political theories of the past two centuries: Kantianism and utilitarianism. Rawls's critics in turn have tended to be inspired (if at some distance) by Hegel. The post-Rawlsian debate has connected directly to the canon, bypassing the gurus.[6]

For me, the challenge posed by Barry in this polemical piece of writing is supplemented by a conversation I had with him a number of years before he published the *Handbook* article. The conversation took place in the kitchen of our mutual friend, Liam O'Sullivan. We somehow got into a discussion of the state of political philosophy as an intellectual discipline, and I guess I displayed a bit more youthful exuberance than Barry thought the state of the discipline warranted (I was in my late twenties at the time). He said that the various research programs – this is what he called them: the Arendtian research program, the Habermasian research program, the Straussian research program, and so on – had all reached a dead end, had exhausted their possibilities. (If I had had this conversation with Barry subsequent to the publication of *Political Liberalism*, he would no doubt have said that the *Rawlsian*

---

[5] It may be worth pointing out that two of these thinkers (Arendt and Oakeshott) *are* in the index of *Political Liberalism*.

[6] Brian Barry, "Political Theory, Old and New," in *A New Handbook of Political Science*, ed. Robert E. Goodin and Hans-Dieter Klingemann (Oxford: Oxford University Press, 1996), pp. 537–538. I have deleted Barry's parenthetical references and folded four paragraphs into one. In note 7 on page 537, Barry informs the reader that he has a more favorable judgment of Isaiah Berlin than of the "gurus" he disdains. Later in this prologue, I explain why my judgment is the reverse of Barry's.

Presumably, part of the reason why Barry is so dismissive of the "gurus" is because (as he sees it) they consider themselves qualified to pontificate about favored visions of life. That is, he thinks that deciding what life is about should be done by individuals *on their own behalf*, rather than by philosophers presuming to reflect grandly on the purposes of life on behalf of everyone else. However, this view of Barry's itself is (or implies) a philosophy of life, as Barry himself elsewhere acknowledges.

research program had also reached a dead end.[7]) Looking back on that conversation today, I cannot help but wonder whether my more hopeful view of the discipline and its intellectual achievements *was* just a product of youth, and whether it can survive more rigorous critical scrutiny at a later (less credulous) stage of life.[8] With luck, writing this book will help respond to such worries.

But let me offer one further set of reflections before we part company with Brian Barry. It has to do with Barry's assertion that many of the thinkers who I am trying to take seriously in this book fall short of providing a genuine "structure of argument" capable of being chewed intellectually. In response, I would suggest that works of theory, not so different from novels, are a way of articulating the lessons of life. Let's say that both novels and ambitious works of theory are crystallizations of wisdom, so to speak. It is not a question of mobilizing rationally binding arguments for the simple reason that human beings are not that easy to convince. They will typically have their own counterarguments, digging in their heels rather than deferring to Reason. "Arguments are a dime a dozen," as Gadamer once put it, glossing Hegel.[9] (I don't endorse that particular formulation, which to my ear sounds too cynical, but I have some sympathy with the spirit of philosophizing that it is meant to evoke.) I believe that Iris Murdoch was right in claiming that philosophy and literature are much more closely aligned than they are generally thought to be.[10] That is, one is off the mark if one casts one as cognitive and the other as noncognitive (or worse, both as non-cognitive, as the postmodernists characteristically treat them). Both are cognitive, but cognitive in a particular way – as I put it earlier, as crystallizations of wisdom rather than as strictly a deployment of cold argumentative reason. This does not mean, of course, that arguments are irrelevant; it just

---

[7] See in particular Barry's hostile references to the post-*Political Liberalism* Rawls in *Culture and Equality* (Cambridge: Polity Press, 2001).

[8] Kurt Andersen, in a review of an edition of Kurt Vonnegut letters in *The New York Times Book Review* (October 28, 2012, p. 27), asks himself why Vonnegut's later novels had nothing like the effect on him exercised by those he read in his youth: "because the '60s were over? Because I was no longer an adolescent?" One's relationship to political philosophers whom one first read in one's youth raises similar questions. Obviously, I am not *asserting* that an intellectual commitment to the importance of these thinkers is reducible to something like mere youthful enthusiasm, but posing this question as a genuine question provokes one to reread them in a way that does not in any way give them the benefit of the doubt.

[9] Hans-Georg Gadamer, *Philosophical Apprenticeships*, trans. Robert R. Sullivan (Cambridge, MA: MIT Press, 1985), p. 43.

[10] "Philosophy and Literature: Dialogue with Iris Murdoch," in *Men of Ideas*, ed. Bryan Magee (Oxford: Oxford University Press, 1982), pp. 262–284. A video of the dialogue can be watched on YouTube.

means that one can recognize something as good theory even if the supporting arguments fall short (as they generally do).

As flagged at the start, I cannot pretend that the twelve philosophers covered in this survey constitute a comprehensive sampling of those who have shaped twentieth-century political philosophy. Without question, there are important thinkers who have been left out, and my own selection is certainly open to challenge. One immediately notices two giants who are missing: Alexandre Kojève and Carl Schmitt. An even more towering twentieth-century philosopher, Martin Heidegger, is a looming presence in the thought of Arendt, Gadamer, Löwith, Rorty, and to some extent Strauss, but Heidegger himself (insofar as there is something corresponding to a political philosophy in his *œuvre*) is not included. Readers may complain (perhaps justifiably) that conservatives such as Oakeshott, Strauss, and Voegelin are overrepresented whereas twentieth-century neo-Marxism is woefully underrepresented. Hence Georg Lukács, another giant, is also missing. The Frankfurt School is represented only by Habermas, in whom the traces of his Frankfurt School roots have become more and more faint as his mature political philosophy has developed over time. Thus major figures such as Max Horkheimer, Theodor Adorno, Walter Benjamin, and Herbert Marcuse have also been slighted.

The political balance among our twelve theorists is a bit more evenly distributed than may be evident at first glance. Three of these theorists – Oakeshott, Strauss, and Voegelin – are fairly clearly on the Right; two – Rawls and Rorty – are liberals; three – Habermas, Foucault, and MacIntyre – are fairly clearly on the Left, though they represent radically different versions of egalitarian politics.[11] Simone Weil is on the Left as well, although T.S. Eliot was right to highlight the difficulty of fitting Weil into conventional political categories when he wrote: "in her political thinking [Weil] appears as a stern critic of both Right and Left; at the same time more truly a lover of order and hierarchy than most of those who call themselves Conservative, and more truly a lover of the people than most of those who call themselves Socialist."[12]

---

[11] As regards Habermas, though, Perry Anderson (*Spectrum: From Right to Left in the World of Ideas* [London: Verson, 2005], p. xv) has made the not unreasonable point that he belongs alongside Rawls among leading "figures of the Centre [since] the ideal that unites the domestic political theory of their later work [is] 'consensus.' If this is not a quintessential value of the Centre, it is difficult to know what would be."

[12] Simone Weil, *The Need for Roots*, trans. Arthur Wills (London: Routledge, 2002), p. x (Preface by T.S. Eliot). Cf. Iris Murdoch, *Existentialists and Mystics*, ed. Peter Conradi (London: Chatto and Windus, 1997), p. 159: "Considering [Weil], our political categories break down."

Hannah Arendt is even harder to categorize on a Right/Left spectrum, as she herself acknowledged.[13] Löwith and Gadamer are also hard to classify politically with any confidence.[14] But it goes without saying that at a certain level of philosophical reflection, labels like liberal, conservative, and radical are intellectually worthless.[15]

The only communitarian I have included is Alasdair MacIntyre, to the exclusion of Charles Taylor, Michael Walzer, and Michael Sandel.[16] John Dewey is a leading twentieth-century liberal (albeit a communitarian liberal) who has been left out. There are no existentialists, such as Jean-Paul Sartre and Albert Camus, included in this book (except insofar as one regards the political philosophy of Max Weber, treated in our second prologue, as an anticipation of existentialism). Postmodernism is represented by one liberal, Richard Rorty, and one antiliberal, Michel Foucault, leaving out Jacques Derrida. Nor have I included other radical European theorists such as Slavoj Žižek, Giorgio Agamben, Jacques Rancière, and Alain Badiou; I have also omitted Roberto Mangabeira Unger, for whom there was once a considerable vogue. Finally, I have left out Isaiah Berlin (who, in common with some of the thinkers I have included, used his studies in the history of ideas in order to transmit a political philosophy).

It may be instructive to say some things about the last political theorist in this list of non-included thinkers, namely Isaiah Berlin, in order to help the

---

[13] *Hannah Arendt: The Recovery of the Public World*, ed. Melvyn A. Hill (New York: St. Martin's Press, 1979), pp. 333–334.

[14] Raymond Geuss has described Gadamer as "a reactionary, distended windbag" ("Richard Rorty at Princeton: Personal Recollections," *Arion*, Vol. 15, no. 3 [Winter 2008], p. 86), but this hardly seems a fair or judicious verdict. Gadamer consistently refers to himself as a liberal. See, for instance, *Hans-Georg Gadamer on Education, Poetry, and History*, ed. Dieter Misgeld and Graeme Nicholson (Albany, NY: SUNY Press, 1992), p. 140; and *Gadamer in Conversation*, ed. Richard E. Palmer (New Haven, CT: Yale University Press, 2001), p. 120. Heidegger, in an angry denunciation of Löwith, claimed that the early Löwith had been "the reddest Marxist" (letter to Elisabeth Blochmann quoted in Richard Wolin, *Heidegger's Children* [Princeton, NJ: Princeton University Press, 2001], p. 97), but whether true or not, this tells us no more about the mature Löwith than Strauss's early self-description as pro-fascist ("Letter to Karl Löwith," *Constellations*, Vol. 16, no. 1 [2009], p. 82) tells us about the mature Strauss.

[15] Cf. Eric Voegelin, *Autobiographical Reflections*, ed. Ellis Sandoz (Baton Rouge: Louisiana State University Press, 1989), p. 46. Gadamer (*Truth and Method*, 2nd rev. ed. [New York: Continuum, 1998], p. 532) called Leo Strauss not a conservative thinker but a radical thinker (*ein so radikaler Kritiker*). Before dismissing Gadamer's description of Strauss, one should consider that Strauss presented his fundamental insight as analogous to a "bomb" that he would eventually detonate (*The Cambridge Companion to Leo Strauss*, ed. Steven B. Smith [Cambridge: Cambridge University Press, 2009], p. 64). Now, admittedly, the adjective "radical" can mean all kinds of things, and Strauss's self-image as a bomb-thrower probably was not what Gadamer had in mind in calling Strauss radical. Still, it underscores the point that Strauss was by no means a conventional conservative.

[16] However, I offer a brief treatment of these other communitarians in the excursus following the MacIntyre chapter.

reader get a clearer sense of why the thinkers we have chosen were chosen while Berlin was not. One can define the theory tradition from Plato
onward as a dialogue between rival conceptions of the good. One can only
participate in this tradition in a meaningful way if one is committed to some
particular determinate view of the ends of life (even if one does not *think*
that one is so committed or theorizes it in terms other than "conceptions
of the good"). I could go through the whole theory tradition, from Plato
to Nietzsche, and discuss the various conceptions of the good articulated
within that great sequence of epic thinkers. Instead I will just comment
briefly on the thinkers I take to be the four most influential political philosophers of the last fifty years (Berlin is not in this group, for reasons I hope
to clarify).

Let's start with a thinker for whom Berlin had limited intellectual respect:
Hannah Arendt. Arendt was committed to a very robust conception of the
good, even though she was never willing to call it that, and would probably have resisted if someone like me had invoked this vocabulary on her
behalf. Arendt was committed to a conception of the human being as a
"civic animal": speaking great words, performing great deeds, and shining
in the glorious light of the public.[17] For Arendt this was what potentially
imbued human existence with its central meaningfulness, and she tended to
presume that the problem of human meaning would be impossible to solve
without it. This was a powerful conception of human life when it was first
articulated in Aristotle's *Politics*[18] and when it was developed in the Italian
Renaissance and it remains a powerful conception today. Perhaps Arendt
was going too far in thinking that it could function as a *comprehensive* purpose in human life (Berlin would certainly have pushed this challenge very

---

[17] The question naturally arises, why do people who are obviously already leading quite interesting
and productive lives as, say, intellectuals get tempted onto the public stage, (Gore Vidal, Vaclav Havel,
Charles Taylor, and Michael Ignatieff are a few examples that come to mind)? For that matter, one
could ask the same question about Barack Obama – clearly an individual with large talents who
did not have to choose politics as the outlet for those talents. Why does politics in particular typically appeal to super-talented or super-ambitious individuals as, so to speak, the preferred vehicle of
supreme ambition (sometimes with quite unhappy results)? Arendt, much more than the other thinkers in this book, promises a possible explanation. Of course, one does not necessarily have to opt for an
Arendtian account, but one needs *some* account comparable to the one that Arendt supplied in order
to answer such questions. That is, there has to be a picture of the conditions of a fully flourishing life,
and some idea of politics as fulfilling those conditions, such that people would be willing to drop or
suspend their otherwise successful lives and take on all the enormous risks and potential grief of a fully
political life.

[18] Clearly, this is not intended to suggest that there is a seamless continuity between Aristotle's idea of
politics and Hannah Arendt's. As will be discussed in the Hannah Arendt chapter, the philosophical
differences between Arendt and Aristotle are very important ones.

hard indeed), but it can by no means be dismissed as a *candidate* among the various rival conceptions of the good. As I just mentioned, Arendt would not have accepted the vocabulary I am applying to her political philosophy, but my own view is that this very vocabulary helps decisively to explain why that political philosophy was received so seriously and why it continues to receive serious attention from a great many theorists.

Although John Rawls himself insists that his political philosophy presumes a "priority of the right to the good," it is possible to speak of a Rawlsian conception of the good, namely setting up and committing oneself to basic political institutions that are fair and just. This is a liberalized version of the conception of human beings as civic animals. Rawls, too, did not want to call this a conception of the good (in fact, *none* of the four thinkers I cite did![19]); yet I think it yields a more coherent account of his political philosophy, just as it yields a more coherent account of Arendt's political philosophy. The ultimate human vocation is moral reciprocity, and citizenship is a crucial aspect of a morally well-developed human life because it provides a privileged locus for this practice of moral reciprocity. We create civic institutions and share practices of mutual provision in order to satisfy the high human purpose of living in a just society.

One might think of Jürgen Habermas as a cross between Arendt and Rawls. He certainly wants a less heroic conception of political life than Arendt offers, but wants more of the pathos of publicity and sharing of a public realm than one can squeeze out of Rawls. What Habermas does is basically drop Arendt's emphasis on "performativity" and play up the idea of public discourse. Habermas's civic animal is a *talking* animal, and it is in the exchange of reasonable opinions that human beings vindicate their political nature.

And lastly, Michel Foucault. The term I have used to encapsulate Foucault's political philosophy is "hyper-liberalism."[20] Unlike standard liberals, Foucault does not think that it is the state alone (with its network of state agencies and state bureaucracies) that is trying to shoehorn us into truncated categories that do violence to our unlimited self-defined identities; the same assertion of power is also associated with schools, factories, hospitals, prisons, and countless other agencies of social "normalization." Power is everywhere,

---

[19] Jeremy Waldron, in a review of Michael Sandel's *What Money Can't Buy* (*The New York Review of Books,* August 16, 2012), remarks that he welcomes Sandel's book because Sandel is "less coy" about his views concerning the ends of life than many or most political philosophers today typically are. Well, one has to ask: why *would* political philosophers be coy about their conceptions of human flourishing? This surely tells us something significant about the state of intellectual life in the present day.

[20] See Ronald Beiner, *Philosophy in a Time of Lost Spirit* (Toronto: University of Toronto, 1997), chapter 9.

and therefore resistance must be everywhere; the omnipresence of power requires the omnipresence of resistance. Foucault would certainly never use the vocabulary of conceptions of the good, which he would see as a "normalizing" discourse par excellence, but I will take it upon myself to say that his conception of the good is: resistance to normalization.[21]

There are various other important political philosophers of the last half-century whom one could discuss in a similar vein (including the other eight thinkers included in this book). Again, let's consider Isaiah Berlin in relation to this idea of political philosophy as a dialogue among conceptions of the good. What is *Berlin's* conception of the good? It consists in an awareness that there is no one definitive conception of the good. Life is a kaleidoscope, and it should be lived in the awareness of a *multiplicity* of worthy ends, a pluralism of the good. The great false seduction of the theory tradition is the idea of a *single* good, the idea of a unitary human telos. The tradition that Plato spawned is inhabited by monistic "hedgehogs" rather than pluralistic "foxes." There is obviously a great deal of truth in this Berlinian insistence on pluralism, but, let's face it, it does not have the drama, the compellingness, the eros, of some actual philosophical claim about *the* nature of the good. There is something *deflating* about Berlin's idea of theory, relative to the four theorists I have discussed, and also relative to the 2,500-year-old tradition that precedes them. The suggestion that human ends are many and no one end is definitive may be true, but it seems a disappointing way to continue the dialogue that Plato began. One cannot pursue a conversation by saying that all points of view contribute to the kaleidoscope of human life (even if that happens to be true!); one can only keep a conversation going by embracing some *particular* point of view and arguing *as if* it expressed some ultimate and authoritative view of life.

My colleague Joe Carens has pressed me forcefully on this point: If Berlin's view concerning moral pluralism happens to be the correct one (and there are plausible reasons to consider it such), the whole debate concerning *the* valid conception of the human good is fatuous, and we should in effect let the debate between the thinkers in this book simply lapse. Truth is truth, and if moral pluralism is the truth, there is no point pursuing a contest

---

[21] Some of the other thinkers included in this book, for instance Leo Strauss and Alasdair MacIntyre, are more open to the vocabulary of conceptions of the good – MacIntyre explicitly so – and therefore, in the case of these thinkers, one does not have to go to the trouble of translating into this vocabulary conceptions of political philosophy that are themselves averse to this vocabulary. Still, it surely tells us something quite significant about the contemporary intellectual situation that so many philosophers are so resistant to a vocabulary that (according to my account at least) is central to what makes political philosophy political philosophy.

between non-pluralists. I have two counter-arguments to Carens's challenge, though I cannot be certain that either is sufficient for the purpose. The first is an anti-neutrality argument. One may flatter oneself that one is being neutral between competing conceptions of the good, but willy-nilly all human beings (including theorists) find themselves gravitating toward *privileged* conceptions of the good. Suspending ourselves above the fray just does not seem to work, humanly speaking. This is an argument deployed recurringly through many of the succeeding chapters of this book. The second argument runs like this: As human beings, we have a *dual* interest in the debate about the human good that the tradition of political philosophy makes available. We have an interest in the truth, of course, and it may be that moral pluralism is true, but we also have an interest in sparking intellectual vitality, in keeping ourselves intellectually engaged and awake, in sustaining and enlivening the human conversation as a genuine debate among living alternatives. To have a coherent conversation, we need robust alternatives. This is similar to Mill's argument on behalf of intellectual liberty. And I am not convinced that a lazy affirmation of moral pluralism will fit the bill ("lazy" because if one knows in advance, or thinks one knows, that no singular normative vision will be able to vindicate itself intellectually, there is no point exerting oneself to articulate such an encompassing normative vision, nor is there a point in exerting oneself to mount intellectual challenges to rival normative visions). If all the alternatives are presumed to have equal validity, the human conversation goes stale. Yes, there are different ways to be human, but as human beings we cannot help wanting to know *which* ways of being human diminish or truncate human experience and which ways allow us to flourish to the utmost. The fact is, reflection in this vein requires that we participate in a dialogue on the human good, rather than merely contemplating the diversity of ways of being human.

Going back to Isaiah Berlin, let me add that I do not think it is an accident that he never wrote a real "treatise" articulating the main themes of his work – on a par with Arendt's *The Human Condition* or Strauss's *Natural Right and History* or Voegelin's *The New Science of Politics* or Rawls's *A Theory of Justice* or Oakeshott's *On Human Conduct*. I think Berlin was averse to this sort of thing because it meant focusing on "one big idea," which he associated with "monism"[22] – the great vice, in his view, of the whole theory

---

[22] It is telling that Berlin, who received APSA's Benjamin E. Lippincott Award in 1984, in contrast with the two dozen other winners of this award, won it strictly for his various essays, not for any particular book.

tradition. Well, again, one might ask whether theory can exist at all without monism in this sense, whether one can have philosophers or an interesting philosophical tradition *without* thinkers obsessed by "one big idea." I would be inclined to say that there is something "post-philosophical" in Berlin's aversion to what he calls monism: his impulse to give equal weight to the full multiplicity of human ends (while a credit to the liberal spirit to which he gave expression) makes it hard to relate to the philosophical tradition as anything other than a *completed* tradition, a tradition we look back upon with retrospective appreciation but one we do not participate in with our own fairly grand epic ideas. In order to have a theory tradition at all, as a dialogue between epic theorists and epic theories, one needs these "monists" with their overwhelming will to articulate single grand thoughts (the idea of justice in the soul for Plato or civic self-rule for Machiavelli and Rousseau or sovereignty for Hobbes or self-legislated duty for Kant or history as the march of liberty for Hegel or class-based emancipation for Marx or nobility and slavishness for Nietzsche and so on). What Berlin was saying with his critique of monism is that he was prepared to study the history of ideas as an intellectual tradition composed of interesting monomaniacs, but that he did not want to *add* to that tradition with some monomaniacal conception of his own (although there is something *slightly* monomaniacal about his obsession with monism). One can ask: how are we in a position to appreciate the full multiplicity of human ends unless "monist" thinkers have succeeded in articulating each of these ends in turn as possessing all-encompassing normative authority?

There is one further point to be made (or maybe it is just another way of formulating the point I have already made). I do not think it requires very much reflection to see why pluralism as a philosophical outlook is *parasitic upon* non-pluralistic philosophies of the good. Pluralism, it should be evident, could not be possible unless philosophers throughout history had exerted themselves to articulate *particular* conceptions of the good in opposition to rival conceptions of the good articulated by rival philosophies. Philosophical pluralism *presupposes* these particular conceptions of the good and pronounces the intellectual rivalry between them ultimately untranscendable: incapable of being intellectually adjudicated. This is the reason (or another way of formulating the reason) why "value-pluralism" is less compelling philosophically than the *particular* philosophical monisms that it claims to encompass and surpass. (What I mean by "less compelling" is that what interests us in the activity of philosophy is to see how far we can go intellectually with some particular vision of the human good. Epic theory does what Flaubert suggested all great art does: it "pursue[s] an idea to its furthermost limits."[23] To be told in advance that *no* vision of the good can in principle vindicate itself in relation to its rivals turns the whole enterprise of philosophy into an exercise in futility. Why should that be interesting to philosophers?)

In short, we should be *grateful* to the monists. The history of political philosophy without the Platos, Rousseaus, Marxs, and Nietzsches would be a much less interesting intellectual tradition than the one we actually have.[24] Berlin never properly acknowledges this, though one might say that it is implicitly acknowledged in Berlin's own intellectual fascination with thinkers who inhabit the extremities, such as Hamann and Maistre. One could make the related point that Berlin's Machiavelli, the "value-pluralist" Machiavelli, is far less interesting than the Machiavelli who embraces a robust commitment to a definite view of how human beings can realize their full humanity (even if the ideal itself is morally problematic).[25] The point I am making can be re-articulated in a way that is perhaps to Berlin's credit (if not as a political philosopher then at least as a citizen): One might hypothesize that Berlin was so appalled by the totalitarian adventures of the twentieth century that he was willing to see political philosophy become philosophically much less interesting as a trade-off for it ceasing to contribute to totalitarian adventures in the future.[26]

Above all, one must ask oneself why political philosophy exists at all. The answer is: political philosophy exists in order to confront human beings with a range of the most intellectually ambitious accounts of the standard

---

[23] Quoted in Philip Roth, *My Life as a Man* (New York: Vintage Books, 1993), p. 241.

[24] Cf. John Stuart Mill's discussion of "one-eyed men" as cited in Beiner, *Philosophy in a Time of Lost Spirit*, p. x. The reference comes from Mill's essay on "Bentham": John Stuart Mill, *On Bentham and Coleridge* (New York: Harper & Brothers, 1962), p. 65.

[25] See Isaiah Berlin, *The Crooked Timber of Humanity*, ed. Henry Hardy (New York: Vintage Books, 1992), p. 8: Machiavelli "merely points out that the two moralities [viz., pagan morality and Christian morality] are incompatible, and he does not recognize any overarching criterion whereby we are enabled to decide the right life for men." Cf. Ramin Jahanbegloo, *Conversations with Isaiah Berlin* (London: Peter Halban, 1992), pp. 53–54. See Perry Anderson, "England's Isaiah," *London Review of Books*, 20 December, 1990, p. 3, for a judgment similar to mine about how Berlin's pluralism yields a fairly insipid reading of Machiavelli.

[26] I do not think it requires that much discernment to see that the problems in Isaiah Berlin's political theory that concern us in this discussion – namely the affirmation of value pluralism as a kind of concession in advance of the impossibility of political philosophy – are fully anticipated (probably in a philosophically deeper, more *Angst*-inflected form) in the theorizing of Max Weber. (However, consider the interesting contrast between Berlin and Weber offered in Anderson, "England's Isaiah," p. 6.) Weber's thought provides what one may regard as a "base line" for the assessment of twentieth-century political philosophy. Our discussion of Weber's more "existentialist" version of value pluralism in the second part of the second prologue should make clear what we mean by this.

by which to judge what makes a human life consummately human – for instance, Hannah Arendt's breathtakingly bold claim that political action furnishes the ultimate existential anchor for a properly meaning-infused human life. And the Berlinian insistence that all such claims ought to shrink themselves down to the point where they are consistent with the truth of moral pluralism seems, by contrast, too lame to be able to sustain political philosophy as the fully robust intellectual enterprise it ought to be. To use Rawlsian vocabulary, "perfectionist" political philosophies cannot avoid committing the great anti-liberal sin of telling human beings how to be human. Anti-perfectionist or non-perfectionist political philosophies, by contrast, are fundamentally oriented to moral pluralism and deliberately limit their philosophical ambitions to articulating principles that will encourage respect for diversity and difference.[27] But how can we *reflect* on what it is to be human unless perfectionist theories are presumptuous enough to confront us with singular (that is, non-pluralist) images of a consummated humanity? That is the guiding question that this book seeks to pose by canvassing "the exemplars."

In order to develop the idea of political philosophy as I understand it, I need to say a few things about the term "horizon" as it figures in the title of this prologue. My idea of political philosophy is captured quite well by John Rawls's idea of a "comprehensive doctrine." The idea is one of enlarging one's lines of philosophic vision – in ever-expanding concentric circles, so to speak – until they constitute a *total* horizon of moral, social, and political existence in its normative dimensions; until one has an *all-encompassing* philosophy of human existence – an authoritative view of what it is to be human or, better, of what it is to be *fully* human. But, of course, for Rawls himself (as I discuss in the Rawls chapter), basing political philosophy on "comprehensive doctrines" (philosophies of life or of the meaning of existence) was something to be rigorously *avoided!* Rawls's worry was that if political philosophy was oriented toward fundamental philosophies of life, people would get fixated on existential disagreements that could never be adjudicated (for example, whether human beings have souls, whether there is a Creator; how one achieves salvation; whether fetuses are persons, etc.),

---

[27] For a very good recent example of a political philosophy that fundamentally privileges moral pluralism, see Samuel Fleischacker, *What is Enlightenment?* (Abingdon, UK: Routledge, 2013). As Fleischacker makes explicit in the preface to another of his books (*A Third Concept of Liberty* [Princeton, NJ: Princeton University Press, 1999], pp. x–xi), his preoccupation with pluralism has been decisively influenced by the thought of Isaiah Berlin.

and we would lose the minimum degree of shared ground that we need in order to uphold an experience of common citizenship. Rawls's conception, one could say, was that political philosophy had to *cease* being political philosophy (for the sake of preserving liberal citizenship). Again, I discuss all this in the Rawls chapter. For now, I can simply point out that if the Rawlsian idea of political philosophy wins out, then political philosophy ceases to be what I want to insist that it *has* to be, namely, the privileged intellectual space wherein human beings reflect, *in the most comprehensive way*, on what it is to be human.

Here is another formulation of the same point: One can say that there is an odd paradox here: Rawls is included in this book, which means that I consider him to be one of the exemplary political philosophers of our time. That in turn means that he offers us a comprehensive doctrine, but his comprehensive doctrine consists in insisting that comprehensive doctrines be kept out of the public domain. That indeed seems paradoxical, and hopefully we will get a better understanding of the paradox when we get to Rawls. (It is not a paradox from *Rawls's* point of view, because he does not believe that he is offering a comprehensive doctrine but rather something else. However, we will have to get into his political philosophy in order to explain all that.) Let me also add: there is a version of the same – or a similar – paradox in Habermas, insofar as he wants to practise a way of doing political philosophy that is rigorously "post-metaphysical"; and we find a similar paradox in Foucault as well, insofar as he is profoundly suspicious of any mode of theory presuming to prescribe norms.

The question we have to start with is: How is political philosophy possible at all? As I examine in the second prologue, and as Max Weber probably illustrates better than anyone, it was not clear to the immediate "post-Nietzschean" generation how it was possible. But then we also have to ask: How can we get along *without* political philosophy? That is, ultimately, how is it possible for human beings to be fully human without ambitious reflection on the meaning of their humanity? Nietzsche, without appealing to nature or human nature or the rationality of history or really without any of the standard "Archimedean points" found in the preceding history of political philosophy, nonetheless found a way of keeping the political philosophy enterprise going. Weber, too, I believe, wrestled with this problem and in fact struggled with it more than Nietzsche did. Yet – to some extent contrary to their own self-understanding – it would seem that both psychoanalysis as practised by Freud and sociology as practised by Weber are intended as forms of the fully comprehensive reflection on human life that I have been speaking about and hence provide good case studies with which to test the more encompassing conception of political philosophy that I have proposed. The second prologue, devoted to Freud and Weber, attempts to do just that.

Here is another way of articulating my "horizon" idea: One finds in Aristotle the idea of an "architectonic science," that is, a science that comprehends or encompasses lesser or subordinate sciences – "architectonic" in the sense that an architect commands and orders into an encompassing whole the activities of bricklayers, plumbers, electricians, carpenters, and so on. (This was Aristotle's way of conceptualizing what his enterprise as a political philosopher consisted in.) One might argue that psychoanalysis for Freud or sociology for Weber count as "architectonic" (i.e., most comprehensive) human sciences in this sense – and therefore correspond to "political philosophy" in my sense. Somewhere in our intellectual life we have to have forms of reflection that try to encompass *everything*. And so any form of thought that pitches its ambitions sufficiently high should correspond both to Aristotle's conception of an architectonic science and to my conception of political philosophy.

Different political philosophies will pick out different aspects of social-political life as salient and normatively meaningful, so that the criteria by which we see a given theory as normatively compelling cannot easily be disentangled from the enterprise of theorizing itself. We can call this the multi-dimensionality of the enterprise of theorizing. It is a good idea (I would suggest) to see this multi-dimensionality as a strength rather than a weakness of normative theory, or what I will call the theory enterprise. Here is an illustration: the juxtaposition of MacIntyre and Habermas yields an argument about what constitutes meaningful deliberation. Habermas will say that public deliberation in a modern society *is* possible, even though he thinks there is not nearly as much of it in liberal societies as he would like to see. MacIntyre, by contrast, thinks meaningful deliberation requires the sharing of a very thick collective way of life of the kind we encounter, for instance, in fishing villages. However, if you ask Nietzsche or Carl Schmitt or Foucault, they will say that deliberation is not remotely central to what defines social and political reality. In fact, there is not even agreement among theorists that a concern with *normativity* is what defines political theory. There are many theorists (Foucault being one example but not at all the only example) for whom a fixation on normative theory is a hang-up that we would be better off discarding.

Let's say something here about the meaning of the idea of normativity, since one cannot begin to grasp what the theory enterprise is about without some understanding of what this means, whether one conceives it to be central to that enterprise, as I do, or rejects its centrality, or tries to reject its centrality, as I said earlier that Foucault does. It is just a fact that people talk to and argue with each other, but this becomes a normative theory when one claims, and develops a complex theoretical framework to defend the claim, that people entering into discourse with each other, trading judgments, challenging each other's opinions, and so on is a crucial part of the human good for human beings (that is, that which makes human beings fully human). Habermas is making a claim of that sort – although he would surely regard my formulation of it as excessively "metaphysical" – and hence for him the obvious reality of human discourse and communication is not merely an empirical fact but part of the normative structure of human life. And similarly for the other political philosophies. The fact that several of the theorists that concern us are nervous about making grand claims about notions such as "the human good" is an interesting, and maybe puzzling, feature of the contemporary situation of theory. We can reflect on all this later as we become more familiar with these theorists, but whether they can actually *avoid* the more grand "metaphysical" notions that they say they want to avoid is another matter. As should be obvious by now, I am extremely skeptical that one can participate in the theory enterprise at all without asserting claims about human nature, the human good, "the good" for human beings, and so on.

Let's return to what I was saying about the "multidimensionality" of the theory enterprise and why we should consider it a strength rather than a weakness of that enterprise. In what follows, we are limiting ourselves to a dozen interestingly different forms of political philosophy (leaving aside Freud and Weber). If they really are truly different in the normative horizons they conjure up through their theorizing, then this yields a dozen different "dimensions" by which to understand social and political reality, which then allows us to penetrate (and appreciate, or at least consider, the normative force of) radically different aspects of political life. For example, in the case of Habermas: communication is viewed as what defines politicalness; in the case of Rawls: the importance of designing institutions of social cooperation that are fair to all participating individuals; in the case of Arendt: the importance of publicness for the sake of publicness; in the case of MacIntyre: the importance of sharing thick collective goods; and so on.

But clearly we cannot just say that these different theories are all valid! The enterprise of theory would be way too easy and lose most of its interest if we became philosophical pluralists to the point of saying that there must be some significant truth in all these theoretical standpoints and leave it at that. As the second prologue explores, that (or at least the claim that they are valid to the extent that one embraces them with unqualified commitment) was basically the sociological standpoint of Max Weber, which prompts two responses: (a) it is hardly a satisfactory basis for doing political philosophy; and (b) even Weber himself had more of a commitment to a particular conception of the human good than his self-professed "polytheism" acknowledges. Trying to gather all the diverse conceptions of the good under one big tent does not work because the various political philosophies are rival claimants to the truth of the human condition. These horizons cannot all be true; nor can they *share* the truth, so to speak, each with their own partial truth. Rather, they are in fundamental competition with each other for the title of being the authoritative articulation of human existence. This competition is adjudicated by human reason, not by something above and beyond human reason. (Hence I reject Weber's conception of ultimate "gods and demons" despite the superficial similarity between Weber's conception and the account of "fundamental competition" I have just presented.) To be sure, the multi-dimensionality of the enterprise makes it extremely difficult to adjudicate rationally between them, but hopefully not impossible. As human beings, we have to have rationally defensible conceptions of what is a properly human life, and therefore we cannot afford to give up in despair, however challenging it may be to weigh the compellingness of the different theories, both with respect to their inner coherence, and, more importantly, with respect to how they stack up intellectually in relation to each other. Political philosophy means being presented with a range of horizon-encompassing views of life where it is possible or meaningful to ask: which is the comprehensive vision of human existence that, in the face of alternatives or rival views, appears most adequate, most compelling, and least vulnerable to intellectual challenges from equally ambitious visions of the human good? Without doubt, this is a tall order! So it should not surprise us or cause excessive concern that after a few thousand years of political philosophy, no theorist has yet actually *fulfilled* the desideratum.

When one speaks of a contest of political philosophies "adjudicated by reason," this cannot mean that one particular political philosophy will manage to come up with a set of knock-down arguments that will defeat all rival views. For if such knock-down arguments were available, somebody would already have discovered them at some previous stage of the history of theory. So that is too much to hope for, and we should not expect such a thing. (The unreasonableness of such an expectation is more or less what some theorists mean when they speak of "anti-foundationalism," or the suggestion that philosophy today must forfeit its foundationalist ambitions.) On the other hand, if we do not at least *aspire* to a theory that presents itself as more rationally compelling than all alternative views, it is hard to see how we can do theory at all. So we somehow have to aim at a conception of what it is to do theory that aspires to an encompassing intellectual framework that possesses rational authority but without the notion that this will generate knock-down arguments that will thrash all alternatives. I am not sure how one does that – striking a balance, one might say, between being too quick to despair of rational argument and getting too hubristic about what rational argument can accomplish – but the fact that one continues with the enterprise of political philosophy (which one does simply by reading these books and exposing oneself to the test of whether one will be persuaded by them) itself embodies a confidence that this balancing-act *is* possible.

The main purpose of this book is to draw up a balance sheet for twentieth-century political philosophy. What lasting insights are supplied by the twelve thinkers I have selected, and is the business of grand theorizing in which they participated still a living enterprise? Above all, does this tradition of epic theorizing have a future? Unless it makes sense to aspire to a rational vindication of one of the horizons available in the theory canon (or a horizon yet to be articulated), even the notion of a dialogue between them ceases to make any sense. And without this dialogue, we are less human. Our humanity requires a dialogue between political philosophies (because being human necessarily involves reflection on *what it is to be* human); and the possibility of such dialogue rests upon the meaningfulness of seeking a rational vindication of one of the participants in this dialogue.

Second Prologue: Freud, Weber, and Political Philosophy

Before we take up our twelve classics of twentieth-century political philosophy, I want to take a preliminary detour into texts by two thinkers who would seem to be involved in intellectual enterprises other than that of political philosophy – namely, Sigmund Freud and Max Weber. Neither Freud nor Weber thought of himself as a political philosopher, nor are they generally treated as such. So why commence a survey of twentieth-century political philosophy with a discussion of one of the twentieth century's greatest psychologists and one of the twentieth century's greatest sociologists? My purpose here is to clarify the scope of political philosophy as well as its unavoidability for *any* thinkers pursuing an intellectual engagement with grand issues of what it is to be human of appropriate breadth and comprehensiveness. That is, I think that looking at Freud and Weber helps to vindicate my idea of political philosophy defined in terms of super-ambitious reflection on the human condition, on "the ends of life," on human experience per se in its normative dimensions. If the enterprise of political philosophy consists in reflecting on the totality of life in its most ambitious normative dimensions, then thinkers like Freud and Weber – "epic" theorists fully on a par with the political philosophers to follow – will be found to be practicing political philosophy whether they think they are or not. And if political philosophy turns out to be inescapable for those thinkers even if they seek deliberately to pursue their grand intellectual projects without it, that in turn will equip us with a better appreciation of why it matters for human beings as human beings. That is, if ambitious thinkers who are more or less determined to steer clear of political philosophy turn out to be far more deeply implicated in it than they want to acknowledge, then it may also be the case that the questions engaged by political philosophy are inescapable for *all of us* (philosophers and non-philosophers, intellectuals and ordinary citizens).

1. Freud and Political Philosophy

Is there a political philosophy in Freud? Answering this question requires an already available answer to the question, what is political philosophy? What is it to offer a political philosophy? My answer to that question would run something like this: Any form of ambitious intellectual inquiry that attempts to reflect on desirable ends of human life and that does so on the basis of some kind of "rational authority" – that is, authority founded on reason-giving rather than authority *tout court* (by appealing, for instance, to holy texts) – is prima facie a mode of political philosophy. I think Freud fairly easily satisfies the requirements of political philosophy according to this (fairly broad) definition.

We all know why Freud is famous. He was the first thinker in the Western canon to articulate the idea of sexual desire as an essential aspect (or maybe *the* essential aspect) of what makes human beings human.[1] Of course, there is no lack of articulations within the canon (especially within Christianity) of the idea of the sinfulness of sexual desire, of how it expresses human sinfulness and as such needs to be disciplined and regulated. Obviously, that was not Freud's theme. On the contrary: he wanted to direct concerted reflection on the question of the effects – the *distorting* effects, one could say – of the *repression* of sex, a perennial project of human societies and clearly one that was not accidental or contingent, not one that merely *happened* to be embraced by particular societies. When Freud speaks of *civilization* (*Kultur*) as an enterprise of sexual repression, he is speaking of a human universal, something that seems inscribed in the human species per se, rather than characteristic of merely this or that society. It is not society X or society Y but civilization *as such* that does this work of sexual repression, and so reflection on what this does to human beings, what its consequences are, and what if anything can be done about it, are addressed at the *universal* level: to humans as humans.

It should already be apparent that we have entered a zone of supremely ambitious reflection – what I called in the first prologue the zone of "architectonic" reflection, or what I also want to call the zone of political philosophy. One response to Freud would be to say that he conceives himself to be an empirical scientist, and that the validity of his psychology stands or falls

---

[1] One of the publisher's reviewers pointed out that this claim might need to be qualified if one gave full consideration to Schopenhauer and Freud's possible debt to Schopenhauer. This suggestion may well be right.

on its capacity to validate its scientific claims. Either human psychology is or is not as Freud describes it; either way, there are no significant *normative* claims being offered. My reply: I am doubtful that any form of thought as intellectually ambitious as Freud's is can be "strictly empirical," unrelated to normative conceptions.

Let me offer some suggestions about what the overarching normative vision might be. Freud starts *Civilization and Its Discontents*² with a discussion about religious experience, provoked by Freud's friend Romain Rolland and Rolland's critical response to Freud's previously published critique of religion, *The Future of an Illusion*. Rolland associates religion with an "oceanic feeling" – a sense of unboundedness or unlimitedness that carries the self beyond its conventional experience of its own boundaries. The self is fundamentally related to something infinite beyond itself; that is, the self, properly experienced, is not just a self (at least if these "feelings" correspond to something real). Freud replies by offering a psychoanalytic explanation of Rolland's report of an oceanic feeling: it points back to our primordial experience as infants, *before* the point where the boundary between ego and object became articulated – for example, before the infant became aware of there being an ontological separation between the lips (its own lips) that demanded feeding and the mother's breast that did the feeding (or chose to withhold itself). So, Freud seems to be saying, there is indeed a kind of quasi-reality to the oceanic feeling, in the sense that it is rooted in a primordial experience that in some sense is still with us (buried deeply in the psyche, as it were – but not *so* deeply that it cannot impinge on *conscious* experience). However, that is its only reality. Beyond that, it is an illusion – something that our own consciousness, our own mental life, bewitches us into believing in.

To appreciate Freud's way of analyzing this, it is important to grasp the significance of his distinction between the ego (*das Ich*) and the id (*das Es*). Consider his suggestion that the ego is a "façade" for the id (pp. 4–5). "The ego extends inwards, with no clear boundary, into [the id as] an unconscious psychical entity." That is: what we take to be ego is really id. Or at least *more* of the ego (the conscious self) than we realize or than we want to acknowledge is, in fact, shaped by and in the service of the id (the unconscious). Whereas in pre-psychoanalytic consciousness, we take ourselves to be (so to speak) 100 percent ego, we are really (say) 50 percent ego and 50 percent

---

² All parenthetical page references to Freud in this section refer to Sigmund Freud, *Civilization and Its Discontents*, trans. David McLintock (London: Penguin Books, 2002).

id with no way of determining exactly where ego stops and id begins. (Or maybe 10 percent ego and 90 percent id! The imagery of "façade" certainly suggests that only the *surface* is ego and everything *behind* the surface is id. This is a much more radical suggestion than merely postulating a realm of the id with some kind of causal effect on the ego.)[3]

As always, Freud's illustration of the distinction between ego and id is telling. On page 28, Freud suggests the possibility (in his view, the *likelihood*) that human beings never cease "longing for" the safety and security of the womb. To be sure, we are not *conscious*, on a day-to-day basis, of longing for the womb. Yet this is not proof that yearning for the womb is not a deep aspect of psychic life. On a Freudian account, this desire for a return to the womb would belong to the id, not the ego. What motivates us psychically stretches far beyond what we can conceptualize as conscious selves. What is immediately accessible to us (the ego) seems to have definite boundaries – thoughts we can conjure up within actual consciousness, close to the surface, so to speak – but this realm of conscious mental life is shaped impalpably by the boundless play of the id *below the surface* (and in pathological cases, deep, deep below the surface). Various things are *on* our mental radar screen, and vastly more is *off* the radar screen; and what is off the radar is intimately related (whether we know it or not) to what is on our radar. That, in any case, is the essence of the Freudian theory.

Okay, so where is the normative vision here? I think the empirical claims (for example, Freud's hypotheses about how to account for Rolland's experience of the oceanic feeling or about the ever-present longing for the

---

[3] For helpful discussion of some of the relevant issues in postulating a kind of "covert" self, or sub-self, hidden in the less visible precincts of our mysteriously functioning mental life, see Colin McGinn, *The Mysterious Flame* (New York: Basic Books, 1999), chapter 5. I have recently noticed with some of my own dreams that my dreaming self (my "id") functions intellectually in pretty much the same way (in the same "style," one could say) as my waking self: thinking, coming up with ideas, formulating sentences, solving intellectual problems, etc. When I wake up, I recognize that more or less the same mind has been performing mental tasks during the dream as when I am conscious. The way this dreaming mind thinks and expresses itself is quite characteristic of my conscious mind as I know it. The sentences composed in such dreams are remarkably similar to sentences I could easily have composed while awake. In short, my intellectual personality in dreams seems to be the same as (or recognizably quite similar to) that in waking life. On such occasions I wake up saying to myself, "That's me; that's how I think." This is a jarring experience (for me, anyway). Is my unconscious merely "mimicking" my conscious mind (by analogy with what parrots do in mimicking voices)? I don't know. If so, the mimicking effect is an impressively convincing one. Or is the opposite the case? Namely, that the unconscious does much or most of the "heavy lifting" with respect to mental activities – for example, coming up with ideas or solving mental challenges – while the conscious mind unfairly walks off with all the credit, so to speak? Again, it is very hard to know. To take note of all this is not to offer a specifically Freudian interpretation of the contents of the id, but it certainly does, to my mind, support Freud's claim that there is a much weaker or more porous boundary between the conscious mind and the unconscious than was assumed before Freud began putting overwhelming emphasis on this issue.

womb) are inseparable from a (tacit) normative claim. Freud says right at the start of *Civilization and Its Discontents* that it is the function of human development, human maturation, to educate us about the distinction between what is ego and what is object. It is possible for people to be pathologically *arrested* in their development, such that the fundamental divide between the ego's mouth and the mother's breast never gets properly or fully acknowledged, or there is some level of the psyche where that acknowledgment fails to occur. Putting it in normative language: human beings *have a responsibility* to mature, to complete their developmental trajectory, and a life that continues to be haunted or determined by its infantile impulses is *a truncated existence.*[4] As Freud puts it (p. 6), "learning how to distinguish between the internal, which belongs to the ego [the infant's mouth] and the external, which comes from the world outside [the mother's breast] … is the first step toward establishing the reality principle," to which we can add that a human life lived oblivious to "the reality principle" is a less than fully human life – a life perhaps damaged by or pathologized by, and certainly truncated by, being arrested in infantile impulses. So in the case of religion, Freud's starting point in this work, the purpose is not simply to *explain* religion (by tracing it back to the realm of infantile desire and infantile sexuality), but also and no less to *criticize* religion (according to Freud's account) as infantile and neurotic. Hence Freud's lament, at the beginning of the next chapter (p. 12), that "All of this [namely, religion's appeal to ideas of providence, compensation for this-worldly failures and disappointments, and supposed responsiveness to human needfulness] is *so patently infantile, so remote from reality* [my italics], that it pains a philanthropic temperament [the implication: Freud himself, despite appearances, is not a misanthrope but, on the contrary, a lover of humanity!] to think that the great majority of mortals will never be able to rise above such a view of life."

That is, sex, or sexual imagination, engages fundamental questions of how it is to live a fully human life. That is *precisely* the question that political philosophy takes responsibility for, and in that sense, Freud – whether this is apparent at first glance or not – is participating in the enterprise of political philosophy. One could perhaps express Freud's normative ideal like this: Look at life with eyes wide open (rather than, to cite the title of a Stanley Kubrick film with a strong Freudian resonance, with "eyes wide shut"). There ought to be a firm boundary between dreaming and waking

---

[4] Cf. Max Weber's rhetoric of maturity versus lack of maturity at the bottom of page 86 of *The Vocation Lectures*, ed. David Owen and Tracy B. Strong (Indianapolis: Hackett, 2004); also page 92.

life. However, this is hardly easy for human beings, because the line between waking consciousness and dream is as porous as the line between ego and id. (Again, this is the message of the Kubrick film, based on a novella by one of Freud's Viennese contemporaries, Arthur Schnitzler.[5]) Life has no "intended purpose" (p. 14), and we are measured as human beings according to our capacity to look this truth in the eye and not flinch! Human beings desire happiness, but the odds are stacked relentlessly in favor of *un*happiness (pp. 14–15). Can we face this truth without cowardice or evasion?

The project of life, in Freud's view, is *to fend off sorrow* (p. 19: "keep suffering at bay"). The famous line that is always quoted from the end of *Studies on Hysteria* – that the purpose of psychoanalysis is to transform "hysterical misery into common unhappiness" – is *no joke*; that is truly Freud's view! Neurosis and psychosis clearly loom large in Freud's view of life because the prospects of human happiness are so meager, and so it is all-too-natural to try to cope with this unavailability of happiness by retreating into various pathological conditions. However, there is also a normative dimension to this; if this is what life is really like, we have a human obligation to be equal to it, existentially speaking, and not wimp out by being cowards or dreamers. That is why Freud is so preoccupied by the question of religion as a form of cowardice (as he sees it).

According to Freud, there is little mystery about "why it is so difficult for people to be happy" (p. 24). He says that there are three fundamental "sources of our suffering: the superior power of nature, the frailty of our bodies, and the inadequacy of the institutions that regulate people's relations with one another in the family, the state and society" (ibid.). That is, we suffer catastrophes beyond our control, we get sick and die, and our social life is organized by institutions that are totally screwed up (*chronically* screwed up, we should add). Even someone like me who does not consider himself a dire pessimist would be hard-pressed to say which part of this diagnosis of the human condition is off the mark!

Civilization and Its Discontents can be read as a philosophical response to the kind of "optimistic" argument laid out most famously in Rousseau's *Second Discourse*, and chapter 3 is where Freud commences that counterargument. (Not that Rousseau is really an optimist either, but explaining his pessimism is a long and complicated story on its own.[6]) To put Rousseau's

---

[5] On Schnitzler's relation to Freud, see Paul Reitter, "The text-life of dreams," *Times Literary Supplement,* August 17 & 24, 2012, p. 24.

[6] For a brief discussion, see Ronald Beiner, *Civil Religion* (Cambridge: Cambridge University Press, 2011), p. 210, n. 27.

case quite crudely, primitive human beings were natural and happy; civilized man, by contrast, is unnatural and miserable. The fundamental issue between Rousseau and Freud in this context is whether the root cause of this human unhappiness is to be sought in a contingent or accidental wrong turn in social development (in the evolution of social man), or whether it is rooted, more primordially, in the essential structures of the human psyche.

In effect, Freud wants to take up Rousseau's challenge (which did not become a less powerful one as the forces at the disposal of modern science continued to grow very dramatically between the eighteenth and twentieth centuries): does civilization, or increased civilization, actually make human beings *happier*? This is not just a debate about human psychology and its capacity or incapacity for happiness. Rather, it engages fundamental questions of political philosophy: what are the possibilities of human flourishing, and (more fundamentally) what does it mean to speak of human flourishing?

At the end of chapter 3 (pp. 33–34), Freud presents a stupendously ambitious theory of the relationship between human psychology and civilizational social evolution. The Freudian theory is that one starts with a set of primordial drives, then one undergoes either the "sublimation" or "repression" of these drives, and then one ends up with civilization (*Kultur*) as a kind of "output." This goes along with a corresponding thesis concerning "the similarity between the process of civilization and the libidinal development of the individual" (p. 34). Freud's example is striking: the individual begins with "anal eroticism"; this drive is sublimated into the urge toward order and cleanliness associated with "the anal character"; and this in turn advances the process of civilization (as an "essential requirement").

We are now getting closer to Freud's central thesis, the core of his analysis of the human condition. *Eros* is at the heart of human life – both human psychological existence and human social existence (one cannot separate the latter from the former). This teaching actually goes back to Plato's *Republic*, which in this respect offers a quite startling anticipation of the pessimistic insights of Freudianism: "surely some terrible, savage, and lawless form of desires is in every man, even in some of us who seem to be ever so measured. *And surely this becomes plain in dreams.*"[7] But unbounded eros is not compatible with living in a civilized state. Hence, civilization

---

[7] *The Republic of Plato*, trans. Allan Bloom, 2nd ed. (New York: Basic Books, 1991), p. 252; my italics. That is, for Plato as for Freud, dreams in particular give one access to the deeper (more disturbing) structures of the life of the soul. To be sure, Plato and Freud have different philosophical responses to this problem, but one should not underestimate similarities in their view of human psychology.

must discipline and regulate eros, giving rise to grave tensions. Because the original unbounded and undisciplined eros is still present in the id,[8] these tensions will never be transcended in a stable way. Therefore, human beings are forever moved by dangerous and unmasterable impulses, and human social (and political) life remains a kind of existential minefield.

Rousseau, in his *Second Discourse*, offers the theory that it was the invention by human beings of *property*, and also the evolution of social vanity (*amour propre*), that led to the onset of civilized existence. Freud has a different (and no less ambitious) hypothesis concerning the dawn of civilization. For Freud, human beings were on the road to civilization as soon as they went from being animals walking on all fours, to being *erect* animals. This provoked an earth-shattering transformation in the nature of human sexuality, involving, first, the *display* of human genitals, and secondly (and relatedly) the shift from eroticism focused on *smell* to eroticism focused on *sight*.[9] For Freud, everything entailed by the process of civilization, for good or ill, follows from that single, decisive transformation in the character of human eroticism. It is important to grasp what is at stake in these competing speculations about the (pre-civilizational) state of nature. It is impossible to have an adequate understanding of what fundamentally moves human beings, what makes them happy and unhappy – essential questions of political philosophy – without a correct conception of what is most *primordial* in human experience and what is correspondingly less primordial. Ultimately, we cannot answer the questions that political philosophy attempts to answer without an understanding of (or at least a theory about) what is most primordial in human longing or human desire. That is what Rousseau and Freud are striving for. Rousseau and Freud are in agreement on why it is necessary to speculate on the transition from the state of nature to the civilized state – they agree on why so much hangs on that speculative enterprise – even though they disagree in the content of their respective theories. (Freud hopes that natural science will one day empirically validate his own speculations, but it is not clear whether the questions of political philosophy can ever be fully settled by deferring to empirical science.) If Freud is right that eros is at the heart of the human condition, and if he is right that there is a fundamental tension between civilization and eros, then – without Freud in any way denying that civilization is the source of many fine things that promote human welfare and without him

---

[8] Consider especially what Freud says on the topic of incest on page 38 and at the top of page 40.
[9] See notes 1 and 3 on pages 41–44.

in any way suggesting that the mastery of nature is not an entirely worthy enterprise (and here, indeed, the contrast between Rousseau and Freud is very striking), there will always be, on a Freudian account, a problem with civilization per se.

Starting in chapter 5, Freud throws in another set of important considerations militating in favor of deep pessimism about civilization – namely, what Freud sees as innate impulses in human beings toward mutual aggression. Christianity says, "Love thy neighbor," but human nature says, "Let my neighbor love me!" However much Christianity and the other religions may wish it were otherwise, the natural situation, in advance of civilization working to bring these impulses under some measure of control, is for human beings to be *wolves*, rather than saints. Here, once again, the ego looks pretty puny when weighed up against the id. As Freud puts it (p. 49), "nothing else runs so much counter to basic human nature" as the injunction that one should love one's neighbor as oneself.

One could say that on a Freudian account, civilization is waging a twofold battle against human nature: the struggle to rein in natural eroticism; and the struggle to rein in natural aggression. On this account: If civilization wins, then human nature is repressed and frustrated. If civilization loses, then human beings are exposed as the wild barbarians that they really are. Either way, we are presented with a picture of the human situation that is far from edifying. Although one would like to embrace a more encouraging picture of human affairs, one has to confess that Freud has plenty of testimony from history on his side. His text was written in 1929, a mere twelve years after the senseless slaughter of World War I. *Civilization and Its Discontents* was published in 1930; three years later, the German people elected Hitler and the Nazis. Six years after that, Europe embarked on an even *greater* exercise in senseless slaughter. Obviously, it was anything but an overstatement when Freud's friend Stefan Zweig wrote: "Each one of us ... has been shaken in the depths of his being by the almost unceasing volcanic eruptions of our European earth."[10] By the end of the twentieth century, Europeans were *still* engaging in senseless slaughter, namely the Yugoslav civil wars of the 1990s. We're not talking about the Middle Ages here. We're talking about affluent Europe several centuries *after* the supposed "Enlightenment"!

---

[10] Stefan Zweig, *The World of Yesterday* (London: Cassell, 1943), p. 5. On page 318, Zweig relates a conversation with Freud in which Freud claimed that the horrors of the 1930s had (unfortunately) entirely vindicated him against critics by whom he "had always been scolded as a pessimist."

It is easy to assume that the Freudian universe is a resolutely monistic universe, that everything is ruled by Eros, or sexuality, but *Civilization and Its Discontents* makes clear that this is not the case. Freud postulates two fundamental forces in the human psyche: Eros and Thanatos, sex and destruction (hence metaphysical dualism, so to speak). At the end of chapter 6, Freud refers to the struggle between these two titanic forces as a "battle of the giants," as "humanity's struggle for existence," pitched "between the life drive and the drive for destruction" (p. 58). It is not going too far to describe this as a "metaphysical" drama.

As we will see in the second part of this prologue, it is not unreasonable to suggest that *both* Freud and Weber are "Homerics" – seeing the world fundamentally through the prism of a cosmic struggle between *warring gods*. In this respect, both are intellectual progeny of Nietzsche.[11] One could say that Freud's foundational philosophical claim was the superiority of Homer to Plato (and to Christianity).[12] The world is not metaphysically unified or harmonious but metaphysically divided against itself, and the outcome of this cosmic struggle is unknown. Freud and Weber accept Nietzsche's claim of the superiority of Homer to Plato: both of them (or rather, all three of them) want to affirm heroism and nobility in a world of resolute conflict. They, like Nietzsche, inhabit a tragic universe, and all three participate in a root-and-branch rejection of Christianity, because the Christian universe – by virtue of being a non-tragic universe – is seen as less noble.[13] (Consider

[11] Relevant Nietzschean texts are plentiful, but one could start with the following: 1. Nietzsche's attack, extending from *The Birth of Tragedy* to *Twilight of the Idols*, on the Socratic (rationalist) tradition as an *anti-tragic* tradition, which Nietzsche casts as an issue of tragic depth versus shallow rationalism; 2. Nietzsche's insistence, in *Genealogy of Morals*, First Essay, section 1, on the existence of "plain, harsh, ugly, repellent, unchristian, immoral truth," in order to challenge the Platonic-Christian presumption of the metaphysical unity of truth, beauty, and goodness; 3. Nietzsche's indictment of Plato for having "destroyed paganism," and correspondingly, for his "preparation of the soil for Christianity" (*The Will to Power*, ed. Walter Kaufmann [New York: Vintage Books, 1968], pp. 242 and 232) – that is, for having helped a fundamentally ignoble view of life displace a fundamentally noble one. For an ambitious attempt to present Nietzsche and Weber as philosophical interlocutors, see Robert Eden, *Political Leadership and Nihilism: A Study of Weber and Nietzsche*, (Tampa: University of South Florida Press, 1983), chapters 2–6. As Eden highlights with his epigraph from "Science as a Vocation" on p. 98, Weber zeroed in on precisely the cultural significance of Nietzsche's debunking of a Platonic faith in the unity of (for instance) beauty and goodness.

[12] See note 28 below, where I cite Simone Weil's rejoinder, on behalf of Plato and Christianity, to Nietzsche, Freud, and Weber. As regards Nietzsche's siding with Homer against Plato, see my discussion in *Civil Religion*, pp. 386–387.

[13] Cf. Weber, *The Vocation Lectures*, p. 82, where Weber refers to the Christian Gospel as "an ethic of ignominy." In the last chapter of *Beyond Good and Evil*, Nietzsche asks, "What is Noble?" Nietzsche very visibly put this question on the agenda for theory, and it is very easy to imagine that his doing so had a decisive impact on both Freud and Weber, and decisively shaped the direction of their theoretical reflections.

the last line of chapter 6 – the nursemaid's "lullaby about heaven" intended to mitigate the "battle of the giants.") Christianity's vision is of a world created by love; Freud replaces love with sex, and then places sex in a life-and-death struggle with violence and destruction.

It has to be said that there is a significant philosophical instability in Freud's account of the relationship between Eros and civilization. In the first half of *Civilization and Its Discontents*, Freud puts the primary emphasis on eros as needing to be policed and disciplined by civilization (for instance, by criminalizing and, therefore, stamping out or seeking to stamp out incest), but after introducing the death instinct as a force or principle of equal primordiality, the emphasis shifts to eros as a fundamentally *unifying* principle, locked in mortal combat with Thanatos as a rival god. This is so to the extent that in chapter 6 (p. 58), Freud refers to civilization as "a process in the service of Eros." That is, Eros is no longer an *anti*-civilizational force or principle but, on the contrary, the inspiration behind – or the primordial causality driving – civilization per se. It is not clear how to resolve this tension in Freud's argument, except perhaps to say that sexuality is *so* central in his view of the world that in thinking about the rise of civilization, it shows up on both sides of the equation (that is, both as pro-*Kultur* and as anti-*Kultur*).

Chapter 7 reprises themes from the Second Essay of Nietzsche's *Genealogy of Morals*: the origins of *conscience*, *guilt*, and *punishment*. Human beings, according to Freud, are innately aggressive, but civilization can inhibit and regulate this aggressiveness by manipulating psychological mechanisms. Conscience, on Freud's account, involves an "introjection" (a throwing inward, the inversion of projection) of human aggressiveness, directing it inward against the ego itself. Freud calls this the super-ego (*das Über-Ich*). In Freud's acute imagery, the emergence of the super-ego as a distinct mental agency within the psyche is akin to civilization "setting up an internal authority to watch over [the ego], like a garrison in a conquered town" (p. 61). One can put oneself in the good graces of external authority by acting virtuously, that is, by forgoing various illicit desires (for example, I may be tempted to falsify my tax returns, but restrain myself from actually doing it), but this obviously does not suffice with respect to the ego's relation to the super-ego, because while the ego can restrain itself from *acting* on its desires, the desires themselves cannot be expelled or expunged. (The wish to cheat on my taxes is there, whether I give in to the wish or overrule it by exercising my sense of probity.) These desires remain present, visible to the ever-present super-ego. (In a later chapter, we will discuss Foucault's compelling image of the Panopticon as a way of conceiving modern society. Freud seems to have anticipated the same conception, except that in the case of Freud, the Panopticon is implanted within our very own souls! This becomes a theme in Foucault as well, so it is not at all unreasonable to see Foucault as, in this sense, an intellectual successor to Freud, or to see Freud as having laid the groundwork for the political philosophy of Foucault. Perhaps another way to put it is to say that themes leading from Nietzsche to Foucault get *mediated* by Freud.)

This conducts us into the sordid realm of guilt and (self-)punishment. Torturing oneself internally for desires that remain present deep in the self cannot help but generate unhappiness; so again, human psychology is, on the Freudian account, marked by "an enduring inner unhappiness" (p. 64). On the one hand, human beings are *defined* by the longing for happiness; on the other hand, it seems as if we are not *built* for happiness – not unlike Rousseau's analysis in the *Second Discourse* that human perfectibility drives us inexorably toward life in society, yet life in society in its very essence makes us miserable. Treading a path pioneered by Nietzsche and also anticipating Foucault's later analysis, Freud makes clear that the punitiveness of external authority, however harsh, looks paltry by comparison to the deeper, more penetrating, and more insidious forms of punitiveness internal to the psyche itself – the mental coercion that the self works upon the self. In place of Aristotle's conception of human beings as "rational animals," Nietzsche and Freud substitute the idea of human beings as *self-punishing* animals.

As is characteristic of Freud, his account of these psychological mechanisms of "introjected" aggression, guilt, and self-punishment are bound up with stories of "primeval" authority and rebellion. The primeval father ruled his sons in a regime of "terrible" aggression. The patricidal fraternity of sons/brothers retaliated by murdering the father. They then *internalized* the authority they had overthrown, both to punish the father for his overbearing authority exercised against them and to punish *themselves* for their own criminal act of rebellion. The father is simultaneously overthrown and reinstalled as a newly internalized authority. Freedom from the father's violence simply becomes another (more oppressive) kind of slavery. (Again, these kinds of narratives of "faux-liberation" later get replayed in Foucault.) This primordial drama, for Freud, is at the heart of the human condition: authority provokes rebellion, which then attempts to atone for its criminality with reestablished, internalized, and in that sense *more* repressive authority. Guilt is inscribed in the very soul of the human psyche. We are guilty not on account of this or that particular misdeed but because of the essential structure of the individual's relation to authority – our primordial criminality, or feeling of criminality (feeling ourselves to be criminal), as Freud presents it. Freud calls it "the fateful inevitability of the sense of guilt" (p. 68). No doubt, Freud would see this kind of explanation as going a long way toward making sense of why the notion of *sinfulness* looms so large in a religion like Christianity.

Human existence is an endless dialectic of love and murderousness (or so it appears in Freud's teaching). Those we truly want to murder (at the "primordial" level, so to speak) are not strangers but our *kin*, those we simultaneously primordially love.[14] Love and murder and guilt are all tangled up together in a supremely potent fatality. It is hardly surprising then, as Freud views it, that the super-ego is charged with such psychological energy, or that the self is capable of such aggression against itself. Freud describes the sense of guilt as "the most important problem in the development of civilization" (p. 71), and this integral relation between civilization and guilt clearly explains, for Freud, the endemic unhappiness in human life. Eros draws human beings into larger communities, beyond the family. However, this line of development, "from the family to humanity as a whole," does not relax the sense of guilt but, Freud insists, *intensifies* it (p. 69). Human experience is fundamentally tragic. Presumably, once the process of civilization draws us into a relation with "humanity as a whole," the "primeval" dynamic of murdering the father, bearing the guilt of that murder, re-inscribing the father's tyrannical authority within one's own super-ego, and all the rest of it simply get inscribed on this much larger social canvas: the macro-society simply reenacts the implicitly pathological patterns associated with the family as the original "micro-society."

Why is there a tension between civilization (*Kultur*) and happiness? A Freudian answer would seem to go more or less like this: Individuals as individuals want to be happy; individuals as creatures of civilization need to be able to live with each other; and the community's defining goal is not to enable individuals to fulfill the happiness they seek, but simply to make them fit with the demands of social life. Freud, then, seems to embrace a version of Rousseau's teaching that human beings are not naturally social but have to be *made* social in ways that inevitably do essential violence to their naturalness (their natural yearnings and natural modes of happiness). At the end of the book (p. 77), Freud offers the following formulation: For

---

[14] I have discussed this theme, linking Freud to other epic figures in the history of political thought canon, in *Civil Religion*, chapter 4.

civilization, "the aim of forming a unified whole out of individual human beings is all-important," and hence the aim of (individual) happiness must be "pushed into the background." There are "two strivings" at stake here – individual happiness and human fellowship. In an optimistic rendering of the human condition, the striving for human fellowship and the striving for individual happiness would be complementary and mutually supportive rather than being in significant tension with each other, but quite clearly that optimistic rendering of the human condition is not one that Freud finds plausible. Consider Freud's insistence on page 81 that he is not arguing for or against civilization, and does not feel competent either to vindicate civilization or to propose alternatives to what is unsatisfactory in human social existence as we currently know it. His fundamental task, rather, is to help human beings see through illusions and gain more accurate self-knowledge. Above all, he offers no consolation. That is, human life must be lived clear-sightedly, without expecting either religion or philosophy to supply reasons to be consoled.

How to characterize Freud as a political philosopher? I would characterize him as a *hyper-pessimistic Enlightenment rationalist*.[15] First of all, he is a rationalist because he believes in the supremacy of reason. (It may seem paradoxical to refer to Freud as a "rationalist" when, in his view, the murky impulses of the unconscious loom larger than the conscious purposes of the rational ego. One can be a rationalist in the sense that one acknowledges reason as the highest standard while seeing most human beings as being in the grip of deep irrationality. Indeed, in my view, *most* major figures in the canon of Western philosophy have been rationalists in just this sense.) He is an Enlightenment rationalist because he wants to bring the sunlight of reason outside the cave to the cave-dwellers inside the cave (to use Plato's imagery); he thinks a scientific view of the world should be deployed in order to disperse the fog of superstition; and he thinks it is the responsibility of scientifically-minded intellectuals like himself to propagate a disenchanted, demystified view of things to the whole society so that everyone will come to a more clear-sighted understanding of their own humanity. (All three of these formulations are really saying the same thing.) But he is a pessimistic or even hyper-pessimistic rationalist because he *does not* think that spreading more enlightenment will make us happier. As already discussed, Freud did

---

[15] Cf. John Gray, "Freud: The Last Great Enlightenment Thinker," *Prospect*, January 2012, pp. 56–60. See also Peter Gay, *A Godless Jew: Freud, Atheism, and the Making of Psychoanalysis* (New Haven, CT: Yale University Press, 1987), chapter 1.

not think that happiness is possible. It is not possible prior to enlightenment and it is not possible subsequent to enlightenment. One might easily assume that being an Enlightenment rationalist entails being an optimist. If so, that in itself supplies an excellent reason for reading Freud. That is because Freud proves that it is indeed possible to be a rationalist, to be committed to the Enlightenment and its legacy, *and* to be, nonetheless, a deep and uncompromising pessimist.

2. Weber and Political Philosophy

In my discussion of Max Weber, I want to zero in on the idea of putting oneself in the service of rival gods. That idea is subversive of political philosophy and is, I think, *intended* to be subversive of political philosophy – namely, political philosophy's commitment to an independent (objective or at least intersubjective) standard of proper human flourishing.[16] But, as with Freud, it is possible that there is a political philosophy here somewhere, whether Weber intended it or not. Let's see if we can clarify what that political philosophy might be.

In line with Nietzsche's idea of Christianity as "Platonism for the people" – that is, Platonism propagated as a kind of mass ideology – Weber's idea represents, or at least is suggestive of, a kind of return to paganism. We do not have a singular, harmonious source of truth, beauty, and justice but rather a plurality of warring gods. As with Freud, we find ourselves in a Nietzschean or post-Nietzschean (at some level anti-Christian) universe. This is already suggested in the titles of Weber's two lectures. Here, "vocation" (*Beruf*) does not mean merely a profession or an occupation (though *Beruf* can be translated according to these more prosaic meanings). It means a "calling" – as in a religious calling, when someone decides to commit himself to the priesthood or commit herself to being a nun.[17] That is, one embraces a view of life as a kind of leap of faith, unconditionally, according to a model of existentialist *engagement*.

We get a powerful expression of such ideas in the first of the two *Beruf* lectures, "Science as a Vocation" (*Wissenschaft als Beruf*), a lecture delivered at the University of Munich on November 7, 1917.[18] The lecture unfolds,

---

[16] See *The Vocation Lectures*, pp. 14–15, where Weber makes explicit his view that Socratically-conceived political philosophy can no longer deliver what it promises.

[17] See ibid., page 1, note 1; page 32, note 1; and page xii.

[18] Interestingly, this lecture was attended by one of the twelve thinkers treated in this book. See Karl Löwith, *My Life in Germany Before and After 1933*, trans. Elizabeth King (London: The Athlone Press,

one could say, within a schizophrenic reality, and this schizophrenic reality, in Weber's view, is intrinsic to our modern condition. On the one hand, the structures of social life that condition our sociological situation are increasingly mechanized and regimented, as if modern society were becoming, more and more, a gigantic mechanism or set of mechanisms. We cannot conjure these away – they are part of how we live and determine what it is to be an inhabitant of modern life. On the other hand, we cannot pursue the way of life that Weber is discussing in this lecture – that of an academic or a paid intellectual or a professionalized teacher and researcher – apart from the passion and commitment that necessarily sustains such a way of life. The first seven or so pages of Weber's lecture[19] focus on the *mechanistic* aspects of academic life: salary, how one obtains employment, the balance between luck and merit in capturing such jobs, what duties have to be performed in order to make one's living in this way, the academic bureaucracies that dispense positions, and so on. But thereafter (starting around page 8), the language of passion and even mania becomes increasingly prominent. Academic life is situated, it appears, at the intersection between mechanism and passion, between being a kind of cog in a giant wheel and being the recipient of almost demonic "inspiration" or possession. To live this life is to experience both disenchantment and "intoxication" (p. 10). On page 11, Weber speaks of the scientist's "inner dedication to his task" and to "serving a cause" – the very opposite of being simply a functionary in a bureaucracy or fulfilling the mundane requirements of a job in a functional modern economy. Weber emphasizes the analogies between science and art – just as the artist cannot be an artist unless he or she receives a kind of divine inspiration, the same turns out to be true of scholarly work. Scholars have to be inspired by grand passions; if it is just a question of doing a job like any other, without a special sense of passion or calling, the activity shrivels into meaninglessness and becomes impossible. In aspiring to be scholars, we are *both* cogs in a larger machinery *and* passion-intoxicated "poets," and it tells us something crucial about the sociological reality in which we live that this tension between machinery and passion somehow has to be reconciled.

What does it mean to live in the modern world? On the most basic level, it means that the conditions of life have been mastered by technical and scientific understanding. Therefore, the world in which we live is a

1994), pp. 160–161, for Löwith's account of the impression made upon him by Weber's lecture, and its climactic peroration in particular.

[19] All in-text page references to Weber's two lectures in this section will be to the edition of *The Vocation Lectures* cited in note 4.

"disenchanted" world – in the sense of a world liberated from magic and supernatural forces, but mastering the world in scientific and technical ways does not necessarily inject more meaning into the world – it may well do the opposite. Hence the implication, which Weber obviously intended, of "disenchantment" in a second, more negative (or potentially negative) sense: living in a world stripped of human significance. Once everything in the world is in principle capable of scientific, disenchanted explanation and control, how are we to sustain the sense that our world is still a world of human significance? What sustains meaning or human meaningfulness in such a world?

In this context, Weber considers the familiar idea of "progress" and its (on his account) unhappy and in fact quite disturbing implications. What does it mean to live in a social world defined by the idea of progress? It means that students will always understand the world better and more reliably than their teachers did; it means that our children and our grandchildren will have a better and more perspicuous grasp of the world than we do, and *their* children and grandchildren will understand things better than they do. Inherent in such a world is the fact that our fundamental goals necessarily elude us. Our purposes as a society (including our purpose to understand the world and understand ourselves) necessarily stretch off to infinity. We will solve certain riddles (at least provisionally) but we will die with other riddles unsolved, and with our best attempts at solutions unraveled and reworked by later generations. Fundamentally, we are no closer to the truth, no closer to definitive understanding, than all our predecessors in the history of civilizations. How does a social world defined by science and its literally "never-ending" progress secure a sense of meaning? How do people living in such a social world fend off despair?

For an artist/scientist of the Renaissance like Leonardo, it was possible to think that there was a unity of purpose between science and art. That no longer holds. For later thinkers, it was possible to think that science and theology, or science and religion, can go hand in hand. Again, Weber is of the view that that unity too has been shattered irrevocably. If it is our view that the meaning of life reposes on individual happiness, and science or scientific progress helps secure the conditions of that happiness, then science and meaning might stand in a harmonious relationship with each other. But, once again, Weber takes it as a given that Nietzsche's "annihilating [cultural] criticism" has delivered a devastating blow to any such optimistic view of things. The result is that there is an unbridgeable gulf between the science and technology that define the collective purposes of contemporary society and ideas of the good that might confer a stable sense of meaning on our existential condition as human beings. Weber has no answer to offer to Tolstoy's assertion that modern science is humanly meaningless; on the contrary, it is clear that in Weber's view, Tolstoy's challenge is unanswerable (p. 17). Is it tolerable to live in a social world whose central driving thrust is a form of human intellectual activity that is better at *dissolving* or *eroding* human meaning than it is at helping to establish it?

What does it mean to devote oneself to science as "a calling"? It means taking on a certain ethic of scientific detachment, a morality of scholarly integrity, one could say. It means caring about the facts for the sake of the facts. It means subordinating one's own political and ethical positions to this ideal of scientific integrity, of upholding the idea that respect for the facts "trumps" one's own political preferences. One does not cease to be a political being when one speaks as a scholar or teacher, but the reality is that these two identities – that of a citizen and that of a scholar – are governed by separate and in fact competing imperatives, and, at any given moment, one has to be aware in a clear-sighted way which of these two different identities one is inhabiting (or which "god" one is serving). And it is at this point in the text – on page 22 – that Weber introduces the theme that most concerns us: "the different value systems of the world," he writes, "are caught up in an insoluble struggle with one another." Nietzsche was right that there is no metaphysical harmony between truth and beauty and goodness and the sacred. Each asserts its claims, and we cannot delude ourselves or succumb to the illusion that we can simultaneously put ourselves in the service of each of these human ideals. We have to *choose*. We find ourselves planted in the midst of "this conflict between the gods of the different systems and values," and so dedicating oneself either to the pursuit of beauty or the pursuit of goodness or the pursuit of the sacred or the pursuit of truth is a quasi-religious commitment. The cause of truth – the cause of scientific integrity and respect for the facts as facts – is aligned with one of these gods, and hence dedicating oneself to the uncompromising pursuit of empirical veracity amounts to submission to a particular deity. Weber cites James Mill (the father of John Stuart Mill) in calling this "polytheism" and states that, in this sense, polytheism is vindicated by "pure experience" (p. 22) – experience uncontaminated by the (false) presumption of a monotheistic civilization that monotheism must be true. The gods we live by are plural, and hence the onus rests on us to choose *which* of these gods will be the ones that we serve.

And Weber goes even further in pushing the rhetoric of his polytheistic vision of the world: "[the different] gods and their struggles are ruled over by fate, and certainly not by 'science'" (p. 23). Presented with the demands of Christian pacifism on the one side and the imperative of resisting evil on the other, we have to *choose*, we have to make an ultimate decision about what is God and what is the devil. When we embrace the Sermon on the Mount, ideas of honor and nobility go out the window, so if we opt for strictly Christian notions of moral purity, we have to face up in a clear-eyed view to the fact that we have turned our backs on conventional conceptions of honor. "[The ancient gods assume] the shape of impersonal forces, arise from their graves, strive for power over our lives, and resume their eternal struggle among themselves" (p. 24).

Weber again uses the language of "serving [a] particular god" on pages 26 and 27, and he insists that serving one god "will *give offense to every other god*" (p. 26; Weber's italics). This again is what his "polytheism" entails: far from being harmonious, the different gods are actually in conflict, so devoting oneself to one god upsets the others and makes them jealous. For instance, Weber insists that we are fooling ourselves if we think it is possible to dedicate ourselves both to religion *and* to science; the reality is that we have to choose between them.[20] Again, "the conflict between these gods is never-ending" (p. 27), so it is not a question of giving support to one cause or one ultimate commitment provisionally, while awaiting an eventual harmonization, so to speak, of the warring gods. The metaphysical reality of conflict between ideals is an *ultimate* one in the sense that it can never be transcended in favor of a more conciliatory vision of the world. "Life is about the incompatibility of ultimate *possible* attitudes and hence the inability ever to resolve the conflicts between them." In other words, Weber's polytheism is itself a metaphysical view – a vision of the ultimate reality of things, in relation to which we can pronounce other more hopeful or more optimistic visions deluded and cowardly.

Our challenge is "to look the fate of the age full in the face" (p. 24). Weber goes so far as to speak of our having been "blinded" by centuries

---

[20] See *The Vocation Lectures*, pp. 21 and 19. Yet again, Weber and Freud appear to be on the same wavelength. Freud is very hostile to "liberalized" versions of religion that might be easier to square with modern science. See, for instance, Freud's staunch rebuke to supposedly more sophisticated versions of religious sentiment that seek to distance themselves from the "infantile" religion of "the common man" in *Civilization and Its Discontents*, p. 12. As Freud strikingly puts it, the common man's religion is "the only one that deserves the name." See also, in the same vein, Freud's letter to Marie Bonaparte dated March 19, 1928: Ernest Jones, *The Life and Work of Sigmund Freud*, Vol. 3 (London: Hogarth Press, 1957), p. 447. For both Weber and Freud, attempts to make religion look more respectable in the eyes of modern science are craven rather than worthy of respect. Interestingly enough, Alasdair MacIntyre has the same view, as one can see from a powerful lecture entitled "Catholic Instead of What?" available on YouTube: https://www.youtube.com/watch?v=j7WWMkIOlsw.

of Christian moral complacency.[21] We need to become "more clearly conscious of [our] situation" as choosers or deciders of our ultimate existential commitments, and the image of a return to polytheism, with its corollaries of metaphysical conflict and struggle, helps to reinforce this awareness of a need for clearer consciousness of our true situation. Again, it is necessary that we face up to the fact that "[we] live in an age alien to God and bereft of prophets" (p. 28), that is, an age governed by the reality of Nietzsche's death of God, and that the scholar violates his ultimate duty as a scholar by living in a state of blindness or oblivion toward our "fate" (p. 28) and the "ineluctable fact of our historical situation" (p. 27). Living in an era of thoroughgoing rationalization and disenchantment asserts moral obligations – above all, the obligation to see one's situation, one's fate, dispassionately and unsentimentally, with intellectual courage. For a "scientist" (that is, a scholar), intellectual integrity is the ultimate ethical duty (p. 31), and what Weber sees all around him and what he depicts again and again in his lecture are failures of moral and intellectual integrity, failures of courage, both in the culture at large ("our youth") and, more particularly, in his fellow intellectuals.

One of the things that we need to reflect on is why the language of "fate" looms as large as it does in this text. Part of the answer, I think, is that Weber is anxious to load as heavy a sense of tragic responsibility on his listeners as he can, and one of the principal themes of ancient tragedy, of course, was the theme of being entangled in a fate beyond one's control. Transposing this theme onto the modern situation, Weber's message is: We want consolation; we want to live in a world that provides help and support for human purposes – a world where the various human ideals can be harmonized and satisfied in an overarching unity, but we are fated to live in an age in which the monotheistic god is dead, different human aspirations are in irresolvable war with each other, and *consolation is out of reach*. We are fated to live in a world ruled by the scientific understanding of the universe, and science does not tell us what to do or how to live our lives; the gap has to be filled by the heroic exercise of choice and decision. We live in a tragic universe, and hard choices or hard decisions are demanded of us. Do we respond to this situation of hard fate with despair and indecision or with equally hard and heroic resolve?

---

[21] This is very similar to Leo Strauss's suggestion, to be discussed in our excursus devoted to the Strauss-Löwith correspondence, that Western civilization had for centuries been "pampered" by Christian providentialism. No doubt, both Weber and Strauss imbibed this idea from Nietzsche.

Weber's rhetoric of tragedy, of heroic resolve, of duty and integrity, of facing up to harsh fate, rises to a climax in his final two paragraphs on pages 30 and 31. Consider for instance this forceful sentence: "To anyone who is unable to endure the fate of the age like a man we must say that he should return to the welcoming and merciful embrace of the old churches." In other words, for people who want to be cowards, fine, be a coward! It is possible for people to turn their backs on modern science and its ethical imperatives, and if people are willing to pay the price for that, fine. However, scholars have a duty to uphold intellectual integrity and to resist the temptations to supply "academic prophecies" that will make good the kind of consolation that rationalizing modernity inexorably strips away.[22] Science cannot put itself in the cultural space formerly occupied by religion: that is intolerable. What one needs as a scholar is "the courage to make up [one's] mind about [one's] ultimate standpoint." "Feeble equivocation" must be rejected; one needs a decisive and clear-eyed embrace of one's god along with an acceptance of whatever conditions are entailed by embracing that particular god. One needs the "finding and obeying" of one's own "daemon" (final sentence of the lecture). If a rationalized or disenchanted view of the universe leaves us without guidance about the proper purposes of a human life, we have to be "manly" and decide these things for ourselves, in accordance with our fate as inhabitants of the kind of social world that has been thrust upon us. (Weber's text is hyper-masculine in its rhetoric, with the unmistakable implication that Nietzsche was right to reject Christianity for its "feminization" of human existence.[23])

I think it is fairly easy to see lines of affinity in all these themes between Weber and Freud. Both of them thought that above all, we have a human obligation not to be fools or cowards – not to cave in in the face of stern and unflinching realities. Both Freud and Weber are deep pessimists. Both of them thought that human beings must rise to a superlatively high standard of human nobility in the face of the harsh demands exerted by a disenchanted and profoundly unforgiving world of brute factuality. Both of them saw the world as tragic, and thought that human beings only rose to being fully human insofar as they comported themselves as self-conscious protagonists in a classical tragedy. This is obviously a very high (and perhaps impossible) normative ideal.

[22] Cf. the warning against "new prophets" in Max Weber, *The Protestant Ethic and the Spirit of Capitalism*, trans. Talcott Parsons (New York: Charles Scribner's Sons, 1958), p. 182.

[23] See, for instance, *The Antichrist*, §§ 58 (contrast between Christian "effeminacy" and pagan "virility") and 59 (contrast between Christianity and Islam at the end of the section).

It may seem even more paradoxical to present Weber as a political philosopher than to present Freud as a political philosopher. This is because of the very heavy emphasis that Weber places on the notion of "value-freedom." Social science, for Weber, is rigorously "value-free." Sociology sticks to the facts and does not try to preach values. Weber was emphatic about that, but my suggestion is that Weber's "values" are themselves expressed in (or "inscribed" in) this very emphasis on value-freedom, as paradoxical as this may sound. Value-freedom, for Weber, was an essential aspect of the pathos of nobility (or pathos of tragic heroism) required in order to face up to a brutally disenchanted world. And "nobility," it goes without saying, is not a value-free conception. What we get in Weber – even more than in Freud – is a philosophic stance of stern facing-up to the realities of life, staring the facts of life squarely in the eye and not flinching. In other words, Weber articulates a view of life oriented to heroes, and, in that sense, his sociological account of modern disenchantment and its human consequences gives Weber what he wants as a normative theorist: a world largely stripped of ready-made meaning, where any meaning that we can draw from the world will have to be fabricated from our own inner resources, which requires a kind of existential heroism and which will dramatically increase the burden resting on our own shoulders to render the world in which we dwell a properly meaningful one.

Needless to say, the themes that I have highlighted in *Science as a Vocation* are also present in *Politics as a Vocation*. Indeed, one can say that the latter text supplies one particular illustration (namely, the case of the modern professional politician) of what Weber has in mind when he speaks, in *Science as a Vocation*'s closing sentence, of "finding and obeying" one's own "daemon." *Politics as a Vocation*, like the text we have already discussed, was delivered as a lecture at the University of Munich; this second lecture was delivered on January 28, 1919, as the editors highlight in their introduction (pp. xxxiv-xxxvii), in the painful aftermath of Germany's defeat in the First World War.[24] It has been rightly described as "the best lecture ever given about politics."[25] Weber's intention is to provide a political education – specifically, an education in political realism as opposed to political idealism. All the sociological

---

[24] On pp. 79–80 of *The Vocation Lectures*, Weber offers what is implicitly but unmistakably a (rather bitter) commentary on the outcome of the war.

[25] Michael Ignatieff, *Fire and Ashes: Success and Failure in Politics* (Toronto: Random House Canada, 2013), p. 148. In the spirit of Weber, Ignatieff calls politics "the noblest and most vexatious of all human activities" (p. 172).

detail laid out on pages 32 to 76 of the lecture is very sobering and *intended* to be sobering. There is a kind of political romanticism in Weber's idea of charisma (in the sense that it bases political authority on a kind of spontaneous magic), but one can think of it as the flip side of a vision of politics that is (very deliberately) as unromantic and anti-romantic as possible. Sociology as Weber practices it involves not only intellectual understanding but also virtues of character, a kind of iron discipline in banishing all sentimentalism and seeing the world as it truly is. The realities of political life are hard, and the person with a true calling for politics, in Weber's view, is one who can see the realities clearly and stare them down.

As before, a key theme of the lecture is the idea of being resolute in deciding upon a "daemon" by which to give meaning to one's life and following through on whatever is required in order to be absolutely true to that daemon. Consider the following text (p. 40): "Whoever lives 'for' politics makes 'this his life' in an *inward* sense. Either he enjoys the naked exercise of the power he possesses or he feeds his inner equilibrium and his self-esteem with the consciousness that by serving a 'cause' he gives his own life a *meaning* [Weber's italics]." What is at stake here is "living for a cause." Being a professional politician means banishing all sentimentalism about the realities of political life. In a modern society, it entails, for instance, accepting the need for ruthless control of a party apparatus. There certainly is nothing edifying about this; consider your average U.S. presidential election! But anyone who abstracts from these realities is not being serious about the vocation they have embraced and, therefore, is failing to honor the god to which they have supposedly pledged absolute dedication. If one has chosen to serve the "god" of modern, party-based professional politics, then one takes onboard everything that goes with worship of that god. One could say that having a sentimentalized view of what the life of political responsibility entails would be akin to deciding to be a monk but thinking that, instead of getting up for 6 A.M. prayers, one will just sleep in when one feels like it. It is not a serious commitment, and, in Weber's view of things, life is always about making serious commitments, commitments that really count. The essence of Weber's view of the world is encapsulated beautifully near the end of *Politics as a Vocation* (*Vocation Lectures*, p. 91): "What matters is the trained ability to scrutinize the realities of life ruthlessly, to withstand them and to measure up to them inwardly." Weber's definition of politics in terms of a monopoly on the legitimate deployment of force or violence is clearly a notable instance of what he means by the "ruthless" determination to look reality in the eye. (Consider the unflinchingness of what he writes

on page 84: "In politics, the decisive means is the use of force"; and also
page 86: the early Christians were right in believing that "whoever becomes
involved in politics ... has made a pact with satanic powers.") For Weber, life
is about commitment – without any hope of consolation or any desire to
smooth off the world's rough edges or cushion its harshness.

These themes are raised again when Weber states that true politicians
require "passion in the sense of a *commitment to the matter in hand*, that is, the
passionate dedication to a 'cause,' to the God or demon that presides over it"
(p. 76; Weber's italics). "Commitment to [politics] must be born of passion
and be nourished by it" (p. 77). Once again, we have the image of a polytheistic choosing of the gods that one will serve, with the insistence that this
choice must be categorical, unconditional. There is nothing half-hearted
about the choice of a god: once this choice has been made, the whole of
one's soul must be bound to it, otherwise it does not count as a "serious"
life commitment – what is referred to, in Weber's rhetoric, as "an authentic
human activity and not just a frivolous intellectual game" (p. 77); or what
he refers to on page 93 as "staunchness of heart." At the bottom of page 77,
Weber describes "the lack of commitment to a cause" as a "mortal sin in
the field of politics." Of course, pure commitment does not suffice. It has to
be backed up by the resolute sense of responsibility that consists in seeing
soberly and clearly the way the world actually works (hence Weber's talk, on
page 77, of "hot passion" being balanced by "a cool sense of proportion"),
since the lack of this very sense of responsibility just proves that one is not
truly committed to the god of politics – to truly political politics, one could
say. (Put otherwise: commitment and responsibility are a "package deal.")
Especially important is the text on page 78 where Weber declares that "the
meaning of human activity" consists in "the tragedy in which all action is
ensnared, political action above all."[26] Politics as a calling encapsulates the

---

[26] Consider Leo Strauss's suggestion that Weber had the kind of soul that craves tragedy: Weber "needed
the necessity of guilt. He had to combine the anguish bred by atheism (the absence of any redemption, of any solace) with the anguish bred by revealed religion (the oppressive sense of guilt). Without
that combination, life would cease to be tragic and thus lose its depth"; *Natural Right and History*
(Chicago: University of Chicago Press, 1974), p. 66. It seems to me that Strauss's formulation (not
just a craving for anguish, but a *double* craving, so to speak) indeed captures something essential about
Weber's intellectual personality. Cf. the related but somewhat different analysis of Weber's "soul," and
how knots in his soul shaped his thought, in Strauss, *What is Political Philosophy?* (Chicago: University
of Chicago Press, 1988), p. 23. And for Eric Voegelin's somewhat different interpretation of the tragic
pathos in Weber, see *The New Science of Politics* (Chicago: University of Chicago Press, 1974), p. 22. One
might also observe that if Weber were merely what he wishes to present himself as being, a pure social
scientist and nothing more, then it would be mysterious why all these theorists (not only Strauss and
Voegelin but also Löwith, Habermas, and MacIntyre) are philosophically so preoccupied by him.

full nobility, the full dignity of human existence precisely because it is a sphere of life where one can come face to face with life's tragedy and participate in worldly action intended to measure up to this tragic character of the nature of things.

Of course, the key question in all this is whether Weber can stay innocent of political philosophy in the way that he presumes he can.[27] After all, he puts some astoundingly grand and far-reaching philosophical notions on the table: the idea that there is something inherently tragic in human life and in the choices we have to make as human beings; the idea that we are implanted in a "fate" entailed by living in an age that thoroughly rationalizes our experience of life, and therefore denudes us of any assurance of help or guidance from nature or science; the idea that therefore our only existential resource is our capacity heroically to *will* commitment to a particular god; the idea that polytheism therefore supplies a truer or more noble view of the demands of life than what we get from a monotheistic civilization (p. 22: polytheism, rather than monotheism, is vindicated by "pure experience"). These, taken individually, and even more so taken together, constitute intellectual claims of exceptional ambition. One could even go so far as to describe them as "metaphysically" ambitious. Needless to say, that defeats Weber's intention to keep "values" out of his sociology.[28]

Weber's basic idea is that we have to choose whether to become Christian saints or upholders of political responsibility.[29] This is only one example of the strict either/or choices that life forces upon us, but for Weber it is a very important example. Borrowing Machiavelli's formulation, which Weber cites on page 91, one has to make a radical choice between the salvation of one's political cause and the salvation of one's own soul.[30] This is

---

[27] I can sum up the message of this book very simply: One can *think* that one can disavow or turn one's back on political philosophy, that one can get along without it, but really one cannot. Overarching reflection on the ends of life is unavoidable. If one pitches it out through the front door, it will slip back in through the back door.

[28] Confronting Simone Weil's diametrically opposite judgment helps us appreciate the "metaphysically" controversial nature of Weber's claims: "Faith is above all the conviction that the good is one. To believe that there are several distinct and mutually independent forms of good, like truth, beauty and morality – that is what constitutes the sin of polytheism"; *The Need for Roots*, trans. Arthur Wills (London: Routledge, 2002), p. 249; cf. page 232.

[29] See page 90: "The genius, or the demon, of politics lives in an inner tension with the God of love as well as with the Christian God as institutionalized in the Christian churches, and it is a tension that can erupt at any time into an insoluble conflict."

[30] Again, the most radical antipode to Weber's view within twentieth-century political philosophy is Simone Weil. See note 21 of our chapter on Weil (as well as the text to which that note is attached). For the articulation of a view much closer to Weber's, see *Hannah Arendt: The Recovery of the Public World*, ed. Melvyn A. Hill (New York: St. Martin's Press, 1979), pp. 310–311.

what political theorists call "the problem of dirty hands." Splitting the difference between these alternatives will produce nothing of human value, and there is no point in looking to anything in the metaphysical structure of the world to try to relieve us of the nakedness of this ultimate decision. Looking to the universe for guidance is itself a mark of existential cowardice. However, it has to be said that no one reading Weber's text and absorbing the rhetoric deployed throughout the text can think that Weber is neutral between the two ethics – that of the unworldly saint and that of the responsible politician – or think that in his own view the two are of equal legitimacy or are equal with respect to human dignity.[31] Real neutrality toward the two competing ethics would be equivalent to saying that it is okay to be a coward in the face of reality, and that is hardly a stance that Weber can endorse.

Especially relevant here is Weber's powerful discussion on page 86 of "the age-old-problem of theodicy" – that is, the problem wrestled with by all the world religions of reconciling God's omnipotence and God's goodness. "How could a power that is said to be both omnipotent and good create such an irrational world of unmerited suffering, unpunished injustice, and incorrigible stupidity?" Weber is obviously in no doubt that the universe is *not* governed by a providentialist deity who looks after human welfare and ensures an appropriate correspondence between how human beings conduct themselves morally and the justice or injustice that the universe metes out to them. He asserts that if human beings were not profoundly disturbed and anxious about the lack of such a cosmic justice, religions would not exist in the first place. ("This problem, the experience of the irrationality of the universe, has always been the driving force of the entire history of religion.") These are "the facts," the nature of the world. Evil cannot be defeated by adopting Christ's counsel of turning the other cheek, therefore politics necessarily involves "a pact with satanic powers." People who cannot face up to this are cowards who (analogously to Freud's rhetoric) cannot rise to maturity; rather, they get stuck at a baby level of existence.

---

[31] As already noted in section 1 of this prologue, crucial here is Weber's reference to the Gospel's teaching of turning the other cheek as "an ethic of ignominy" [*Würdelosigkeit*; literally: forfeiture of one's dignity] (p. 82). Weber adds, "except for a saint," but it is not clear why what is ignominious or lacking in dignity for all other human beings is not also ignominious or lacking in dignity for a saint. Consider also Weber's discussion on page 92 of the pseudo-serious character of appeals to an ethics of conviction by contemporary politicians (that is, his strong suspicion that they lack "*inner gravity*"); and page 93's contemptuous treatment of those who will resort to "a mystical escape from the world" when they realize that they are not humanly equal to the demands of politics ("*not* equal to the challenge of the world as it really is") – and in particular, not equal to the "polar night of icy darkness and harshness" that awaits Germany.

The rhetoric attacking metaphysical cowardice – cowardice in facing up to the way the world really is – runs (at least implicitly and often explicitly) throughout Weber's text; yet obviously "coward" is not a value-free term. In deploying this rhetoric, Weber violates the strictures of his own sociology, but deployment of this rhetoric is not accidental, a careless slip; it is central to how Weber sees social life.

Weber may be right that science cannot *prove* that way of life A is rationally superior to way of life B or way of life C, but it does not follow from that that we have no rational standards by which to judge the normative attractions and normative drawbacks of different visions of life or different conceptions of the human good. Nor does it follow that we are required (unless we are cowards) to solve the problem of how to live by a heroic exercise of pure volition, pure willing. That seems like a nihilistic, or potentially nihilistic, view of things. There are people who can commit themselves to their chosen gods with utter dedication – for instance, terrorists like Bin Laden or Timothy McVeigh – but who choose ends of life for which no good case can be made, and who, precisely through their heroic willing of an uncompromising view of life, place themselves wholly outside the boundaries of human rationality. (Weber sometimes writes as if existential extremism, in itself, is humanly admirable, which is a very dubious proposition!) To be sure, in doing philosophy, we should retain a steady appreciation of the limits of human reason and never lose our awareness of the untranscendable *finitude* of human life and human judgment. However, that applies to all aspects of science and philosophy, not just political philosophy. It certainly does not give us a reason to give up on the enterprise of reflecting on the ends of life.

I

Hannah Arendt: The Performativity
of Politics

Endowing Life with Splendor

There are many things that are questionable or unpersuasive in the political philosophy of Hannah Arendt, but there is one thing that entitles her to the high rank she continues to occupy among twentieth-century political philosophers, namely that she is a brilliant spokesperson for the view that politics possesses a privileged status among the panoply of human activities, and that she supplies an especially powerful articulation of why politics in particular is what truly humanizes human beings.

It may seem obvious that there is a performative dimension to politics. After all, politicians cannot get elected unless they succeed in presenting themselves in ways that voters find attractive and compelling and that capture voters' emotions, engage their sense of identity, and elicit their trust.[1] What seems much more surprising is that this aspect of political life can be presented normatively and, as we discover when we read *The Human Condition*,[2] can in fact be made the basis of a strikingly bold political philosophy.

What is immediately striking about Arendt's articulation of her political philosophy in *The Human Condition* is all that is *missing* from it: no account of the modern state; no account, really, of citizenship or the rights and duties of the citizen; no account of the problems and dilemmas of modern states

---

[1] For an excellent account of this in the context of the 2008 U.S. presidential election, see Jeffrey C. Alexander, *The Performance of Politics: Obama's Victory and the Democratic Struggle for Power* (Oxford: Oxford University Press, 2010). As Alexander makes explicit on pages 278–281, Arendt is one of the theorists informing the story that he tells about the Obama campaign. Alexander's book translates into sociological language what is basically an Arendtian vision of politics and applies it much more directly to contemporary political processes than Arendt herself ever does.

[2] All parenthetical page references in this chapter are to Hannah Arendt, *The Human Condition*, 2nd edition (Chicago: University of Chicago Press, 1998).

(e.g., problems of fair distribution, or of how to balance equality and liberty, or of just and unjust wars).[3] On the contrary, the purpose of her political philosophy is to give an account of why much of what the modern state does, much of how it conceives itself as a set of institutions, is questionable when judged by the standard of an uncompromisingly authentic understanding of the political qua political. She shifts us to a completely different universe of political experience, and she does that very deliberately.

There is certainly no lack of intellectual ambition in Arendt's account of politics for the sake of politics. As she makes most explicit in an unforgettable passage at the very end of her book *On Revolution*, Arendt's fundamental ambition is to establish politics as the sphere of human experience where human beings turn a potentially futile, ephemeral, and basically meaningless existence into a form of human existence that is non-futile, non-ephemeral, and rich with meaning. That is a tall order! And for a thinker who is emphatic that philosophy must relinquish its formerly overly hubristic metaphysical aspirations, her own brand of political philosophy seems itself to border on claims of a metaphysical order. Here is the text from *On Revolution* to which I refer:

[Sophocles in *Oedipus at Colonus* wrote:] "Not to be born prevails over all meaning uttered in words; by far the second-best for life, once it has appeared, is to go as swiftly as possible whence it came." There he also let us know, through the mouth of Theseus, the legendary founder of Athens and hence her spokesman, what it was that enabled ordinary men, young and old, to bear life's burden: it was the polis, the space of men's free deeds and living words, which could endow life with splendor.[4]

This is Arendt's whole political philosophy in a nutshell, with the key idea being that politics is meaning-conferring. Without politics, without a common space in which human beings speak and act, life is empty and meaningless, but with politics (assuming it is available according to Arendt's exacting understanding of it – not at all something one can take for granted!), life is capable of "splendor." And one particular human activity makes the

---

[3] Indeed, one largely sympathetic book review went so far as to suggest that "the book makes no pretensions to political philosophy"! James P. Scanlan, "Man as Laborer, Dehumanized," *The Review of Politics*, Vol. 22, no. 2 (April 1960), p. 299. Obviously, I do not go along with this judgment, but I can more or less understand why a reader of *The Human Condition* would come to the judgment that Arendt must be doing something other than political philosophy.

[4] Hannah Arendt, *On Revolution* (New York: Viking Press, 1965), p. 285. Ross Douthat ("Puddleglum and the Savage," *New York Times*, Nov. 24, 2013, p. SR 12) suggests that what animates critics of modernity in general is "the desire for grace and beauty, for icons and heroes, for a high-stakes dimension to human affairs that a consumerist, materialist civilization can flatten and exclude." This encapsulation obviously fits Hannah Arendt extremely well.

difference between a world where life is worth living (a life with splendor) and a world where life is empty and trivial (a life without splendor). Can one imagine a more philosophically ambitious set of claims than that? But this is precisely the scale of the existential propositions Arendt's theorizing puts on the table.

Whatever one's ultimate judgment on this conception, I would urge students of Arendt's political philosophy not to be too quick in dismissing her vision of politics as just a nostalgia-driven romanticization. I once met a political theorist (Kent Moors) who had been a speechwriter for Bobby Kennedy. He would sit in the back seat of limousines with Kennedy on the way to campaign events; Kennedy would cross out lines he did not like, and Moors would rewrite them before they arrived at the venue. One can well imagine that for someone in such a situation, life at that moment would take on a kind of enhanced reality whereas the rest of one's life, by contrast, might come to feel as if it had diminished reality – a sense of "flattened" reality, one might say. Clearly, the same sort of thing would apply in the case of those immediately involved in the civil rights movement (arguably, the highest manifestation of the political witnessed within the lifetime of those of my generation). Here, Arendt's idea of endowing life with splendor has some real purchase. Nor in the Bobby Kennedy example is it just a matter of being exposed to the aura of an exceptionally charismatic individual. I do not think it is far-fetched or implausible to say that the common world in which we all have a stake felt as if it had collapsed when Bobby Kennedy or Martin Luther King Jr. was assassinated, in a way that it did not when, say, John Lennon was assassinated. If this is right (if it is not itself the product of a romanticized and nostalgic view), then it suggests that there are at least rare moments – associated with the political agency of the greatest and most tragic figures – when the Arendtian experience of politics is within the ken of mere moderns.[5]

What I want to do in the discussion that follows is to clarify the basic structure of Arendt's argument for the centrality or privileged status of politics among the various human activities. Why should politics have this privileged

[5] The closest I have come to this sort of thing within my own life-experience (namely, politics as a mode of enhanced reality) was a cloak-and-dagger visit to Prague in the spring of 1983 under the auspices of the Jan Hus Educational Foundation. The project of the Czech dissident intellectuals with whom I met was to fashion a "world" in precisely the Arendtian sense – a world that was private in 1983 but had become fully public a mere six years later. They read Arendt in *samizdat*, and then built a society in which her books could be freely published in Czech. For an account of all this, see Barbara Day, *The Velvet Philosophers* (London: The Claridge Press, 1999).

status? Why should life be endowed with splendor by virtue of our participation in the political realm rather than our participation in the sphere of economic life, or cultural life, or family life, or religious life, or various other spheres in which we live out our human existence? Why does my own individual existence as a person with particular parents, a particular spouse, particular children, particular neighbors, and a particular job in the larger economy not suffice to give me a meaningful life? Moreover, one might well ask, why should we single out one particular sphere of human activity or human experience as a privileged site, so to speak, for the realization of human ends? Why not leave individuals to decide this for themselves? Why not aim at political and societal neutrality with respect to these different spheres of life? This liberal-neutralist conception is of course a staple of contemporary liberal political philosophy. (And market liberals would add, why not leave it to the market?) In response, I would suggest that it is quite naïve to think that any society does anything other than privilege certain ways of being human. Let's simplify. Suppose there are merely three competing conceptions of the human good:

- According to vision of the human good number 1, the center of human existence consists in being faithful to God's will, fulfilling what God expects of us.
- According to vision of the human good number 2, the center of human existence consists in building up a shared civic existence by working to strengthen and enhance civic relationships and civic solidarity, that is, how we relate to each other as citizens among fellow citizens.
- According to vision of the human good number 3, the center of human existence consists in focusing one's energies on economic life – what to produce, how to earn a living, how to exercise consumer preferences; in short, individual and collective decisions about what to sell, what to buy, how to invest one's savings, and so on.

Once these three possibilities have been laid out, there is no question that our society strongly privileges the third.[6] If so, one must admit a necessary role for theory in questioning whether our society has put its money on the right horse, so to speak. That is, we need to raise the question of whether the vision of human good that we as a society have favored is indeed the appropriate locus for human flourishing. So when Arendt is asserting her own ranking of the political over the economic, this is not necessarily a

---

[6] For a forceful argument about how, in contemporary liberal society (especially the United States), vision of the human good number 3 has comprehensively displaced vision of the human good number 2, see Michael Sandel's recent book, *What Money Can't Buy* (New York: Farrar, Straus and Giroux, 2012).

mark of her overbearing philosophical hubris; rather, she is challenging an existing societal ranking with a counter-ranking.

It is often thought that Arendt is updating Aristotle's ancient argument for "man as a naturally political animal," and that therefore the structure of her argument is in some basic sense "neo-Aristotelian." I think this represents a fundamental misunderstanding, and if it matters not just *what* one argues, but the basis *on which* one erects one's argument, it is important to set this right. (My teacher, Charles Taylor, always presumed Arendt to be a kind of neo-Aristotelian, but he was not the only one to get this wrong.[7]) Arendt is not an Aristotelian, not only because she consistently criticizes Aristotle no less than she consistently criticizes Plato; she is not an Aristotelian because for her, the argument about the privileged status of politics among the various human activities is not an argument about "the human telos" – not an argument about human nature or how we realize our innate human ends. I'm not sure she really has thought this through satisfactorily, because if participation in a political realm allows us to endow our lives with splendor in a way that is unavailable through other forms of human experience, then that certainly looks like an argument for a certain conception of human flourishing, even if she does not conceptualize it that way. Arendt has the notion that human beings are defined by *who* they are, not *what* they are, and that priority of the *who* over the *what* strongly militates against appeals to an objective human nature in constructing one's political philosophy. If she is right about that, then Plato and Aristotle were wrong to found their political philosophy on teleological conceptions – notions of what it takes for human beings to flourish as human beings. However, as I have already intimated, I think it is quite questionable that Arendt can avoid the notion of a flourishing human life in the way that she hoped to avoid it. While we certainly do not wish to exempt Arendt from philosophical criticism, neither do we want to be insensitive to the kind of argument that Arendt intended her argument to be.

So, what kind of argument is it? The fundamental argument hangs on the foundational distinction between "life" and "world." Theorists like Arendt who pride themselves on being anti-foundationalist, anti-metaphysical, or post-metaphysical tend to insist that there are no "Archimedean points."

---

[7] Jürgen Habermas, in *Theory and Practice*, trans. John Viertel (London: Heinemann, 1974), p. 286, n. 4, implies that Arendt's argument is fundamentally inspired by Aristotle. That is a misreading. The same error of considering Arendt as a representative of "the Aristotelian tradition" occurs in Habermas, *The Philosophical Discourse of Modernity*, trans. Frederick G. Lawrence (Cambridge, MA: MIT Press, 1987), p. 48.

But one of my theses is that there is always an Archimedean point when we are dealing with a political philosophy that is a genuine political philosophy, and this distinction between life and world is Arendt's Archimedean point.[8] Life is ephemeral; we are born and we struggle to feed ourselves, clothe ourselves, and house ourselves, and then we die. Intrinsically, an individual life lived at the level of life as such leaves nothing behind. It is biological existence, and what remains of biological existence after death is merely a corpse, hardly more significant than what existed before the conception of the biological creature. World, by contrast, is durable (or relatively durable). It provides a framework of shared spectacles, shared memories, and shared narratives that outlive (and transcend in meaningfulness) our individual lives in their bare individuality. Life is subjective; world is inter-subjective. The purpose of life is to sustain its biological existence; the purpose of world is to confer inter-subjective meaning on lives that would otherwise lack it. We need the worldliness of the world in order to live individual lives that are something more than a transient, ephemeral, meaningless coming on the stage and moving off the stage.[9] That is the core of Arendt's political philosophy.

Of course, all of this generates another important question: If the distinction between life and world, the ephemerality of the former and the durability or relative durability of the latter, grounds Arendt's political philosophy, why is it specifically the political dimension of existence that constitutes the worldliness of the world, and what exactly does political mean in this privileging of the political in such an account of the meaningfulness of human life? These questions are far from easy to answer, and Arendt generally leaves us to reconstruct the answers from her narratives about the Greeks and the

---

[8] Arendt's 1954 lecture, "Concern with Politics in Recent European Philosophical Thought," concludes with talk about articulation of "a new political philosophy" and "erection of a new fundament": see Hannah Arendt, *Essays in Understanding 1930–1954*, ed. Jerome Kohn (New York: Harcourt Brace & Company, 1994), p. 445. *The Human Condition* obviously became the fulfillment of this theoretical program. As just noted, Arendt's philosophical rhetoric is typically anti-foundationalist, but her suggestion in this text seems to me correct; one cannot aspire to the articulation of a new political philosophy (or any political philosophy) without endeavoring to erect an intellectual "fundament" upon which it will stand. On page 443 of the same text, Arendt acknowledges the Heideggerian provenance of what is arguably the key conception of her own political philosophy, namely the idea of "world." In "Love and Worldliness: Hannah Arendt's Reading of Saint Augustine," in *Hannah Arendt: Twenty Years Later*, ed. Larry May and Jerome Kohn (Cambridge, MA: MIT Press, 1996), pp. 269–284, I trace Arendt's preoccupation with worldliness back to her very early dialogue with St. Augustine.

[9] Why does worldliness require a public world? Suppose I amass a personal library, or a private art collection. Isn't this a way of fashioning a world for myself, sheltered against the flux of nature? (As a grand example, think of Freud's astonishing museum-like study at 20 Maresfield Gardens in London.) Why doesn't a worldly dwelling-place that is private rather than public satisfy Arendt's conception of worldliness? Arendt never tells us.

history of political thought rather than addressing them directly and giving her own systematic account.

Let's look at some actual passages from *The Human Condition* that express Arendt's ideas of life and worldliness and give us a better understanding of how Arendt's notion of the political relates to those ideas.

The meaningfulness of everyday relationships is disclosed not in everyday life but in rare deeds, just as the significance of a historical period shows itself only in the few events that illuminate it. (p. 42)

That is, what we are doing when we connect ourselves to a public realm that bestows a political identity on us is not simply servicing our material needs as creatures who have to be fed, kept healthy, and rescued from poverty and have a menu of other material necessities satisfied; rather, we are doing something on a "higher" level – humanizing ourselves, giving ourselves a stake in some more epic narrative that gives us a sense of collective destiny beyond the mundane realities of our individual lives. Or rather, increasingly, our modern societies are failing to do this, and are leaving us bereft of that higher identity, that higher consciousness of participating in enduring "events"; as a consequence, we are consigned to the purely mundane level, living lives of futility without lasting significance. What happens on the public stage provides "illumination," the lighting up of a shared experience.[10] Without these privileged happenings in a shared space of appearances, we are left with mere obscurity and triviality.

One might add that Arendt's theme in this aspect of her political theory flows into her famous (or infamous) "banality of evil" thesis as developed in her book *Eichmann in Jerusalem*.[11] The thesis, put simply, is that human beings are capable of unprecedented kinds of evil, totalitarian evil, insofar as the conditions of life in modern mass societies "banalize" them, reduce them to utterly shallow, thoughtless, and pedestrian placeholders in an anonymous social machinery. This thesis may be true or false; again, it is a set of claims of staggering ambition. But it is worth highlighting because it clarifies how big the stakes are for Arendt's argument in *The Human Condition*: if human beings really do need a sense that they are tied to something grand and "larger than life" being performed in the public world that all citizens share

---

[10] Cf. the phrase "make shine" in the passage from page 55 quoted later.

[11] For a good account of the moral and intellectual limitations of Arendt's depiction of Eichmann, see Mark Lilla's essay, "Arendt and Eichmann: The New Truth," in the November 21, 2013 issue of *The New York Review of Books*. As Lilla nicely puts it, Arendt judged Eichmann "in light of her own intellectual preoccupations, inherited from Heidegger, with 'authenticity', the faceless crowd, society as a machine, and the importance of a kind of 'thinking' that modern philosophy had abolished."

as citizens, modern societies pay a very large price, not just with respect to banalized everyday life but even with respect to people's capacity for evil-doing of the worst kind when life is systematically reduced to an unrelent-ingly petty and pedestrian existence. In that sense, the themes of *The Human Condition* are directly related to the pathologies of modern evil analyzed in *Eichmann in Jerusalem*.[12]

Here is another important passage:

To live together in the world means essentially that a world of things is between those who have it in common, as a table is located between those who sit around it; the world, like every in-between, relates and separates men at the same time. [But with the rise of mass society,] the world between them has lost its power to gather them together, to relate and separate them. The weirdness of this situation resembles a spiritualistic séance where a number of people gathered around a table might suddenly, through some magic trick, see the table vanish from their midst, so that two persons sitting opposite each other were no longer separated but also would be entirely unrelated to each other by anything tangible. (pp. 52–53)

The claim here is that the world of modernity involves a process of "de-worlding," so to speak. Because it is not our own individual existence, but rather the presence of a shared public world, that allows us to defeat or transcend (to some extent) the mortality and fleetingness of all human things, this loss of a tangible shared world (if Arendt's highly metaphorical descriptions are persuasive) threatens to deprive us of what we most need as human beings. Or that, at any rate, is the kind of claim she is making.

Only the existence of a public realm and the world's subsequent transformation into a community of things which gathers men together and relates them to each other depends entirely on permanence. If the world is to contain a public space, it cannot be erected for one generation and planned for the living only; it must transcend the life-span of mortal men. Without this transcendence into a potential earthly immortality, no politics, strictly speaking, no common world and no pub-lic realm, is possible.... The common world is what we enter when we are born and what we leave behind when we die.... Such a common world can survive the

---

[12] Of course, the politics of Nazism is not exhausted by the banality of an Eichmann. On the contrary, the Nazis offered grand deeds galore – monumental rallies in monumental stadiums, epic architecture on the grandest scale, a politics of grandeur deliberately modeled on the Roman Empire. The chal-lenge might be put to Arendt that European fascism's evil politics of grandeur comes much closer to meeting Arendt's standards of non-instrumental politics, of politics for the sake of politics, than anything one encounters in liberal-bourgeois societies (hence the attempts by some contemporary theorists to highlight affinities between Arendt and Carl Schmitt). In an important sense, the goal of the national-socialist "Reich" was precisely Arendtian immortality, and if (God forbid) World War II had had a different outcome, no doubt their "great deeds" would have lived on in collective memory for the duration of the fascist tyranny. Herein lies the enormous peril of celebrating politics apart from its content and its ends.

coming and going of the generations only to the extent that it appears in public. It is the publicity of the public realm which can absorb and make shine through the centuries whatever men may want to save from the natural ruin of time. [In the past but "not any more,"] men entered the public realm because they wanted something of their own or something they had in common with others to be more permanent than their earthly lives. (p. 55)

This is what is at stake: mortality versus immortality.[13] In its ultimate meaning, politics is not about serving the mundane purposes of members of society who share concerns about whether they will be impoverished or prosperous, healthy or sick, sheltered from nature or exposed to the elements. Something much bigger is at stake: whether our lives are limited in their scope to our own paltry existence or whether human beings are oriented to a sense of human meaningfulness grander than these paltry individual lives. "Worldliness" ultimately means that human beings are aware of this grander experience of the common world and our stake in it; "worldlessness" or "world-alienation" means that as a society or as a civilization we have fallen into oblivion about these higher stakes.[14] (There are unmistakable echoes in these passages of Heidegger's philosophy, shaped as it is by the idea of *Seinsvergessenheit*, that is, "forgetfulness of Being" or spiritual destitution.) What we need above all as human beings is "a space in which things are saved from destruction by time" (p. 57), and her thesis is that the way in which we negotiate the relationship between what is public and what is private in the modern world more and more robs us of this space where we are sheltered from flux.

We see from all of these passages that the key theme in Arendt's political philosophy is the theme of *tangibility*. I think it is undeniable that this theme speaks in a very powerful way to our contemporary situation (quite possibly in a more powerful way than when Arendt wrote her book). We live today in a world where virtual reality seems increasingly to be eclipsing

---

[13] In contrast to the existentialists, for whom preoccupation with the inescapability of death led naturally to thoughts of the absurd, Arendt was determined to shift the focus from mortality to natality: Why be preoccupied by the reality of death when the miracle of birth is just as much of a reality in human life? Nonetheless, it remains true that Arendt was no less haunted by the problem of death than the existentialists were.

[14] The idea of world-alienation (one of Arendt's key ideas) is also present in Karl Löwith, as we will see in our chapter devoted to Löwith. (On page 10 of *Der Weltbegriff der neuzeitlichen Philosophie* [Heidelberg: Carl Winter Universitätsverlag, 1960], Löwith calls it *Weltverlust*.) However, for Löwith, the world from which we are alienated is the cosmological world, not a world in the sense of a human mega-artifact. Still, there are substantial overlaps between Löwith's intellectual concerns and those of Arendt. (Both, of course, were schooled by Heidegger, and reflect – and react against – his modes of responding to modernity.)

non-virtual reality; where we are more likely to buy a book online than in a tangible bookshop; where we are more likely (or soon will be) to read an e-book than a physical book; where we are more likely to have electronic conversations than conversations facing each other in physical space; where we are more likely to participate in electronic public space than in physical, tangible public space; where we are more likely to sign electronic petitions than march in physical political rallies; and so on. When we take a photograph, it is an electronic (that is, an ephemeral) image rather than a tangible imprint of an image on a physical film. University teaching, for good or ill, seems to be moving toward interaction via computer screens rather than in a physically shared space. The tangibility of our world seems to have eroded and may well go on eroding.[15] All of this makes Arendt look amazingly prescient, and rightly so!

To be sure, the concept of ephemerality is a relative one. As Keynes famously put it in *A Tract on Monetary Reform* (1923), "In the long run we are all dead." That is, ephemerality is inscribed in our human condition – it is something that neither theory nor practice will ever cure in the way that we may wish it could be. If I carve a sculpture in marble (a pretty durable material!) or, say, as pharaoh order my slaves to build the pyramids in Egypt, that is an impressive standard of tangibility and durability relative to most things that human beings fabricate during their short duration on earth. But the marble sculpture, or indeed the pyramids, will eventually perish into dust. Still, Arendt's claim (interesting but contestable) is that it matters a great deal to us as human beings what kind of durability/ephemerality is normal for us in this or that particular social environment. Her claim is that human life will be *impoverished* if (as she thinks is increasingly the case in our own form of society) the things around us lack sufficient durability or sufficient staying power to constitute a meaningful world as a kind of anchor for a human life that would otherwise be intolerably fleeting.

Here is a good passage from "What Is Freedom?" that again expresses the core Arendtian conception of politics:

If … we understand the political in the sense of the polis, its end or *raison d'être* would be to establish and keep in existence a space where freedom as virtuosity can appear. This is the realm where freedom is a worldly reality, tangible in words which can be heard, in deeds which can be seen, and in events which are talked about, remembered, and turned into stories before they are finally incorporated into the

---

[15] In *Sweet Tooth* (Toronto: Alfred A Knopf Canada, 2012), a novel set in the early 1970s, Ian McEwan notes how the main character has replaced cotton handkerchiefs with paper tissues: "The world was starting to become seriously disposable" (p. 129). Indeed!

great storybook of human history. Whatever occurs in this space of appearances is political by definition, even when it is not a direct product of action. What remains outside it, such as the great feats of barbarian empires, may be impressive and noteworthy, but it is not political, strictly speaking.

Again, we have the characteristic Arendtian notion that *something* must be elevated above the common run of human beings living merely to preserve their biological existence – something grand enough, memorable enough, sufficiently deserving of being "narrativized," to transcend the depressing flux of an animal-like existence. Anything grand enough to fit this description gets included in Arendt's conception of the political, and anything that seems to falls short of this dimension of meaning generation is dismissed as nonpolitical or sub-political. Needless to say, these remarkable claims raise more questions than they answer. The polis achieved this order of heroic existence, but do contemporary political institutions offer similar possibilities? Do we have to return to the ancient polis in order to be truly political? Is there a way to reconcile the kind of mundane purposes typically served by modern states (e.g., providing a decent level of subsistence for the whole society) and the much grander "existential" purposes that for Arendt constitute the political as political? To the extent that there is a radical difference between what "public realm" meant for, say, the Greeks and what it means for us, is Arendt saying that the political (or the authentically political) does not exist at all in modern liberal-bourgeois societies? Are we necessarily fated to live lives that are nonpolitical, lives deprived of the very possibility of being political? Is there a stark either/or here, such that we have to choose between remaining animals living basically meaningless and necessity-defined lives and being truly autonomous "Homeric" heroes in the epic Arendtian sense?

One of the aspects of Arendt's vision of politics that seems most questionable is her insistence that politics is only politics when one participates in it *for its own sake*, that is, politics for the sake of politics. Here is an important statement of that view (again from Arendt's essay, "What Is Freedom?"):

Action, to be free, must be free from motive on one side, from its intended goal as a predictable effect on the other. This is not to say that motives and aims are not important factors in every single act, but they are its determining factors, and action is free to the extent that it is able to transcend them.[16]

---

[16] Hannah Arendt, *Between Past and Future: Eight Exercises in Political Thought*, enlarged ed. (New York: Viking Press, 1968), p. 151; cf. *The Human Condition*, p. 206: "Greatness ... or the specific meaning of each deed, can lie only in the performance itself and neither in its motivation nor its achievement." See also Hannah Arendt, *Thinking* (New York: Harcourt Brace Jovanovich, 1978), p. 131: according to the Greek experience of virtuosity, what counted was neither the "intention of the actor, nor ... the consequences of his deeds" but rather simply the sheer performance itself; hence we see that in

She continues two pages later:

Freedom as inherent in action is perhaps best illustrated by Machiavelli's concept of *virtù* [whose] meaning is best rendered by "virtuosity," that is, an excellence we attribute to the performing arts (as distinguished from the creative arts of making), where the accomplishment lies in the performance itself and not in an end product which outlasts the activity that brought it into existence and becomes independent of it.[17]

This is a radical view, and it seems hard to square with our common experience of politics. Political action, she suggests, is a "performing," not a "making"; but is it true that people would get involved in political agency if they were not fundamentally oriented toward the "end product which outlasts the activity"? Would we admire or praise political actors who were in it simply to show off their virtuosity, as if they were *pure* actors in the theatrical sense, rather than fellow citizens working to promote a shared common good?

Suppose I sign up with the Obama campaign. This is certainly a form of political agency, and it is meant to connect me to events unfolding on the public stage that will generate narratives, generate meanings, and to some extend sustain a larger-than-the-individual public meaning. But I have to have some conception of what *civic ends* are being promoted by this activity. I may volunteer my time to work for Obama because I think his presidency will narrow the gap between rich and poor; or because I think having him in the White House will lessen the chances of reckless foreign wars; or because I think that his policies will decrease the chances of global warming; or because I think he's entitled to a second term as a reward for winning medical insurance for 36 million previously uninsured Americans. And so on. Conversely, if I sign up with the Romney campaign, I may think that a Romney presidency will accelerate a return to American prosperity, because I think the economy only works properly when taxes are very low on the very rich; or because I think Obamacare infringes too much on individual liberties; or because I think Obama's conduct on the international stage is driven too much by idealistic cosmopolitanism and not enough by cold hard American national interests. Now of course I *may* also think that active political participation is an intrinsic human good, because being a good human being incorporates ideas of being a citizen among citizens, and

Arendt's final work, *The Life of the Mind*, she was still committed to the same basic concepts. Indeed, it perhaps would not be overstating matters to say that the idea of performance as non-reducible to either its motivation or its outcome constitutes the central idea of Arendt's political philosophy.

[17] *Between Past and Future*, p. 153.

this ideal of citizenship is hollow unless I'm active in *practicing* my citizenship. That is a reasonable conception, but it is an added bonus, so to speak. It wouldn't make sense if I carried it so far that I would simply toss a coin to determine whether I put my citizenship into practice on the Obama side or the Romney side – driven by the belief that what matters is politics for the sake of politics, hence the *content* of the politics, or the civic purposes served by the politics, are correspondingly less important. That seems a somewhat crazy view, although Arendt, as I have quoted her, seems to tread perilously close to just that kind of view.

What prompts her to embrace such an implausible account of political action? Arendt was determined at all costs to avoid a vision of politics that *instrumentalized* it, that conceived it as merely means to ends that were non-political – that conceptualized political agency as a kind of "making." If I am working in a brick-making factory, the meaning of the activity consists in producing the bricks, not brick-making for the sake of brick-making. It is not impossible to say that brick-making per se is a meaning-generating activity, but we typically do not think of it along those lines; people take jobs producing bricks because someone is paying them to fabricate those bricks, not because brick-making in itself is an intrinsically humanizing activity. However, Arendt was determined to give an account of the political where one *could* say this about political activity, regardless of what it produced or failed to produce. I think we can see why it was important to Arendt to distinguish political agency as a privileged form of human activity in this sense (a human activity elevated above the prosaic or banal character of all other human activities); still, portraying the domain of political action in the way that she did cannot help but do a certain measure of violence to the way we experience real politics and how ordinary citizens conceive the nature of their activity on those occasions when they insert themselves into broader political happenings. Caring about politics means caring about what the political outcomes are; and a celebration of political life that abstracts from the civic goods that politics secures or aspires to secure will not come remotely close to capturing what the political actors themselves understand to be the politicalness of what they are doing.

Of course, when one considers Arendt's own more directly political writings – for instance, her interventions on the politics of Zionism or her assaults on the Nixon regime during the Watergate era – she too is oriented toward the *contents* of this politics versus that politics, not just the performative dimension of political self-disclosure for the sake of political self-disclosure. What matters is *getting one's politics right*, not just participating for the sake of participating.[18] And how could it be otherwise if one is actually taking the trouble to exert oneself as a political actor (including the exertion of writing political commentaries)? To repeat the formulation I have already offered, caring about politics means caring about what political outcomes result from one's political activity.

I've conceded that Arendt's conceptualization of the political falls well short of being a plausible view. Still, we can – and I think we should – admire the intellectual radicalism of her theoretical project. In fact, I think she deserves full credit for doing exactly what I suggested, in the first prologue, political philosophers *should* be doing, articulating a totalized view, an all-encompassing horizon for reflecting on the ends of a human life. That is indeed what we get with Arendt's conception of political action for the sake of political action, engendering meaning in an otherwise meaning-deprived biological existence. It may or may not be a plausible representation of our experience of politics, but it gives us a philosophy of human life of the appropriate order of intellectual ambition.

Labor, Work, and Action

There is both a positive aspect and a negative (or critical) aspect to Arendt's political philosophy. The positive aspect – her celebration of political life and political action – has already received some discussion. It remains to give some attention to the negative aspect – her critique of labor and her (less harsh) critique of work. Arendt fashions her political philosophy by constructing a hierarchy of labor, work, and action, and it is only by situating worldly political action in the context of her views about the other two activities that concern her in *The Human Condition* that one comes fully to appreciate how she conceptualizes it and why she celebrates it.

In effect, Arendt is asking: What is it in human life that renders the lives of human beings lives that are properly or fully or consummately human? (As discussed elsewhere, phrasing it like this makes it sound like a "theory of the good," but of course my view, in tension with Arendt's self-interpretation of her kind of theorizing, is that that is exactly what it is, and justifiably so.) Do we live lives that are properly human by simply preserving ourselves and reproducing our biological existence? Do we live lives that are properly human by constructing artificial environments (art, architecture,

---

[18] I pursue related issues in "Rereading 'Truth and Politics'," *Philosophy and Social Criticism*, Vol. 34, nos. 1–2 (January–February, 2008), pp. 123–136.

constructions of urban existence) distinct from nature? Or do we live lives that are fully or consummately human by enacting stories of collective life that are memorable and worthy of subsequent narration? Arendt puts her money, as we already know, on the third of these alternatives, and she writes *The Human Condition* in order to try to articulate, in a way that is persuasive to her readers, why she ranks these three activities in the way that she does.

Let's start with labor, since the distinction between work and labor is arguably more intellectually compelling and more persuasive than Arendt's theory of action. The following text gives a good sample of the flavor of Arendt's writing on the topic of labor:

> Labor's products, the products of man's metabolism with nature, do not stay in the world long enough to become part of it, and the laboring activity itself, concentrated exclusively on life and its maintenance, is oblivious of the world to the point of worldlessness. The *animal laborans*, driven by the needs of its body, does not use this body freely as *homo faber* uses his hands, his primordial tools....A mass society of laborers, such as Marx had in mind when he spoke of "socialized mankind," consists of worldless specimens of the species mankind. (p. 118)

Here we have the idea of labor as part and parcel of "the metabolism with nature," the idea of labor's incapacity to create a world or fashion something durable, the idea of "a mass society of laborers," as opposed to a public of political actors with authentic personalities. In short, we have the idea of the laboring "process" as more animal than human. All of these notions are central to the kind of story Arendt wants to tell about labor vis-à-vis work.

One important part of the story is that what became *The Human Condition* started out as, or was intended to be, a book about Marx and Marxism. For Marx, as she understands Marx, labor is the defining human activity. It is what makes human beings human. It is how we set ourselves off against the rest of nature. Labor is a properly *humanizing* activity.[19] (Hegel had his own version of this doctrine, and in important ways, the Marxian teaching is simply a reworking and adaptation of notions that were first articulated in Hegel, but we don't need to go into that in any length. Marx understood himself to be developing ideas drawn from Hegel; Arendt was fully aware of this, of course, and we as readers of Arendt are aware of it too. But Arendt, in

---

[19] See, for instance, *The Human Condition*, p. 101: for Marx, labor is "the expression of the very humanity of man." As we will see in Chapter 7, labor as a properly and essentially humanizing activity is also a central view of Simone Weil's, although Weil maintained a fairly critical stance toward Marx and Marxism. For a good discussion, see Robert Sparling, "Theory and Praxis: Simone Weil and Marx on the Dignity of Labor," *The Review of Politics*, Vol. 74 (2012), pp. 87–107.

The Human Condition, was primarily concerned with the Marxian version.) Arendt wants to ask, as a philosophical question: Is this actually true? *Is* labor the properly humanizing human activity, or should we look elsewhere for the activity that allows human beings to be fully human?

What is at stake here seems in one sense quite reminiscent of the political philosophy of Aristotle, with its emphatic distinction between "mere life" and "the good life."[20] Politics, for Aristotle, is essential to human life because it instantiates a vision of the good life, and that very much looks like the kind of claim that Arendt is making as well: we need politics because it opens up a domain of human experience that allows us to elevate ourselves above the mundane demands of mere life, mere biological preservation and reproduction, in its meaningless circularity. However, there are key differences. For Aristotle, everything is subsumed under the idea of human nature; politics is important because it helps to realize the naturalness of the good life, of the natural human telos. Nature provides us with our constitutive ends, and our vocation as creatures of nature is to fulfill those ends (including by becoming political, by rising to a properly civic existence). For Arendt, in stark contrast, our human vocation is not to *realize* what is natural but to *transcend* it. That is, she assumes a radical cleavage between nature and freedom: humanizing ourselves is an exertion of human freedom, and freedom becomes meaningful insofar as we raise ourselves above the merely natural. Her dualism would perhaps be tidier if her philosophy simply opposed action to labor, but with her tripartite account of human activities, a bit of a puzzle arises about where to situate work (the middle category). If Arendt's ontology divides the world between nature and freedom, is work on the nature side or the freedom side? My view is that she tends to depict work as a kind of accessory to action.[21]

---

[20] It is also easy to notice a certain analogy between Arendt's opposition of action and work and Aristotle's seemingly parallel distinction between *praxis* (acting) and *poiesis* (making). For Habermas and those influenced by his reading of Arendt, this parallel suffices to establish Arendt as a neo-Aristotelian. Of course Aristotle would never have claimed (and was right not to claim) that *praxis* is non-teleological.

[21] Admittedly, there are complexities in Arendt's theory that have the effect of upsetting this philosophical hierarchy. Her official view is that *action* assumes the full burden of rescuing us from our natural condition of flux and futility, but action can only serve this meaning-generating function insofar as it generates narration-worthy events. Yet the actual "durability" of these stories rests upon the efforts of poets and historians because action itself is not durable but ephemeral or fleeting. (This theme receives further development in Arendt's Kant Lectures. See Arendt, *Lectures on Kant's Political Philosophy*, ed. Ronald Beiner [Chicago: University of Chicago Press, 1982], pp. 5, 56, and 77.) It requires the poetry of a Homer or the historiography of a Thucydides to render the deeds of Achilles or Pericles literally memorable in the sense of being *capable* of remembrance. Yet Arendt quite clearly associates *these* activities with the category of work. (See *The Human Condition*, chapter 23; for instance, page 167: "Because of their outstanding permanence, works of art are the most intensely worldly of all tangible

Arendtian metaphors easily suggest themselves here. If human beings rise to the possibility of endowing their merely natural existence with enduring meaning by *performing* in a public space visible to their peers, someone has to build the *stage* on which that performance takes place. That is *work*, fabricating a worldly space that resists the natural flux of biological life. A tree is governed by its own biological necessity, its own biological rhythms, but if I cut down the tree with a saw and then use a hammer and nails to turn it into a worldly artifice, I have transcended nature in a significant way. The assumption is that we are forging something *more durable, less subject to natural flux*, than the wood from which we have built this worldly artifice. To put it in Heideggerian language, I am conjuring into existence a human dwelling-place, and without such sites for properly human "dwelling," it is impossible to have an existence that is properly human or humanized, that is, something more than what is purely nature (defined by immersion in the rhythms and necessities of biological life).

It seems clear from these considerations that the jump from labor to work involves an enormous step forward toward what Arendt regards as satisfying the conditions of a properly human life, as Arendt understands this. If we could not fabricate enduring furniture of the world, human fabrications resistant to the flux of biological existence, then any notion of human "worldliness" or "durability" (key Arendtian conceptions) would be out of reach. Yet Arendt is insistent that this human activity of fabricating a durable world for ourselves is ontologically subordinate to something higher. Why? At this second stage of the argument, she puts tremendous emphasis on the idea of the ends-means character of work as work. If I am building a piece of furniture or building a stage on which a performance will take place, I have a definite idea of the *end* at which I am aiming with my sawing and hammering of the wood. I deploy these tools in order to fashion something quite definite. The activity is instrumental to the achievement of the end. And here Arendt takes it pretty much for granted, and makes it central to her argument, that a non-instrumental human activity is of ontologically higher status than an instrumental activity. Again, as discussed in the previous section of this chapter, much hangs on the idea that action – authentic action enacted before a genuine public – is indeed non-instrumental, enacted for

---

things; their durability is almost untouched by the corroding effects of natural processes.") Without enduring works of poetry or enduring works of historiography, the meaning-generating exertions of political action are for naught. Hence there is an important (perhaps decisive) sense in which not only is work an accessory to action, but action is no less an accessory to (in this sense the ontologically privileged activity of) work.

its own sake, qua performance rather than qua achievement or hoped-for achievement of these or those particular ends. As already discussed, this is a highly problematical view; it is hard to see why a political actor would go to the trouble of standing up in a public space and trying to mobilize political sympathies in one direction or another without a pretty strong commitment to the political ends that one takes to be the right ends. That is, politics conceived as performance for the sake of performance seems of questionable coherence. It seems to do a certain measure of violence to our intuitions about why people commit themselves to political activity in the first place. However, *without* this fairly radical claim about the non-instrumental character of (political) action, it becomes harder to see why action has the ontological privilege over work that Arendt asserts for it in her political philosophy.

One of the distinctive things about the political philosophy of *The Human Condition* is that we get a *celebration* of work vis-à-vis labor, and we get a *critique* of work vis-à-vis action. This suggests that getting a handle on the middle position of work in this three-way ranking is the hinge of the whole argument. Let's consider some texts:

The things of the world have the function of stabilizing human life, and their objectivity lies in the fact that – in contradiction to the Heraclitean saying that the same man can never enter the same stream – men, their ever-changing nature notwithstanding, can retrieve their sameness, that is, their identity, by being related to the same chair and the same table. In other words, against the subjectivity of men stands the objectivity of the man-made world rather than the sublime indifference of an untouched nature.... Only we who have erected the objectivity of a world of our own from what nature gives us, who have built it into the environment of nature so that we are protected from her, can look upon nature as something "objective." Without a world between men and nature, there is eternal movement, but no objectivity. (p. 137)

The most important task of the human artifice [erected by work] is to offer mortals a dwelling place more permanent and more stable than themselves. [That is, it is our very *mortality* that requires us to fashion an artificial world distinguished by its relative *im*mortality (i.e., at least relative to ourselves).] (p. 152)[22]

---

[22] Of course, artificially created objects vary enormously in their duration or lifespan. As discussed elsewhere in this chapter, it is possible that in contemporary life, the durability of the things around us is constantly being diminished (e.g., the same pair of shoes that used to last me five or ten years now last a maximum of six months). We know from a visit to the museum that it was possible for the ancient Egyptians to fabricate artifacts capable of surviving processes of natural decay for *thousands of years*; very few (if any) of the products of contemporary work will have that kind of staying-power. Although Arendt herself does not attempt to pursue this kind of exercise, it would be quite easy and natural to draw from *The Human Condition* a form of Arendtian cultural critique that measures contemporary norms of object-durability against the standards set by other more immortality-oriented cultures and civilizations.

18

The implements and tools of *homo faber*, from which the most fundamental experience of instrumentality arises, determine all work and fabrication. Here ... the end justifies the means; it does more, it produces and organizes them. The end justifies the violence done to nature to win the material, as the wood justifies killing the tree and the table justifies destroying the wood. Because of the end product, tools are designed and implements invented, and the same end product organizes the work process itself.... During the work process, everything is judged in terms of suitability and usefulness for the desired end, and for nothing else. (p. 153)

Utilitarianism [constitutes] the philosophy of *homo faber* par excellence, [a philosophy that systematically subverts] the distinction between utility and meaningfulness, which we express linguistically by distinguishing between "in order to" and "for the sake of." [In a society of craftsmen permeated by the ideal of usefulness, the] "in order to" has become the content of the "for the sake of"; in other words, utility established as meaning generates meaninglessness. (p. 154)

One can see in this succession of four quotations how Arendt swings from celebration to critique. We need work because work allows us to build a stable world for ourselves that elevates us above nature and elevates us above the preservation of life merely for the sake of preserving life. But at the same time we need a kind of activity that transcends work, because work – crucially oriented as it is to the fabrication of specific products – is locked into a mentality of "instrumentality," is fixated on a means-to-ends way of thinking. I need to build a house, so I need to secure the materials and deploy the tools that allow me to build this house. What counts is the fashioning of the desired product, not any kind of human meaningfulness associated with the activity per se. Work cannot generate meaning because its exclusive focus on utility, on attaining its designated ends, militates against the kind of non-instrumentalist experience associated with the generation of meaning. Action, by contrast, *can* generate meaning, because it unfolds a type of human experience that is not so tightly bound to, and certainly is not exhausted by, instrumentalist (means-ends) considerations; hence Arendt's relentless emphasis on the performativity or virtuosity of action. That, in any case, is the basic line of thought.

An important part of Arendt's argument is that Plato *devalued* the political sphere by presenting politics as (merely) a form of "making," wherein the statesman conceives an "idea" of what the state should look like and then "uses" politics (as the maker of furniture uses his hammer) to realize that pre-conceived vision of the end. Politics thereby becomes merely an instrument for the achievement of something outside politics; hence its instrumentalization. One sees the logic here, but Arendt's alternative – a vision of politics that transcends or has its ontological status independent of what its ends are – does not seem a viable one. We would be better off, it seems, with a conception of political action that incorporated *both* the idea of its being geared toward particular ends *and* having an intrinsically worthwhile significance in its own right.[23] However, this conception would not have the philosophical radicalness Arendt desires in according categorical superiority to action over work.

In any case, all of this helps to make sense of characteristic features of Arendt's philosophical description of action: its spontaneity; its unpredictability; its capacity to generate the novel and the unprecedented; the idea that because we are bound together in a fabric of human *inter*action ("the web of relationships") that no one individual or group of individuals controls, we never know what will result and what ends will be accomplished or not accomplished.[24] It is a leap in the dark. Once again, Arendt is focused very intensely on the contrast with "work" (as she conceptualizes it): In work, the wood and hammer and nails are fully under the control of the craftsperson who is manipulating these things in pursuit of the desired end. But with action, because it is intrinsically collective and interpersonal, we never have much of anything under our control, and the unpredictability of the outcome is part of the essence of what defines the activity. For instance, the people who got the Occupy movement going likely did not have a conception of mobilizing large numbers of people all around the world; they simply put something collective in motion, and events took off on their own. Or with the first stirrings of the Arab Spring, again, these individuals did not say to themselves, "Let's start a political movement that will put an end to Mubarak and Gadhafi and Assad." They simply acted in a setting visible to other potential actors, and the "web of relationships" did

---

[23] Hence, when Arendt wrote in "What Is Freedom?" that "action, to be free, must be free from motive on one side, from its intended goal as a predictable effect on the other," it might have been better to write something like the following: "what constitutes free action as free action is not only its motives and goals but also its performative dimension." Simply inserting this "not only" (hence retracting her suggestion that action can actually *transcend* teleological considerations and still be coherent as action) would have dramatically increased the plausibility of Arendt's theory of action.

[24] Arendt's characteristic emphasis on spontaneity, unconditionedness, and novelty as the defining traits of genuine action is clearly related to her prior reflection on the nature of totalitarianism (in her book *The Origins of Totalitarianism*). Having experienced the lowest, most abysmal possibility in human life (a life regimented by all-encompassing, uniformity-enforcing ideologies), Arendt's thought seems to be that what we want is to swing to the opposite end of the human condition, the highest and most humanizing possibilities of human existence. So it makes sense (she seems to assume) that these highest possibilities would be, so to speak, a mirror image of the lowest, the highest therefore inverting what is most abysmal about the lowest. Hence, if totalitarianism is *anti*-human by virtue of representing anti-pluralism and a life dictated by fixed and rigid ideologies, then what is *most human* is associated with what is open-ended and spontaneous. This, I think, helps to account for emphases within Arendt's phenomenology of action that otherwise appear as a bit extreme.

the rest. These examples indeed show that Arendt's conception of acting as something other than a process of "making" does have some real substance to it. It is not just a figment of her own theoretical imagination. However, one can also question (as I have already questioned) whether any of these actors would have initiated their political performances on the Arendtian basis of performing for the sake of performing. A political performance is always ends-oriented, even if it *also* has the consequence of constituting a realm of shared publicity or politicalness that is worthwhile as an end in itself. In order to pursue the latter conception, Arendt tends to abstract from this indispensable ends-oriented dimension, or sometimes even writes as if it were beside the point (or, more radically, as if it were serving to *undermine* what makes action action).

It would be utterly damning to say of any political actor that he or she put on a good show, but did not accomplish anything and did not even really try to. I think everyone can recognize that Barack Obama has a certain measure of genius when it comes to the performative aspect of politics, but ultimately the success or failure of his political career will be judged (quite rightly) on *what he was able to do* with the power that he won with his performative gifts. Does it follow, then, that Arendt's conception of action simply misfires? I don't think so. Her account captures a certain slice of political experience, and she wants to suggest that appreciating what is disclosed in these very special and very rare moments is crucial in understanding why a shared experience of politics is existentially privileged, so to speak. If one found oneself standing amidst the hundreds of thousands of Czechs assembled in Wenceslas Square during the Velvet Revolution of November and December of 1989 (or even if one merely watched these events on TV), it does not seem unreasonable to think of this as an Arendt-style "immortalizing" moment, elevating one above the banalities of day-to-day life and giving one stories of collective struggle and solidarity ("public freedom," in Arendtian vocabulary) worthy of being told to one's grandchildren. Or if one happened to be on the Mall in Washington, D.C. on January 20, 2009 as the United States inaugurated its first black president, a similar account would apply. Such performances do not even have to be stories of political success. Consider Tiananmen Square. Arguably, it was no less memorable and meaning-bestowing, even though it signally failed to achieve its purpose (and similarly with the intended Green Revolution in Iran). The key idea here is *agency*. When the citizens of Czechoslovakia were oppressed by an autocratic regime, they were subjects but not actors; they did their jobs, they obeyed the laws, they tried to stay out of trouble with the authorities, and so on. But when they started demonstrating in the streets of Prague in November of 1989, they were doing something quite different: they were taking their destiny into their own hands, they were *acting* (that is, asserting genuine agency). These are genuine experiences, and Arendt may well be right that they contribute more to a sense of human meaningfulness than other, more pedestrian human activities. Still, it remains misleading to conceptualize this as performance for the sake of performance, virtuosity for the sake of virtuosity, cut off from the essentially constitutive "motives and goals" of the actors who enact these great deeds.

Of course, there is another, perhaps even bigger problem with Arendt's political philosophy. Few people will be lucky enough, privileged enough, to participate in the kind of miraculous happenings that Arendt takes as her model, and that figure in my examples of Arendtian politics. If Arendt's argument is that this is the kind of thing required in order to rescue human beings from a biological cycle of flux and futility, how will meaningfulness be secured for all those human beings who are *not* lucky enough or privileged enough to participate in such happenings? Above all, for Arendt, *ordinary* politics will not suffice; for meaning-constitution, one needs a politics of performative virtuosity.[25] There has to be the lighting-up of a shared space of luminous collective meaning. That is a transcendently high standard for judging politics, and it seems inevitable that most of what unfolds in the sphere of civic life will look simply too pedestrian, too mundane, to satisfy the Arendtian demand for ultimate meaning. As seems obvious, this problem goes together with Arendt's attempted exclusion of, or abstraction from, the ends-oriented aspect of politics. To the extent that individuals or groups enact politics in order to achieve specific purposes (better healthcare provision, a fairer tax system, more judicious environmental policies, wiser foreign-policy decisions, and so on), the more politics will gravitate toward politics as we ordinarily experience it, and gravitate away from the more meaning-generating performative politics Arendt celebrates.

---

[25] Cf. Alan Ryan's critical response to Sheldon Wolin's conception of politics: "Like Hannah Arendt, who first put the thought in his mind, Wolin has always thought that little of what we call politics deserves that label. Or rather, he expressed that idea by contrasting the *political* with (mere, everyday) *politics*." There is, according to Ryan, "an incoherence in Wolin's [and by extension, Arendt's] idea of 'the political.' It is too tightly tied to his enthusiasm for extraordinary politics that will go beyond passive citizenship, and one cannot – logically – want everything to be extraordinary" ("Visions of Politics," *The New York Review of Books*, June 27, 2002, pp. 37, 38). See also George Kateb: "all normal politics is [for Arendt] estranged politics, that is, the normal ... is alien to her" (*Hannah Arendt and Leo Strauss: German Émigrés and American Political Thought After World War II*, ed. Peter Graf Kielmansegg, Horst Mewes, and Elisabeth Glaser-Schmidt [Cambridge: Cambridge University Press, 1997], p. 185).

We have spoken of Arendt's emphasis on the *spontaneity* of action, its *unpredictability* and its tendency to generate what is *novel*. For Arendt, action that simply repeats routinized behaviors, that conforms to what is already present in the world, that remains in the same rut, so to speak, is not really action. Action, properly speaking, has to generate something new. People act to *change* the world, not simply to play out the routines that are already entrenched. This, in effect, constitutes one half of her theorization of action. The other half is her relentless emphasis on *human plurality*. Of course, this has already been invoked in her account of action's unpredictability, because the unpredictability is in large measure a function of different people interacting in ways that are impossible to predict before the interaction actually gets underway. But one could say that she is interested in plurality not just because it contributes to action being capable of generating what is new and unpredictable; she is also interested in plurality for its own sake, because a political philosophy that neglects plurality, or understates its importance, will necessarily fail to grasp what is essential about our experience of politics. Consider this passage from a lecture she delivered in 1954:

One of the decisive handicaps of philosophy in its dealings with politics has always been to speak of man in the singular, as if there were such a thing as one human nature, or as if originally one man inhabited the earth. The trouble has always been that the whole political sphere of human life exists only because of the plurality of men, because of the fact that one man would not be human at all. In other words, all problems of political philosophy begin where traditional philosophy, with its concept of man in the singular, stops.[26]

This formulation (and parallel formulations in *The Human Condition*) is more problematic than it first appears. Suppose Arendt is confronted with individuals (of whom there are a countless multitude!) who insist that political life constitutes no part of what makes life meaningful for them; according to life as *they* experience it, political life is utterly tangential. Life, for them, has its meaning entirely in living as pure individuals, seeking individuals ends that are important to them strictly as individuals, indifferent to and unconcerned with the lives of fellow citizens or indeed that of people living anywhere on earth, near or far. What then becomes of Arendt's assertions about action in a public sphere as a uniquely humanizing activity of human beings as human beings, or as having philosophical priority among other possible human activities? How does she cope with this kind of manifestation of human plurality? For this is surely part of the phenomena that define our

[26] *Essays in Understanding 1930–1954*, ed. Kohn, p. 447, n. 25.

experience of plurality – for instance, the view that politics must contribute little to the meaning of life, because living a life according to God's plans for us encompasses the *whole* of what makes life meaningful for human beings (hardly an uncommon view).[27] Does not *her own* political philosophy then start to take on the appearance of being a set of propositions about "man in the singular" (no less than the political philosophies of Plato or Aristotle or any later thinker in the political philosophy canon)? Put otherwise, is it not the case that *any* political philosophy that defers unconditionally to human plurality (Isaiah Berlin's political philosophy, for example, comes to mind) must by that very token refuse to assert claims about what are the properly humanizing ways to be human (that is to say, thereby *ceases to offer* a political philosophy)?

---

[27] Arendt is a committed theist. See, for instance, what she says about atheism in *Men in Dark Times* (Harmondsworth, UK: Penguin, 1973), p. 72; cf. Alfred Kazin, *New York Jew* (New York: Alfred A. Knopf, 1978), p. 199. In a 1954 letter to Karl Jaspers (Hannah Arendt/Karl Jaspers, *Correspondence 1926–1969* [New York: Harcourt Brace Jovanovich, 1992], p. 244), she expresses bemusement about Leo Strauss's "orthodox atheism," but Arendt never intellectually confronts in a serious way the view that God rather than politics (or, in her terms, eternity rather than immortality) is what should be relied upon to secure human life against the threat of meaninglessness. Rather, she tends to make the (surely premature) assumption that religion in modern society has lost both its cultural sway and its political salience.

2

Michael Oakeshott: Life's Adventure

The political philosophy unfolded in *On Human Conduct* certainly lacks nothing for radicalism.[1] The core of Michael Oakeshott's theorizing is the idea that, as the mandate of the modern state expands, the possibility of living life as the self-sufficient adventure it is meant to be contracts. *On Human Conduct* is above all a reflection on the nature of the state. It can hardly be an accident that Hobbes and Hegel, two of the figures within the canonical theory tradition who most deeply engaged Oakeshott intellectually, were also utterly preoccupied with the project of theorizing the state.[2] There is no question that Oakeshott wants a severe constraining of the scope of state activity, but this view of the state would not have the philosophical character that it does if it were not tied to views about what it is to live life.

An ordinary sort of human life, such as we all must lead, is inhabiting and responding to a present composed of objects and happenings ... related to ourselves as the objects of our attention and concern.... Each of us occupies such a present as his own; it is a personal present.... My Venice is not your Venice, and this grove of trees, which to me now is a shelter from the rain or a place to play hide-and-

---

[1] Michael Oakeshott, *On Human Conduct* (Oxford: Clarendon Press, 1975). All parenthetical references in this chapter are to this book.

[2] See page 109, where Oakeshott singles out Aristotle, Hobbes, and Hegel as the three philosophers of the civil condition "from [whom] we have the most to learn." Given Oakeshott's antipathy to teleological understandings of political life, Aristotle seems like an odd choice. One might say the same about Hegel, except that Oakeshott (fairly idiosyncratically) reads Hegel in a non-teleological fashion. On p. 257, he refers to Hegelian *Geist* as "an adventure, not a teleological process"; for an incisive commentary, see pp. 22–23 of Perry Anderson, "The Intransigent Right," in Anderson, *Spectrum* (London: Verso, 2005), pp. 3–28. (In the late 1970s, I had a conversation with Oakeshott in which he expressed puzzlement about how Charles Taylor went from *The Explanation of Behaviour* to his work on Hegel. I responded that Taylor's interest in teleology explained the link between the two books, to which Oakeshott replied that there is no teleology in Hegel!) As regards Aristotle, Oakeshott, in a note straddling pages 118 and 119, advances an interpretation according to which the human good instantiated in the polis "is not for [Aristotle] a substantial good but a formal condition."

seek, to another (or to me in different circumstances) may be a defence against soil erosion.[3]

Oakeshott's guiding conception comes out most clearly when he distinguishes between an association "of pilgrims, travelling to a common destination" and an association "of adventurers," each wandering in a unique direction (p. 243). As individuals, we have a responsibility to respond reflectively to the worlds in which we find ourselves and to exert practical intelligence in comporting ourselves to those worlds of practical existence. An overactive state, for Oakeshott, is a clear sign that individuals are abdicating that responsibility or seeking ways to lessen the burden of exercising reflective intelligence. (More precisely, the problem is not an overactive state but a state that takes itself to be purposive *at all*.) When Oakeshott speaks of the "individual *manqué*" (p. 275), he implies a kind of duty to be the sort of individual who is not an individual *manqué*, and he urges us to repudiate visions of the state that (he thinks) encourage or facilitate such moral abdication.

Here are some passages from *On Human Conduct* that further develop Oakeshott's key idea:

What is postulated of the agent is not "free will" but intelligence. Conduct is specified as actions and utterance, wise or foolish, which have reasons, adequate or inadequate, but not causes.... Diverse images of human circumstance abound in medieval art and literature, the human condition was allegorized and theorized in many different idioms, "free will," rationality, or an ever unresolved tension between passion and reason; but everywhere a human life is portrayed as an individual self-enactment, not a passage in a cosmic process, and human association as dramatic and intelligent, not organic, relationship.... This condition may be greeted with various mixtures of revulsion, anxiety, and confidence; it is both gratifying and burdensome. The sort of self-fulfilment it promises is partnered by a notorious risk of self-estrangement or self-destruction.... But few who reflected upon this combination of "freedom" and responsibility could avoid the conclusion of the seventeenth-century poet: 'Tis glorious misery to be born a man. (pp. 235–236)

Oakeshott goes on to write that the modern European state embodies a "recognition of this condition as the emblem of human dignity and as a condition for each individual to explore, to cultivate, to make the most of, and to enjoy as an opportunity rather than suffer as a burden" (p. 236). An authentic understanding of human conduct discloses a "self [bearing] a substantive personality ... whose resources are collected in a self-understanding; and conduct is recognized as the adventure in which this cultivated self

---

[3] Michael Oakeshott, *On History and Other Essays* (Oxford: Basil Blackwell, 1983), pp. 10–11.

deploys its resources, discloses and enacts itself in response to its contingent situations, and both acquires and confirms its autonomy" (pp. 236–237). The human agent "is what he understands himself to be, his contingent situations are what he understands them to be, and the actions and utterances in which he responds to them are self-disclosures and self-enactments. He has a 'history,' but no 'nature'; he is what in conduct he becomes" (p. 41).[4]

How does this philosophical account of the self-disclosing and self-enacting personality relate to theoretical reflection concerning the modern state? If the glory of the modern European state is to have helped to make possible (or give expression to) a self-enacting, autonomous individual, "a collected personality, autonomous on account of its self-understanding and its command of resources it has made its own" (p. 237), then it is essential that the state be conceived in a way that fully honors what it is to be an individual rather than an individual *manqué*.[5] The heart of the political philosophy unfolded in *On Human Conduct* reposes on a distinction between two understandings of collective life. According to the first, human beings join in an association for reasons that are essentially purposive, in that they seek some satisfaction and decide to seek it jointly. Oakeshott calls this *enterprise association*, which he defines as a "relationship in terms of the pursuit of some common purpose, some substantive condition of things to be jointly procured, or some common interest to be continuously satisfied" (p. 114). Such joint associations of seekers of satisfactions, such as a society of poets or a society of innkeepers,[6] may constitute rules for themselves, but any given rule "would be judged by its propensity to promote or to hinder the pursuit of [the society's constitutive] purpose. That is to say, [the rules] are instrumental to the purpose which itself constitutes the ready and appropriate criterion for judging their propriety" (p. 116). Poets want to advance the shared interests of poets; innkeepers want to advance the shared interests of innkeepers; and each group conjures into existence its own club or fraternity in order to promote these jointly held purposes. People gather into

---

[4] Cf. Oakeshott, *The Vocabulary of a Modern European State*, ed. Luke O'Sullivan (Exeter: Imprint Academic, 2008), p. 296: "the endless adventure of being human." For an instructive account of Oakeshott's preoccupation with what it is to live life in its full authenticity, see Glenn Worthington, "Michael Oakeshott on Life: Waiting with Godot," *History of Political Thought*, Vol. 16, no. 1 (1995), pp. 105–119. Worthington argues that, for Oakeshott, self-disclosure and self-enactment refer to different aspects of the process of constituting an authentic self, but that distinction is not one that we need to pursue for our purposes.

[5] Recall again the important text from page 236, quoted in the previous paragraph, in which Oakeshott refers to the modern European state as embodying proper recognition of individual autonomy "as the emblem of human dignity," to be explored, cultivated, made the most of, and enjoyed as an opportunity rather than suffered as a burden.

[6] These are Oakeshott's examples.

these societies partly because they, not unreasonably, presume "that where many are related in procuring a joint satisfaction the wished-for outcome is more likely to be achieved" and partly because they appreciate "the warmth it is alleged to generate" (p. 117).

The other kind of association is quite different. Oakeshott calls it *civil association*. Civil association is conceived as association oriented toward participation in the civil condition as a distinct "practice," as well as the legislation of rules acknowledgment of whose authority constitutes the civil relationship. Hence this account hangs on Oakeshott's discussion of participation in a practice:

> To be related in terms of a practice is precisely not to be associated in the reciprocal satisfaction of wants or in making or acknowledging "managerial" decisions in the pursuit of common purposes; it is relationship in respect of a common recognition of considerations such as uses or rules intelligently subscribed to in self-chosen performances. It is formal, not substantial relationship; that is, association in respect of a common language and not in respect of having the same beliefs, purposes, interests, etc., or in making the same utterances. (pp. 120–121)

> There are, then, two categorially discrete modes of human relationship to be reckoned with: the one substantial, concerned with the satisfaction of chosen wants and from which an agent may extricate himself by a choice of his own, the other formal and in terms of the considerations which compose a practice. (p. 121)

Oakeshott clearly puts much emphasis on the idea that his theorizations are just abstractions from historically and therefore contingently evolved human institutions, but there is nonetheless something faintly metaphysical about how the term "categorially" figures in the passage just quoted. A practice-based relationship or association is one constituted not by substantive purposes but by formal rules, and as far as understanding of the state goes, everything rests on whether it resides on one side or the other of this crucial distinction. "Since the civil condition is not enterprise association and since *cives* as such are neither enterprisers nor joint-enterprisers, it follows that they are related solely in terms of their common recognition of the rules which constitute a practice of civility" (p. 128). Civil association "begins and ends in the recognition of rules" (ibid.). "Rules do not enjoin, prohibit, or warrant substantive actions or utterances; they cannot tell agents what to do or to say. They prescribe norms of conduct; that is, abstract considerations to be subscribed to" (p. 126). Hence, a vision of state focused on rules in their formality is radically distinct from one oriented to purposes with a particular content. Or at least, Oakeshott hopes to sketch a conception of law that abstracts as much as possible from substantive outcomes.

In chapter 3 of *On Human Conduct*, Oakeshott introduces a somewhat different vocabulary to capture the same basic dichotomies: *Universitas* constitutes a "corporate mode of association" joining persons together "in respect of some identified common purpose [or] acknowledged substantive end" (p. 203). A *societas*, by contrast, "is not that of an engagement in an enterprise to pursue a common substantive purpose or to promote a common interest.... It [is] a formal relationship in terms of rules, not a substantive relationship in terms of common action" (p. 201). As is evident from these definitions, the *universitas/societas* distinction is a historical interpretation that exactly parallels the enterprise association/civil association distinction as a philosophical interpretation. Now it is in the context of the historical interpretation that Oakeshott acknowledges that the actual reality of the modern state is a complicated hybrid, or hodge-podge, of these two "categorially discrete" conceptions. Here is the crucial passage:

As the equivocal character of a state unfolded itself, the inability of either *societas* or *universitas* to sustain itself as an adequate representation of it, and their incapacity to merge in order to compose a new and more adequate identity, were exposed.... Irreducible, unable to combine, and rejected as alternative accounts of the character of a state, they may be recalled as the specification of the self-division of this ambiguous character. A state may perhaps be understood as an unresolved tension between the two irreconcilable dispositions represented by the words *societas* and *universitas*....This tension ... has acquired some new features and has imposed a particular ambivalence upon all the institutions of a modern state and a specific ambiguity upon its vocabulary of discourse: the muddle in which we now live where "law," "ruling," "politics," etc., each have two distinct meanings.... It is this tension ... which is central to the understanding of the character of a modern European state and the office of its government. (pp. 200–201)[7]

It may be that Oakeshott does not come right out and say that, as far as the state goes, one side of this tension represents a legitimate function of state activity and the other side an illegitimate one. Still, Oakeshott is clear that the state as we know it bespeaks a "muddle" in the fundamental vocabulary by which modern Europeans express their notions of politics. It is

---

[7] Cf. page 320: "my contention is that the modern European political consciousness is a polarized consciousness, that these are its poles and that all other tensions (such as those indicated in the words 'right' and 'left' or in the alignments of political parties) are insignificant compared with this."

a muddle between the idea of the state as "a nomocracy whose laws are understood as conditions of conduct, not devices instrumental to the satisfactions of preferred wants" (p. 203) and the idea of the state as "teleocratic, [overseeing] the management of a purposive concern" (pp. 205–206). Again, Oakeshott does not quite state flat-out that the nomocratic conception of the state is the normatively superior one,[8] whereas the teleocratic conception is a usurpation; however, there is no question that his (often strident) rhetoric points in that direction, and one would have to be pretty tone-deaf not to detect that leading political thinkers of European modernity engage Oakeshott's sympathy or engage his strong antipathy depending on whether they are taken to be upholders of a *societas* state or ideologists of a *universitas* state.[9] Notwithstanding Oakeshott's effort in the final two paragraphs of the book to soften his anti-teleocratic rhetoric, no reader of *On Human Conduct* could reasonably think that he is neutral between these two conceptions of the state (or two poles of European political consciousness), or that his primary endeavor is a descriptive one. Consider the passage near the end of the book where Oakeshott argues that purposive associations ought to involve the freedom to associate or to not associate, depending on whether one shares or does not share the purposes being pursued, but in the case of the state, this freedom "of association and disassociation" is clearly out of the question, since it is by definition a compulsory association.[10] Hence: "The member of [a teleocratic] state enjoys the composure of the conscript assured of his dinner. His 'freedom' is warm, compensated servility" (p. 317). In the same context he writes, "a state understood in the terms of enterprise association," because it enforces a common purpose even upon those who disapprove of that purpose, reveals itself "to be a somewhat rickety moral

---

[8] He does say, though, that "while those who are disposed to take the other path [viz., the path of *societas*] are, perhaps, fewer and are often denigrated as frivolous individuals merely out for the walk, no European alive to his inheritance of moral understanding has ever found it possible to deny the superior desirability of civil association without a profound feeling of guilt" (p. 321).

[9] On pages 244–263, Oakeshott enlists a large company of theorists on behalf of the *societas* conception: Machiavelli, Bodin, Hobbes, Spinoza, Locke, Madison, Burke, Paine, Montesquieu, Hume, Kant, Fichte, Hegel, Tocqueville, and J.S. Mill. By contrast, on pages 287–292, Oakeshott brings forth a gallery of villains who champion the *universitas* conception: Francis Bacon, Fourier, Comte, Owen, Louis Blanc, Marx, Bellamy, Beatrice Webb, and Lenin; cf. page 269. Interestingly, Oakeshott gives substantial emphasis to the encouragement given to the teleocratic conception by the urge on the part of the Church to treat the state "as a religious corporation": see pages 281–282. In the same vein, see the discussion on pages 220–221 of the Church's aspiration to found a Christian theocracy: "a sacerdotal *universitas* [that] remained a profoundly influential dream, passages of which have often been plundered by governments in modern times."

[10] Cf. page 242: "a state, on any reading of its character, is a comprehensive, exclusive, and compulsory association."

construction, *but that is a matter which I have refrained from exploring in order not to prejudice the investigation of its substantive character*" (ibid.; my italics). What is suggested here by Oakeshott, which only the most credulous of readers could take at face value, is that his primary theoretical intention is descriptive or analytic, not normative or prescriptive. But his suggestion may be true in the limited sense that Oakeshott (as the good "Hobbesian" liberal that he is) is less concerned with arguing in favor of a positive vision of politics than with arguing against ideas of politics that he thinks impede the (more important) business of self-enactment.

Oakeshott, throughout his intellectual career, was deeply committed to the idea that it was not the job of the political philosopher to supply prescriptions for the conduct of political life. Practice, in his view, regulates itself by evolving "a self-moved manner of activity" that maintains coherence, that is, deals with any incoherencies in its own way of life that might arise, by drawing on its immanent resources as "an inheritance" of practical wisdom, a "concrete whole ... having the source of its movement within itself," rather than putting itself "in debt to something outside itself."[11] However, his account of the state as a civil association seems so far removed from the modern state as we know it that one struggles to interpret it as anything other than a normative criticism of the existing state and, hence, as the prescriptive recommendation of a kind of state that would not be subject to such normative criticism. On page 109, Oakeshott goes out of his way to emphasize that his account of civil association "is ideal not in the sense of being a wished-for perfect condition of things but in being abstracted from the contingencies and ambiguities of actual goings-on in the world," but it is hard to escape the suspicion that a picture of civil association as "ideal" in the former sense is present in his theorizing as well.[12] If Oakeshott does

---

[11] Michael Oakeshott, *Rationalism in Politics and Other Essays* (London: Methuen and Co., 1977), pp. 115–116, 113.

[12] Cf. pages 121–122: "since we are concerned with an ideal character and not an ambiguous going-on like the Kingdom of Denmark, [the reader] may find himself at a loss even to know how to decide [which way to turn]. But I have not distinguished these two modes of human association in order to put this alternative before him or myself. That human beings may be associated in terms of the pursuit of a common purpose is beyond doubt, but what I am concerned with and what I have identified as the civil condition is not this." Is it really credible that Oakeshott, in writing *On Human Conduct*, did not intend to present one of these visions of political existence as more normatively attractive and the other as less normatively attractive? See also pages 180–181: "As a mode of human intercourse the civil condition is an ideal character glimpsed here or there in the features of human goings-on, intimated in some choices and dispositions to choose and in some responses to actual situations, but it nowhere constitutes a premeditated design for human conduct." It is as if Oakeshott is desperate to avoid seeing his political philosophy being turned into yet another ideology.

not have some normative purpose in mind, why is he exerting himself to delineate this particular abstraction from the contingencies and ambiguities of actual goings-on?

Every modern state that we know of tries to secure enabling conditions for a prosperous economy for its citizens. Every modern state builds hospitals and bridges and funds opera houses and parks. Every modern state tries to expand literacy and reduce poverty. Modern states provide a clean water supply, regulate pollution, and fend off potential epidemics, and they also seek to provide security against terrorist threats. In what sense are these not all common purposes of various kinds? Oakeshott's line about the "tension" between *societas* and *universitas* within the bosom of the modern state allows him to make some measure of concession to the reality that states pursue common purposes. But he is deeply hostile to the state as a purposive association, however much he realizes that nothing short of a libertarian revolution will dislodge it. Oakeshott is very emphatic in highlighting the fact that the state's responsibility for the conduct of wars helped to entrench and legitimize the idea of the state as an enterprise association (pp. 272–274), while acknowledging at best only very grudgingly that, for instance, the defeat of Hitler was a legitimate, and indeed imperative, common purpose (pp. 146–147). Is Oakeshott really proposing a non-teleocratic vision of the state where adventurer–individualists take it upon themselves to assume responsibility for bridge-building and regulation of pollution? It certainly *seems* that that is what he is proposing, except that he then denies that he is proposing anything at all.

Oakeshott, going back to his earliest philosophical writings, always insisted on the autonomy of practical experience – including (perhaps especially) its autonomy in relation to the world of philosophy. In his very first book, he insisted that what is "accomplished in the mental fog of practical experience" is in no way inferior to the achievements of the philosophically "clear-sighted." Indeed, when it comes to "leading the world," we would be better advised to depend on men and women of practice than on "those who are fashioned for thought and the ardours of thought":

Practice is the tireless pursuit of a more satisfying way of life.... From the standpoint of practical experience there can be no more dangerous disease than the love and pursuit of truth in those who do not understand, or have forgotten, that a man's first business is to live.... The practical consciousness knows well enough what is inimical to its existence, and often has the wisdom to avoid it.[13]

---

[13] Michael Oakeshott, *Experience and Its Modes* (Cambridge: Cambridge University Press, 1978), pp. 320–321; the book was originally published in 1933.

This idea of the rightful autonomy of practice,[14] which it would not be going too far to describe as one of his key notions, induced in Oakeshott a strong and consistent resistance to the idea of philosophy as the source of prescriptions for practice: political philosophy "will not help us to distinguish between good and bad political projects; it has no power to guide or to direct us.... It must be understood as an explanatory, not a practical, activity,"[15] and the offering of specific prescriptions carries us, illegitimately, from the realm of understanding to the realm of practice. Again, to quote the early Oakeshott:

> Philosophy is without any direct bearing upon the practical conduct of life.... It has certainly never offered its true followers anything which could be mistaken for a gospel.... Nearly always a philosopher hides a secret ambition, foreign to philosophy, and often it is that of the preacher. But we must learn not to follow the philosophers upon these holiday excursions.... And instead of a gospel, the most philosophy can offer us (in respect of practical life) is an escape, perhaps the only complete escape open to us.[16]

Oakeshott's response to the political philosophy of Hayek is telling in this respect: while Oakeshott approves of Hayek's politics, he strongly disapproves of Hayek's casting of this politics in the form of "a doctrine." Hayek, as an anti-planning theorist, thereby participates, according to Oakeshott, in "the same style of politics" as the compulsive planners (namely the politics of "rationalism").[17] What is not clear here is what it means to theorize politics while avoiding the snare of offering a doctrine. In what sense is Oakeshott himself not offering a doctrine?[18] Suppose we are persuaded by

---

[14] This may suggest the idea of the "primacy" of practice in relation to philosophy. John Gray, in a review of *On History*, argues that it would be wrong to interpret Oakeshott in this way. As Gray puts it, Oakeshott's approach is to conceive "distinct idioms of activity, each of them autonomous of the rest and none of them capable of being ranked in any sort of hierarchy" (*Political Theory*, Vol. 12, No. 3, August 1984, pp. 449–453, at p. 451). On this view, Oakeshott is as much concerned to assert the autonomy of philosophy in relation to practice as to assert the autonomy of practice in relation to philosophy. In this context, Gray also alludes to Richard Rorty's appropriation of Oakeshott, criticizing it as a mistaken projection of Heideggerian and Wittgensteinian notions onto Oakeshott.

[15] *Rationalism in Politics*, pp. 132–133.

[16] *Experience and Its Modes*, pp. 1, 3.

[17] Ibid., p. 21. Oakeshott consistently portrays "rationalism" as a universal contagion. See, for instance, his editor's introduction to Thomas Hobbes, *Leviathan*, ed. Michael Oakeshott (Oxford: Basil Blackwell, 1960), p. lxiii, referring to the "fantasies of the *saeculum rationalisticum*, amid the dim ruins of which we now live."

[18] Timothy Fuller writes: "Like Hume, Oakeshott is a political skeptic about a world suffused by the ideological deformation of philosophy"; "Michael Oakeshott: The Philosophical Skeptic in an Impatient Age," in *Political Philosophy in the Twentieth Century*, ed. Catherine H. Zuckert (Cambridge: Cambridge University Press, 2011), pp. 142–153, at p. 150. This buys into Oakeshott's conceit that it is the "rationalists" who offer doctrines whereas he himself does not. Yet the idea that the state that considers itself responsible for pursuing common purposes on behalf of its citizens by that very fact enlists

Oakeshott that one misinterprets the moral foundation of the modern state when one conceives it according to the image of an enterprise association rather than that of a civil association. Suppose that we are active participants in politics or government, and reading *On Human Conduct* has opened our eyes to the fact that everything we hitherto took to be encompassed within the natural purposes of civic life are in fact corruptions of it. Is it really the case that Oakeshott's theorizing offers no practical guidance in such a situation? Wittgenstein famously suggested that philosophy leaves the non-philosophical world untouched ("leaves everything as it is"[19]), and there is plainly a parallel conception here. But it's hard to see why Oakeshott introduces his distinction between enterprise association and civil association if he is not aiming at clarifying a confusion or rectifying a mistake,[20] and insofar as the confusion does get clarified or the mistake does get rectified, surely this makes a difference to the actual conduct of political life. I think that one can go along with Oakeshott's wish not to reduce theory to the provision of a roadmap for political actors without divorcing theory and practice as radically (and implausibly) as he does. Despite his emphatic view that theory "has no power to guide or to direct us," it would be puzzling or perverse for someone who had read *On Human Conduct* and found its arguments persuasive to persevere in a form of political agency resting on an understanding of the political that those arguments had sought to challenge, especially if one thought that it had succeeded in debunking a hegemonic view of the state. In this respect, there is something more than a little paradoxical in the Oakeshottian theoretical enterprise.[21]

Such paradoxes also abound in *Rationalism in Politics*. The book is a relentless critique of the idea that politics ("attending to the arrangements of a society") is in any given instance founded on "a premeditated ideology," that is, on "independently acquired knowledge of the ends to be pursued." The idea here is that one forms a rational plan or design for how the world should be, and then proceeds to put this rational plan or design into practice. Such a political ideology is supposedly "the product of intellectual

those citizens into "warm, compensated servility" (quoted above) *is* a doctrine, and not a particularly skeptical one.

[19] Ludwig Wittgenstein, *Philosophical Investigations*, 3rd ed., trans. G.E.M. Anscombe (New York: Macmillan, 1968), p. 49.

[20] Cf. *Rationalism in Politics*, p. 31: "Rationalism in politics, as I have interpreted it, involves an identifiable error, a misconception with regard to the nature of human knowledge, which amounts to a corruption of the mind." Also, page 122: "The ideological style of politics is a confused style."

[21] Here is an instance of something one frequently encounters in the political philosophy of Oakeshott (as well as in other political philosophies): a valid and helpful insight that is pushed to such a philosophical extremity that it forfeits its coherence.

premeditation," and those who hold such a view of political life presume that "because it is a body of principles not itself in debt to the activity of attending to the arrangements of a society, it is able to determine and guide the direction of that activity."[22] Political reason, in other words, exists in abstraction from political practice, and the latter is, both empirically and normatively, founded on the former. Such views, according to Oakeshott, are misconceived from top to bottom. Yet Oakeshott again insists that understanding the world of political practice rightly – correcting the ratio-nalistic distortions of it – leaves that world fundamentally untouched. Lenin may have thought that he was reshaping Russian society by means of a revolutionary ideology, but this was nothing but a rationalist misconception of political practice: "The Russian Revolution (what actually happened in Russia) was not the implementation of an abstract design worked out by Lenin and others in Switzerland: it was a modification of *Russian* circum-stances."[23] It would appear to follow that what we take to be political revo-lutions are not revolutions at all but just (as all politics is) "the amendment of existing arrangements by exploring and pursuing what is intimated in them."[24] And since what was in fact at work in the Russian Revolution was simply the playing-out of adjustments in the de facto tradition of behavior of Russian society, pointing out Lenin's mistake about what he took to be his own contribution to the revolution changes nothing; hence, no mean-ingful prescriptions for a transformed practice follow from, or could follow from, Oakeshott's critical analysis of the fallacies and self-misunderstanding embodied in rationalism.

Here is another telling example:

The legal status of women in our society was for a long time (and perhaps still is) in comparative confusion, because the rights and duties which composed it intimated rights and duties which were nevertheless not recognized. And, on the view I am suggesting, the only cogent reason to be advanced for the technical "enfranchise-ment" of women was that in all or most important respects they had already been enfranchised. Arguments drawn from abstract natural right, from "justice," or from some general concept of feminine personality, must be regarded as either irrelevant,

---

[22] *Rationalism in Politics*, p. 118.

[23] Ibid., p. 126n.

[24] Ibid., p. 124. We have quoted Oakeshott's views about the Russian Revolution (which seem particularly paradoxical), but he applies similar lines of thought to the American and French revolutions; see pages 25–28 and 120–121. A revolution cannot really be a revolution, because political activity per se (qua practical activity) must be (merely) the amendment of an existing tradition of behavior, just as texts that are generally taken to articulate ("independently premeditated") political principles are not what they appear, but instead constitute mere "abridgments" of traditional practice modified over time.

or as unfortunately disguised forms of the one valid argument; namely, that there was an incoherence in the arrangements of the society which pressed convincingly for remedy.[25]

Despite appearances, extension of the franchise to female voters was not the consequence of political agency connected to a set of independent moral principles but simply the official acknowledgment of an already-transpired evolution in the society's practices – an acknowledgment serving to mend an incoherence by closing an unfortunate gap between the society's "technical" rules of civic membership and the de facto reality of life in that society. So: the theory of women's rights was indeed a "premeditated" rationalist ideology of just the kind that Oakeshott bitterly criticizes and polemicizes against, yet it ultimately made no difference to the practical outcome since the change in rules governing the franchise did no more than consecrate after the fact a transformation that had already occurred at the level of modes of life. Oakeshott may well be the most gifted writer of all the theorists surveyed in this book, and it is all too easy to be hypnotized by the artistry of his prose, but I confess that it is hard for me to make sense of this as a coherent view. If rationalizing ideologies are in the end innocent in their practical effects, why all the polemics? Moreover: if practice really is fully autonomous, then philosophical insights into its true nature (including Oakeshott's) also cannot have any effect on how the world of practical experience actually unfolds. Such Oakeshottian paradoxes (and again, they run throughout *Rationalism in Politics*) seem to be generated by a rationalist fixation of his own – namely, Oakeshott's stubborn theoretical commitment to the idea that boundaries between different modes of experience (science, history, practice, philosophy) are categorically untraversable. If one conceives political philosophy as a quest for ideas of justice or freedom or political community that are presumed to possess universal normative validity – a normative validity that one seeks to display through the construction of a set of persuasive rational arguments – then Oakeshott's political philosophy looks like a systematic effort to deflate the conceits of political philosophers, showing or trying to show that these ideas have no relevance at all to the actual practice of politics. Characterizing the Oakeshottian enterprise in

---

[25] Ibid., p. 124. Notice the clear implication of this text: It is not just radical transformative ideologies that violate Oakeshott's vision of the autonomy of practice; *any* appeal to justice, *any* appeal to a set of transcendent principles mistakes "rationalism" for genuine practice. Any political philosophy (whether Lenin's or Hayek's) that takes itself to be a guide to practice misconceives what practice is. Political actors who take themselves to be motivated by a conception of justice are deluding themselves; at the same time, Oakeshott takes it upon himself to legislate "the one valid argument" – namely, pursuing the intimations of an already-existent tradition of behavior.

these terms (which I think is faithful to his lifelong project) should help to explain the paradoxes I have tried to highlight.[26]

When one considers Oakeshott's political philosophy in juxtaposition to Hannah Arendt's, one sees striking commonalities between them – both are hostile to political rationalism, or to any endeavor to guide politics by principles that transcend politics; both are captivated by the idea of action as self-disclosure. Hence a brief comparison between these two political philosophies seems in order.[27] Arendt (for her own reasons) is just as hostile to a "teleocratic" conception of the state as Oakeshott is. Essential to Arendt's political philosophy is the idea that there must be a clear and inviolable "distinction between a private and a public sphere of life correspond[ing] to the household and the political realms."[28] But the rise of modern societies, in her view, has brought about momentous developments whereby "the dividing line is entirely blurred, because we [moderns] see the body of peoples and political communities in the image of a family whose everyday affairs have to be taken care of by a gigantic, nation-wide administration of housekeeping."[29] Hence, there are clear affinities between Oakeshott's political philosophy, with its determination to avoid a vision of politics focused on the satisfaction of collective purposes, and the political philosophy of Arendt; yet there are also dramatic differences, which we should not fail to note. As we saw in the preceding chapter, in Arendt's view, the lives of human beings can be imbued with meaningfulness, rather than being left bereft of meaning, insofar as they share a public realm that gives them a space of appearances within which they can enact exemplary political deeds worthy of being retained by the memory of posterity. (The praxis of citizens of the Greek polis was imperishably memorable, and if our appearance in the fleeting gap between birth and death is to have some meaning, our praxis has to be no less memorable.) Therefore, the administrative conception of politics criticized by

---

[26] How is a theorist committed to such a view supposed to apply *any* criticisms, modest or ambitious, to the conventions, norms, or habitual behaviors that have managed to insinuate themselves into the historically evolved practical life of a particular society? And yet there does not seem to be any lack of criticisms of modern politics in Oakeshott (recall again his evocation of the "fantasies of the *saeculum rationalisticum*, amid the dim ruins of which we now live," quoted above). Hence the ineluctable sense of paradox with respect to the normative status of Oakeshott's own theorizing.

[27] For a useful comparison of their respective ideas about political judgment, see Peter J. Steinberger, *The Concept of Political Judgment* (Chicago: University of Chicago Press, 1993), chapter 1.

[28] Cf. *On Human Conduct*, p. 219.

[29] Hannah Arendt, *The Human Condition* (Chicago: University of Chicago Press, 1958), p. 28. This helps explain Arendt's appreciation for Oakeshott, as expressed in Arendt, *Willing* (New York: Harcourt Brace Jovanovich, 1978), p. 239, n. 130.

Arendt in our quotation from *The Human Condition* is, she thinks, a fatal one because it rules out possibilities of existential grandeur attaching to collective action in the authentic sense. That, to put it very mildly, is not Oakeshott's view.[30] Consider the following remarkable passage from the introduction he wrote for Hobbes's *Leviathan*:

> The end in politics is conceived [by political philosophy] to be the deliverance of a man observed to stand in need of deliverance. This, at least, is the ruling idea of many of the masterpieces of political philosophy, the *Leviathan* among them.... We may, then, enquire of any political philosophy conceived on this plan, whether the gift of politics to mankind is, in principle, the gift of salvation itself, or whether it is something less, and if the latter, what relation it bears to salvation.... For politics, we know, is a second-rate form of human activity,[31] neither an art nor a science, at once corrupting to the soul and fatiguing to the mind, the activity either of those who cannot live without the illusion of affairs or those so fearful of being ruled by others that they will pay away their lives to prevent it.[32]

One cannot imagine a view of politics more far removed from Arendt's. Arendt's purpose is to deny that politics should properly occupy itself with the mundane ends of social life (the nation's "housekeeping") in order to elevate the political to the highest possible existential plane. Oakeshott's purpose is exactly the opposite: for him, one must deny that a civil association, rightly conceived, is teleocratic so as to keep its scope as modest as possible – thereby preventing politics from impinging on the capacity and willingness of the genuine individual to design the adventure that is his or

---

[30] It is almost as if Oakeshott is addressing himself to Arendt when he speaks of the "inherently episodic character of the diurnal adventures of self-disclosure which compose a human life" that agents seek falsely to mask by pursuing "purposes more enduring than those of a single agent and his immediate associates: the iniquity of oblivion eclipsed by posthumous glory" (p. 84). For Oakeshott, by contrast with Arendt, self-enactment is "an episodic and an inconclusive engagement" (ibid.). The discussion on page 105 of wanting to redeem human sorrows "by putting them into a story" also reads very much as if it were crafted with Arendt in mind: "to do this is to give up the story-teller's concern with the topical and the transitory and to endow occurrences with a potency they cannot have.... It is not to tell a story but to construct a myth."

[31] Cf. *Rationalism in Politics*, p. 112: "For most people, political activity is a secondary activity – that is to say, they have something else to do besides attending to" the general arrangements to which politics attends. See also *On Human Conduct*, p. 162.

[32] Editor's introduction to Hobbes, *Leviathan*, ed. Oakeshott, p. lxiv. What immediately provokes this response from Oakeshott is a statement in Hobbes's preface to the Latin edition of *Leviathan* referring to "the State [as] an artificial man made for the protection *and salvation of* the natural man." (Salvation from the state of nature, though, surely counts as an extremely modest form of salvation!) The Oakeshott text reads very much like an indictment of the tradition of political philosophy as a whole (running from Plato to Hannah Arendt), but on the next two pages (the concluding pages of his introduction), Oakeshott hastens to exculpate the leading canonical political philosophers (including Hobbes) from this apparent indictment.

her own life.[33] Oakeshott's philosophy is about enjoying where you are, not about getting to some improved destination, so politics as a vehicle for transporting people (collectively) from a so-so point A to a better point B is not something that ranks highly in his scheme of life.

For Brian Barry, as we saw in the first prologue, what we are presented with here are simply the grand pronouncements of two authority-claiming gurus; Arendtians will plump for Arendt's vision, and Oakeshottians will plump for Oakeshott's vision, and neither one nor the other has any special rational privilege. I don't find this very satisfactory. As human beings, we cannot help having a human interest in knowing whether politics is a "second-rate form of human activity" or whether it is that which "endows life with splendour" and hence enables us "to bear life's burden." (Of course, we aren't obliged to restrict our choices to Arendt and Oakeshott: it may be that these are both exaggerated views, and that a more just estimation of the importance of political life lies between these two extremities.) I don't see how we can opt simply to remain agnostic on this major question of human existence; and I don't see why, in principle, political philosophy cannot deliver ambitious answers to such ambitious questions. Moreover, to say, as a Rawlsian liberal for instance says, "Let different individuals embrace different comprehensive doctrines, and let the liberal state organize a framework of civic cooperation based on abstracting from these rival existential commitments" involves its own kind of metaphysical presuppositions (as we will try to show in our Rawls chapter). Does this mean that either Oakeshott or Arendt has a knockdown argument to guarantee the triumph of his or her own vision? Of course not. The political philosophies of Oakeshott and Arendt (and others) are simply extended narratives intended to heighten the persuasiveness of their grand judgments about what is or is not important in human life, and in my view, the more intellectual ambition brought to bear in the fleshing-out of these narratives, the stronger their claim to be considered bona fide political philosophies. Nor is it clear why political philosophers should not be in the business of articulating, as ambitiously as they are able to, meta-judgments of this kind. The fact that any particular such narrative displays intellectual weaknesses, or falls short of winning over

---

[33] Notwithstanding the reciprocal antipathy between Arendt and Strauss, Strauss, when he stated that political philosophy is oriented to freedom and government as "mankind's great objectives ... which are capable of lifting all men beyond their poor selves" (*What is Political Philosophy? And Other Studies* [Chicago: University of Chicago Press, 1988], p. 10), was much closer to Arendt than either of them was to Oakeshott.

readers who are critically-minded (and have every right to be critically-minded!), does nothing to invalidate this mode of philosophizing. To borrow a favored trope of Oakeshott's,[34] the human conversation on these issues is still continuing. But what kind of conversation are we left with if ambitious answers to existentially ambitious questions, such as those engaged by Arendt and Oakeshott, are to be excluded from the start?

---

[34] See Oakeshott, "The Voice of Poetry in the Conversation of Mankind," in *Rationalism in Politics*. As we discuss in the Rorty chapter, Oakeshott's idea of "a conversation [in which] the participants are not engaged in an inquiry or a debate; there is no 'truth' to be discovered, no proposition to be proved, no conclusion sought" (*Rationalism in Politics*, p. 198) was one that significantly influenced Rorty's views about philosophy. (One can also see anticipations of Rorty in Oakeshott's emphasis on contingency, as well as in his theme of the "inconclusive" or "fugitive" self, as opposed to an essential or essentialized self.) It is hard for me to grasp why one would trouble oneself to trade opinions in a conversation unless one aspired to discovering which opinions were true, but Oakeshott and Rorty obviously thought otherwise. In the Oakeshott view embraced by Rorty, philosophers appeal to truth so that they can "trump" the contributions to the conversation by poets, historians, men and women in the sphere of practice, and so on – that is, voices in the conversation that ought to be equal to the voice of philosophy. I can see why this is an attractive conception, and I can certainly see why it is improper for philosophers to claim for themselves some privileged voice. What I do not see is that it is possible to abstract from notions of truth, whether the conversation is one that is hogged by philosophers or whether it is one where philosophers and non-philosophers have equal standing.

3
Leo Strauss: The Politics
of Philosophy

What Defines Straussianism

The first thing that needs to be said about Leo Strauss is that he is set apart from the other theorists treated in this book insofar as attitudes toward him divide between those who demonize him and those who worship him. For his followers, he is the definitive guide to how one does political philosophy – the "only Star and compass," to borrow a phrase of Locke's. For those who demonize him, he is a kind of Rasputin who secretly pulls the strings of world events, even to the extent of inspiring a war that erupted thirty years after his death![1] Let me say very directly that neither of these polarized attitudes – demonizing, worshipping – is an appropriate way to respond intellectually to a political philosopher, and in what follows, I am determined to treat him exactly as I treat the other thinkers who figure in this book – by giving him credit for helpful insights and criticizing him (exactly as we criticize the others) when he produces ideas that come up short with respect to coherence or persuasiveness. That is, he should be treated on exactly the same level as all the others, as neither a beast nor a god, borrowing this time a phrase of Aristotle's.

Esotericism is the heart of Strauss's political philosophy. It is his key insight; it defines the hermeneutical methodology he founded and propagated; above all, it animates his experience of intellectual life. It is normatively significant because it implies fundamental forms of (perennial) human inequality that pose a challenge to much of modern political philosophy. The issue Strauss raises, and intends to raise, is the existence of different and normatively incommensurable communities. The question is: who are the

---

[1] For an amusing rendition of this anti-Straussian narrative, see Jonathan Franzen, *Freedom* (Toronto: HarperCollins, 2010), pp. 266–267. However, I must say that I find it more than a little far-fetched to trace the second Gulf War, and the errors of political judgment that it embodied, back to the seminar that Paul Wolfowitz took with Strauss in 1966 on the political philosophy of Montesquieu (which is basically what one would have to do in order to blame Strauss for the 2003 war in Iraq).

human beings with whom we can share the secrets that really matter, and why is it necessary for us to share these secrets only with these particular human beings and guard them from all the rest? The fundamental issue is nicely expressed in Allan Bloom's statement that "[Strauss's] politics were the politics of philosophy and not the politics of a particular regime."[2] What is "the politics of philosophy," and why should it be philosophically privileged in relation to politics in a more conventional or more familiar sense?

Although Strauss's insight is presented as a *discovery*, it is of course implied by his whole philosophy that he is not the originator of esotericism. On the contrary, unless the intellectual practice of esotericism has been in existence for millennia, Strauss's mode of interpretation as a way of doing political philosophy makes no sense. Therefore Strauss's "discovery" is necessarily an uncovering (that is, an exoteric revelation) of an insight into the need for esotericism practiced by philosophers going all the way back to the ancients. In that sense, Strauss's own practice of philosophy requires that there is nothing original about his awareness of esotericism as an intellectual possibility; it is common knowledge among philosophers qua philosophers. Consider, for instance, the following passage in Freud:

The writer lives in fear of censorship, so he moderates what he says and distorts his meaning. Depending on the strength and sensitivity of that censorship, he finds himself compelled either to cease certain forms of assault entirely or to speak in innuendoes rather than direct terms, or he must hide his offensive statement behind a seemingly innocuous mask – for instance, by narrating incidents between two mandarins in the Middle Kingdom when what he really has in mind are civil servants in his own country. The stricter the censorship, the more detailed the mask and often the more amusing the means by which the reader is nevertheless set on the trail of the true meaning.[3]

---

[2] Allan Bloom, *Giants and Dwarfs* (New York: Simon and Schuster, 1990), p. 240.

[3] Sigmund Freud, *Interpreting Dreams*, trans. J.A. Underwood (London: Penguin, 2006), p. 155. There is also a significant allusion to esotericism in Freud, *Civilization and Its Discontents*, trans. David McLintock (London: Penguin Books, 2002), p. 12. It is worth noting that this is by no means the only important affinity between Strauss and Freud. They also share the notable commitment to a view of intellectual life as *riddle-solving*. See, for instance, *Interpreting Dreams*, pp. 280 and 285. As Janine Burke discusses in *The Sphinx on the Table* (New York: Walker & Company, 2006), chapter 8, not only was Freud rather obsessed with images of the Sphinx, but he also had a distinct self-image as Oedipus. It seems very improbable that Strauss picked up this view of intellectual life from Freud. It is much more probable, in my view, that both of them shared an inspiration traceable back to *Nietzsche*: it is hardly accidental, for instance, that the very first section of *Beyond Good and Evil* refers to Oedipus and the Sphinx.

Quite relevant here is the following text from Leo Strauss, *Thoughts on Machiavelli* (Glencoe, IL: The Free Press, 1958), p. 50: "Concealment as practiced by Machiavelli is an instrument of subtle corruption or seduction. He fascinates his reader by confronting him with riddles. Thereafter the fascination with problem-solving makes the reader oblivious to all higher duties if not all duties." The obvious question here is whether a similar form of seduction/corruption is being practiced by Strauss.

This text in Freud was published roughly forty years before Strauss's "discovery" of esotericism in 1939–1940 (as documented especially well in a wonderful account by Laurence Lampert).[4]

The key text is a letter from Strauss to Jacob Klein dated February 16th, 1938 in which he writes: "When in a few years I explode this bomb (in case I live so long), a great battle will be kindled."[5] The "bomb" to which Strauss refers is the necessary incompatibility between philosophy and Judaism (and by extension, philosophy and all religions).[6] There is certainly some exhilaration in this discovery or re-discovery by Strauss. But not only exhilaration! He also expresses a kind of dread and revulsion at the dark secret that he has (inadvertently?) chanced upon in the course of his studies of Maimonides. Maimonides is not what he seems – not an orthodox exponent of philosophical Judaism, but rather, an esoteric "Averroist" who subverts Judaism for the in-the-know philosophers.[7] Philosophy is above all the assertion of the unspeakable abyss that separates philosophers and non-philosophers.[8]

---

[4] Laurence Lampert, "Strauss's Recovery of Esotericism," in *The Cambridge Companion to Leo Strauss*, ed. Steven B. Smith (Cambridge: Cambridge University Press, 2009), pp. 63–92. Of course, it makes sense to refer to Strauss's "recovery" rather than "discovery" of esotericism, for again, if esotericism did not already exist as a pervasive intellectual practice across the millennia of the philosophical tradition, there would be nothing for Strauss to discover.

[5] Lampert, "Strauss's Recovery of Esotericism," p. 64. The natural conclusion to draw from the letters highlighted by Lampert is that Strauss was fundamentally a *"libertin érudit"*; indeed, I really cannot see what other conclusion *can* be drawn.

[6] Cf. Rousseau's suggestion that "Philosophy" (i.e., philosophy per se) = esotericism = atheism in Rousseau, *The Discourses and Other Early Political Writings*, ed. Victor Gourevitch (Cambridge: Cambridge University Press, 1997), pp. 41–42, note. See also John Toland, "Clidophorus; or of the Exoteric and Esoteric Philosophy," one of four essays composing *Tetradymus* (1720); as well as J. Judd Owen 's illuminating commentary "Toland and Strauss on Esoteric Writing," in *Recovering Reason*, ed. Timothy Burns (Lanham, MD: Lexington Books, 2010), pp. 209–221.

[7] Without intending to do so, Paul Rahe, in *Against Throne and Altar* (Cambridge: Cambridge University Press, 2008), discloses a fundamental incoherence in the Straussian project. If (as Rahe rightly affirms) Strauss reads Plato and the Platonic tradition through the lens of the esotericism of Alfarabi and Averroës, and if (as Rahe argues in chapter 2 of *Against Throne and Altar*) Averroism – i.e., a commitment to bolstering religion for the vulgar who need it while subverting it for the philosophers who do not – is the fundamental driving force behind the philosophical enterprise of Machiavelli, then it is not really true that Machiavelli represents an ultimate caesura between ancients and moderns. On the contrary, the Western philosophical tradition, for Strauss, is Averroistic from start to finish. The only difference between ancients and moderns is that the ancients do a better job of concealing, or at least obscuring, this Averroism. (Robert Bartlett is the Straussian who comes closest to acknowledging – however guardedly – this implied unity of ancients and moderns: see *The Idea of Enlightenment: A Post-Mortem Study* [Toronto: University of Toronto Press, 2001].) For Strauss (as Rahe allows us to see – again, despite his own intentions), philosophers qua philosophers are Averroists, which means that the distinction between ancients and moderns loses much of its force. Similar implications can be drawn from Strauss's telling expressions of solidarity with Spinoza as quoted by Steven B. Smith on pp. 398–400 of "Leo Strauss's Discovery of the Theologico-Political Problem," *European Journal of Political Theory*, Vol. 12, no. 4 (October 2013), pp. 388–408.

[8] I am sure this sounds more dismissive than I mean it to be. Strauss no doubt felt the full force of the enormous existential gulf between, on the one hand, his origins in an orthodox household in a small

Esotericism as the defining mark of the philosopher is something that presents an irresistible allure for students who are led to think of themselves as having been made privy to secrets that have been guarded for millennia. The greatest thinkers are the greatest human beings, and by learning about esotericism, students conceive themselves to have been granted entrance to this most elite of elite clubs (or at least allowed to sneak in by a side door).[9] But the problem (which Strauss never addresses in a satisfactory way) is that the club is no longer an exclusive one once esotericism has been made public and the secrets have been published in books that anyone can purchase and read.[10] There is in Strauss an unfortunate failure to acknowledge (a) that in modern liberal societies, esotericism has become redundant, and (b) that it has been and continues to be an unconditionally good thing for philosophy that esotericism is no longer required. In a sense, what Strauss accomplishes (paradoxically) is the completion of the Enlightenment, by making the hidden purposes of philosophy accessible to the multitude in a more radical fashion than the historical Enlightenment of the seventeenth and eighteenth centuries managed to do. Strauss is the ultimate Enlightener, while he presents himself as the one modern philosopher trying to put the genie back in the bottle – that is, to resist the Enlightenment's efforts to weaken the separation between the few and the many.

Philosophers and Non-Philosophers

There are three major themes in Strauss's work: The first is his account of esotericism in Western political thought. The second is his theme of the opposition between nature and history. The third is a narrative about "the decline of the West," and how it "tracks" a corresponding decline in the history of Western philosophy. The most compact restatement of this third theme is that Western theory, starting with Machiavelli, moves away from nature and moves toward history and historicism as the governing ideas of modernity,

---

community in provincial Germany, and on the other hand, his early encounter with towering philosophical spirits like Husserl and Heidegger. Not surprisingly, Strauss experienced these as two distinct worlds that could not be easily harmonized or bridged, and he deserves credit for giving that experience philosophical expression. But rigid orthodoxy and the kind of radical thinking that subverts everything fixed are extremities, between which lie a wide range of other human possibilities.

9 Especially relevant here is Nietzsche, *Beyond Good and Evil*, § 30 – perhaps the *key* text in appreciating what esotericism meant for Strauss. Cf. Alexandre Kojève, "The Emperor Julian and His Art of Writing," in *Ancients and Moderns*, ed. Joseph Cropsey (New York: Basic Books, 1964), p. 95: "literary camouflage could serve to form an elite."

10 The obsolescence of esotericism is even more evident in the age of the Internet. On YouTube, one can now listen to an audio of Strauss exposing, in his own voice, the secrets of Maimonides!

and this in turn puts us on a slippery slope toward pervasive relativism and the incapacity of Western societies to give a confident account of their own underlying principles. Hence theme number 3 is clearly very closely related to, and bound up, with theme number 2. All of these Straussian themes are important and influential, and all of them are problematic.

We have already begun to discuss esotericism. Let's take a step back and fill in more of an account of what esotericism is and how it figures in Strauss's broader political philosophy. We can then move on to the other two familiar trademarks of Strauss's theorizing. The theme of esotericism receives much less explicit treatment in *Natural Right and History*, although it cannot help but inform the interpretations of canonical theorists that Strauss offers in that book. Rather, the best and most important treatment of esotericism as defining Straussian political philosophy is offered in another of Strauss's books – namely, *Persecution and the Art of Writing*. Since esotericism is a crucial component of what defines Straussianism, and since it figures less prominently (or at least less explicitly) in *Natural Right and History*, let me start with a thematic discussion of the issue of esotericism as Strauss unfolds it.[11]

Without question, Strauss's greatest contribution as a political philosopher was his powerful, intellectually radical, and often brilliant readings of great texts in the history of political theory. But these readings – at least subsequent to Strauss's "discovery" of esotericism in the early months of 1938 (he wrote a few important books prior to this discovery, but these works are, so to speak, "pre-Straussian" or "non-Straussian") – are inseparable from Strauss's idea of philosophy as an esoteric enterprise. What is esotericism? The basic idea is that texts can be read at multiple levels, having one meaning for one audience and a different meaning for another audience, and the philosophical audience knows that the texts by fellow philosophers contain this subversive meaning intended only for them; hence it is possible for readers who are the intended recipients of the esoteric meaning actually to clue into the text's true teaching, while the broader or more vulgar readership receive the merely "exoteric" (vulgar) meaning of the text. (The prefixes "eso-" and "exo-" mean "inside" and "outside," so the in-group – the

---

[11] In "Esotericism and the Critique of Historicism" (*American Political Science Review*, Vol. 100, no. 2 [May 2006], pp. 279–295), Arthur M. Melzer has argued that Strauss's preoccupation with esotericism is justified as a way of refuting historicism (since historicism cannot be true if philosophers are communicating with each other, esoterically, across the whole philosophical tradition). This suffices as a justification of esotericism (and Strauss's obsession with it) only if one presumes (as Melzer does) that Strauss was right to place the emphasis that he did on historicism as the great bogeyman of the modern West. As should be amply clear from what follows, I do not share that view.

philosophers – share the true teaching while the outsiders – the multitude – get the vulgar teaching.)

Why would anyone write like this? And why would it reshape one's whole understanding of political philosophy, and the intellectual tradition that defines political philosophy as an enterprise spanning the centuries, to imagine philosophers of the past writing in this way? Strauss's idea here is by no means crazy, and a few simple reminders about the history of philosophy suffice to render his notion of esotericism intelligible. In Strauss's view, it is not an accident that the first key figure in what became the history of political philosophy, Socrates, was executed as a subversive by his fellow citizens. This was already an unmistakable signal that there is, in human society qua human society, a natural cleavage between those governed by opinion (the multitude) and those governed by the search for truth (the philosophers). Strauss rightly highlights in his famous essay on "Persecution and the Art of Writing" the list of persecuted philosophers: Anaxagoras, Protagoras, Socrates, Plato, Xenophon, Aristotle, Avicenna, Averroes, Maimonides, Grotius, Descartes, Hobbes, Spinoza, Locke, Bayle, Wolff, Montesquieu, Voltaire, Rousseau, Lessing, and Kant.[12] It is a formidable list! The lesson: non-philosophers must live by *doxa*, and they will kill, or at least suppress and intimidate, those who disturb the reign of *doxa*. But philosophy by its very nature is a challenge to the reign of *doxa*. To be a philosopher is to love truth more than one loves the dogmatic opinions of one's own society. Hence the long history of persecution of philosophers is in no way accidental.

No one can deny that Socrates was persecuted by his society, and so were a large percentage of succeeding great thinkers who sought to continue with the intellectual enterprise that Socrates had started. The more controversial Straussian claim is that this relationship between philosophers and non-philosophers is natural, and any attempt to renegotiate the relationship between philosophers and non-philosophers unavoidably violates nature. That claim is much less plausible. Think of a society like contemporary Iran and how it treats its intellectuals. Trying to live a Socratic life in that society certainly would land one in prison, or worse, make one the target of a *fatwa*. If one lived in Iran and wanted to pursue a Socratic life, one would certainly be well-advised to write esoterically, and trying to write non-esoterically would have the same consequences as those suffered historically by the people on Strauss's list (Anaxagoras, Protagoras, Socrates ...). Now Strauss's idea

---

[12] Leo Strauss, *Persecution and the Art of Writing* (Chicago: University of Chicago Press, 1988), p. 33.

is that that kind of relationship between philosophers and the larger society is the natural situation, and trying to change that is either futile or guaranteed to produce something worse than what one gets in the "natural" situation. However, clearly all of us live in post-Enlightenment societies where intellectuals can pretty much write what they think. If I write a "Socratic" book challenging the opinions current in my society, no one comes to arrest me and toss me in prison. On the contrary, I can earn a high salary as a professor and live a fairly cushy life. Strauss himself, at least from the age of forty-five onward, lived in such a society.[13] Why did he not welcome this new situation where philosophers were no longer required to write esoterically? I don't believe that Strauss ever gave an adequate answer to that question, but it appears that his view was that this particular "violation of nature" went along with a larger package of anti-natural or counter-natural aspects of modernity that were on the whole bad for society, and, in particular, that the reconciliation between philosophers and non-philosophers effected by the Enlightenment diminished the cultural status of philosophers as the singular beings that they really are and therewith attenuated the fundamental idea that nature itself dictates binding standards of what is higher and lower in human life.

One would assume that the sensible thing to say in this situation is that while it is true that pre-Enlightenment philosophers were certainly exposed to the threat of persecution, which very much affected how they were able to write, and equally true that being aware of this fact can generate new and interesting insights about what their uncensored thoughts might have been, esotericism is now irrelevant in the post-Enlightenment era in which we live. Philosophers (at least in Western liberal societies) can in fact now write what they think without risking death or imprisonment, and the whole society profits from this historically achieved liberty of thought and expression. Yet Strauss cannot bring himself to say this. Why not? Because for him the antagonism between the polis and philosophy in pre-Enlightenment societies is *natural*. Hence the Enlightenment, in his view, is not a liberation from oppression and superstition (i.e., a historical achievement) but rather a

---

[13] All of this seems so obvious that it is hard not to draw the conclusion that Strauss was simply captivated by his own meta-narrative (of the naturalness of the antagonism between the polis and the philosopher). But aren't the other thinkers treated in this book no less hypnotized or bewitched by their own meta-narratives? Perhaps this is even an essential attribute of the epic theorist qua epic theorist: unless their meta-narratives have this capacity to bewitch (including being capable of self-bewitching the very theorists who articulated them), these meta-narratives would lack the intellectual power to make a specific contribution to what Hobbes (*Leviathan*, chap. 15) memorably called "the conversation of mankind."

violation of nature – the price of which is that modern human beings suffer moral disorderliness in their social and political lives. This seems to me a perverse view. (How can it be other than perverse to say, or even imply, that the norm of persecution in an illiberal society like Iran is natural while the norm of intellectual liberty in liberal societies is unnatural?) However, it has the (to Strauss attractive) consequence of postulating an essential and universal rather than historically contingent relation between philosophy and esotericism.

Let's concede that certain great thinkers of the past wrote in a way that made esoteric meanings available to privileged readers of equal intellectual caliber while concealing these meanings from less philosophical readers. Why should that matter to us? For starters, let's remind ourselves that Strauss made this "discovery" in 1938. The context is relevant. Europe was in the throes of one of the most abysmal political crises that humankind had ever experienced, hurtling toward the most devastating of all wars – a cataclysmic war of ideologies, with genocidal regimes emplanted in both Germany and Russia. Millions of people would be slaughtered for purely ideological reasons.[14] The slaughter was just about to start, and there was no question that the nations of Europe were sliding down a precipice toward unprecedented political horror and dehumanization. In short, humanity was going to hell! So the question for Strauss, as for others of his generation, was: what defined the precipice? What had gone so dramatically wrong that human beings turned into beasts, and polities turned into machines producing genocidal degradation? Strauss was not alone in reaching the judgment that modernity as such had led human beings over this cliff. That is, something in the very nature of the modern organization of social life had violated what nature had intended human societies to be, and the price of this violation of nature was ultimately the war of ideologies that was present to everyone's eyes in the Europe of 1938. Where had modernity come from? It came from the great thinkers of the sixteenth and seventeenth centuries who had revolted against the sounder philosophies of antiquity and medievalism.

This does not mean that the intellectual revolutionaries who spawned modernity necessarily abjured esotericism. Hobbes and Spinoza and Locke

---

[14] One cannot help marveling at the accuracy with which this was foreseen by Nietzsche (in 1888): "[W]e shall have upheavals, a convulsion of earthquakes, a moving of mountains and valleys, the like of which has never been dreamed of .... [T]here will be wars the like of which have never yet been seen on earth" (*Ecce Homo*, "Why I Am a Destiny," § 1). But needless to say, Nietzsche conveys nothing of the sense of moral horror that would be appropriate to such a prediction.

were also subject to the persecution of philosophers (quite properly, all three are on Strauss's list of persecuted philosophers in "Persecution and the Art of Writing"). So they too wrote esoterically, and they too can be submitted to Straussian readings of their texts. But they rejected the view of society that ancient philosophers like Plato and Aristotle took for granted, and hence the esoteric/exoteric distinction becomes, in their hands, something contingent, something in principle capable of cultural and political transformation. So, Hobbes and Spinoza and Locke still wrote esoterically, but they aspired to a reorganization of social life that would make it possible to *transcend* the distinction between the esoteric and the exoteric, between the philosopher and the multitude. The idea was for philosophy to be at the service of the whole society, to help it to be educated to be more tolerant and less superstitious, and once this process of education had achieved its ends, society in general would have reason to be friendly, or even grateful, to the intellectuals who had helped liberate it from intellectual bondage.[15] There is a name for this project: "the Enlightenment." Strauss's whole life-work is a never-ceasing polemic against the Enlightenment (which in his view began, disastrously, with the writings of Machiavelli), and Strauss's appeals to "nature" capture the fundamental rhetoric by which he polemicizes against the Enlightenment as a supposedly "anti-natural" intellectual project. For Strauss, Plato demarcated for all times and all places the essential relation between the philosophers and the non-philosophers in his fable of the cave[16]: only singular philosophers can ascend up out of the cave, and any notion of going back into the cave for the purpose of enlightening the multitude can only have extremely unhappy consequences both for the society and for the philosopher himself. (It would be okay to go back into the cave if non-philosophers accepted the rule of wise philosophers, but this is, as Strauss emphasizes, a utopian possibility.) This is what nature dictates, and defying nature is both futile and ultimately catastrophic. It is in this sense that the Enlightenment project is counter-natural.

As we suggested at the very start of this section, one of the main things that distinguishes Strauss's mode of political philosophy is a narrative about

---

[15] In the last paragraph of chapter 14 of *De Homine*, Hobbes tells a story about a process of popular enlightenment during the rise of the Protestant Reformation. When the Church discredited itself through its arrogant dogmatizing and its shameless corruption, it not only aroused the Reformers; it also allowed ordinary people to come to see how they had been hoodwinked. The lesson: the multitude is not just a multitude; the people are *educable*. Hobbes here encapsulates what he and the others were aiming at with their project of enlightenment.

[16] See Leo Strauss, *Natural Right and History* (Chicago: University of Chicago Press, 1953), pp. 11–12.

civilizational decline: the morality and politics of ancient city-states were healthy, and these were succeeded by early-modern societies whose morality and politics were conspicuously less healthy, which were succeeded in turn by late-modern societies (societies where modernity had reached full maturation) that were flat-out pathological. How does Strauss make good on such an ambitious claim about the slide from virtuous Sparta to decadent modernity? He does so via a set of interpretations of the political philosophy canon, from Plato to Heidegger. *Natural Right and History* lays out the full trajectory of Strauss's interpretation, which is why this book is generally read as Strauss's master-work. If we want to understand why ancient Spartans were virtuous and we moderns are not, we need above all to understand why Thucydides and Plato and Aristotle represent the absolute high points of the intellectual life of the West, and why the towering thinkers of the modern period – Machiavelli and Francis Bacon and Spinoza and Locke and Rousseau and Kant and Nietzsche, to say nothing of Hegel and Marx – are, by comparison, intellectually corrupt. These latter thinkers all participate in a betrayal of the vocation of philosophy, and with this betrayal goes a fundamental spiritual corruption of the West as a whole.

Teasing a political philosophy out of Strauss is particularly challenging because – notwithstanding all his polemics against "historicism" – Strauss's emphatic preoccupation with interpreting grand texts of the Western canon conveys the strong impression that what he offers is not a trans-historical political philosophy at all but strictly an account of the *history* of political philosophy. He offers what the post-modernist, Jean-François Lyotard, called a "meta-narrative" – and a particularly ambitious one. This does not mean that there is not a political philosophy in Strauss (any more than the challenges of teasing political philosophies out of Freud and Weber mean that there are no political philosophies in those thinkers). The foundation on which Strauss erects his political philosophy is the idea that all societies knowingly or unknowingly (more likely the latter) base their structures of political order on the thinking of their greatest thinkers. So if there is a moral and spiritual decline, so to speak, in the sequence of great thinkers that defines the history of political philosophy, this will be reflected in a process of moral and spiritual decline in the societies or civilizations founded on those philosophies. (Again, think of Plato's image of the cave with the silhouette-puppeteers determining what the cave-dwellers believe, determining their horizons of experience within the cave.) It is on the basis of this line of thinking (never exactly spelled out but definitely implicit in

Strauss's work) that Strauss pursues his critique of modernity via a critique of the history of political philosophy.

Strauss does not really tell us in any detail how diminished appeals to "nature" as a rock-hard philosophical standard within the theory canon, and correspondingly beefed-up appeals to history as a kind of substitute-standard, contribute to significant moral decline in Western societies.[17] How exactly do ordinary citizens of a liberal society lose their virtue as a result of developments within the history of philosophy? Do they have a sophisticated enough awareness of the history of philosophy to be influenced by the waning of Plato and the waxing of Locke? Or do they somehow merely absorb, by an obscure process of osmosis, spiritual pathologies at work in the philosophical tradition and replicate in their own souls processes of moral and spiritual decline taking hold in the souls of philosophers distributed across the centuries? In order to vindicate his ambitious meta-narrative of a mirroring of decadence in society and decadence in philosophy, Strauss would have to be able to explain precisely how this works.[18] It would be a difficult case to make, and Strauss takes an easy way out by not trying.

It must be noted that the intriguing figure of Martin Heidegger occupies a special place in Strauss's narrative of civilizational decline. Arguably, Heidegger was the greatest philosopher of the twentieth century. That was certainly Strauss's opinion, and Strauss was by no means alone among leading political philosophers in holding that view. (Hannah Arendt, for instance, fully shared the same view.) But Heidegger was also, from 1933 onward, a fervent supporter of Adolf Hitler and the Nazis, and during that same fateful year (1933) held office as a quasi-official of the Nazi state, serving for one year as rector of the University of Freiburg. It seems reasonable enough to ask what Strauss asked: What had gone wrong with the history of philosophy such that the philosophical tradition's most eminent and intellectually powerful representative in twentieth-century Europe could be so

---

[17] Allan Bloom, in *The Closing of the American Mind*, does offer such a narrative. But the kind of account that he offers (Woody Allen channelling Martin Heidegger, or Louis Armstrong channelling Nietzsche via Bertolt Brecht) is so flippant that it is hard to take it very seriously.

[18] Arguably, a similar objection can be put to Alasdair MacIntyre – namely, that he treats his complaints about the contemporary social order as a refutation of contemporary philosophy, and treats his complaints about contemporary philosophy as a refutation of the prevailing social order, hence presuming (I think misleadingly, and without sufficient argument) that there is a one-to-one correspondence between one and the other. In *The MacIntyre Reader*, ed. Kelvin Knight (Notre Dame, IN: University of Notre Dame Press, 1998), pp. 146–150, MacIntyre more or less claims that the narrative history of individuals, the narrative history of the social orders in which they are embedded, and the narrative history of successive stages in the history of moral philosophy run on parallel tracks (and do so because they are all entangled with each other).

bereft of civic and moral judgment? Strauss thought he had an answer to this question. Strauss's story is that Nietzsche and Heidegger were "radical historicists," and therefore, with Heidegger, Western civilization's long slide from nature to history reached its logical completion.[19] Any idea of appealing to trans-historically valid moral or political standards had by now been completely thrown out the window. The West's greatest philosophers had succumbed to relativism and nihilism, and therefore the West itself had been flung into the abyss of relativism and nihilism.

I find this analysis very questionable. We need some counterfactuals here. Would modernity be any different if Nietzsche had died in infancy or if Heidegger had never been born? What reasons does Strauss give us for thinking that it would be? In fact, it would be extremely difficult to come up with a plausible story whereby intellectual history loomed larger than sociology in understanding the genesis and evolution of advanced modernity (or any other epoch in human history, for that matter).

Nietzsche and Heidegger, in their different ways, were profound critics of the times in which they lived, no less so than Strauss, probably more so. If it were true, as Strauss asserts, that Nietzsche and Heidegger founded their philosophies on the idea of "deferring to History,"[20] then they could not be severe critics of modernity, yet that is precisely what they are. So it makes little sense to trace their moral and intellectual pathologies, whatever they were, to something called "historicism." True, there is a murky fatalism in both Nietzsche and Heidegger – they were attracted to (sometimes quasi-mystical) notions of a metaphysical destiny to which human beings are subject and to which neither mere human reason nor mere human volition are equal. Those conceptions may or may not be philosophically defensible. But the idea that it was excessive deference to history and insufficient deference to nature that explains what went wrong with Nietzsche and Heidegger does not seem plausible. And even less plausible is Strauss's claim that this

---

[19] See especially Leo Strauss, *Natural Right and History*, pp. 25–32; and Leo Strauss, *What is Political Philosophy?* (Chicago: University of Chicago Press, 1988), pp. 26–27. The fact that Heidegger's name does not appear in the index of *Natural Right and History* does not prove that Heidegger is not central to the purpose of that work.

[20] *What is Political Philosophy?* p. 27. Historicism, in Strauss's view, is inherently decadent because it means acceding to or adapting oneself to a process of historical change that is invariably one of moral decline. Holding fast to nature, by contrast, is associated with a stance of upholding the cause of civic and moral virtue *unbendingly*. The commitment of Nietzsche and Heidegger to common morality was shaky, to say the least, so Strauss interprets this culmination of radical modernity as vindicating his thesis about the relation between historicism and morality. Here I endorse the view of Robert Pippin cited in the next note – namely, that Strauss is much too quick in drawing his philosophical conclusions.

same failing accounts for all that is wrong with modern Western culture and modern Western politics.[21]

Natural Right

What does Strauss mean by natural right? One of the many puzzles that confront the reader of *Natural Right and History* is that Strauss begins the book by presenting himself as a champion of the natural right doctrine of the American Founders, as if he were aligned with Thomas Jefferson.[22] That, in turn, would align Strauss with John Locke and the pre-Lockeian and post-Lockeian Enlightenment. Yet *Natural Right and History* makes clear that Strauss is a root-and-branch critic of all that. Where does that leave Strauss as a champion of natural right?

He has to insist that there are two fundamentally different versions of natural right, ancient and modern, and that the ancient doctrine is the one

---

[21] David Wootton writes, in criticism of Quentin Skinner ("The Hard Look Back," *Times Literary Supplement*, 14 March, 2003): "[Skinner] is interested in the ways in which ideas shape behavior, but scarcely at all in the ways in which behavior shapes ideas." This kind of criticism could be made with far greater force against Strauss.

This example of a too-quick jump from the idea of Heidegger as a supposedly radical-historicist philosopher to the conclusion that we inhabit a radically historicist epoch illustrates a tendency on the part of Strauss to offer woefully short-circuited arguments where we need much fuller (and slower) elaboration in order to be convinced. Cf. Robert B. Pippin, "The Modern World of Leo Strauss," in *Hannah Arendt and Leo Strauss*, ed. P.G. Kielmanegg, H. Mewes, and E. Glaser-Schmidt (Cambridge: Cambridge University Press, 1997), p. 151, n. 31, concerning Strauss's Rousseau-to-historicism "slippery slope" argument: "The ride is so fast that many potential safe stops on the way down are too hastily ignored." Pippin, not unfairly, makes a similar criticism of Arendt. By comparison with both Strauss and Arendt, Pippin commends Hans Blumenberg as offering an analysis that is "much more historically specific, sensitive to nuances, to what made ... the project of modernity ... unavoidable" (*Hannah Arendt and Leo Strauss*, p. 168). Cf. page 147: Strauss, unlike Blumenberg, "neglects the larger issue of the *motivations* for the modern revolt against antiquity."

[22] See the good discussion of Jeffersonian natural right offered by Jeffrey Sikkenga in *Civil Religion in Political Thought*, ed. Ronald Weed and John von Heyking (Washington, D.C.: Catholic University of America Press, 2010), chapter 8. Note Strauss's appeal to the Declaration of Independence on the very first page of *Natural Right and History*. (Moreover, my own copy of the book, the paperback edition of the 8th impression, features the Declaration of Independence on its cover.) This surely has to be chalked up to Strauss's (fairly easy-to-penetrate) rhetoric. When we think of the Declaration's famous first sentence of the Preamble, Strauss is unquestionably attracted to the assertion of "self-evident truths" as a contrast to modern relativism and historicism, but he is clearly much less enamored of the *content* of the particular self-evident truth that the Preamble asserts (namely universal human equality); cf. Alan Gilbert, "Do Philosophers Counsel Tyrants?" *Constellations*, Vol. 16, no. 1 (2009), pp. 109–110 and p. 122, n. 28. This duality in Strauss's stance toward the Founding (embrace of its appeal to a natural standard; rejection of its egalitarianism) defines a pervasive tension in Straussianism in general. For a quite sharp encapsulation of this tension, see the paradoxical syllogism on page 58 of Catherine and Michael Zuckert, *The Truth About Leo Strauss* (Chicago: University of Chicago Press, 2006). I explore aspects of Strauss's anti-egalitarianism in *Philosophy in a Time of Lost Spirit* (Toronto: University of Toronto Press, 1997), chapter 13 (including the appendix to that chapter).

to which he gives his allegiance.[23] So what then defines that ancient teaching on natural right? With Strauss, it is generally easier to say what natural right is not than to say what it is. It certainly is not a theory associated with appeals to history.[24] Nor is it associated with characteristically modern doctrines of individual rights, contractual consent, general will, utility, or autonomy. If there is something that can be affirmed with confidence in regard to Strauss's commitment to a conception of natural right that is philosophically valid, it is that the relevant theory is situated within the domain of what Strauss calls "classic natural right" (the principal account of which is given in *Natural Right and History*, chapter 4).

For Strauss, the heart of the distinction between *physis* and *nomos*, as apprehended by the theorists of classic natural right, is their distinction "between genuine virtue and political or vulgar virtue" (p. 121).[25] The regime specifies the virtue required by citizens of that regime, but that specification is located within the domain of *nomos*. Classic natural right exists insofar as it ultimately makes available, at least among the philosophers who seek it, a true understanding of "genuine virtue," as distinct from the conceptions of virtue promulgated by this or that regime. All societies yield a range of opinions, partial conceptions of justice, that are intelligible in the light of something more than opinion, a more comprehensive or more philosophical understanding of justice (pp. 124–125). Socratic dialectic is dedicated to showing that partial opinions about justice necessarily contradict themselves, hence proving their inadequacy in relation to "the one true view of justice" (p. 125), which is the object of philosophical aspiration. Does philosophy,

---

[23] In his preface to the 7th impression of *Natural Right and History* (p. vii), Strauss refers tellingly to his "inclination to prefer 'natural right,' *especially in its classic form* [my italics]." The equivocation in this text suggests that modern natural right is a kind of second-best to ancient natural right; he prefers the ancient version, but if it were no longer available, he would settle for the modern version (presumably on account of its superiority to the alternative, namely historicism, and beyond that, "radical historicism," or nihilism). But that is an odd suggestion, given that the champions of modern natural right (Hobbes, Locke, Rousseau) are in Strauss's view fully implicated in the decisive turn away from nature that is coeval with (Machiavelli-inaugurated) modernity. Hence, strictly speaking, modern natural right cannot serve as a, so to speak, "back-up" for ancient natural right.

[24] It is not at all impossible to combine historicism with a doctrine of natural right. As my colleague Alan Brudner drew to my attention many years ago, if one consults the full original title of Hegel's *Philosophy of Right*, one sees that Hegel actually subsumes his political philosophy under the rubric of "*Naturrecht*." A doctrine of natural right, for Strauss, is any articulation of authoritative standards for human life that have their source in something less malleable than subjective will or social convention. Arguably, the Hegelian idea of history satisfies this criterion. If the unfolding of history is rationally ordained rather than merely contingent, as it certainly is for Hegel, then it makes available standards of judgment that are, so to speak, deliverances of *physis* rather than *nomos* – even if these standards do not reveal themselves as authoritative until a fairly late stage of the unfolding of human history.

[25] All parenthetical references in this section are to *Natural Right and History*.

therefore, supply "the one true view of justice"? Strauss seems to concede that it does not, for he refers to "the unfinishable character of the quest for adequate articulation of the whole" (ibid.). We know that the opinions that circulate within all societies are partial, and we know that they are partial in relation to an assumed whole – that the contradictoriness of a given opinion "points beyond itself" (ibid.) to something non-contradictory or comprehensive. Philosophy is the search for this non-contradictory whole, but philosophy's quest is Socratic, that is, "unfinishable"; it is the human quest for the divine.

Classic natural right affirms that nobility or human excellence *exists*. Modern natural right, akin to ancient hedonism, presumes that the higher can always be reduced to the lower, but classic natural right never makes this mistake. The higher is the higher: the soul is higher than the body, and the higher parts of the soul are higher than the lower parts of the soul. Classic natural right gives us an adequate understanding of the soul, and its hierarchical structure, that modern natural right can never give us.[26] "The various human things which are by nature noble or admirable are essentially the parts of human nobility in its completion, or are related to it; they all point toward the well-ordered soul, incomparably the most admirable human phenomenon" (p. 128). Once again, classic natural right is committed to a doctrine of parts and whole. The suggestion seems to be that souls are more important than regimes, because regimes always rest on partial opinions concerning justice, whereas souls – so it seems to be implied – are in principle capable of "completion." If philosophy cannot make available a complete understanding of justice (because the Socratic quest is an "unfinishable" quest, that is, a human quest for the divine, for the more-than-human), perhaps it can make available a complete understanding of the well-ordered or fully excellent soul.

In the end, I do not see how the outcome of classic natural right, as presented by Strauss, can be anything other than a largely negative one. It can serve to debunk the leading philosophies of modernity because (on Strauss's account, anyway) they don't even *aspire* to the idea of the whole, the idea of an ordered completion, to which the ancient philosophers

---

[26] It is not impossible to find such doctrines among modern political philosophers. For one interesting example, consider James Harrington, *The Commonwealth of Oceana*, ed. J.G.A. Pocock (Cambridge: Cambridge University Press, 1992), pp. 10–11, 18–19 and 273–275; cf. J.G.A. Pocock, Historical Introduction to *The Political Works of James Harrington* (Cambridge: Cambridge University Press, 1977), pp. 53–54, 112–113, and 120–121. Presumably, Strauss would say that Harrington did not think through the contradiction between his Platonism and his Machiavellianism.

aspire. But can classic natural right actually make available the whole, the completion, that it promises? With respect to its character as a doctrine of the just city, it offers truisms: true justice is natural rather than conventional, the idea that people should not rob from or cheat each other is grounded in the natural sociability of human beings, the just city or best regime is oriented toward human excellence, and so on. This is the kind of incontestable morality cited in the verses from *1 Kings*, chapter 21 and *2 Samuel*, chapter 12 that feature as Strauss's epigraphs for *Natural Right and History*[27]: people should not steal from each other, and virtue is superior to vice – as if the modern slide toward historicism implies a repudiation of this natural wisdom, necessitating in reaction a defense of basic common morality, which would be a fairly ridiculous thesis.[28] It is true that Strauss also appeals to the Platonic-Aristotelian idea of the just political community as a collective striving for human excellence (pp. 130–135), which suggests an idea of natural right as the vision of a community of excellence (which Strauss argues is limited to the historical experience of the ancient polis just because other types of political community are not on the intimate scale required for a shared commitment to the collective pursuit of moral and civic excellence).[29] Clearly, the natural right conception of the ancient philosophers is oriented toward a politics of character, a politics of the soul. Ancient politics on this account is claimed to be superior to modern liberal politics because it privileges the shared pursuit of human excellence, and thus provides a standpoint from which it is possible to repulse modern egalitarian notions that are seen as pretexts for leveling. Arguably, there is a substantive political philosophy here endorsing an aristocratic conception of politics, but this too is in a sense more negative than positive: it cannot point to any particular city as *realizing*

[27] The second of these two texts is a parable presented by the prophet Nathan to King David dramatizing David's famous sin against Uriah the Hittite. Putting the two epigraphs together, one gets the strong sense (though it is hard to be certain) that modernity, in its privileging of history over nature, is cast as the wicked and greedy rich man who robs the poor man both of what he cherishes as ancestral and of what is in fact his only solid possession, namely morality in its purity and simplicity.

[28] Arguably, it is Strauss's hope of giving some modicum of plausibility to this thesis that explains the enormously inflated significance that he attaches to Machiavelli as the supposed key inspirer of modernity. Since it is obviously much easier to portray Machiavelli as an enemy of common morality, Strauss's strategy is then to suggest that the anti-morality of Machiavelli somehow stains and contaminates modernity as a whole.

[29] "Only a society small enough to permit mutual trust is small enough to permit mutual responsibility or supervision – the supervision of actions or manners which is indispensable for a society concerned with the perfection of its members; in a very large city, in 'Babylon,' everyone can live more or less as he lists" (p. 131). Is every modern state, for Strauss, an instance of Babylon?

such a project of collective self-perfection[30] but it can point to actual societies (in fact, all societies on the modern scale, according to Strauss) as proving themselves unjust by virtue of their egalitarianism. The just city is oriented toward excellence, and excellence discriminates between superior and inferior souls, hence regimes erected on egalitarian principles are ipso facto unjust (pp. 134–135). The idea of the best regime in the ancient model privileges wisdom over equality (pp. 140–141),[31] thus in principle the endorsement of the highest Platonic-Aristotelian ideal serves as a basis for impugning the theoretical principles that underlie all modern regimes as such. Nobility in the highest sense is the ultimate standard of Platonic-Aristotelian politics, although Plato and Aristotle were wise and moderate enough to temper their yearning for nobility with an appreciation of the realities of non-ideal political life (pp. 141–143), and virtually nothing in the modern experience of politics, on Strauss's account, preserves even a trace of these ancient ideals. Strauss's claim is that ancient natural right is superior to modern natural right because the ethical-civic ideal embraced by the most important philosophers of the ancient world conjures up a higher standard of human life than the ideals embodied in modern principles (and by extension, the politics of antiquity is humanly superior to the politics of modernity). However, if (as Strauss himself emphasizes) the best regime of Plato and Aristotle is an *imaginary* regime (a mere construction of philosophical speech), this seems altogether too easy a basis upon which to award the ultimate prize to antiquity.

Natural right is a vision of justice, and ancient natural right shows itself to be superior to modern natural right because the ancient philosophers imagined a society in which the wise are supreme, the unwise defer to the wisdom of the wise, and all citizens participate in a cultivation of general good character that emanates, so to speak, from the city's ability to commit itself to a firm assertion of ultimate human hierarchy (of higher souls and lower souls). But given the fact that this is a merely imaginary dispensation, it hardly presents itself as a satisfactory solution to the question of how human societies should realize justice within the boundaries of their

---

[30] "The best regime, which is according to nature, was perhaps never actual; there is no reason to assume that it is actual at present; and it may never become actual. It is of its essence to exist in speech as distinguished from deed" (p. 139).

[31] It privileges wisdom over equality *philosophically*, but as Strauss emphasizes again and again, it does not do so *in practice* (since political life of its very nature requires moderation and compromise). Hence, the clear implication is that ancient political philosophers who found themselves living in modern egalitarian societies would be open to substantial prudential accommodations with the very different principles on which modern societies organize their civic life.

civic life.[32] At least it does seem to be a determinate conception insofar as it affirms "the essentially political character of the classic natural right doctrine" (p. 144). Yet precisely this aspect of ancient natural right gets put very much in question in the remainder of chapter 4. In fact, Strauss's reference to "the essentially political character" of Platonic-Aristotelian natural right is immediately followed by a discussion of how the ancient philosophers and the Christian thinkers who followed them were in basic agreement that "man's ultimate end," therefore natural right itself, "is trans-political" (p. 145) – for the Christians, because "the best regime simply is the City of God" (p. 144) and for the philosophers, because "political life as such is essentially inferior to the philosophic life" (p. 145). To be sure, a large gulf that had not previously been evident in Strauss's account now opens up between the Platonic and Aristotelian political philosophies (156), so that determining the political or trans-political character of classic natural right will depend heavily on whether one sides with Plato, for whom quite emphatically "the only life which is simply just is the life of the philosopher," or with Aristotle, who tries his best to keep his reflection on civic justice immune from "the dialectical whirlpool that carries us far beyond justice in the ordinary term toward the philosophical life."[33] Whereas most of the chapter had given us a strong impression of the singularity of "classic natural right," as an undivided doctrine, so to speak, Strauss now (on pp. 146–164) puts heavy emphasis on the diversity of natural right teachings available prior to the rise of modernity. Strauss (pp. 163–164) is quite clear on his rejection of "the Thomistic doctrine of natural right" (that is, the version of natural right that comes to be called natural law), but beyond that, we are left in quite a state of uncertainty and puzzlement about where Strauss stands amidst what is now a bewildering multiplicity of natural right doctrines. However, if the fundamental question is whether

---

[32] A recurring theme of chapter 4 (pp. 141, 152–153, and 160–165) is that, since philosophers are unlikely to be able to rule the unwise, and since in any case political life is intrinsically situation-bound, much scope will have to be given to the exercise of prudential discretion. Natural right in the proper sense defines the ultimate *ends* of political (and indeed human) existence, not the correct decisions in such-and-such unforeseeable circumstances. Trying to apply natural right directly, unmediated by principles of consent (where consent is assumed to involve an admixture of unwisdom), would have the effect of "dynamite" upon the society (p. 153). So Strauss is very resistant to an idea of standards of justice that one might even attempt to apply to actual societies, since he thinks the results are virtually certain to be disastrous. If so much of political life will in practice come down to prudence, why does so much hang on the utopias of philosophical rule dreamed up by philosophers?

[33] In this context, Strauss (p. 156) contrasts Aristotelian "sobriety" with Platonic "divine madness." Of course, this contrast may be less philosophical than rhetorical (that is, a function of Aristotelian rhetoric), for there is little reason to think that Aristotle is less committed to the superiority of the philosophical life than Plato is.

natural right is fundamentally political or fundamentally trans-political, the key issue is how Strauss relates to the radical Platonic privileging of the philosophical life over the political life.

This inevitably draws us back to Strauss's all-important reference (cited earlier) to the distinction "between genuine virtue and political or vulgar virtue" (p. 121) – which in turn inevitably raises the issue of the status of politics in the light of ancient natural right.[34] The "essentially political character of the classic natural right doctrine" (p. 144) turns out to be essentially non-political or trans-political. Again, Strauss underscores that the Biblical view that its morality is "of infinitely higher dignity than the best regime" (p. 144) is anticipated by the ancient political philosophers themselves when they affirm that "political life as such is essentially inferior in dignity to the philosophic life" (p. 145). Here the crucial passage is on p. 151. In the previous pages, Strauss had been exploring fundamental contradictions in the human city as such (that is, all human societies) as possible sites for the "truly just" (p. 148). He now refers to "other reasons which force men to seek beyond the political sphere for perfect justice or, more generally, for the life that is truly according to nature." Prominent among these other reasons is the need to *compel* the wise to rule in the just polis, "because their whole life is devoted to the pursuit of something which is absolutely higher in dignity than any human things – the unchangeable truth. And it appears to be against nature that the lower should be preferred to the higher." It follows directly from this train of thought that political justice now presents itself as a merely instrumental good:

If striving for knowledge of the eternal truth is the ultimate end of man, justice and moral virtue in general can be fully legitimated only by the fact that they are required for the sake of that ultimate end or that they are conditions of the philosophic life. From this point of view the man who is merely just or moral without being a philosopher appears as a mutilated human being.

From here, Strauss raises the question of whether there is a full identity between justice and morality or whether there is a diremption in the idea of justice ("two entirely different roots"). That is, the question is whether

---

[34] As specified in an earlier footnote, a doctrine of natural right, for Strauss, is any articulation of authoritative standards for judging the ends of human life. Nothing in this definition requires that it be essentially an *intra*-political ordering (although it will generally have implications for how human affairs are ordered within the domain of the political). Hence *trans*-political doctrines such as Plato's privileging of the philosophical life or Augustine's privileging of the City of God count, for Strauss, as doctrines of natural right. The question is whether Strauss's own idea of natural right (which he never spells out as such) is intra-political or trans-political.

moral virtue "is not, in fact, merely political or vulgar virtue," implying a higher morality available only to higher human beings. It seems obvious that this is what the reference to "genuine virtue" on p. 121 had meant to flag, and it has the inescapable implication that what divides philosophers from non-philosophers, genuine virtue from vulgar virtue, is more salient, for Strauss, than what unites them.[35]

Ultimately, the philosophers' utopias that Strauss invokes from *The Republic* and *The Politics*, with their visions of a best regime where justice, virtue, and wisdom prevail, are misleading with respect to Strauss's deeper philosophical purposes, and may have been intended to be misleading. To be sure, this utopian vision of perfected civic life and incorruptible morality is of service to Strauss in his determined polemicizing against modernity (modern relativism, modern decadence, modern nihilism). But at bottom it is a dream, and Strauss is insistent that one must not apply dreams to reality unless one wants to incur disaster. Ultimately, the idea of ancient natural right functions primarily as an assertion of human hierarchy (the high as naturally rather than conventionally high, the low as naturally rather than conventionally low). And the human hierarchy that truly matters to Strauss is the natural superiority of philosophers (those who live the Socratic life) to non-philosophers (those who live vulgar, non-Socratic lives).

It may help give us some perspective on Strauss's tendency to fetishize the ancients (including the ancient experience of philosophy) to ask: What would *Plato and Aristotle* have made of the astonishing series of cognitive revolutions that unfolded between the seventeenth and twentieth centuries? Considering the monumental progress achieved not just in mastering the world but also in understanding it, it is not at all obvious that *their* verdicts on modernity would have been as harsh as Strauss's is. After all, the Greek philosophers cared passionately about truth, about understanding the world rightly; and no one (not even Strauss[36]) can deny that

---

[35] Strauss's account of what fundamentally defines classic natural right falls well short of full clarity, and sometimes one gets the impression that muddying the waters serves Strauss's purpose. As regards my own interpretation, I would put my money on the views encapsulated in the last paragraph as capturing the core of natural right as Strauss understood it.

[36] See *Natural Right and History*, pp. 7–8. According to MacIntyre, we cannot forgo a teleological understanding of the universe without lethal consequences for our moral life, but only a religion like Christianity makes available such a teleological conception (*The MacIntyre Reader*, ed. Knight, pp. 152 and 267). Hence in his view teleology is rescued from oblivion by theology. I do not believe that such a solution is available to Strauss. (In an important letter to Karl Löwith dated January 10th, 1946 [*Independent Journal of Philosophy*, Vol. 4, p. 108], Strauss invokes the unbelief of the philosopher as

post-Enlightenment science and mathematics (Newton, Darwin, Maxwell, Lorentz, Planck, Einstein, Bohr, Schrödinger, Heisenberg, Dirac, Hawking, Higgs) has infinitely eclipsed ancient understandings of the world. For Strauss, the ancients are superior to the moderns because the ancients prize the contemplative life and the moderns subordinate the contemplative life to the vulgar imperatives of practical life. But what defines the contemplative life? For Strauss the contemplative life, the life of the philosopher, is fundamentally defined by its insight into the superiority of the philosophical or Socratic life. It is hard not to notice that there is something unattractively narcissistic about this conception of philosophy.[37] If, on the other hand, one conceives the contemplative life as oriented toward a fully veridical comprehension of the world, then one is likely to arrive at a completely different assessment of the Enlightenment (triggered by despised moderns like Descartes, Bacon, Hobbes, Spinoza, and Locke) as well as of modernity itself. As Gadamer once remarked, "Philosophy can never be in contradiction with science so long as philosophy remains science [*Wissenschaft*]."[38] That is, driving a wedge between philosophy and science is *philosophically* unacceptable. And since there are aspects of ancient philosophy that are hard to square with the discoveries of modern science, to put it mildly, that automatically gives a sizeable advantage to the moderns in the quarrel between ancients and moderns (as Strauss understood perfectly well, and as ancient philosophers themselves would not have hesitated to acknowledge).

philosopher. There is no reason to doubt that Strauss is including himself in this universal consensus among "genuine" philosophers.)

Let me hasten to make clear: I do not mean to assert dogmatically that the question of whether we inhabit a teleological or a non-teleological universe has been definitively settled. See Thomas Nagel, *Mind and Cosmos: Why the Materialist Neo-Darwinian Conception of Nature Is Almost Certainly False* (Oxford: Oxford University Press, 2012), for an argument that this remains, both scientifically and philosophically, very much an open question. (Nagel, unlike MacIntyre, does not think that natural teleology is a credible view only if it piggybacks on theism.) The point here (which applies not only to Strauss but also to Löwith and MacIntyre) is simply that lamenting the loss of Greek wisdom will do little to settle the issue one way or the other.

[37] Cf. Terry Eagleton, *The Meaning of Life: A Very Short Introduction* (Oxford: Oxford University Press, 2008), p. 93: "the idea that reflecting on the truth of existence is the noblest goal of humanity has had its allures – not least, needless to say, among intellectuals. It is pleasant to feel that one has tuned in to the meaning of the universe simply by turning into one's university office every morning. It is as though tailors, when asked about the meaning of life, should reply 'A really fantastic pair of trousers,' while farmers should propose a bumper harvest." In my view, Strauss is ultimately preoccupied with philosophy less as a mirror of the world than as a mirror of itself (or of a fetishized version of itself), with the consequence that one ends up with less of a political philosophy than was promised.

[38] *Gadamer in Conversation: Reflections and Commentary*, ed. Richard E. Palmer (New Haven, CT: Yale University Press, 2001), p. 98. Gadamer goes on to affirm an unbroken faith in "the unity of reason."

Gold Souls

In a footnote earlier in this chapter, I suggested that riddle-setting and riddle-solving is central to Strauss's practice of the philosophical life. The purpose, for Strauss, is to set apart those with gold souls from those with bronze souls.[39] There is at least one Straussian riddle that I think I can claim to have solved. Halfway through "What Is Political Philosophy?" Strauss, for no particular reason (it is not obviously related to the rest of his narrative), goes into a long digression on Socrates ("the Athenian") in *The Laws*. My thesis is that it is really a meditation on Strauss's experience of exile. His account of "Athenianizing" the Spartans (or the citizens in a Cretan/Spartan regime) is (according to my interpretation) really a discussion (esoteric, of course!) of "Germanizing the Americans." This connects with Tocqueville's presentation (at the beginning of Volume 2 of *Democracy in America*) of the Americans as an unphilosophical or anti-philosophical people. Rather than remaining a foreigner in such a culture, one alternative (Strauss seems to be saying) is to remake the culture so that one is no longer a foreigner. If Socrates, forced into exile, can turn Cretans into Athenians (supplying a proper home for philosophy, etc.), Strauss can do the same for America. Creating a Straussian school was a way for Strauss to "Athenianize"/Germanize the United States. Our first reaction to the notion of a "politics of philosophy" may well be that such a thing makes no sense or has no possible content, but my reading of "What is Political Philosophy?" perhaps offers some suggestion of what Strauss and his disciples may have had in mind in imagining that the politics of philosophy was of greater importance than the politics of citizens and states.

---

[39] There is a terrific Gene Hackman film entitled *Heist* (written and directed by David Mamet), which came out in 2001. In the film, everyone is trying to outsmart everyone else. Who will get the last laugh? Who will be the last one standing in a situation where life is a competition to outsmart everyone else? This might seem like a bit of a far-fetched comparison, but I think that there is an aspect of this in Strauss: for Strauss, the philosopher is the one who sees through every subterfuge, penetrates every veil, solves every riddle. It is not without reason that Stanley Rosen claimed that Strauss's ultimate aim was self-deification (*Hermeneutics as Politics* [New York: Oxford University Press, 1987], pp. 17 and 107).

4
Karl Löwith: In Awe of the Cosmos

Of the twelve thinkers surveyed in this book, Karl Löwith has surely been the one whose subsequent influence on political philosophers has been the most modest. There is no Löwithian school and no shelf of books devoted to his thought and legacy. It would be fair to say that he, along with Gadamer, contributes the least to the formulation of immediate (or even remote) prescriptions for the organization of political life. Still, a strong case can be made that his thinking about fundamental issues of modern life is no less worthy of our attention than that of the other thinkers covered in this book; in particular, there is a tragic sensibility in Löwith that seems to capture a deep truth about the human condition. Moreover, his chosen themes continue to have a pre-eminent relevance in the social world we currently inhabit. The relationship between nature and humanity, and the urgent need for a renegotiation of that relationship, comes up in several of the other thinkers we discuss, but arguably it is Löwith who makes this issue central to his philosophical reflection to a greater extent than any of the others.[1] To that extent, he surely deserves more recognition than he has yet received. In considering Löwith, it must be said that it is far from obvious exactly what follows for contemporary social and political life from the notion of a cosmos that Löwith wants somehow to resurrect. Still, it seems reasonable to expect (or at least to hope) that the more we are reminded of our

---

[1] The other thinker who has also (presciently) put this question at the top of his philosophical agenda is of course Hans Jonas (another post-Heideggerian). See above all *The Imperative of Responsibility: In Search of an Ethics for the Technological Age* (Chicago: University of Chicago Press, 1984). For a philosophical review of Jonas's argument, see my essay "Ethics and Technology," in *Democratic Theory and Technological Society*, ed. Richard B. Day, Ronald Beiner, and Joseph Masciulli (Armonk, NY: M.E. Sharpe, 1988), pp. 336–354. In a similar vein, consider also Hannah Arendt's critique of the human instrumentalization of nature in chapter 21 of *The Human Condition*. I once heard Gadamer offer the suggestion that it was possible to consider Heidegger as a kind of prophet of Green politics. In line with that suggestion, it does not seem accidental that all of these thinkers were shaped by a Heideggerian education.

species' puniness in relation to nature – and it is certainly an important part of Löwith's intellectual purpose to drive home this reminder – the more we will be forced to rein in our tendency to comport ourselves on this planet as if we were lords of the universe. (One should perhaps also make the countervailing point that the more we direct our gaze outwards toward the cosmos, the less it will seem to matter what kind of mess we human beings make on our own obscure planet.)

I'd like to begin by situating Löwith in relation to two of the other thinkers treated in this book, namely Strauss and Habermas. From Habermas's standpoint, Löwith turns his back on modern historical consciousness in a way that is deeply questionable.[2] From Strauss's point of view, by contrast, Löwith himself continues to be mired in historicism – which, as we saw in the preceding chapter, Strauss considers to be the defining vice of modern intellectual life (and also of modern political life insofar as the vices of political life reflect the vices of intellectual life). Now these two opposing characterizations of Löwith, when we juxtapose them, seem quite puzzling, and it seems hard to imagine that both could be right. (Of course, it is possible that *both* are off the mark.)[3] So let's examine the matter more closely.

Let's start with Strauss and Löwith. It is impossible to grasp their respective positions without noticing the intriguing fact that each of them appears as a historicist when seen from the perspective of the other. What this tells us is that not only do they have very different conceptions of historicism, but they also have very different conceptions of nature as something that can be appealed to in order to rescue us from historicism. Löwith appears as a historicist from Strauss's point of view because he takes for granted that centuries or millennia of historical experience crucially shape the views of social life held by those who have lived through this or that history (Christianity, the Copernican revolution in astronomy, the Reformation, the French Revolution, and so on).[4] And Strauss appears as a historicist

---

[2] As Gadamer points out, it seems likely that, apart from the ancients, the three main sources influencing Löwith's rejection of any faith in history were Goethe, Burckhardt, and the anti-historicist Nietzsche of the *Untimely Meditations*; Hans-Georg Gadamer, *Philosophical Apprenticeships*, trans. Robert R. Sullivan (Cambridge, MA: MIT Press, 1985), p. 174. In addition, while Heidegger was in no sense an anti-historicist, his trenchant analysis of modern "subjectivization" heavily shapes Löwith's critique of historicism (as it does Hannah Arendt's parallel critique).

[3] Another possibility would be that Löwith changed his views about history and historicism between the exchanges that he had with Strauss in the 1930s and 1940s, and the later writings targeted by Habermas. As is noted by many commentators on Löwith (including Habermas himself), there is, from first to last, a striking consistency in Löwith's lifework; therefore, this does not strike me as a plausible thesis. Probably the simplest explanation is the one that I propose in the next note.

[4] See the discussion, in the excursus that follows this chapter, of the dialogue between Strauss and Löwith devoted to such questions. Habermas, in his critique of Löwith, puts objections to Löwith

from Löwith's standpoint because nature, for Strauss, is something that is to be apprehended fundamentally in relation to human doings – the ranking of good and bad, noble and ignoble, excellent and mediocre, and so on. Löwith would regard this as a species of historicism at least in the weak sense that it enlists nature on behalf of what is exclusively a vision of the proper ordering of *human* affairs, rather than attending to nature *for the sake of nature*. What I mean is captured by a passage in "Nature, History, and Existentialism" referring to how we are estranged from nature when we engage in "historical appropriation of the natural world": historicism, according to Löwith, "made nature relative to us, with the effect that actually nothing natural was left over."[5] There may be a certain sense in which Strauss's doctrine of natural right does this as well (again, because "nature" is located by Strauss entirely in the realm of human doings, so as to determine our ranking of what is humanly better and worse). Historicism in the full sense, interpreted in a Löwithian way, renders the realm of human affairs, the realm of historical happenings, *so* central that concern with nature drops away altogether. It would certainly be a stretch to accuse Strauss of historicism in the latter sense; still, it would be hard to maintain that nature in the sense of the grandeur or majesty of the cosmos figures significantly in Strauss's intellectual concerns.

Löwith, like Strauss, is preoccupied with the antinomy of nature and history. But whereas nature, for Strauss, refers to the naturalness of the Greek polis (both with respect to the kind of political community that it was and with respect to the mode of theorizing it spawned), nature for Löwith has a different signification altogether. Perhaps a helpful way to put this would be to say that Strauss adheres to a strictly *anthropological* idea of nature and of the relevance of nature to political philosophy, whereas Löwith insists upon a *cosmological* conception of nature. If one looks back to the Greeks, one clearly finds an appeal to nature and the natural in both of these two senses, but arguably, in the case of say Aristotle, Löwith would be right in

---

that seem puzzlingly similar to those that Löwith puts to Strauss. Löwith sometimes oscillates between emphasizing history as what is through-and-through transient and emphasizing history as revelatory of what is constant and enduring in the human as human. Clearly, the latter theme is what provokes Habermas's challenges; the former theme, on the other hand, is what comes out in the debate with Strauss. Let me add, finally, that it is not obvious that Löwith's two themes are incompatible – they just *look* that way when viewed in relation to stances to history as different as Strauss's and Habermas's. (See note 33 below: the kernel of Löwith's "Stoic" wisdom is that empires rise and empires fall, but the human as human remains constant.)

[5] Karl Löwith, *Nature, History, and Existentialism and Other Essays in the Philosophy of History*, ed. Arnold Levison (Evanston, IL: Northwestern University Press, 1966), p. 20. All subsequent parenthetical page references refer to this volume.

maintaining that nature in the cosmological sense (as constituting those eternal entities contemplated by *theoria*) would be categorically privileged over any merely anthropological conception of what is natural.[6]

As regards Habermas's critique of Löwith's anti-historicism, consider the following sharp challenge in "Karl Löwith: Stoic Retreat from Historical Consciousness":

> We find ourselves in a situation in which the conditions for survival have become exorbitant, in the sense of being incompatible with forms of life that have taken on the bewitching appearance of "quasi-naturalness" by persisting for millennia. In such a situation of analytically definable alternatives between mortal dangers and changes in just such naturelike forms of life, historical experiences of the plasticity of human nature should not get shoved under the cover of the taboos supplied by a doctrine of invariants.[7]

This sounds similar to the worries about "an apotheosis of nature, naturalness, and natural law that would be nothing but an impotently doctrinaire critique of history" expressed in Gadamer's critique of Strauss (which is developed in close proximity to Gadamer's critique of Löwith).[8] I will have more to say about the Habermasian critique of Löwith and whether it does sufficient justice to Löwith's philosophy, but first, let's say more about what actually defines that philosophy.

There is a certain way of narrating the history of civilizations, inspired by Löwith, that prompts one to marvel at humankind's arrogant preoccupation with itself. It is a story of consistent, and in fact ever-increasing, "species

---

[6] In *Truth and Method*, 2nd rev. (English) ed. (New York: Continuum, 1998), p. 532, Gadamer states that Strauss's critique of historicism "seems to me more radical" than Löwith's. It is not clear why Gadamer says this. If one seeks a philosophical appeal to nature that is at the furthest possible remove from the apotheosis of history, then it strikes me that nothing can be more radical than Löwith's anti-historicism. That is certainly Löwith's intention. As Gadamer puts it on page 174 of *Philosophical Apprenticeships*, "Löwith seeks to bring [cosmological] nature to bear as the constant of reality, the granite that bears all," and it is hard to see that the Straussian invocation of natural right offers anything comparable to this.

[7] Jürgen Habermas, "Karl Löwith: Stoic Retreat from Historical Consciousness," in Habermas, *Philosophical-Political Profiles*, trans. Frederick G. Lawrence (London: Heinemann, 1983), pp. 79–97, at p. 89. The meaning of these sentences is hardly transparent. Translated into much simpler language, I think Habermas is saying that the stakes have become sufficiently high in contemporary political life that we are all exposed to very considerable peril if we are not prepared to strive for significant transformations in our social and political practices – say, with respect to the human propensity for fighting endless wars (see page 88). Hence the critique applied to Löwith by Habermas is that in this context, Löwith's pessimistic fatalism – his inclination toward the view that whatever the frantic ups and downs of human historicity, things basically stay the same in human affairs – is itself a politically dangerous stance.

[8] *Truth and Method*, 2nd rev. ed., p. 541.

narcissism."[9] Naturally, all human civilizations prior to Copernicus assumed our planet to be the center of the cosmos. One cannot really blame these pre-Copernican epochs for lacking the cognitive resources to grasp the true facts about our place in the universe. Much more striking is the presumptuousness built into the various historical religions, especially the three monotheistic religions. The Hebrew and Islamic scriptures would have us all believe the conceit that the Creator was so fixated on our particular planet that He dispatched a succession of prophets to reveal His preferences to us as privileged objects of divine attention. Christianity considerably ups the ante in relation to the monotheistic faith that preceded it and the monotheistic faith that followed it by suggesting that the Deity dispatched to our planet not only mere prophets but one of His own relatives! Could human beings really believe themselves to be that important within the larger cosmic scheme of things?[10]

One might easily assume that this grossly inflated human self-conception would be finally punctured when it was discovered, on the basis of the combined efforts of Copernicus, Brahe, Galileo, and Kepler, that the universe in which we live is so far from being a geocentric one that in fact we find ourselves planted on an infinitesimal speck floating obscurely in immeasurable space. Does this discovery dent human hubris and conceit? Actually, not at all. According to Löwith, the history of philosophy in the centuries following Copernicus and Kepler does not adjust our cosmic stature in a manner that is commensurate with what we now know about our place in the universe, following on from the refutation of geocentrism, but on the contrary *elevates* still higher our sense of our own importance relative to the rest of the universe. How does it do that? The Greeks, because their

---

[9] What I here term "species narcissism," Freud calls humanity's "naïve self-love" (*naiven Eigenliebe*): see Sigmund Freud, *Introductory Lectures on Psychoanalysis*, trans. James Strachey (London: Penguin Books, 1991), p. 326. Cf. Hannah Arendt, *Between Past and Future: Eight Exercises in Political Thought* (New York: Penguin, 1993), p. 89: "The modern age, with its growing world-alienation, has led to a situation where man, wherever he goes, encounters only himself." The text is from "The Concept of History," originally published in 1958; the idea it expresses is so close to Löwith (who is not cited) that it could virtually have been lifted straight from one of his essays – except that the idea of "world-alienation," as Arendt develops it in *The Human Condition* (in sharp contrast to Löwith), privileges "world" in the sense of the artificial *human* world. In this passage, on the other hand, Arendt is referring to a process of alienation from *both* nature and history: "In the situation of radical world-alienation, neither history nor nature is at all conceivable. [It leads to a] twofold loss of the world – the loss of nature and the loss of human artifice." Let me acknowledge helpful e-mail exchanges concerning the Arendt-Löwith relationship with Waseem Yaqoob, who has also noticed the striking affinities between Arendt and Löwith.

[10] Recall Nietzsche's unforgettable image of the mosquito that imagines itself to be "the flying centre of the world" (*The Portable Nietzsche*, ed. Walter Kaufmann [New York: Viking Press, 1968], p. 42).

universe was a geocentric one, were able to inhabit an enfolding cosmos with perfectly orbiting heavenly bodies; our post-Copernican universe, by contrast, is neither geocentric *nor is it a cosmos.* Lacking a cosmos, we post-Copernicans have turned inward, filling the cosmic vacuum by focusing ever more attention on ourselves and our own history (as if our *historical experiences* had cosmic importance).

Views about Nature and Spirit within German Idealism loom very large in Löwith's account of just how far the moderns have departed from the cosmocentric worldview of the Greeks.[11] This tradition, culminating in Hegel (but whose effects extend far beyond Hegel), is according to Löwith fixated on the idea of the ontological superiority of self-consciousness to what lacks self-consciousness: Hegel's "ontology of consciousness ... originates with the Christian experience of the self and results in a devaluation of nature which does not know itself, in contrast to a 'spirit' or 'mind' [*Geist*] which does" (p. 138). Human beings know that they are human, know that they stand in relation to nature, and reflect both on nature and on themselves; nature does none of this. It just *is.* Let's cite some passages from *Nature, History, and Existentialism* that convey Löwith's intellectual response to what is at stake in the German-Idealist philosophy of spirit. In "Hegel and the Christian Religion," Löwith refers to "the proud depth of [Hegel's] disdain for nature. It was this disdain which led him to describe the stars as only a sort of 'light eruption, no more astonishing than a crowd of men or a mass of flies'" (p. 201). "The physical world ... had, for Hegel's 'eye of reason,' no genuine reality. The truth of the world is its 'ideality'" – that is, nature as mediated by Spirit (p. 199). In "The Quest for the Meaning of History," Löwith writes: "Marx liked to quote Hegel's remark that the most criminal thought is more magnificent and sublime than all the wonders of the starry skies because the criminal, as mind, is conscious of his thoughts whereas nature does not know itself. Marx is no longer astonished by those things which are by nature what they are and cannot be otherwise" (p. 141).[12]

---

[11] In *The Legitimacy of the Modern World*, trans. Robert M. Wallace (Cambridge, MA: MIT Press, 1985), p. 27, Hans Blumenberg accuses Löwith of taking at face value German Idealism's own (inflated) sense of itself as having both inherited and fulfilled the spiritual mission of Christianity. This seems like a fair challenge.

[12] In *The Mysterious Flame* (New York: Basic Books, 1999), pp. 15–16, Colin McGinn compares the fact of consciousness to cosmological phenomena precisely in regard to the issue of which of these – mind or cosmos – deserves to astonish us more. McGinn argues that however much we find (say) black holes wonder-inducing, it is reasonable to view consciousness (whether human or animal) as even more wonder-inducing. We see from this that one does not have to buy into the intellectual extravagancies of German Idealism in order to find something like Hegel's view a plausible one. Perhaps a better or more faithful way of putting McGinn's point would be to say that our own consciousness

Hegel, Feuerbach, and Marx were all agreed "that nature is there 'for man' – [that] spirit is there for spirit,"[13] which suggests to Löwith that "the radical secularization of man [interpreted in a Feuerbachian way as an overcoming of man's self-alienation] corresponds to a similarly radical humanization of the world" (p. 197).

In a 1959 text entitled "Curriculum Vitae," Löwith puts rather sharply his challenge to the philosophical movement that (for him) culminated in Marxism: "He who wants to 'change' the world – who wants it to be different from what it is – has not yet started to philosophize, and mistakes the world for world *history*, and that for a human creation."[14] For Löwith, the whole anthropocentrizing trajectory of modernity (which is given philosophical expression by Hegel and his successors) derives ultimately from *Christianity*: "By refining substance into subjectivity [in Hegel's terms], Christianity produced a revolutionary 'reversal' in world-history. Man is no longer looked upon as a creature included in the cosmos, [subject] not to the highest law of freedom, but to unchanging necessity. Instead, the divine is placed at the peak of self-consciousness" (p. 191). It may have taken many centuries for Western thought to draw out the full entailments

or self-consciousness is itself one of the truly astonishing products of whatever natural processes are unfolding themselves in the cosmos; therefore, while it would be unreasonable not to feel a sense of wonder in regard to stars and black holes, it would be no less unreasonable for a sense of wonder in regard to consciousness to be left out of our sense of wonder in the face of the cosmos.

[13] The idea that "spirit is there for spirit" becomes clearer when we relate it back to a Hegel text that Löwith quotes on page 189: "God ... cannot reveal Himself to nature, that is, to stones, plants, and animals because He is spirit." But if humanity displaces God, or in the Feuerbachian sense comes to see that the divine Spirit is really itself, then this same denigration of nature gets replicated in humanity's self-apprehension as spirit.

[14] Karl Löwith, *My Life in Germany Before and After 1933*, trans. Elizabeth King (London: The Athlone Press, 1994), p. 160. "Curriculum Vitae" was originally delivered as an address to the Heidelberg Academy of Sciences. Why is world history *not* a human creation? According to Löwith's way of thinking, the Hegelian-Marxian presumption that the historical world is a matter of "self-production" abstracts from the essential truth that historical man "is also a creature of nature and not a self-made *homunculus*"; historicist thought "forgets that historically existing man is only in the world because the world of nature produced him" (*Nature, History, and Existentialism*, p. 140). See also Löwith, *Nietzsche's Philosophy of the Eternal Recurrence of the Same*, trans. J. Harvey Lomax (Berkeley: University of California Press, 1997), p. 187: "a teaching about man is groundless if it does not have as a supporting basis either a metaphysical *God* or the *physis* of the world; for man does not exist through his own powers [*der Mensch ist nicht da durch sich selbst*]."

Löwith's theme of human beings deluding themselves into thinking of themselves as self-making is undoubtedly influenced by Heidegger. See, for instance, Heidegger's "metaphysical" critique of the Marxist doctrine of the self-production of man: "Man produces himself as he produces his shoes." Martin Heidegger, *Four Seminars*, trans. Andrew Mitchell and François Raffoul (Bloomington, IN: Indiana University Press, 2003), p. 32; cf. pp. 52 and 76–77. Nonetheless, Löwith views his critique of Western anthropocentrism as also applying to *Being and Time*. See, for instance, *Nature, History, and Existentialism*, p. 18; and Löwith, *Der Weltbegriff der neuzeitlichen Philosophie* (Heidelberg: Carl Winter Universitätsverlag, 1960), pp. 7–8.

of this revolution in consciousness, but if the stars make little impression on us, we can ultimately thank (i.e., blame) Christianity's having dislodged us from the pagan sense of being creatures of fate. The Greeks inhabited a literally "awesome" cosmos,[15] whereas we Christianity-shaped moderns are fundamentally oriented toward spiritual freedom as the truly supreme thing in the universe. Hence we see little in the physical universe that warrants a sense of reverence.[16]

However, Löwith tells the story of modern anthropocentrism a little differently than I have. In Löwith's telling, the jolt to human self-regard administered by Copernicus does not offer an opportunity for human beings to shuck off their species narcissism. *On the contrary*, by decentering humanity's sense of its place in the universe, the Copernican revolution made human beings *all the more desperate* to focus their sense of the human destiny on the supposed providentialism inscribed in human affairs.[17] This led to modern historicism, which on Löwith's account is an even more extreme version of species narcissism.

Why does historicism aggravate (or, perhaps better put, express the essence of) the problem of anthropocentrism? What historicism means, according to Löwith's understanding of it, is not simply preoccupation with the sum total of happenings that populate the realm of human affairs, distributed in a linear temporal sequence. Rather, it means regarding this temporal sequence as capable of delivering an ultimate redemption for human beings, equivalent to (and replacing) the redemption promised (but left undelivered) by eschatological religion. It involves "immanentization of the eschaton," to employ Voegelin's categories.[18] If the idea is that in a secularized world, history, and history alone, will fulfill the consummate human destiny that had previously been expected from Jewish or Christian or Islamic narratives of salvation,

---

[15] According to the argument of Jan Assmann in *Moses the Egyptian* (Cambridge, MA: Harvard University Press, 1998), there is nothing specific to the Greeks in this experience of the divinity of the cosmos; it is to be found in *all* pre-monotheistic civilizations. Assmann calls it "cosmotheism."

[16] *Nature, History, and Existentialism*, p. 160: "the myth [of Prometheus] reveals a holy awe in the face of every assault upon the powers of nature, upon the physical cosmos which the Greeks regarded, in sharp contrast to human powers, as something divine. All such awe seems now to have vanished." Needless to say, one finds similar themes and intellectual concerns throughout the work of Hans Jonas; see, for instance, the appeal on page 89 of *The Imperative of Responsibility* to "Being (or instances of it), disclosed to a sight not blocked by selfishness or dimmed by dullness," as an object of reverence.

[17] The fundamental transformation away from "the pre-modern concept of an essential human existence within an orderly *cosmos* ... [occurs] as a consequence of the astronomical discoveries of the sixteenth century" (p. 24).

[18] See Chapter 6.

then the hopes invested in the historical process will vacuum up all spiritual energies, without remainder, so to speak. Our relationship to the natural world will come to seem paltry – as paltry as, in Löwith's reckoning, our relationship to the historical world is in fact. To quote again from a passage we cited earlier: "So-called historicism would be harmless if it had merely historicized and relativized the so-called spiritual world." But what historicism actually does is reshape in a fundamental way our experience of the naturalness of nature, such that "what still remains of natural things seems to be a mere leftover of that which has not yet been thoroughly subjected by man" (p. 20). "*Physis* ... is almost nonexistent for historical thought, while history ... has, so it seems, become everything" (p. 141).

Löwith asks: "Why does the natural light of the stars mean less to us – almost nothing – than a traffic light? Obviously because the meaning of a traffic light is in its purpose, while the light of sun, moon, and stars has no human and artificial purpose" (p. 21). Is there a cure for the experience of our historical being as all-consuming, as Löwith presents it? The only possible remedy, in Löwith's view, would be some kind of recovery of the experience of nature as a genuine cosmos, "as something divine." The prospect of such a philosophical recuperation of the ancient idea of *physis* accounts for why Löwith never ceases to be captivated by Nietzsche's metaphysics of the eternal recurrence. But it turns out that Nietzsche was far too infected with late-modern conceptions of volition and creativity to be capable of a true recuperation of antiquity.[19] Ultimately, Nietzsche founds his eternal recurrence idea on an appeal to the will, and the will corresponds to a *linear*, not circular, mode of temporality: "All this is entirely un-Greek, not classic, not pagan, but derived from the Hebrew-Christian tradition, from the belief that world and man are created by God's purposeful will. Nothing is more conspicuous in Nietzsche's godless philosophy than the emphasis on being creative and willing, creative by willing, like the God of the Old Testament."[20] "The Greeks felt awe and reverence for fate; Nietzsche makes the superhuman effort to will and to love it."[21] One thing that is not

---

[19] This is discussed further at the end of the excursus following this chapter. Cf. Habermas, *Philosophical-Political Profiles*, pp. 79–80, citing Löwith's view, arrived at by juxtaposing Nietzsche to Burckhardt, that Nietzsche lacked the composure or serenity required in order to effect a bona fide "return to the cosmological world perspective of the Greeks." However, it seems obvious that if recapturing the Greek sense of cosmos requires, among other things, overturning modern astronomy, Nietzsche would not have been able to return to this world perspective (or enabled the rest of us to return to it) no matter how serene he had been.

[20] Karl Löwith, *Meaning in History* (Chicago: University of Chicago Press, 1949), pp. 221–222.

[21] Ibid., p. 221.

quite clear in Löwith's thought is whether the project that was attempted in Nietzsche but failed to attain its goal can be pursued with more success in some other way. It is possible (probable?) that there is no solution.

Habermas quotes an ancient fragment that he says captures well the fundamental "leitmotif" of Löwith's thought: "In days to come, on account of the [weariness: *Überdruß*] of humans, the cosmos will not be a source of astonishment and will not appear to be a worthy object of prayer. This greatest of all goods in its totality, the best object of contemplation there has ever been, is, or will ever be, will have become endangered."[22] In a similar vein, Gadamer points out that no ancient text encapsulates Löwith's central intellectual concerns better than the pseudo-Aristotelian work, *On the Cosmos*.[23] Near the start of that text, we read the following:

[As regards men who have laboriously described to us either the nature of a single region or the plan of a single city or the dimensions of a river or the scenery of a mountain] ... one should pity [them] for their small-mindedness in admiring ordinary things and making much of some quite insignificant spectacle. They are thus affected because they have never contemplated what is nobler – the Universe and the greatest things of the Universe; for if they had properly attended to these things, they would never marvel at anything else, but all else would appear insignificant and, compared to the surpassing excellence of these things, of no account.[24]

As Gadamer and Habermas rightly suggest, Löwith indeed has ancient texts like these in mind when he, for instance, writes in his "Curriculum Vitae" text: "Only the natural world moves and exists of its own accord. No matter how far human beings manage to appropriate nature by cultivating it and extending their dominion over it, it will never become our environment, it will always remain itself."[25] If we fail to marvel at it in an act of contemplative awe, that counts as a decisive indictment of us as individuals and, more to the point, as a species. Nature in its self-subsistent splendor will still exist long after our species perishes and our planet is no more.[26] "We cannot exist

---

[22] Habermas, *Philosophical-Political Profiles*, p. 81; quoted on page 10 of *Der Weltbegriff der neuzeitlichen Philosophie*.

[23] Gadamer, *Truth and Method*, 2nd ed., p. 532. An ancient text that is equally inspirational for Löwith is Heraclitus fragment no. 30, with its conception of the cosmos, in its eternity, not only surpassing human beings but even surpassing the gods. See *Der Weltbegriff der neuzeitlichen Philosophie*, pp. 9 and 22.

[24] *The Complete Works of Aristotle: The Revised Oxford Translation*, ed. Jonathan Barnes (Princeton, NJ: Princeton University Press, 1991), Volume I, p. 626. Löwith himself cites an adjacent passage from the same text on pp. 9–10 of *Der Weltbegriff der neuzeitlichen Philosophie*; cf. pp. 21–22. See also *My Life in Germany Before and After 1933*, p. 167.

[25] *My Life in Germany Before and After 1933*, p. 166.

[26] We all know that this is true. But it has implications far beyond the kind of historicism that is Löwith's immediate target. Yes, we can ask how the willingness to invest energy in changing the world survives

without the world for one moment, but it can quite easily exist without us."[27]

So we know the desideratum, namely reorientation away from what is "of no account" and back toward what is truly worthy of reverence. What we *don't* know is how we are supposed to secure this desideratum, living as we do in a civilizational epoch where our relation to nature is thoroughly disenchanted by modern science. With respect to the intrinsic character, so to speak, of nature and history, nature is a cosmos and history is a chaos: "The natural world is a world rather than chaos because it is in itself ordered by nature or a cosmos. The so-called historical world is equally then a world only if there is order within it.... All knowledge of history, however, attests to the fact that ... any such system of laws is of relative duration, is broken, dissolved and needs to be forever created anew."[28] But the question is: do we *experience* the natural cosmos as a cosmos? On Löwith's own account, we do not (owing partly to developments in modern science and partly to our experience of ourselves as fundamentally historical beings), and it is far from clear how our contemporary experience of nature and history can be reconstituted such that we once again experience the cosmos as a cosmos.

The common rap against Löwith (articulated most sharply by Habermas[29]) is that he is an apostle of Stoic withdrawal. Is this Habermasian character-ization of Löwith a fair one?[30] There are two possible ways of answering Habermas's critique. First, one can ask, why does Habermas think that there is something necessarily anti-historical or anti-political in Löwith's protest

---

the knowledge that eventually all will perish. But we can raise the very same question about the willingness to invest energy in, for instance, writing an ambitious work of philosophy. In other words, *anything* that human beings do requires some degree of abstraction from our own individual finitude, the finitude of our species, and ultimately the finitude of our planet.

[27] *My Life in Germany Before and After 1933*, p. 167; cf. *Nature, History, and Existentialism*, p. 140.

[28] *My Life in Germany Before and After 1933*, pp. 165–166.

[29] See the essay on Löwith cited in note 7. As Habermas puts it on page 80 of that essay, Löwith aims "to steer clear of the cliffs of historical consciousness." On page 82, he describes Löwith's philosophy, rather more polemically, as "a repristinized Stoic world view" – an aspiration to overcome "a histor-ically diagnosed menace" through means that have been purged of history (namely an intellectual revival of Stoic naturalism). Obviously, thus characterized, there is a clear analogy between Löwith's project and that of Strauss – namely to *use* history in order to break free of history and thus return to nature – except that, as already discussed, what concerns Löwith under the rubric of nature is radically different from what concerns Strauss. Habermas's critical depiction of Löwith is echoed in chapter 4 of Richard Wolin, *Heidegger's Children* (Princeton, NJ: Princeton University Press, 2001); see, for instance, the repeated references to "Stoic detachment" in the last section of that chapter, entitled "Löwith's Retreat from History." The ascription of "detachment" also figures prominently in Gadamer's portrait of Löwith: see *Philosophical Apprenticeships*, p. 169.

[30] Again, the debate with Strauss discussed in the excursus following this chapter is relevant.

against the hubris asserted again and again in human history (and not least in the unfolding of advanced modernity)? After all, Stoicism, for Löwith, is not an incitement to withdrawal but rather a warning against hubris. Moreover, Löwith is obviously not uninterested in the often perverse political-historical consequences of human beings absurdly overestimating the importance of their place in the cosmos. Consider, for instance, Löwith's invocation of the "supra-historical wisdom" of Scipio in the latter's irrefutable observation, following Rome's destruction of Carthage, "that the same fate which the power of the Romans had just visited upon their enemy would someday befall Rome, just as it had formerly befallen Troy" (p. 137; Löwith's source is Polybius). Löwith adds: "We can hardly conceive of a modern statesman who, after the victorious outcome of the last world war, would reflect, as did Scipio after the destruction of Carthage, that the same fate which has just been meted out to Berlin will someday befall Washington and Moscow. The modern historical consciousness, whether it is based on Hegel, Marx, or Comte, does not know how to unite the remote future with the remote past because it does not want to admit that all things on earth come and go" (ibid.).[31] Arguably, the history of human empires (right up to the present) flows from human beings somehow coming to believe that they leave a more permanent impression on the world than they really do. Or consider Löwith's suggestion that "the English, French, and Russian revolutions would not have taken place without the faith in progress, and secular faith in progress would hardly have come into existence without [monotheism's] original faith in an ultimate goal of human existence" (p. 23). In other words, the suggestion is that the history of modern revolutionary politics (from Cromwell onward) flows from human beings being duped by monotheistic religion into seeing more providential purpose in human life than is really there. And so on. In any case, there is no evidence that Löwith was in any way indifferent to how the philosophical themes that are of concern to him play out in the world with respect to their possible consequences for political and historical life. As he himself puts it (p. 138): "It would be foolish to suppose that [viewing history as contingent rather than providential] makes factual history superficial."

That is the first of our two proposed responses to Habermas. But as a second response, one can turn back against Habermas a counter-challenge

---

[31] Cf. *Nature, History, and Existentialism*, p. 161: "we know of nothing which lasts forever"; and pp. 139–140: "only the natural world is really the all-inclusive or universal 'world.' Our historical human world is something transitory within the natural world and can disappear like Icarus in [Bruegel's] painting ... [as if] nothing at all has happened."

from Löwith. Why is it so obvious to Habermas that our relation to history is central to the meaning of human existence? True, the coming generations *may* bring progress in the realization of Habermas's ideal of a political community oriented toward communication rather than oriented toward power.[32] However, given what we know of the mutability and transience of human affairs[33] – the unpredictable ups and downs of history, its frustratingly constant inconstancy, so to speak – who is to say that the future won't bring the very opposite of such progress (or worse, perhaps simple obliteration of our self-important species)? If one lived in the nineteenth century and took the various philosophies of history seriously, one might have had reason to invest hope in what the twentieth century would have to offer. As it was, it turned out to be a century marked, from its first to its last decades, by senseless slaughter, and its middle decades saw genocidal horror of an intensity which few other epochs of human history could match.[34] One should not make the mistake of thinking that because Löwith sees more meaninglessness than meaning in what fickle history has to offer, therefore he must look to some *non*-historical sphere to secure the sense of meaning that history fails to supply. If so, Löwith would have to accept, for instance, the truth of ancient cosmology, or the validity of Christian doctrines of salvation; and there is no reason to believe that he does.[35]

---

[32] In the last sentence of Lecture 11 of *The Philosophical Discourse of Modernity*, Habermas denies that his theory of a process of normative rationalization unfolding in the course of modernity "draw[s] upon the constructions of the philosophy of history." I suspect that Löwith would see more philosophy of history in Habermas's theorizing than Habermas wants to acknowledge.

[33] This theme is articulated very emphatically throughout the texts that concern us in this chapter; see, for instance, the texts quoted in note 31 above. However, in Lecture 1 of Karl Löwith, *Permanence and Change: Lectures on the Philosophy of History* (Cape Town: Haum, 1969), Löwith explores the idea that the relentless transitoriness of historical happenings does not rule out the experience of an enduring "human essence." Referring to the characters portrayed in Tolstoy's *War and Peace* in the context of Napoleon's invasion of Russia, Löwith comments that "the really human in these human beings remains essentially unaltered by history" (p. 17). Löwith's point is that even though we experience history as ceaseless change, we could not experience the human as properly human unless history itself at the same time made available an experience of "some sort of permanence, duration, constancy" (p. 12). All of this in turn suggests that there is a way of countering the feeling of being at the mercy of the flux-ridden vicissitudes of human affairs from *within* our experience of history. For another very powerful statement of this theme of history as constancy, see Löwith, *Martin Heidegger and European Nihilism*, ed. Richard Wolin (New York: Columbia University Press, 1995), p. 95.

[34] No one can deny the justice of Humphrey Bogart's unforgettable crack in the Billy Wilder version of *Sabrina*: "The twentieth century? I could pick a century blindfolded out of a hat and pick a better one."

[35] As Löwith nicely puts it in "Curriculum Vitae" (*My Life in Germany Before and After 1933*, p. 164), his agreement with Christian theology is limited to the *negative* doctrine that "the wisdom of this world would pass as a folly in the eyes of God." See also page 166: a Hegel-type "faith in world history ... has become as implausible as the preceding faith in divine guidance and providence."

As will be obvious to anyone who is familiar with Löwith's biography, and as he explicitly acknowledges in his "Curriculum Vitae" address, Löwith's five years in Japan made a very strong impression on his thinking about the West.[36] (*From Hegel to Nietzsche* was written in Japan.) Clearly, he acquired a picture of venerable Oriental wisdom as a reproach to the franticness of the Occident. The fact that Asia excels the West in its "mature insight into the frailty of all things human" is, for Löwith, tellingly illustrated by the traditional Japanese practice, after wars, of sending their leading statesmen and generals into monastic retreat (p. 138). However, as the discussion in "Curriculum Vitae" also emphasizes, it was in no way possible for Löwith to assimilate into Buddhist culture. Experiencing and admiring – and quite possibly over-idealizing – the culture of the Orient was something he could do strictly as a mere outsider, as an exile from the frenzied West. Löwith's account of modernity is a *lament*, and no more than a lament; he directs the bulk of his intellectual energy against historicism simply because in his view it stokes up a faith in the meaningfulness of human affairs that unfortunately seems groundless.[37] History itself instructs us in the folly of putting too much stock in history: "If there is anything which history teaches us, then it is plainly that history is nothing on which one can hold fast and on the basis of which one could orient one's life. To want to orient oneself on history, while tossed around in the midst of it, would be like wanting to hold on to the waves in time of shipwreck."[38]

I do not endorse Löwith's judgment that embracing the prospect of social and political progress in the future is almost guaranteed to be a delusion. As is also the case with respect to other very pessimistic thinkers included in this book, I tend to think that Löwith's anti-historicism was a reaction – an understandable reaction – to the catastrophes of the mid-twentieth century.[39] But neither do I dismiss it, à la Habermas, as deriving from a blindness or indifference to the importance of history.

[36] See *My Life in Germany Before and After 1933*, pp. 162–163; cf. Wolin, *Heidegger's Children*, p. 76. See also *Nature, History, and Existentialism*, p. 144, criticizing the Western philosophical tradition (including Heidegger) for over-privileging the Occident.

[37] On page 32 of *Permanence and Change*, Löwith calls this "the faith in the absolute relevance of the most relative"; cf. *Nature, History, and Existentialism*, p. 143.

[38] *Permanence and Change*, p. 33.

[39] Löwith bore the imprint of catastrophe, as many of our twelve thinkers do. (Cf. Habermas, *Philosophical-Political Profiles*, p. 95.) Yet, in *Permanence and Change*, he makes the important point that human beings have a surprising aptitude for bouncing back from catastrophe: "Most astounding in history are not only the tremendous changes, the losses and damages which mankind suffers on their account, but rather more, that, and how, again and again mankind restores itself after loss and [catastrophe] and raises itself up again upon the ruins of the past as if almost nothing had happened" (p. 16). There seems an important human truth captured in this observation.

I once had a brief discussion about Löwith with Allan Bloom, who had attended Löwith's classes in Heidelberg. Löwith had said to him that at the end of the day, the truth may be boring – and, Bloom quipped, Löwith didn't fail to put this maxim into practice with his own teaching! But there is nothing boring about Löwith's mature philosophy; his critique of modernity is no less bracing and intellectually robust than anything we get from Arendt or Strauss or Voegelin or Gadamer. Löwith gives us the worries about modern hubris that we also get from Heidegger and Arendt and Strauss and Voegelin, but without the ambitious positive claims that eventually trip up these other theorists. There seems to be a certain vein of skepticism in his thought that renders him in some ways less vulnerable to criticism than the others. Perhaps this is just another way of saying that Löwith offers us less of a full-blown political philosophy than we get from these other critics of modernity; still, the negative or critical claims advanced by Löwith remain important and interesting (and philosophically distinctive) and, hence, are worthy of renewed attention.

Let us conclude with one important challenge. Consider the following statement from Löwith's "Curriculum Vitae" text: "The naturalness of nature, *physis*, has been lost through modern physics."[40] Reading this statement, one inevitably wonders why Löwith's privileging of nature over history did not lead him to greater appreciation of modern science (including the attempt by quantum mechanics to ponder and hopefully unravel the nearly unfathomable mysteries of the atom, as well as the attempt by post-Einsteinian cosmology to ponder and hopefully unravel the nearly unfathomable mysteries of the stars and galaxies). For pure science at its peak – no less than Aristotle's famous first sentence of the *Metaphysics* appealing to the inherent human desire for knowledge, or Kant's awe at "the starry heavens above,"[41] or Löwith's own longing to recapture the ancient experience of nature as "the granite that bears all" (Gadamer)[42] – is surely driven by

[40] Löwith, *My Life in Germany Before and After 1933*, p. 164; cf. *Permanence and Change*, pp. 9–10. See also *Der Weltbegriff der neuzeitlichen Philosophie*, p. 21: "eine Physik ohne *physis*."

[41] In "Kant, the Sublime, and Nature" (in *Kant and Political Philosophy: The Contemporary Legacy*, ed. Ronald Beiner and William James Booth [New Haven, CT: Yale University Press, 1993]), I offer a "Löwithian" interpretation of the famous passage at the end of the *Critique of Practical Reason* in which Kant discusses "the starry heavens above" as a source of awe. What I try to show is that while the passage in the 2nd *Critique* seems to assert a parity between the sublimity of the starry heavens above and the moral law within, the account of the sublime in the 3rd *Critique* depicts sublimity in nature as a *projection* of our own inner sublimity, and in that sense ultimately reduces the sublimity of the starry heavens *to* the sublimity of the moral law. Cf. the challenges put to Kant on pages 88–90 of Jonas, *The Imperative of Responsibility*.

[42] Cf. Johannes Fritsche's suggestion that Löwith knowingly or unknowingly replicated familiar Heideggerian tropes of hankering after a resurrection of a primordial pre-Socratic experience of

wonder at the cosmos.[43] Löwith's idea seems to be that modern physics has *contributed to* (perhaps contributed decisively to) modern historicism (the absolutizing of history and the sidelining of nature) by debunking ancient ideas of the cosmos.[44] This seems to imply, rather perversely, that modern science ought to be blamed for replacing false ideas about nature with true (or truer) ones. On page 17 of *Permanence and Change*, Löwith refers to the "modern mistake, which broke up the single physical cosmos into a multiplicity of historical worlds." If this "mistake" follows from, or is somehow related to, developments in modern science, how are we supposed to return to the idea of a unitary and harmonious cosmos without undoing the cognitive progress achieved by, for instance, modern astronomy (which is obviously not a viable option)? On page 28 of *Nature, History, and Existentialism*, Löwith writes: "How can one feel at home in a universe ... which is said to have come into existence through an explosion?" But if the universe *really did* come into existence through an explosion, we surely cannot conjure up some non-existent or alternative universe just for purposes of restoring our sense of rapport with nature.[45] My guess is that Aristotle himself, if he

physis that had been steadily effaced by the history of the West, reaching its nadir in modernity as the final nihilistic culmination ("From National Socialism to Postmodernism: Löwith on Heidegger," *Constellations*, Vol. 9, no. 1 [2009], p. 86). Fritsche rightly cites Habermas as one of the sources of this view of Löwith. Similar thrusts against Löwith can be found on pages 78–79 and 97–100 of Wolin, *Heidegger's Children*; see, for instance, p. 98: Löwith's "uncritical celebration of [*das Ursprüngliche*, the primordial] is quintessentially Heideggerian."

[43] John Gray is right to distinguish between science as science, and science as it intersects with the sometimes sensible but often delusional projects of human beings. See *The Immortalization Commission* (Toronto: Doubleday Canada, 2011), p. 235: "The end-result of scientific inquiry is to return humankind to its own intractable existence. Instead of enabling humans to improve their lot, science degrades the natural environment in which humans must live. Instead of enabling death to be overcome, it produces ever more powerful technologies of mass destruction. None of this is the fault of science; what it shows is that science is not sorcery. The growth of knowledge enlarges what humans can do. It cannot reprieve them from being what they are."

[44] Cf. the text by Nietzsche cited by Richard Wolin in the introduction to Löwith, *Martin Heidegger and European Nihilism*, p. 17, in which Nietzsche bemoans modern science's effect of "dissolving everything which is firmly believed." Clearly, there is a similar pathos in Weber's account of "rationalization" (of how modern science drains meaning out of received worldviews) in *Science as a Vocation*, as we discussed in our second prologue. But Weber's rhetoric of manliness is: Don't whine about this. Face up to it! Treat it as a test of one's character, of one's essential fibre as a human being.

[45] If Löwith's central intellectual purpose is to urge us to attend to the universe for the sake of the universe, rather than reducing everything to anthropocentric concerns, then he surely shouldn't be complaining about the fact that the universe fails to arrange itself in order to satisfy our need for feeling at home in the cosmos. (Think of Bohr's rejoinder, at the famous 1927 Fifth Solvay International Conference, to Einstein's unhappiness with the probabilistic character of quantum mechanics – a story related in Neil Turok, *The Universe Within* [Toronto: House of Anansi, 2012], p. 81. Einstein: "God does not play dice!" Bohr: "Einstein, stop telling God how to run the world.") Richard Feynman famously said that "nobody understands quantum mechanics." Well, if we are fated to live in a universe from which we are alienated because it seems ultimately to defeat our efforts at comprehending it, we may

were alive today, would welcome contemporary physics, and celebrate it for doing a better job – infinitely better! – of what he was trying to do.

How can we make nature an object of *theoria* unless we exert ourselves to secure the most cognitively adequate account of the natural world? And the fact is that that is precisely what modern physics seeks to do.[46] (Think of the colossal resources invested in the Large Hadron Collider at CERN, which is fundamentally driven by questions located within *pure science*, not by hopes of technological applications. It may well be true that Löwith and the other post-Heideggerians, as well as presumably Heidegger himself, take the "metaphysical" implications of modern technology to be so huge that one is pretty much obliged to view modern science through the lens of its embodiment in technology. But that seems a skewed – and unfair – view of science as science.) Presumably, Löwith could respond that modern physics somehow fails to respect "the naturalness of nature" because it does not attend to the world as an overarching cosmos, but instead breaks the world down into discrete aspects capable of being intellectually mastered. That amounts to the suggestion that the Greek apprehension of nature was superior to the modern apprehension of nature (or at least that the Greek apprehension of nature proves its human superiority with respect to supporting the proper *existential stance* toward nature). Yet as already suggested, I very much doubt that even Aristotle, if he were alive in the twenty-first century, would find that a sustainable view (because he would *agree* with contemporary scientists that the absolutely key test in regard to superiority is the issue of which view of nature is *cognitively* superior). Moreover, insofar as we privilege the ancient apprehension of the world on account of its being conducive to the right sort of existential stance, then we are seemingly treating nature with a view to how it will shape *human* concerns – which is exactly the kind of anthropocentric reception of nature that Löwith's whole philosophy is designed to protest against.

---

just have to resign ourselves to this fate (though science in its essence obviously means *refusing* to resign ourselves in the sense of ceasing to try).

[46] Obviously, Löwith is not the only post-Heideggerian critic of modernity to whom one can apply this kind of challenge. In the previous chapter, I put a similar challenge to Leo Strauss.

5

Excursus on Nature and History in the Strauss-Löwith Correspondence

As critics of Strauss and Straussianism have never ceased to emphasize, a view of political philosophy that puts esotericism at the heart of the whole enterprise poses unique hermeneutical challenges. Nods and winks are by definition harder to interpret than theoretical affirmations assumed to be sincere. How do these hermeneutical challenges affect the enterprise of interpreting Strauss himself? Can a theorist who sees esotericism as central to the nature and identity of philosophers be trusted not to engage in significant esoteric writing of his own?[1] One sure way of surmounting this problem is to turn from Strauss's public texts to his private texts, philosophical views confided to a good and trusted friend in a context where the imperatives of politic communication (as Strauss and Straussians understand this) are not applicable.[2] In particular, we may be able to gain privileged access to

---

[1] This applies especially to the "theological-political problem" – the paramount theme of Strauss's whole lifework (as he himself emphasizes). For me, what Laurence Lampert has to say on this topic is exactly on-target: "It is no accident that Strauss, an unbeliever from beginning to end, is believed by many of his adherents to be a believer if an odd one: he acted as if the conflict between unbelief and belief was less a stalemate than tipped in favor of revelation"; see "Strauss's Recovery of Esotericism," in *The Cambridge Companion to Leo Strauss*, ed. Steven B. Smith (Cambridge: Cambridge University Press, 2009), p. 90. That is, Strauss disguised his views so effectively that it even fooled some (many?) of his own followers (and this despite the relentless schooling they received from him on the wiles of esotericism!). See the eye-opening quote from Strauss cited by Anne Norton in *The Legacy of Leo Strauss*, ed. Tony Burns and James Connelly (Exeter: Imprint Academic, 2010), p. 182 (implicitly identifying Jewish faith with "science fiction"), along with Norton's commentary. See also note 2.

All of this illustrates very well the perils of founding philosophy on esotericism. We can call it the problem of the final veil. Suppose I am a disciple of Leo Strauss, determined to penetrate his true meaning. I make my way through three, or seven, or twelve veils meant to confound the vulgar. How do I know that there isn't a thirteenth veil? How do I know that the last veil I penetrated is the final veil?

[2] For a pertinent discussion, see Werner J. Dannhauser, "Leo Strauss in His Letters," in *Enlightening Revolutions*, ed. Svetozar Minkov (Lanham, MD: Lexington Books, 2006), pp. 355–361. Consider in particular Strauss's admission to Gershom Scholem, cited by Dannhauser (p. 360), that Strauss writes his commentaries as in effect a heretic (an "Epicurean"). Christopher Hitchens writes: "Straussians believe in religion and not in God"; *Unacknowledged Legislation: Writers in the Public Sphere* (London: Verso,

Strauss's most important ideas by eavesdropping on his epistolary exchanges with Karl Löwith on the all-important theme of nature versus history.

Consider Strauss's remarkable letter to Löwith of August 15, 1946, containing the following astonishing statement of what Strauss believes with respect to what is fully natural:

I *really* believe ... that the perfect political order, as Plato and Aristotle have sketched it, *is* the perfect political order. Or do you believe in the world-state? If it is true that genuine unity is only possible through knowledge of the truth or through search for the truth, then there is a genuine unity of all men only on the basis of the popularized final *teaching* of philosophy (and naturally this does not exist) or if all men are philosophers (not PhDs, etc.) – which likewise is not the case. Therefore, there can only be closed societies, that is, states. But if that is so, then one can show from political considerations that the small city-state is in principle superior to the large state or to the territorial-feudal state. I know very well that *today* it cannot be restored. [We live precisely today in the *extremely* unfavorable situation; the situation between Alexander the Great and the Italian *poleis* of the thirteenth to fifteenth century was considerably more favorable.] But the famous atomic bombs – not to mention at all cities with a million inhabitants, gadgets, funeral homes, "ideologies" – show that the contemporary solution, that is, the completely modern solution, is *contra naturum*. Whoever concedes that Horace did not speak nonsense when he said "Expel nature with a hayfork, but it always returns," concedes thereby precisely the legitimacy *in principle* of Platonic-Aristotelian politics. Details can be disputed, although I myself might actually agree with everything that Plato and Aristotle demand (but that I tell only you).[3]

This is a truly stunning account of Strauss's (otherwise largely unavowed) intellectual commitments as a political philosopher. It is stunning for two reasons: stunning because of its provocative content, and no less stunning because of the esotericist suggestion at the end. Let's start with the latter. The ending of the passage states that Strauss cannot enunciate his true intellectual commitments as public doctrine; he can only disclose it in private, like whispering a secret. But then Strauss cannot lay out his intellectual grounds for holding these beliefs – that is, cannot develop his political philosophy *as* a political philosophy. As he says, "details can be disputed"; indeed they can! However, this requires a public exchange of philosophical reasons, and this is what Strauss shies away from. What this tells us is that philosophers conduct their intellectual business by whispering to each other, not

2000), p. 219. I am not sure that this is true of Straussians in general, but I do not see any reason to doubt that it *is* true of Leo Strauss himself.
[3] Karl Löwith and Leo Strauss, "Correspondence Concerning Modernity," *Independent Journal of Philosophy*, Vol. 4 (1983), pp. 107–108. What I show as an interpolation in square brackets is a footnoted addition by Strauss.

by trading reasons and counter-reasons. The implications that this has for the whole enterprise of philosophy are more than a little disturbing, since it elevates (enormously!) the existential authority of philosophers, without them having to lay out in public arguments the grounds or reasons (in all their "details") that should be required to *vindicate* this authority.

Let's go through Strauss's statement a bit more slowly in order to weigh the problematic character of his claims. Now Strauss (contrary to the image many people have of him as a guru of stern arch-conservatism) was a deliberately playful writer – playfulness was an integral aspect of his conception of theory – and so one cannot rule out that part of what is going on in this letter is a playful pulling of Löwith's leg. But the opening ("I *really* believe") suggests that Strauss was not just horsing around. He makes the truly extraordinary suggestion that if Löwith rejects the idea of the world-state, then he *must* accept the Greek polis. Why? "Political considerations" will convince us "that the small city-state is in principle superior to the large state," but Strauss does not spell out what these political considerations are. The fact that the Greek polis was defined by the institution of slavery, or that the city-states put most of their civic energies into fighting wars against each other, or that they accorded absolutely no civic status to women, seems not to detract from the naturalness of those states, for Strauss. Nature demands "the closed state," and this is somehow automatically equated with the ancient polis. In a later letter, Strauss at least fills in the content somewhat: "a *surveyable, urban*, morally serious society, based on an agricultural economy, in which the *gentry* rule"; such a society is *natural* in the sense of being "the most reasonable and most pleasing."[4] Modernity, by contrast, is deemed through-and-through counter-natural. Again, why? Modern states are too big to be surveyable, they are certainly not "morally serious," their fundamental ethos is egalitarian rather than aristocratic, founded on bourgeois rather than agrarian economies, and their life revolves

---

[4] Ibid., p. 113 (letter dated August 20, 1946); cf. *Natural Right and History* (Chicago: University of Chicago Press, 1953), p. 142. It is very telling that Strauss immediately adds: this "does not mean at all that *I* would want to live in such a polis (one must not judge everything according to one's private wishes)." Qua philosopher, Strauss would prefer to live in a more diverse and more democratic and more modern society, with the human variety of such a society helping to stimulate philosophical reflection (just as Athenian democracy helped to stimulate the philosophical imagination of Socrates and Plato). Of course, in all likelihood the vast majority of the inhabitants of a modern state would have no more desire to live in ancient Sparta or ancient Crete than Strauss would, but for Strauss this desire for diversity and democracy on the part of non-philosophers is of no consequence. He has legislated that the ancient polis, with its moral-political seriousness, is more natural than modernity, with its gadgets; hence, if a return to the polis were possible (which it probably isn't anyway), the moral-political welfare of non-philosophers would demand such a return to nature.

around "gadgets," of which atomic bombs are the ultimate consummation. Abandon nature and that's what you get!

According to Strauss's argument, the unnaturalness of the world-state entails the naturalness of the ancient polis — as if these are the only meaningful alternatives. Vindication of the polis, he says, rests upon "political considerations," but again, he does not spell out what these political considerations are.[5] And so on. To say that these super-ambitious claims require far more intellectual fleshing-out and defense than Strauss gives them would be a massive understatement. One would have no reason to complain if Strauss had articulated and defended these views in works other than this private letter to a friend. Given that Strauss published no less than *fourteen* books of political philosophy, one would have thought that he had ample opportunity to do so. If, as the letter to Löwith seems to suggest, these are core convictions of Strauss's, one might have expected the public defense of these articles of philosophical belief to occupy a high place on Strauss's list of priorities as a political philosopher. Here the closing line to Löwith is once again crucial: "but that I tell only you." However, if this was Strauss's actual view of the best regime, why did he not *articulate* it as such, and explain *why* he considered it superior to the alternatives (instead of merely appealing to the authority of antiquity)? If this was a philosophical judgment, why was it intended only for Löwith's eyes or ears? Strauss does not seem to think that refusing to justify *or even disclose* fundamental intellectual commitments impugns what he is supposed to be doing as a political philosopher.

There is one central paradox underlying the intellectual enterprise of Strauss. (There are in fact *many* paradoxes in Strauss, but the others do not have the centrality that this one does.) In Strauss's view, historicism is the fundamental plague that accounts for the undoing of Western philosophy. But rather than conducting his own intellectual activity as the articulation of timelessly valid principles for the understanding of political life, he offers precisely a historical narrative unfolding within the history of ideas.[6]

---

[5] Admittedly, Strauss does provide a highly compressed account on pages 130–131 of *Natural Right and History*; cf. note 29 of our chapter on Strauss. The key argument seems to be that in a society that tries to perfect itself with respect to virtue, all citizens must know each other and trust each other enough to participate in this project of reciprocal perfection. Large cities inevitably turn into a version of Babylon (governed by license rather than virtue), and in that sense, all modern societies correspond to Babylon. It is a severely abbreviated argument, but it does provide a bit more of an account than the letter to Löwith supplies.

[6] See *Natural Right and History*, p. 33, where Strauss writes that in order to liberate ourselves from the intellectual hegemony of historicism, we need "an understanding of the genesis of historicism that does not take for granted the soundness of historicism"; and p. 7: today we are "in need of historical studies." See also the suggestion on page 157 of *Persecution and the Art of Writing* (Chicago: University of Chicago Press,

If there are timelessly valid principles of political life, why not attempt to present them? This is, for instance, what political philosophers such as the early Rawls, Ronald Dworkin, Jeremy Waldron, and countless other contemporary liberals do in their grounding of liberalism: that is, try to provide an account of what normative principles define a liberal regime, and why those principles are normatively compelling. (Admittedly, the Rawls of *Political Liberalism* disavows this enterprise, at least with respect to the transcultural, trans-historical character of the principles involved, for reasons that will be examined in the chapter on Rawls, but this U-turn on the part of late Rawls does not invalidate the enterprise per se.) In principle, couldn't Strauss do the same, and thus prove his inoculation against the historicist virus? Esotericism is supposed to protect the philosopher against the wrath of the multitude. But let's face it, it also protects Strauss against the intellectual obligation to justify his claims.

What does it mean to assert that political philosophy must orient itself toward "nature" as an ultimate philosophical standard, and that it has dire long-term consequences for society as a whole if political philosophers cease appealing to nature, or if this appeal is somehow diluted or replaced by appeals to something else (e.g., history)? As regards the first part of the preceding question, this can mean different things, depending on what "orienting oneself to nature" is intended to mean. In other words: this can have modest or not so modest interpretations, and the plausibility of the claim hangs on which of these interpretations is being offered. Let me explain.

If one believes, as I do, that political philosophy – explicitly or tacitly, avowedly or unavowedly – necessarily involves reflection on the human

1988) that if we have the misfortune to find ourselves living in an epoch thoroughly dominated by historicism, the best we can hope to do is to gain access to "the original meaning of philosophy ... through recollection of what philosophy meant in the past." But if philosophy, correctly practiced, addresses itself to what is timeless, why not let historicism stew in its own juice and skip directly to a non-historical articulation of a valid vision of moral and political life (which, contrary to what Strauss stubbornly avers, is what many or most contemporary theorists and philosophers continue to do)? It may be that Strauss believes that Plato and Aristotle have already achieved this, but a bit of skepticism would be in order here. On the paradox of Strauss endeavoring to repudiate historicism by means of historical inquiry, cf. *Truth and Method*, 2nd rev. ed. (New York: Continuum, 1998), p. 533: Strauss's "argument against what he calls historicism is itself based primarily on historical grounds"; and p. 534: "What Strauss is concerned with is still conceived within historical thought." As I discussed in the previous chapter, there are strong parallels here between Strauss and Löwith. See, in particular, Löwith's statement of how he conceives his own enterprise as quoted by Habermas on page 84 of *Philosophical-Political Profiles*, trans. Frederick G. Lawrence (London: Heinemann, 1983). Finally, consider as well Eric Voegelin, *The New Science of Politics* (Chicago: University of Chicago Press, 1952), p. 2, where Voegelin rightly points out that "political science [meaning: political philosophy] cannot be restored to the dignity of a theoretical science in the strict sense by means of a literary renaissance of philosophical achievements of the past."

good, the human telos, then that itself constitutes an appeal to a normative conception of human nature – that is, an implicit appeal to nature. One invokes an idea of human flourishing which is in turn the invocation of a foundational standard – which it is not unreasonable to think of as invoking what the ancients called *physis* as opposed to *nomos*. However, political philosophers reflect on such conceptions and aspire to articulate them philosophically; they are not asserted as self-evident truths. Strauss's idea is a little different. In Strauss's view, the notion of natural right implies that uncorrupted human beings have immediate access to what nature teaches.[7] Only after centuries of malconditioning by misguided philosophy are human beings detached from this immediate apprehension of what is natural.[8] That is, philosophers must first blind themselves to nature before ordinary human beings as well fall victim to this blindness. This is the "hayfork" idea that Strauss borrows from Horace: modern philosophy, with its worship of history, is the hayfork that attempts to drive away nature, and all the pathologies of modernity represent nature's revenge.

Political philosophy as a process of reflection on what human flourishing consists in invokes the idea of *physis*, or something like it, as an object of intellectual *aspiration*. The kind of dogmatic assertions one encounters in Strauss's letters to Löwith are a different matter entirely.

Of course, we also want to know how Löwith responded to Strauss's provocative suggestions. Strauss apparently knows what nature mandates, even though he is extremely economical in his provision of a theoretical account that backs up his claims about what is natural. Löwith's responses do a very good job of explaining why some intellectual humility and caution is called for:

Whatever one might say against progressive models of history, I do agree however with them inasmuch as I also find that Christianity fundamentally modified ancient "naturalness." With a cat or a dog "nature" does indeed always come out again [in accordance with Horace's maxim], but history is too deeply anchored in man for

---

[7] See *Natural Right and History*, pp. 31–32, referring to "the evidence of those simple experiences regarding right and wrong which are at the bottom of the philosophic contention that there is a natural right."

[8] This is part of what Strauss has in mind with his famous image of "the cave beneath the cave" (*Persecution and the Art of Writing*, pp. 155–156). Yes, non-philosophers are slaves to *doxa*. But modern philosophy somehow removes them in a far more profound sense from nature. According to Strauss, philosophy is supposed to liberate at least the philosophers from *doxa*, and thus bring them closer to nature. Under the modern dispensation, however, philosophy does the opposite: it renders the philosophers themselves more oblivious to nature, and this, Strauss seems to think, has a kind of spillover effect on non-philosophers.

Rousseau or Nietzsche or your future hero of natural being and understanding to succeed in restoring something which already died out in late antiquity. The "simplest" touchstone would be – as Nietzsche saw quite correctly – the restoration of the ancient relation to sexuality as something natural and *at the same time* divine. Even Goethe's "nature" is no longer that of antiquity. And I can imagine even less a natural social order. The world-state is certainly nonsense and *contra naturam*, like all historical institutions created by man. Only when you are able to convince me that stars, heaven, sea and earth, generation, birth and death give you, the "simple" man!, natural answers to your unnatural questions, will I be able to agree to your thesis.... To what extent our de-naturalization traces back to Christianity is hard to say, but certainly it is not only our historical *consciousness* which has changed, but our historical *being*.[9]

The atomic bomb teaches me nothing at all that I would not have known already without it.... Where do you ... draw the line between natural and unnatural? For the Greeks it was – I commend them for this – completely natural to consort with women, youths, and animals. The bourgeois marriage is just as unnatural as pederasty, and Japanese geishas are just as natural for the man as O. Wilde's friend was for him. – The creation of a perfect order – be it social and political or in private morals – is always afflicted with the unnatural – simply *qua* order.[10]

It does not follow from these arguments (or at least I don't think it is intended to follow) that all is *nomos* (the teaching of the sophists). Rather, I think Löwith's point is that all human societies are a complicated entanglement of *physis* and *nomos* – over against Strauss's inclination to view the ancient stance toward the world as pure *physis* and the modern stance toward the world as pure *nomos*. Just because the Greeks had a more confident grasp of the distinction between *physis* and *nomos* does not prove that they had privileged insight into what defines the *content* of what is morally and politically natural for human beings. The moderns do not have any special privilege with respect to grasping the human telos just because they are more

---

[9] Löwith and Strauss, "Correspondence Concerning Modernity," p. 109. Habermas, in the title of his essay devoted to Löwith in *Philosophical-Political Profiles*, refers to Löwith's "Stoic Retreat from Historical Consciousness." As is clear from the debate with Strauss, Löwith took historical consciousness, and indeed historical being, far more seriously than Habermas appreciated. Gadamer, too, seems uneasy about the extent of Löwith's appeal to the natural in reaction against modern historicism. See his critique of Löwith in *Truth and Method*, 2nd rev. ed., pp. 499–500 and 531–532. In effect, Gadamer's point is that the teaching of eternal return cannot simply be read off from the stars and the heavens, but surely Löwith knows this perfectly well. Gadamer rightly acknowledges that Löwith's anti-historicist appeal to the natural (like Nietzsche's and like that of the Stoics) is a reaction to "the desperate disorder of human affairs" (p. 532). That is, it is on the basis of an apprehension of history's lack of ultimate or metaphysical meaning, and hence very much *from within* historical consciousness, that Löwith conceives his fundamental project, with its concerted rejection of the unconvincing projections of cosmic meaning asserted both by modern philosophies of history and by the theological-eschatological teachings on which they modeled themselves.

[10] Löwith and Strauss, "Correspondence Concerning Modernity," p. 110.

attuned to human historicity, but neither is it the case that the ancients have any special privilege on account of their greater *innocence* of historicity. For Löwith, wisdom consists in having the intellectual modesty to acknowledge that neither nature nor history gives us ready access to an understanding of what constitutes the proper humanity of human beings.[11]

There was another, earlier exchange of letters between Strauss and Löwith in 1935 (that is, eleven years or so before the other letters we've discussed). And there is a truly extraordinary passage in one of those letters that we should take note of before leaving the Strauss-Löwith correspondence. Here is the text: Nietzsche's doctrine of eternal return "is *asserted convulsively* by Nietzsche only because he had to wean us and himself from millennia-old pampering (softening) [*Verwöhnung/Verweichlichung*] due to belief in creation and providence. The rebellion against the indifference of the universe, against its aimlessness, which lies at the root of modern civilization, is an essential part of this pampering."[12] An amazing set of suggestions: Modernity is not identified with the liberation from feudalism, or the triumph over superstition, or the recognition of the equal dignity of all human beings, or any of the various other things that might give one cause to celebrate or at least welcome it as a new dispensation. Rather, it is conceived in the image of indulging spoiled children who have been thoroughly schooled in the foolish idea that the universe cares about their welfare, and who therefore have to go on being spoiled with unnecessary technologies (Strauss's "gadgets") and other forms of indulgence. It is not only Nietzsche who holds this view; Strauss does too. And not only does Nietzsche see through these decadent notions and struggle to resist them in himself; he sets himself the project (in Strauss's words) *"to wean us" from the (Christianity-inspired) softness and decadence of modernity*. Wow. How exactly is a merely intellectual conceit dreamt up by a fairly eccentric thinker supposed to do *that*?

---

[11] It is clear that Gadamer, like Löwith, thought that Strauss went overboard with his appeals to nature against history: If one gives sufficient weight to Aristotle's insight into the absolute difference between the practical or the phronetic and the merely technical (which he thinks Strauss failed to do), then "Aristotle can help us avoid falling into an apotheosis of nature, naturalness, and natural [right] that would be nothing but an impotently doctrinaire critique of history" (*Truth and Method*, 2nd rev. ed., p. 541). As we discuss in a later chapter, for Gadamer the main exemplars of the kind of philosopher's hubris that he is anxious to avoid are Hegel and Heidegger, but as this characterization of Strauss makes clear, such hubris, from Gadamer's point of view, is present in Strauss as well.

[12] Letter of June 23, 1935, *Independent Journal of Philosophy*, Vol. 5/6 (1988), p. 183. The German words insinuate the image of a mother spoiling her child with goodies that the child doesn't need. That conjures up Strauss's whole conception of modernity, which he clearly recognized was in close alignment with Nietzsche's conception of modernity.

Like Nietzsche (about whom Strauss famously confessed that he was so "dominated and bewitched [by him] between my 22nd and 30th years, that I literally believed everything I understood of him"[13]), Strauss perceives monotheistic religion, and especially Christianity, as, so to speak, the "wimpification" of the West, and sees modernity as *in service to* this wimpification. Nietzsche in a sense is more ancient than modern, and far from being in thrall to his own particular historical epoch (as Strauss elsewhere suggests), actually provides insights into the limits of Christian and post-Christian experience that help Strauss appreciate the superiority of antiquity.

What this suggests to us is that Strauss is not nearly as thoroughly anti-Nietzschean as he wants to make himself out to be.[14] True, Nietzsche participates in, and in some important sense represents the intellectual climax of, the philosophical tradition inaugurated by Francis Bacon aiming at human mastery of nature (a line of critique a version of which can also be found in Heidegger, and which quite clearly casts Nietzsche on the side of the moderns). But for Strauss, and also for Nietzsche, the ancients were more in tune with the harsh realities of nature, and in pursuing his war against Christian "pandering," Nietzsche wanted some manner of return to the ancients. Plainly, that is what Strauss wants as well.[15] In a late commentary on Nietzsche published in *Interpretation* in 1973, the year Strauss died, Strauss twice declares: "nature ... has become a problem for Nietzsche and yet he cannot do without nature."[16] Hence we see, both in the 1935 letter to

[13] Ibid.: the quotation occurs in the very same letter we are now discussing. Strauss was thirty-five years old when he wrote this letter, hence a mere five years past the point when he says he parted ways with Nietzsche. Tellingly, Strauss writes at the start of this letter that he cannot help taking a keen interest in Löwith's Nietzsche book as the "old Nietzschean that I – was" (*als alten Nietzscheaner, der ich – war*). What the dash surely indicates is that it would be more natural for Strauss to write "the Nietzschean that I *am*," and that it requires effort (and hesitation) on his part to write "was." Everything that follows in the letter emphasizes his residual affinities and sympathy with Nietzsche.

[14] Strauss once famously contrasted a preference for Jane Austen with a preference for Dostoyevsky as a vivid way of capturing the difference between the sound taste of antiquity and the decadent taste of modernity (*On Tyranny*, ed. Victor Gourevitch and Michael S. Roth [New York: The Free Press, 1991], p. 185). But Strauss's evident taste for Nietzsche gives us a glimpse of Strauss as, so to speak, a lover of Dostoyevsky pretending to be a lover of Jane Austen.

[15] Sometimes Strauss associates nature with the humble morality of ordinary human beings (as in *Natural Right and History*'s invocation of Biblical morality in its two opening epigraphs), sometimes he associates it with classical utopianism, and sometimes he associates it with the facts of life in their harshest aspect. Whether this represents merely a tension in Strauss's thought, or a contradiction or incoherence, or simply an appeal to opposing rhetorics, would require a long discussion. The debate with Thomas Pangle published in my book *Philosophy in a Time of Lost Spirit* lets us see, I think, that it is not entirely easy to pin down exactly what is being appealed to in the Straussian appeal to nature.

[16] "Note on the Plan of Nietzsche's *Beyond Good and Evil*," in Leo Strauss, *Studies in Platonic Political Philosophy* (Chicago: University of Chicago Press, 1983), pp. 183 and 190. For an ambitious commentary on Strauss's essay, see Laurence Lampert, *Leo Strauss and Nietzsche* (Chicago: University of Chicago Press, 1996).

Löwith and in the 1973 essay in *Interpretation*, a more complex and ambivalent relation to Nietzsche than the straightforward denunciation of him as a radical historicist offered in *Natural Right and History*.[17]

Other passages in the letter offer additional help in making clear Strauss's debt to Nietzsche and the sense in which he did and did not desire to transcend him. Strauss very much sympathizes with Nietzsche's project, which consists in "repeating antiquity at the peak of modernity" (p. 183) – a formulation that Strauss borrows from Löwith and strongly endorses. But trying to recapture antiquity from within modernity (let alone the peak of modernity) means having to polemicize *against* modernity – *krampfhaft*, as Strauss puts it: frantically or desperately – with the result that one loses the "calmness" or serenity associated with the ancient stance toward nature.[18] As Strauss explains, the intended teaching (namely the doctrine of eternal return) is calm (*ruhig*), but its promulgation, from within modernity and against modernity, is necessarily overwrought or even hysterical. This just goes to show why the project of recuperating antiquity from within modernity is self-defeating. The existential challenge of enduring the idea of eternal return is intended to restore "a truly natural morality," but "one must ask whether or not Nietzsche himself became untrue to his intention to repeat antiquity, and did so as a result of his confinement within modern presuppositions or in polemics against these" (p. 184).[19] This helps to explain Strauss's project of seeking to recuperate antiquity by trying to stand *outside* modernity (if such a thing is possible). This discussion with Löwith thereby allows us to see that Strauss's wholesale repudiation of modernity was driven not by his rejection of Nietzsche but by his fidelity to Nietzsche (that is, his intention of pursuing Nietzsche's project, but doing so in a way that was less

---

[17] See *Natural Right and History*, p. 26, where Nietzsche is identified as the pivotal figure in the transition from historicism to "radical historicism."

[18] In "What is Political Philosophy?" Strauss repeatedly emphasizes *serenity* as defining what is distinctive about ancient political philosophy. See, for instance, Strauss, *What is Political Philosophy?* (Chicago: University of Chicago Press, 1988), pp. 23 and 28. Cf. what Gadamer says concerning Löwith's version of neo-Stoicism: "We should look at the eternal cycle of nature, in order to learn from it the equanimity that alone is appropriate to the minuteness of human life in the universe"; *Truth and Method*, 2nd rev. ed., p. 532. See also Löwith, *Nature, History, and Existentialism*, ed. Arnold Levison (Evanston, IL: Northwestern University Press, 1966), p. 125, invoking ancient skepticism's "ideal of unshakable equanimity, of passionless ataraxy." (And of course one finds in ancient Epicureanism no less emphasis on the importance of achieving serenity.) As Löwith makes clear at the end of his book on Nietzsche, Jacob Burckhardt was Löwith's model of the noble equanimity that eluded Nietzsche.

[19] The journal editor helpfully lets us know in an endnote that Löwith underlined Strauss's phrase "*wahrhaft natürliche Moral*," and placed both an exclamation point and a question mark in the margin next to this phrase. My guess is that part of the reason why Löwith found Strauss's notion of a "natural morality" problematical is that, for Löwith, only *nature* (the cosmos, the sempiternal heavens) is natural.

self-defeating). In fact, reading this early letter to Löwith, one has to wonder: Was Strauss's whole subsequent philosophical project (the project of fleeing the insanity of modernity by seeking sanity in the ancients) a matter of pursuing an agenda that was set for him by Nietzsche?[20] We can add: in light of the Löwithian themes sketched in the previous chapter, it seems quite possible that the project as formulated here by Strauss – the *serene* return to ancient serenity, so to speak, rather than the convulsive return to antiquity – was not Strauss's alone, but one he in fact shared with Löwith.[21]

[20] It is especially telling that when Strauss, in a more or less esoteric setting (in 1970), comes to disclose his ultimate conception of moral life, he appeals specifically to Nietzsche (and indeed appeals to him, in effect, as a spokesperson for views also to be found in Plato and Aristotle). Even more tellingly, the Nietzschean conception to which he appeals is the idea that philosophers go along with morality not for genuinely *moral* reasons, to promote purposes they share with all human beings, but rather, *instrumentally* – in the service of purposes that are specific to them as philosophers. See "A Giving of Accounts," in Leo Strauss, *Jewish Philosophy and the Crisis of Modernity*, ed. Kenneth Hart Green (Albany: SUNY Press, 1997), p. 465. Cf. page 463 on philosophy as "transpolitical, transreligious, and transmoral."

[21] Cf. Habermas's characterization of Löwith's intellectual project at the top of page 80 of *Philosophical-Political Profiles*.

6

Eric Voegelin: Modernity's Vortex

Eric Voegelin is another theorist of the crisis of modernity. His crisis is a crisis in how modern societies stand in relation to the reality of transcendence. Like Karl Löwith, who was discussed in Chapter 4, Voegelin subscribes to an ambitious version of the secularization thesis[1] – that is, the thesis that modern philosophies take the extravagant form that they do because they think that they, and they alone, can fulfill the expectations of human salvation that were aroused by eschatological religions, and which those religions proved themselves (in the modern view) incapable of satisfying. Modernity as modernity rejects the reality of transcendence and, hence, replaces it with its own substitute realities or surrogate realities. These latter generate a whole range of violent pathologies, and these pathologies, viewed in the aggregate, constitute *the* crisis of modernity. That is the broad meta-narrative; the rest of Voegelin's political philosophy is devoted to working out the details.

The term "modernity" figures in the titles of two of the six chapters in *The New Science of Politics* (namely chapters 4 and 6). The book as a whole is clearly directed toward coming to an understanding of fully-unfolded modernity at its worst (as Voegelin apprehends it), and this purpose is served by, among other things, tracing the specific pathology back to political, religious, and intellectual tendencies in early modernity. (Chapter 5, for instance, offers an interesting interpretation of the rise

---

[1] It would not be entirely unwarranted to view Voegelin as a kind of Karl Löwith on steroids! For a text that nicely captures Voegelin's proximity to Löwithian themes, see *The Collected Works of Eric Voegelin, Volume 33: The Drama of Humanity and Other Miscellaneous Papers 1939–1985*, ed. William Petropulos and Gilbert Weiss (Columbia, MO: University of Missouri Press, 2004), p. 380: with modern ideologies, the idea of providence "is perverted in the sense that it is imagined as a human foreknowing of things and not as divine knowledge[;] then when you get [the] alienation of being immanentized, you believe still … in the providence, only you assume that the providence is supplied by human beings." For evidence of Voegelin's debt to Löwith, see for instance notes 8, 9, 21, 22, and 27 of chapter 4 of *The New Science of Politics: An Introduction* (Chicago: University of Chicago Press, 1974); all parenthetical page references to follow refer to this work.

of Puritanism and its political consequences.) However, Voegelin in no sense loses sight of premodern (and especially ancient) ways of thinking and ways of conceiving political order, for the premodern and the non-modern is at all times Voegelin's authoritative standard for judging what he considers the far less philosophical thinking proper to modernity. Indeed, Voegelin gives us a leading example of a mid-twentieth-century critic of modernity whose critique of modernity is inspired not by Heidegger but by Plato. Perhaps one could say the same about Leo Strauss, but Voegelin takes Platonic metaphysics seriously in a way that Strauss certainly does not.[2] (For Voegelin, all metaphysics is simultaneously theology, and therefore it is impossible to say, either in the case of Plato or in that of Aristotle, where metaphysics stops and theology begins: for him they are indistinguishable.)

The guiding premise of the political philosophy of Voegelin, like those of others included in this book such as Strauss, Löwith, Oakeshott, and Arendt, is that, by the middle of the twentieth century, Western civilization had totally gone to hell. And from a mid-twentieth-century perspective, it pretty much *had*, so the premise is far from implausible. The West had been sucked into a vortex of evil ideologies; hence the job of political philosophy was to figure out how on earth this had come about. What is distinctive about Voegelin's narrative in relation to the others is that he thinks the story cannot be disengaged from the issue of modernity's denial and distortion (as he sees it) of the legacy of Western monotheism, and, one would assume, of Christianity in particular. Voegelin's theorizing presents the purest case of a theocentric political philosophy.[3] Reality is a manifestation of the divine, and all pathologies in the political world derive from a perverse will to shun or turn one's back on this reality. It is not surprising that a theocentric vision of this kind will find much that is questionable about modernity. Really, it is pretty much guaranteed to find modernity through-and-through questionable, and this is indeed Voegelin's stance.

Is it appropriate then to speak of Voegelin's political philosophy as a specifically *Christian* political philosophy? Mark Lilla has helpfully highlighted a significant complexity in Voegelin's stance toward Christianity:

---

[2] Of course, Simone Weil is another theological/metaphysical-Platonist critic of modernity. But as we will see in the next chapter, her appropriation of Plato is strikingly different from Voegelin's.

[3] Ellis Sandoz cites a text in which Voegelin endorses Marcus Aurelius's description of the philosopher as "the priest and servant of the gods": see Sandoz, "The Philosopher's Vocation: The Voegelinian Paradigm," in *Political Philosophy in the Twentieth Century*, ed. Catherine H. Zuckert (Cambridge: Cambridge University Press, 2011), p. 81. Cf. *The New Science of Politics*, p. 26, n. 1.

[Voegelin's] hydraulic notion of a religious drive that reappears in secular life if it is denied access to the divine has been a staple of Counter-Enlightenment thought since the nineteenth century, especially among Christian theologians protesting the course of modern history. But the theologians had a clear remedy in mind: return to the one true faith. Was this Voegelin's remedy as well? It was not – though reticence about his own religious views led more than a few of his conservative readers to think it was. Voegelin, who was raised a Protestant, wrote casually about the 'transcendent' or 'divine' as if its existence were unquestionable, but he never expressed any particular doctrinal faith about it and was openly critical of Christianity, which he blamed for preparing the advent of modern politics.[4]

A few comments are in order. First, consider Lilla's statement that Voegelin "was openly critical of Christianity" in light of the following eye-opening Voegelin text:

Great masses of Christianized men who were not strong enough for the heroic adventure of faith became susceptible to ideas that could give them a greater degree of certainty about the meaning of their existence than faith. The reality of being as it is known in its truth by Christianity is difficult to bear, *and the flight from clearly seen reality to gnostic constructs will probably always be a phenomenon of wide extent in civilizations that Christianity has permeated.*[5]

Moreover, no reader of *The New Science of Politics* can fail to see that the critique of seventeenth-century Puritanism as anticipating the forms of "immanentist" politics in the centuries that followed forms a very important theme of the book (in fact, one of its most important themes). And in his *Autobiographical Reflections*, Voegelin does highlight the fact that post-Reformation Christianity more generally has fed into and perhaps shaped what Voegelin finds most damaging in secular modernity: "beginning with the Reformation [sectarian fringe movements] moved more and more into the center of the stage; and the replacement of Christian by secularist expectations [of a new transformative world] has not changed the structure of the problem."[6] Does all of this entail a reproof of Christianity as such?

---

[4] Mark Lilla, "Mr. Casaubon in America," in *The New York Review of Books*, June 28, 2007. Cf. what I say about Voegelin in *Civil Religion* (Cambridge: Cambridge University Press, 2011), p. 364, n. 17. As the following remarks make clear, I no longer regard it as helpful to describe Voegelin as a "Christian-theocratic" thinker; however, I do still think that Lilla and I were both right to point to Voegelin's complicated stance toward the mixed legacy of Christianity (which receives support from our next Voegelin quotation).

[5] Eric Voegelin, *Science, Politics and Gnosticism* (Chicago: Henry Regnery, 1968), p. 109; my italics. Voegelin here seems to verge on the thought that the problem of Gnosticism for modern politics inheres not merely in the fact that it is a Christian *heresy*; the deeper problem is that there is something latently or potentially Gnostic about *Christianity itself*. In that sense, Lilla seems right to say that Voegelin "blames" Christianity "for preparing the advent of modern politics."

[6] Eric Voegelin, *Autobiographical Reflections*, ed. Ellis Sandoz (Baton Rouge: Louisiana State University Press, 1989), p. 121. Cf. *The New Science of Politics*, p. 134: "the Reformation [is to be] understood as the successful invasion of Western institutions by Gnostic movements."

Presumably, Voegelin would distinguish between, on the one hand, the existential core of Christianity, which is purely transcendentalist rather than corruptly immanentist, and on the other hand, the often blatantly worldly forms taken by or encouraged by Christianity (of which Puritanism is merely one historical example), which indeed serve in practice to deflect transcendental concerns to the immanentist sphere.

One can certainly concede to Lilla that there *appears* to be a not trivial tension in Voegelin's position insofar as he has not the slightest doubt that human beings have access to the divine, yet seems unable or unwilling to commit himself to any particular doctrine of divinity among the large diversity of such doctrines that are historically on offer. However, during a discussion that took place in Montreal on March 12, 1976, Voegelin basically answered the challenge just posed. He suggested that all known world religions (encompassing not only monotheistic religions like Judaism and Islam but also African forms of paganism, Hinduism, Buddhism, and so on), and Plato as well, "have all experienced the same Divine Reality and there is only the one God who manifests Himself, reveals Himself, in a highly diversified manner all over the globe for all these millennia of history that we know."[7] (Of course, this has the effect of turning *all* religions into monotheistic religions.) So from this point of view, Christianity in particular (and even more so any particular *version* of Christianity) presents itself as unacceptably parochial. This would then sufficiently explain why Voegelin never presents himself as a Christian as such, let alone as an adherent of some specific Christian denomination. If anything I write in this chapter suggests to the reader that Voegelin privileges monotheistic religion, or Christianity in particular, that impression would have to be qualified or corrected in light of the discussion I have quoted. (But again, it might be said that Voegelin thereby engages in a monotheistic appropriation of religions that take themselves to be non-monotheistic.)

Another notable feature of Voegelin's critique of modernity is that his version is not anti-historicist in the way that some of the other versions are, or at least say they are[8] – for instance, the critiques of modernity in

---

[7] "Conversations with Eric Voegelin at the Thomas More Institute for Adult Education in Montreal," in *The Drama of Humanity*, ed. Petropulos and Weiss, p. 326; cf. Sandoz, "The Philosopher's Vocation," pp. 86–87. Interestingly, one can find quite similar ideas in Joseph de Maistre: see my discussion in *Civil Religion*, pp. 340, 349, and 355.

[8] Cf. Levison's introduction to Karl Löwith, *Nature, History, and Existentialism*, ed. Arnold Levison (Evanston, IL: Northwestern University Press, 1966), p. xxxvii: "Löwith's argument may be objected to on the grounds that it is excessively historicist in character.... [Genuinely to refute the contemporary philosophies that Löwith regards as nihilistic would be a matter] of showing that the fundamental

Strauss, Löwith, and Arendt. Leaving aside important differences among their respective accounts, Strauss, Löwith, and Arendt all assert that part of what is wrong or most problematic about modernity flows from the over-preoccupation of human beings with their own history. Although Voegelin clearly views certain philosophies of history as expressing precisely the kind of pathological "immanentization" that most exercises him – notably that of Hegel[9] – he is clearly himself a strongly committed historicist: "The existence of man in political society is historical existence; and a theory of politics, if it penetrates to principles, must at the same time be a theory of history." (p. 1)[10] History makes available the range of experiences with which political philosophy grapples, and hence abstraction from history removes the content to which theory orients itself and from which it draws its standards: "Theory is bound by history in the sense of the differentiating experiences. Since the maximum of differentiation [associated by Voegelin with the Christian idea of divine grace] was achieved through Greek philosophy and Christianity, this means concretely that theory is bound to move within the historical horizon of classic and Christian experiences" (p. 79). Voegelin's historicism is easy to illustrate, at least relative to Strauss. By far the clearest illustration is Voegelin's idea that Plato was surpassed by Christianity with respect to the "differentiation of consciousness" made possible by the latter: "full differentiation comes only through Jesus, not through Plato."[11] That is, the experience of full differentiation is in principle

principles on which the philosophy in question is based are false and that another set of principles is true or at least more likely to be true"; and this is something that neither Löwith nor Strauss nor Arendt attempts to do.

[9] See Voegelin, *Science, Politics and Gnosticism*, p. 73, on Hegel as a "gnostic magician." Cf. *The Drama of Humanity*, ed. Petropulos and Weiss, pp. 275–276 (Hegel's philosophy as "sorcery and alchemy") and p. 308 (Hegelianism as an "ideology"). On page 2 of *The New Science of Politics*, Voegelin describes Hegel's political philosophy as "the first major earthquake of the Western crisis."

[10] This is the first sentence of *The New Science of Politics*. Cf. *Autobiographical Reflections*, chapter 23.

[11] *The Drama of Humanity*, p. 281. Cf. *The New Science of Politics*, p. 77: "the Platonic-Aristotelian complex of experiences was enlarged by Christianity in a decisive point." On pages 76–77, Voegelin distinguishes between the "cosmological truth" represented by the early empires; the "anthropological truth" as it "appears in the political culture of Athens and specifically in tragedy"; and the "soteriological truth" made available by Christianity. Voegelin's suggestion, in effect, is that Plato and Aristotle (with respect to the experiences of ultimate reality that they articulate) fall somewhere midway between anthropological truth and soteriological truth; that is, the notion seems to be that there was a genuine intimation of the experience of a saving transcendence in (especially) Plato, but that this pagan intimation or anticipation underwent a quantum leap in fulfillment with the bursting onto the scene of history of the Christian Incarnation. As regards the vocabulary of "differentiation," this is contrasted with "compactness" of experience or consciousness. Developments in articulated symbolism "from rite, through myth, to theory," represent a movement from relative compactness to relative differentiation in the articulation of experienced reality (p. 27). In line with this conception, one could say that for Voegelin, just as theory is more "differentiated," less "compact," than myth, so the same may be said concerning Christian consciousness in relation to Platonic-Aristotelian philosophy.

not available to Plato because it presupposes a mode of historical experience that has not yet come on the scene; possibilities of consciousness or experience of reality are put within reach subsequent to the historical disclosure of the Christian Gospel that are simply beyond the ken of human beings (including great philosophers) prior to the advent of Christianity.[12] This is a conception that would certainly never be conceded by Strauss!

A proper political science, as Voegelin again expresses his conception on the first page of *The New Science of Politics*, is located at the point of intersection "where the principles of politics meet with the principles of a philosophy of history." For Voegelin, we need very serious inquiry into the history of civilizations in order to come to a proper understanding of the range of symbolizations by which human beings represent the divine to themselves, and thereby confer order on their political existence. Voegelin's decades-spanning lifework was entitled *Order and History* – a title that suggests pretty clearly that only a meditation on how civilizations conceive and put into practice principles of cultural and political order *through history* will answer the questions that a political philosophy needs to answer. Presumably, this is not a philosophy of history in the sense in which it is criticized by Löwith or Arendt (namely, Christian providentialism transferred onto the realm of human happenings)[13]; as regards philosophy of history in *that* sense (as we find it paradigmatically in Hegel and the intellectual heirs to Hegel), Voegelin is exactly as anti-historicist as Löwith and Arendt are.[14] Still, it has

---

(But on page 78 he states that Plato gives one the sense of "moving continuously on the verge of a breakthrough" to the Christian insight into God's reciprocation in grace of human yearning for the beyond.)

[12] It would seem natural to assume that this declared superiority of Christ to Plato with respect to differentiation of consciousness presupposes a (religious) commitment to Christianity, and therefore relies upon revelation as opposed to reason. However, as we discuss later on in this chapter (see note 35), Voegelin categorically repudiates any distinction between reason and revelation; hence it must be as a *philosopher* or as a *political philosopher* that Voegelin upholds this view, rather than as a committed or believing Christian. (The universal validity of the spiritual experience disclosed by Christianity is asserted by Voegelin in his telling use of the word "supposedly" in the sentence on page 60 where he refers to "the epoch of Christ which supposedly is relevant for Christians only.") A non-Voegelinian would say that the claim is affirmed on the basis of "secular reason," but the very same Voegelinian doctrine of the invalidity of a reason/revelation distinction renders it impossible to put the point in these terms.

[13] Unlike Löwith, Voegelin does not reject eschatology. On the contrary: see *Autobiographical Reflections*, chapter 27. But Voegelin insists that eschatology must be confined to the sphere proper to eschatology. This is in his view the horrible deformation associated with modernity: it transfers the eschatological to a domain of political realization, thus fatally corrupting both politics and what ought to be located beyond politics.

[14] Hence Voegelin's claim that Löwith had successfully demolished all Hegelian and Hegel-inspired historicism: see *The Collected Works of Eric Voegelin, Volume 11: Published Essays 1953–1965*, ed. Ellis Sandoz (Columbia, MO: University of Missouri Press, 2000), p. 237. As regards Arendt's anti-historicism, see, for instance, her polemics against the Hegelian conception that world-history is the ultimate tribunal

the look of a kind of philosophy of history, and Voegelin acknowledges it to be such. Löwith observes (probably with Oswald Spengler's theories about Occidental decline in mind): "Not only the radically secular philosophies of progress of Condorçet, Saint-Simon, Comte, and Marx are oriented eschatologically toward the future: so are their more recent transformations which appear as negativistic theories of progressive decay."[15] If so, one wonders why the narratives of decline elaborated by Arendt, by Strauss, and by Löwith himself don't count as philosophies of history. I suspect that they do.

It would be wrong to cast Voegelin's own philosophy of history as utterly fixated on absolute despair, although his rhetoric usually sounds grimly apocalyptic. There are moments when he allows himself to express cautious hope of a return to sanity, of a recovery of reality and realism. One such moment is the passage in the last chapter of *The New Science of Politics* where he anticipates "the probable reaction of a living Christian tradition against Gnosticism in the Soviet empire," and the parallel backlash of "Chinese, Hindu, Islamic, and primitive civilizations [against] prolonged exposure to Gnostic devastation and repression" (pp. 165–166). "The date of the explosion," he ventures, "is less distant than one would assume" (p. 166).[16] Universities at the moment are "brothels of opinion," but one cannot rule out a revival of science through the emergence of "new organizational forms, outside the organization of the universities," which might in turn eventually ("after some fifty years") spur universities themselves to return once again to being truth-oriented institutions.[17] In one place, Voegelin even goes so far as to say, "Oh, personally I'm quite optimistic" – meaning that the received ideologies have already been thoroughly discredited, and that "we have in our time a very peculiar generation of scholars who all are clear about" the intellectual exhaustion of previously dominant ideologies (though they have no clue about what should come next).[18] One could say that there's a dialectical logic at play here (ironically, not at all unlike that

---

(*die Weltgeschichte ist das Weltgericht*): *Lectures on Kant's Political Philosophy*, ed. Ronald Beiner (Chicago: University of Chicago Press, 1982), pp. 4–5; cf. pp. 56–58 and 77.

[15] Löwith, *Nature, History, and Existentialism*, p. 136.

[16] This passage occurs in a book originally published in 1952. It would be hard to deny that subsequent history has accorded Voegelin some measure of vindication, at least in regard to the role of Polish Catholicism in overturning the Warsaw Pact, the revival of the Russian Orthodox Church, and the continuing vibrancy of Tibetan Buddhist culture in the face of the Chinese domination of Tibet.

[17] *The Drama of Humanity*, pp. 306–307; cf. page 303: "Science is flourishing today – except in the universities."

[18] *Published Essays, 1953–1965*, pp. 247 and 237. Voegelin said these things in the context of a discussion that took place in 1965.

in Marx's view of capitalism). The more horrendous Gnostic modernity is, the more urgent becomes the pressure for human beings under its sway to come to their senses. (This is what in other familiar contexts we tend to call a "dialectical" conception of history.) Ultimately, human beings estranged by Gnostic fantasies must grasp that their longings to bring about salvation on earth are hopeless and misguided, and they will let go of these Gnostic fantasies or rebel against them, and return to the reality that has been repressed.

As has already been anticipated in our discussion of Voegelin's historicism, the central category of Voegelin's political philosophy is "Gnosticism." I am not sure whether Voegelin ever quite defines what this particular vocabulary signifies for him, or spells out why it figures so prominently in his theorizing, though such an account can certainly be extrapolated from *The New Science of Politics*.[19] (To be sure, Voegelin introduces and constantly deploys a fairly extensive philosophical vocabulary of his own construction, much of it drawn from Plato and Aristotle, which empowers his disciples to communicate with each other in "Voegelinese," without feeling obliged to detach themselves from the vocabulary enough to be able to ask themselves whether Voegelin's notions are actually rationally persuasive.[20] But of course it would be unfair to depict this as a problem unique to Voegelin and the Voegelinans.) Yet we know that Gnosticism, as a historical phenomenon as opposed to a category of political-philosophic analysis, refers to one of the notable heresies at the time of early Christianity. This clearly tells us that Voegelin regards modernity, from the start and consistently thereafter, *as a form of religious heresy*. For Voegelin, liberalism is not less "Gnostic" than are fascism and communism: John Rawls is as much a Gnostic as were Nietzsche and Marx. It is definitely suggested in the final chapter of *The New Science of Politics* that the totalitarian ideologies of the twentieth century were merely the carrying-to-their-logical-conclusion of Gnostic tendencies already present in the liberal-egalitarian political philosophies of early

---

[19] But see *The Drama of Humanity*, ed. Petropulos and Weiss, p. 338, where Voegelin concedes that *The New Science of Politics* probably gave more weight to the Gnosticism idea than was warranted. On the next page he appeals to "magic" as a more suitably expansive notion: "*Magic* means the attempt to realize a desired end that cannot be realized if one takes into account the structure of reality." For a good summary of what Voegelin associates with the idea of Gnosticism, see Elizabeth C. Corey, "Voegelin and Oakeshott on Hobbes: Gnostic but not Rationalist?" which is posted on the website of the Eric Voegelin Institute: http://www.lsu.edu/artsci/groups/voegelin/society/2002%20Papers/Panel22002.shtml.

[20] No doubt, Voegelin would protest here that I am myself relying on a notion of rationality that is "ideological," existentially "corrupt," or intellectually deranged (and probably all three).

modernity.[21] Indeed, it would hardly be an exaggeration to say that for Voegelin, modernity is not a late-flowering development of Western civilization but on the contrary, an apostate *subversion* of Western civilization.

It is important to note that for Voegelin, Gnostic doctrines of salvation on earth are not merely a set of misguided theories to be engaged with on the intellectual plane. Instead, and crucially, these doctrines are to be traced to a "pnemopathological condition"[22] evidencing malformed souls on the part of those who adopt such doctrines; in fact, this is a distinctive trait of Voegelin's mode of theorizing. Hence in *The New Science of Politics*, after making the point that a Gnostic conception of history involves a "fallacious immanentization of the Christian eschaton," he adds that "the fallacy looks rather elemental": otherworldly salvation is one thing, and what transpires within history and historical experience is categorically different. So what accounts for this "fallacy"? "Obviously one cannot explain seven centuries of intellectual history by stupidity and dishonesty.[23] A drive must rather be assumed in the souls of these men which blinded them to the fallacy" (p. 121). In other words, what has gone off the rails during these seven centuries is not something specifically *intellectual*, but rather something amiss in the souls of those who embraced the views concerned. Following Plato, philosophy in the proper sense is associated with the well-ordered soul, which places itself in confrontation with non-philosophical souls subject to a variety of dislocations or derangements (p. 63). However, *the* problem for Voegelin is that the norm in modernity is for the philosophers themselves to suffer from deranged or dislocated souls.

The theme of the lectures that became *The New Science of Politics* is "representation." On the face of it, this seems rather strange, since it is recognizably a theme of modern liberal political thought, and this, one might expect, would have the effect of drawing Voegelin away from the ancients and toward the political thought of modernity. This is relevant to explaining why Thomas Hobbes looms so large in Voegelin's book, since of course the

---

[21] See Hannah Arendt's challenge to this Voegelinian view in *Essays in Understanding 1930–1954*, ed. Jerome Kohn (New York: Harcourt Brace and Company, 1994), p. 405.

[22] *Science, Politics and Gnosticism*, p. 101. Cf. *The New Science of Politics*, p. 139 (Voegelin in this text is referring to Calvin).

[23] Joachim of Flora looms as large in Voegelin's version of the story of Western spiritual corruption as he does in Karl Löwith's version. Joachim dated the start of his postulated "Third Realm" ("the age of the Spirit") at 1260, hence the "seven centuries" referred to by Voegelin. See *The New Science of Politics*, pp. 110–114; for the corresponding account in Löwith, see *Meaning in History* (Chicago: University of Chicago Press, 1949), chapter 8 and appendix I.

problem of political representation, and the question of the legitimacy of the Sovereign qua representative, is central to the political philosophy laid out in *Leviathan*. But political representation, in Voegelin's hands, reacquires something of the character of a premodern concept. What is Voegelin's account of representation?

For Voegelin, at bottom, the purpose of a given political order is to "represent" the meaning of existence and give political expression to a conception of the nature of cosmological reality as experienced by members of the political order. Every society has to articulate a vision of itself to itself if it is to have any kind of presence "on the historical scene" (p. 36). This involves a notion of *existential* representation, embodied in a construction of political order that enacts symbolic projections of what the society stands for far deeper than what we associate with the representative institutions of a standard modern liberal democracy, for instance. Voegelin says that he practices "the Aristotelian procedure of examining symbols as they occur in reality" (p. 34), with the clear implication that the symbols in question engage visions of human existence in relation to cosmic (and ultimately divine) reality. Prior to Plato, according to Voegelin, what a political society represented was "cosmic truth"; subsequent to Plato, it came to represent another principle as well, namely "anthropological truth" (p. 61; cf. pages 76–77). This new Platonic revelation is of "permanent" validity, relevant "today quite as much as in the time of Plato" (p. 61). And ultimately, once Christianity comes on the scene, what a society represents (or ought in principle to represent) is the "soteriological truth" made available by the Christian dispensation (p. 77). For a society to be genuinely represented in its political structures, whatever they happen to be, means the symbolic disclosure of where that society stands, not only in relation to other societies, but ultimately in relation to the cosmos, to the nature of the human psyche,[24] and to God; and that vision of its metaphysical purpose, or its stance vis-à-vis the truth of existence, must be given historical articulation. Relative to this conception of existential representation, Voegelin would surely say that all contemporary thinking about political representation looks unspeakably shallow.

What is at stake in political representation, on Voegelin's account, is what a given political order expresses to the world (by way of either affirmation or

---

[24] For Voegelin, "psyche" is interpreted not merely psychologically, but as an "opening" toward transcendent reality (p. 67). Hence, the anthropological principle is not strictly anthropological, and Plato's "discovery" is, so to speak, already proto-soteriological. See also page 75.

rejection) with respect to the truth of the soul and the ordering principles of the cosmos as a whole – that is, ultimately, God and how human existence relates to God.[25] The "process in which human beings form themselves into a society for action shall be called the articulation of a society" (p. 37). "Articulation, thus, is the condition of representation. In order to come into existence, a society must articulate itself by producing a representative that will act for it" (p. 41). And again, these representations of political order are only meaningful insofar as they get unfolded more or less monumentally on the scene of history: "Political societies as representatives of truth ... occur in history" (p. 59). Every political order, from the Mongol empire in the thirteenth century to the Soviet Union in the twentieth century, asserts a claim of truth concerning "cosmic order"; just as the "Mongol Khan was the representative of the truth contained in the Order of God," so the General Secretary of the Central Committee of the CPSU represents "the truth of a historically immanent order" that has directly supplanted the truth of cosmic order (pp. 58–59). The content has changed, obviously, but the epic character of what political representation fundamentally represents has not changed (and never will). So what gets highlighted in this way of conceptualizing representation is "nothing less than the historical process in which political societies, the nations, the empires, rise and fall" (p. 41). Hence the contest of visions of political order now takes on the character of what may be conceived as a drama of near-metaphysical proportions. A struggle of interests between two rival states is no longer merely that. Instead, it is a competition about which vision of the existential representation of human beings in relation to God and the cosmos is to yield and which is to prevail.[26] Banal or prosaic images of what is at stake in political life thus melt away; the stakes in symbolizations of political order could not be grander or more awesome. It is as if Voegelin responds to the banalization of political experience within contemporary social science by projecting a vision of political existence that goes as far as possible in the opposite direction – that is, claiming a meaning for politics by which it assumes the highest kind of metaphysical import.

Just as the stakes are raised in the understanding of political existence, so the stakes are similarly raised with respect to political philosophy in relation

---

[25] "The truth of man and the truth of God are inseparably one" (p. 69). Cf. page 70: "the anthropological principle ... requires the theological principle as its correlate."

[26] Voegelin's account of Greek tragedy at the end of chapter 2 suggests that this work of existential representation is in some sense better accomplished by the tragedians than by the statesmen of the polis. This in turn is somewhat reminiscent of Shelley's famous dictum about poets as the true legislators of the world.

to the political order that a given political philosophy confronts. What was at stake in the philosophy of Plato was whether what would be represented existentially in the Greek polis would be spiritual truth or spiritual lies.[27] What was at stake in the *theologia civilis* of Hobbes was whether Gnostic revolutionaries inspired by a perverse interpretation of Christianity could be permitted, without intellectual challenge, to seize the seat of power in England.[28] What was at stake in Hegel was whether "Joachitic immanentization" (p. 119) would install itself as the defining meaning of the modern state.[29] Surely no less, Voegelin wants to impress upon us, should be at stake in the practice of political science or political philosophy in the twentieth (or twenty-first) century.

Is there a "conception of the good" and a vision of the ideal organization of social and political life in Voegelin? Given the overwhelmingly ambitious character of his theorizing, one would certainly presume that there must be; still, I am tempted to say no. Voegelin does not give us a positive doctrine of justice, or human rights, or citizenship, or an account of the civic purposes that properly define a community of citizens – apart from the purpose of "representing" the existential yearning for a connection to the divine that he thinks marks the decisive difference between ordered and disordered human communities. Instead of this, we get hermeneutics spanning the whole of the Western tradition and anti-modern *Kulturkritik* (both of which are often quite penetrating), along with an abundance of overheated polemics. The most obvious philosophical prescription offered by Voegelin is for human beings in their political existence to be "realistic" – to reject the "dream-worlds" or "magic-worlds" by which the various murderous ideologies try to seduce us, and to attend to or attune ourselves to non-ideological realities, and to divine reality (or the divine ground of reality) in particular. There are two considerations that seem to militate against Voegelin being able to provide prescriptions more specific than this. First, as Voegelin sees it, there are a wide range of symbolic orders throughout

---

[27] This is a central topic of *The New Science of Politics*, chapter 2.

[28] Needless to say, Voegelin's response to Hobbes is highly ambivalent. Insofar as Hobbes was motivated to push back against the politics of the saints, the intention of his political theory was anti-Gnostic. But of course Hobbes had his own complicity in "the Gnostic dream world" of modernity (p. 161). Hence the purpose of Voegelin's interpretation of Hobbes in chapter 5 of *The New Science of Politics* is not to champion him as a satisfactory adversary of Puritan politics (although sympathy with Hobbes is not entirely absent from Voegelin's account); his story is more one of battling competing Gnosticisms.

[29] See note 9 above.

history that supply human beings with articulations of existential order – civilizations, each of which manages to ground the existence of human beings in an apprehension of transcendence (expressed in a particular symbolic articulation: a "symbolization"). Human civilizations thereby provide a foundation for coherent political order. These structures, both symbolic and eventually intellectual, are *historical* achievements, concrete embodiments of "historical existence" (to use the phrase introduced in *The New Science of Politics*'s first sentence), and there would be something ludicrous about stepping outside history in order to legislate a philosophically prescribed way for human beings to structure their political living-together.[30] In Voegelin's view, it would be too easy, surely, for such a project to turn into another reality-twisting ideology.

Secondly, Voegelin appears too fixated on the pathological side of modern politics to offer positive prescriptions. His enterprise is the diagnosis of political *disorder*, which he traces in every case to *spiritual* dysfunction; his self-assigned role is to be the analyst of what he calls "the putrefaction of Western civilization."[31] For Voegelin, when human societies fail to generate a proper vision of order, this always has the same explanation: estrangement from the divine, and the concocting of phantom pseudo-realities to supplant the genuine ground from which we have thus alienated ourselves. And modernity seems uniquely pathological in this regard: it is bereft of order in an unprecedented way, one might say, because its structures of cultural and intellectual consciousness represent an unprecedented blindness to the fact of transcendence, a historically unique insensitivity to the mystery of being that joins the mystery of human existence with the mystery of the divine in a binding and sustaining state of "existential tension," as Voegelin terms it. (What does "existential tension" mean? I imagine it means that human beings feel themselves pulled toward the divine such that, once they experience that pull, they are thereafter unable to dwell strictly in the realm of the human; they are always subject to a spiritual pull *out* of the human, in the direction of whatever transcendent mystery is exerting this gravitational attraction. Hence existential tension, in its simplest signification, refers to the indissoluble tension between the human and the divine planted in the

---

[30] In Chapter 8, we will discuss Gadamer's view that Plato and Aristotle had no ambition, by articulating (preexisting) conceptions of the good, to reconstruct a new principle of life for the Greek polis. They were analysts of the decadence of the polis, full stop. Voegelin's view seems to be strikingly similar. Cf. *The Drama of Humanity*, p. 306: "Plato was perfectly clear when he wrote his [dialogues] that Athens was doomed"; cf. *The New Science of Politics*, pp. 74–75. If Plato had been serious about wanting philosopher-kings, he too would have been merely an ideologist.

[31] *Published Essays, 1953–1965*, p. 15.

very nature of existence.) Voegelin would undoubtedly classify Heidegger as another magic-dispensing Gnostic; yet there seems to be a definite Heidegger-type "forgetfulness-of-Being" thesis being enunciated here.

As we discussed earlier to some extent, Voegelin is averse to committing himself to any particular doctrinal theology because, it appears, he regards all such theologies and all such doctrines, including those proffered by Christianity, as attempts to abate the impenetrable mysteries of existence.[32] And it may well be that Voegelin is leery about embracing some positive vision of how human beings should enact their political existence – as opposed to the merely negative work of diagnosing pathologies[33] – for similar reasons: namely, that it too comes unacceptably close to taking on the appearance of a kind of Gnostic hubris, of a desire to abate or dissolve the mystery of human existence. In fact, it counts as a form of Gnosticism made much worse by imagining that unaided secular reason is sufficient for this purpose of abating the mystery, that is, by submitting the fundamental purposes of existence to an exhaustively profane interpretation. In a 1965 lecture entitled "In Search of the Ground," Voegelin says of Karl Löwith that he decisively refuted the nineteenth-century historicism that flowed out of Hegel. "But that doesn't mean that Löwith now knows what to do."[34] In other words, in common with other leading intellectuals of the time, the demolition of false philosophies does not equip Löwith with a positive philosophy of his own. That's a fair point. Yet does Voegelin have a solution any more than Löwith does?

The decisive objection to Voegelin's political philosophy is almost too obvious to need spelling out. Voegelin is convinced that he is privy to an ontological reality that the majority of the inhabitants of advanced modernity are blind to, or – worse – are subliminally aware of but are committed to actively suppressing. If contemporary politics is a bloodbath – an endless spectacle of murder and spiritual corruption – then this blindness to or

---

[32] Cf. *The Drama of Humanity*, p. 282, on Christian theology as a "deformation" of "the symbolism of the Gospel."

[33] Again, in our Gadamer chapter, we will offer the suggestion that Gadamerian political philosophy is centrally defined by (merely) the critique of sophism, and notwithstanding all the grand gestures in Voegelin's style of theorizing, there is a sense in which the same may be true of Voegelin. In any case, it is evident that the theme of philosophy versus the sophists is an important one for both Gadamer and Voegelin: see, for instance, *The Drama of Humanity*, pp. 318 and 371. The latter is a question put to Voegelin by Gadamer at a conference in Toronto in 1978 in which they both participated. The whole conference is available in a fascinating DVD (which can be purchased on Amazon) entitled *Voegelin in Toronto*.

[34] *Published Essays, 1953–1965*, p. 15.

suppression of divine reality supplies a sufficient explanation. If one desires *chutzpah* in a theorist, then this surely meets that criterion (and Voegelin may in fact satisfy the criterion more fully than any other thinker covered in this book). Yet it is difficult to know how to position Voegelin in relation to a larger dialogue encompassing political philosophy in general when he flatly refuses to accept the legitimacy of any reason/revelation distinction.[35] Indeed, he regards that distinction as a civilizational disaster of very large proportions. It goes without saying that we would very much *want to* include Voegelin within the reciprocal dialogue that defines the broad company of political philosophers (both those treated in this book and the many others who could have been added).[36] But the perplexing fact is that Voegelin himself resists inclusion by virtue of insisting upon the acknowledgment of divine reality as the necessary starting-point for any such dialogue.[37]

For Voegelin, reason is *nous* in the sense that it is apprehension of a divine ground of reality.[38] Philosophy is "noetic," that is it arises from a set of

---

[35] See *The Drama of Humanity*, ed. Petropulos and Weiss, pp. 325 and 327–329: what gets referred to as "natural reason" is really a product of divine grace, so the idea that one can hive off a realm of the rational from the experience of the divine, or vice versa, is categorically mistaken. Cf. Sandoz, "The Philosopher's Vocation," pp. 82 and 86, as well as Voegelin as quoted in note 8 and on page 88. For Voegelin, it is equally true (and for the same reason) that any distinction between philosophy and theology would also be both the destruction of philosophy and the destruction of theology. As discussed earlier, what Voegelin means by revelation is not Christian revelation, or even Judeo-Christian revelation (or that of monotheism, for that matter), but the revelation of a divine presence common to *all* world religions (and Plato too). However, it is important to note that the text quoted by Sandoz in note 8 ("In my view there is neither natural reason nor revelation, neither the one nor the other. [The idea of 'revelation'] is *a theological misconstruction*") suggests that Voegelin *rejects* revelation in the sense that the very category already commits one to a reason/revelation distinction, and Voegelin utterly rejects that distinction.

[36] Interestingly, Hannah Arendt seems to have been more open to Voegelin as a philosophical interlocutor than she was to Strauss or indeed any of the others. Arendt wrote in a letter to the wife of Karl Jaspers that *The New Science of Politics* (which Arendt read as soon as it was published) was "the first fundamental discussion of the real problems since Max Weber"; see Hannah Arendt/Karl Jaspers, *Correspondence 1926–1969*, ed. Lotte Kohler and Hans Saner (New York: Harcourt Brace Jovanovich, 1992), p. 203. I don't have a theory to explain this, though there must be an explanation. In the same letter to Gertrud Jaspers, Arendt also said that Voegelin's political philosophy "is on the wrong track," so obviously Arendt's intellectual respect for Voegelin should not be mistaken for acceptance of his views.

[37] In *Published Essays, 1953–1965*, p. 119, Voegelin states: "experiences of transcendence … are historical facts, and it is necessary to begin by accepting them as such"; cf. page 121: "I have simply described a fact [in characterizing the modern West in terms of a closure of the soul]." Accordingly, he regards dialogue with people who deny transcendence as tantamount to reasoning with a madman, or trying to pursue a rational discussion with someone who denies the facts staring him or her in the face. This does not seem a productive basis for intellectual exchange, although maybe Voegelin would say that modern secularists or agnostics are just as dogmatically closed to opposing views, but simply express their own dogmatism a little less bluntly or rudely.

[38] See, for instance, *Autobiographical Reflections*, p. 109: "the discovery of "the *Nous* as the ground of being [defines] the theophanic core of Classic philosophy"; and *The Drama of Humanity*, pp. 315 and 329.

primordial experiences in the soul, spiritual experiences, and all genuine philosophers have these experiences. Philosophers who don't have these experiences – who are not theocentric in their mode of philosophizing but try to philosophize instead on the basis of human-centered secular reason – are not philosophers at all but "sorcerers" or "magicians" or "alchemists." Christianity is correct (is the ultimate source of philosophical wisdom) when it informs us that we exist because, so to speak, God loves us. All world religions and all human cultures, going back thousands of years if not tens of thousands of years, are agreed on what makes reality real, namely the fact that it is rooted in divinity, and it is a unique derangement of modernity to have alienated itself from that universal truth. Voegelin's view receives unsurpassable expression when he writes: "The general deculturation of the academic and intellectual world in Western civilization furnishes the background for the social dominance of opinions that would have been laughed out of court in the late Middle Ages or the Renaissance."[39]

Suppose one were to say that Voegelin's theocentric view is itself a fantasy.[40] Or suppose one were merely to say that he is incapable of giving us reasons to be intellectually persuaded by his views if we aren't already predisposed to hold them in advance of reading his work. Voegelin wouldn't say that this is an intellectually competing view with which he has to engage intellectually; on the contrary, he would say that it is a form of spiritual corruption, a "pneumopathological condition" to be diagnosed, to be denounced, and to be combated. To be sure, Voegelin is no Habermas: "You can't put a Hindu, a Confucian, a Western ideologue of the communist persuasion, and one of the liberal persuasion together into one room and have anything result from their talking at one another. It's no dialogue."[41] To put it very simply: there is no Gadamerian doctrine of a (secular) fusion of horizons in Voegelin. For Voegelin, no less than for Alasdair MacIntyre, meaningful dialogue requires a sharing of thick philosophical premises, with the not-trivial added requirement that inhabiting the right intellectual

---

[39] *Autobiographical Reflections*, p. 49. Cf. *Published Essays, 1953–1965*, p. 126: "we are living today in a civilization where the confusion of ideas is such that everything that Plato had rejected as *philodoxie* is called philosophy." Similarly vehement is Voegelin's judgment pronounced upon denizens of the contemporary academy as "intellectual pimps for power" (Eric Voegelin, *Order and History, Volume 3: Plato and Aristotle* [Baton Rouge: Louisiana State University Press, 1957], p. 37), as well as his already-cited reference to contemporary universities as "brothels of opinion" (*The Drama of Humanity*, p. 306). As is obvious from these (all-too-characteristic) samples of Voegelin's rhetoric, Strauss's crisis rhetoric looks quite moderate and subdued by comparison with Voegelin's.

[40] Cf. the challenge put to Voegelin by Lucien Goldmann on pp. 119–120 of *Published Essays, 1953–1965*.

[41] *The Drama of Humanity*, p. 274. Cf. *The New Science of Politics*, p. 65, for the suggestion that "a theoretical debate" is only possible among people equipped with a certain kind of soul.

framework presupposes a consciousness that is spiritually healthy rather than spiritually deformed. That does not look like a very propitious basis for open dialogue with those who (in Voegelin's opinion) fall short of having rightly-constituted souls. At this point, readers of this chapter may be starting to wonder if, at least in the case of Voegelin, Brian Barry wasn't so far off the mark after all with his suggestion that with respect to the epic theorists, one has to respond to them in a mode of swallow-whole-or-spit-it-out.[42] However, even in the case of Voegelin, I would resist Barry-type aspersions against epic theory – namely, the idea that Voegelin is simply setting himself up as a "guru." Voegelin is immensely learned; he reflects on the history of philosophy, the history of civilizations, and the meaning of human cultures at an impressively deep level; and non-Voegelinians, even with their ill-constituted souls, can learn a lot from reading his work. Still, I would concede to Barry that, given Voegelin's views about the noetic character of reason and the experiential character of philosophy (as well as the rejection as "Gnostic" of competing visions of how to practice philosophy), there is indeed something quite problematic about trying to engage intellectually with Voegelin if one is not already a fully-committed Voegelinian.

---

[42] In "Prospects of Western Civilization," in *Published Essays, 1953–1965*, pp. 113–133, the transcript of a discussion with leading intellectuals such as Raymond Aron, Arnold Toynbee, and Lucien Goldmann that took place in Cerisy-la-Salle in 1958, Voegelin's claims are met with broad skepticism. All that Voegelin is able to do by way of response is to insist, fairly unconvincingly, that his own arguments are pitched at the "analytical" (i.e., philosophical) level, whereas those of his interlocutors are located merely at a "pre-analytical" or "rhetorical" (i.e., sub-philosophical) level.

7

Simone Weil: The Politics of the Soul

What centrally motivates Simone Weil as a political philosopher is well captured in the title of Part 1 of *The Need for Roots*: the soul, what the soul needs, and what politics can contribute toward meeting the needs of the soul. *The Need for Roots* (written in early 1943 and first published as *L'Enracinement* in 1949)[1] was composed as a set of reflections, commissioned by the Free French headquartered in London, on a desirable reconstruction of French social and political life, in anticipation of the eventual expulsion of the fascists who were then in command of France. For all the idiosyncrasies and even perversities of the text, Iris Murdoch was right to describe the book as "one of the very few profound and original political treatises of our time."[2] Weil's project is to give an account of what constitutes a truly well-ordered soul, and then, on the basis of that account, to offer proposals about how France, subsequent to its liberation, could be set on a suitable cultural, economic, political, and (especially) spiritual foundation. Something truly essential about her vision of politics is conveyed when she writes on page 213 that "the true mission of the French movement in London is, by reason even of the military and political circumstances, a spiritual mission before being a military and political one." If political philosophy in the grandest sense is aimed at the articulation of a comprehensive conception of the good, Weil's practice of political philosophy easily meets that standard.

One of the central themes that concern us in our encounter with leading political philosophies of the twentieth century (as we will see in succeeding chapters) is the relation between politics and truth, or what happens

---

[1] Simone Weil, *The Need for Roots: Prelude to a Declaration of Duties towards Mankind*, trans. Arthur Wills (London: Routledge, 2002); all parenthetical references to follow refer to this work. I am grateful to Aldo Bruzzichelli for having alerted me, many years ago, to the importance of this book.

[2] Iris Murdoch, "Knowing the Void," in Murdoch, *Existentialists and Mystics*, ed. Peter Conradi (London: Chatto and Windus, 1997), p. 159.

to political philosophy when a commitment to the primacy of truth flags in the thought of leading political philosophers. The issue of truth, and its importance for politics, is absolutely central to the political philosophy of *The Need for Roots*; hence this theme, in its Weilian version, can be an important reference-point for judging later thinkers interested in downplaying or displacing it as the decisive anchor of political reflection. As the good Platonist that she is, there is certainly nothing halfhearted or conditional about Weil's commitment to the primacy of truth. In Weil's view, modern society is fatally corrupted by its indifference to truth, and no society is worthy of approval until its inner compass is firmly oriented toward the distinction between what is and isn't true. In a remarkable passage, Weil comes close to suggesting that France deserved to be conquered by Hitler, and deserved this because it was spiritually corrupt (p. 239).[3] And for Weil, deterioration in the reverence for truth is one good index, perhaps the best index, of being spiritually corrupt (hence the telling statement on page 36 that "the need for truth is more sacred than any other need").[4] "Truth is the radiant manifestation of reality" (p. 250). Truth is inseparable from love because "to desire truth is to desire direct contact with a piece of reality [and to] desire contact with a piece of reality is to love" (pp. 250–251). Something of this kind of Platonism is expressed in a beautiful passage from Cormac McCarthy's *No Country for Old Men*, which may therefore be of some relevance in getting attuned to the spirit of Weil's thinking:

We come here from Georgia. Our family did. Horse and wagon. I pretty much know that for a fact. I know they's a lots of things in a family that just plain aint so. Any family. The stories gets passed on and the truth gets passed over. As the saying goes. Which I reckon some would take as meanin that the truth cant compete. But I dont believe that. I think that when the lies are all told and forgot the truth will be there yet. It dont move about from place to place and it dont change from time to time. You cant corrupt it any more than you can salt salt. You cant corrupt it because that's what it is.[5]

Part of what makes this a "Weilian" text is the emphasis on incorruptibility at the end. A friend of Weil's, Louis Bercher, put the apt challenge to her that

---

[3] Cf. page 96, referring to the "moral bankruptcy" of France; and page 100: "The French people, in June and July 1940, were not a people waylaid by a band of ruffians, whose country was suddenly snatched from them. They are a people who opened their hands and allowed their country to fall to the ground."

[4] Cf. page 36, where she suggests that mendacity is so pervasive in a modern society like France that one cannot help feeling that "one reads as though one were drinking from a contaminated well." See also page 102: "we live in an age so impregnated with lies that even the virtue of blood voluntarily sacrificed is insufficient to put us back on the path of truth."

[5] Cormac McCarthy, *No Country for Old Men* (New York: Vintage Books, 2006), p. 123.

her version of Christianity was a Cathar-like heresy because of her preoccupation with purity. Bercher wanted her to see that corruption is part and
parcel of the human condition. "Simone didn't deny this, but she didn't give
in to my point either."[6]

Within the catalogue of needs of the soul offered in Part 1 of *The Need
for Roots*, one encounters the striking (and surprising) fact that by far the
longest discussion is devoted to freedom of opinion. Hence, that particular
analysis may give us a helpful window into what is distinctive about Weil's
style of theorizing. One might expect that a theorist privileging freedom of
opinion among the needs of the soul would draft a J.S. Mill-type vision of
maximal liberties, but the polestar of Weil's theorizing is Plato, not the principles of the Enlightenment or of liberalism.[7] As is clear from the very first
sentence of the book (as well as its subtitle), Weil's theorizing is fundamentally oriented toward obligations or duties, not rights.[8] One cannot fail to
notice that "order" precedes "liberty" in her list of spiritual needs. And her
account of freedom of opinion is certainly not one that remotely resembles
a liberal account. Summarizing Weil's political vision in Part 1 of *The Need
for Roots* (and giving special attention to the "Freedom of Opinion" section
that also interests us), Conor Cruise O'Brien rightly observes that it is "a
rather disconcerting sketch [of the kind of reconstruction of French society
that the Free French might carry out after the liberation]. A France reconstructed on Weilian lines ... would have had no political parties, no trade
unions, no freedom of association. It would have had a rigid, primitive, and
eccentric form of censorship – one that would permit Jacques Maritain
to be punished for having said something misleading about Aristotle."[9]
O'Brien goes on to allege (plausibly) that what she is really aiming at is
"a rule of the saints," and he suggests that "in practice an effort by mortal

---

[6] Simone Pétrement, *Simone Weil: A Life*, trans. Raymond Rosenthal (New York: Pantheon Books, 1976),
p. 419.

[7] The secular Enlightenment and "1789" are accused by Weil of "infinitely increasing" the plague of
"uprooting": see Simone Weil, *Gravity and Grace*, trans. Emma Crawford and Mario von der Ruhr
(London: Routledge, 2002), p. 162. As I discuss in Chapter 11, I suspect that that is MacIntyre's view as
well, though he never quite spells it out as explicitly as Weil does.

[8] That first sentence reads: "The notion of obligations comes before that of rights, which is subordinate
and relative to the former" (p. 3). Hence her insistence on the "disastrous mistake" committed by "the
men of 1789" (p. 275). For a good account of Weil's critique of the vocabulary of rights, see Edward
Andrew, "Simone Weil on the Injustice of Rights-Based Doctrines," *The Review of Politics*, Vol. 48, No.
1 (Winter 1986), pp. 60–91.

[9] Conor Cruise O'Brien, "Patriotism and *The Need for Roots*: The Antipolitics of Simone Weil," in *Simone
Weil: Interpretations of a Life*, ed. George Abbott White (Amherst, MA: University of Massachusetts
Press, 1981), p. 96.

and fallible men to 'apply' *The Need for Roots* would probably have resulted in something quite like Vichy France ... but minus collaboration with the Nazis, and with de Gaulle at the top instead of Pétain."[10]

That would seem plenty to prick our theoretical interest! Let's now take a closer look at the arguments by which Weil arrives at these (if not perverse certainly paradoxical) conclusions. Curiously, but crucially, Weil begins the section by trying to drive a wedge between freedom of opinion (which she affirms) and freedom of association (which she criticizes). Why would a theorist who regards "complete, unlimited freedom of expression for every sort of opinion, without the least restriction or reserve" as "an absolute need" of the soul (p. 22) want to curtail freedom of association? Freedom of expression, she insists, "is a need of the intelligence, and that intelligence resides solely in the human being, individually considered. There is no such thing as a collective exercise of the intelligence. It follows that no group can legitimately claim freedom of expression, because no group has the slightest need of it" (p. 26). "When a group starts having opinions, it inevitably tends to impose them on its members" (p. 27) – a consideration that convinces her that liberty would be enhanced rather than diminished by a purge of all political parties, a view in whose support she invokes Rousseau (p. 28). But in pursuing this analysis, Weil is especially preoccupied by the question of trade unions and their proper mission. Even before Vichy, she declares, the unions had become living corpses, no longer "the expression of working-class thought, the instrument of working-class integrity" (p. 30). To restore a post-Vichy trade union movement, one would have to put less emphasis on wages and more emphasis on "everything to do with justice" (p. 31). Workers are no less vulnerable than the bourgeois are to the "moral death always brought about by an obsession in regard to money" (p. 29). O'Brien is overstating things a bit when he refers to Weil's desire for an *abolition* of trade unions, but it is certainly correct that she dwells more on the French unions as agents of coercion (or potential coercion) than as agents of collective liberty. Here is the enigma of Weil's political thought in a nutshell: a passionately committed champion of the working class, but a principled critic of syndicalism! The solution to this enigma, as to all enigmas in her thought, has to be found in her Platonism. For Weil, it is impossible to reflect on the topic of liberty of opinion (or any other topic) in abstraction from

[10] Ibid. O'Brien adds that Weil showed "characteristic courage and integrity" in acknowledging affinities between her vision for France and what was already present in Vichy France. The relevant text in *The Need for Roots* is on page 30 noting the Vichy Government's abolition of autonomous trade unions; cf. page 64.

the question of the "sick" soul versus the "healthy" soul (pp. 22–23). Trade unions strike Weil as spiritually "dead" when they focus on something as vulgar as obtaining improvements to material earnings and benefits (beyond the alleviation of dire poverty). Instead, workers' associations, like all human communities, should be fundamentally judged by the extent to which they promote or injure spiritual well-being. In any case, Weil's view is that it is a mistake to think that a soul can be perfected by trying to coordinate itself with anything collective; the healthy soul must commune with itself and attend to its own integrity.

Little remains of Weil's commitment to "complete, unlimited freedom of expression for every sort of opinion, without the least restriction or reserve" by the time we get to the last section of Part 1 of *The Need for Roots*, the section on "Truth."[11] Weil opines that the population must be protected from "offences against the truth" (p. 37).[12] "There are men who work eight hours a day and make the immense effort of reading in the evenings so as to acquire knowledge. It is impossible for them to go and verify their sources in the big libraries. They have to take the book on trust. One has no right to give them spurious provender" (p. 36). For that purpose, one must set up "special courts enjoying the highest prestige" where, in egregious cases, "prison or hard labour" must be meted out to those putting into print "any avoidable error." As we already know from O'Brien in his passage criticizing Weil, she considered Jacques Maritain's suggestion that the injustice of slavery hadn't been on the moral radar screen of Greek society at the time Aristotle wrote in defense of it as worthy of indictment "before one of these tribunals" (ibid.). Would Maritain be punished with jail-time or hard labor, or would a heavy fine suffice?[13] How would judges be selected to serve on

---

11 On page 22 we read that unlimited freedom of expression "is an absolute need on the part of the intelligence," but on page 39 (cf. page 25) we read that "protection against suggestion and falsehood" constitutes "the human soul's most sacred need." How is one supposed to reconcile these two seemingly opposed sacred needs? Yet even in the "Freedom of Opinion" section, Weil recommends the punishment of novelists who violate "the moral principles recognized by law" (p. 25), on the grounds that their novels affect the practical conduct of their readers. And going even further, she calls for "repression" (*répression*) of publications and radio broadcasts that contribute to "baseness of tone and thought, bad taste, vulgarity or a subtly corrupting moral atmosphere" (p. 26).

12 She is particularly hostile to newspapers, which she accuses of "stupefying" their readers rather than helping them to think (p. 38; cf. pp. 24 and 26). She regards journalism as verging on "organized lying" (p. 37). Her solution is to ban journals that publish more frequently than once a week.

13 In the case of some other writer (say, Hannah Arendt), Weil's suggestion might be interpreted as a kind of arch irony, but Weil is not that kind of writer: she's absolutely serious. Presumably, Weil could distinguish between "facts," which must be rigorously accurate – on pain of punishment for departures from strict accuracy – and "opinions," which must be granted maximal liberty. But her example of Maritain as an offender against the trust of his readers hardly supports such a distinction. She says that

these tribunals? Weil's suggestion: require that they "be trained in a school where they receive not just a legal education, but above all a spiritual one, and only secondarily an intellectual one" (p. 39). As a good Platonist, Weil's main concern is not to liberate opinion from illiberal restrictions but rather to submit the opinions of those with poor souls to oversight by those with more perfectly developed souls. "Freedom of opinion" is on Weil's list of the needs of the soul, but for Weil truth trumps opinion to the extent that her account of freedom of opinion really *negates* freedom of opinion.[14]

Consonant with her Platonic emphasis on the spiritual integrity of the individual soul, Weil was deeply suspicious of collective life in its various social and political dimensions (as we have already seen in the preceding discussion of her views concerning opinion and truth). She thought that a suitably "precise" social science would be "founded upon the Platonic notion of the enormous animal, or the apocalyptic notion of the Beast" (p. 291).[15] Social reflection is less a matter of understanding how human virtues are grounded in social life than of apprehending how this great beast, society, could be "broken in," that is, domesticated. Established political institutions, too, strike her as beastly, or at least as brutally mechanical. Like Alasdair MacIntyre and to some extent like Arendt among our other "classics," Weil is more sympathetic to syndicalist democracy, or guild democracy, than she is to the characteristic principles and institutional forms of the contemporary state (see page 294). "One may say that, in our age, money and the State have come to replace all other bonds of attachment" (p. 99) – a view of our modern condition that coincides perfectly with MacIntyre's.[16]

Maritain deserves "censure" because his claim constitutes "an outrageous calumny against an entire civilization" (p. 38). Yet she herself rises to the defense of this "calumniated" civilization as if it were not, through and through, a slave-based society. Weil's judgment on Aristotle and Thomas Aquinas is suitably severe (see page 241), but as Iris Murdoch points out ("Knowing the Void," p. 160), Plato is strangely given a free pass.

[14] This is one respect among others where Weil's political philosophy presents itself as the very antithesis of Hannah Arendt's – a topic about which we will have a bit more to say in a later section of this chapter. My own view is that Arendt fell far short of giving an adequate account of the relationship between politics and truth. But if the main alternative to Arendt's view is the Platonic view that "opinion" is associated with the corrupted soul, as opposed to the apprehension of truth in its purity by the rightly-ordered soul (the kind of view that seems expressed in Weil's account), then this has the effect of making Arendt's view look a lot more attractive than it otherwise would.

[15] Cf. page 137: "Plato found the right expression when he compared the collectivity to an animal"; and p. 131. See also *Gravity and Grace*, pp. 164–169; and Gary A. Lewis, "Consent to the Universe," in *Democratic Theory and Technological Society*, ed. R.B. Day, R. Beiner, and J. Masciulli (Armonk, NY: M.E. Sharpe, 1988), p. 285, for a discussion of the importance of this theme in Weil; as well as O'Brien, "Patriotism and *The Need for Roots*," p. 96.

[16] As regards the Weil-MacIntyre parallel, it strikes me as interesting that while both are champions of "rootedness" and critics of the culture of individual choice associated with liberalism, the religious

She refers to the modern state as "a cold concern" and a source of "moral torment" (p. 114); she speaks of "the State's cold, metallic touch" (p. 133; cf. page 114). Weil is a champion of a certain kind of patriotism (loyalty toward what is worthy of loyalty, willingness to sacrifice on behalf of deep attachments): "men feel that there is something hideous about a human existence devoid of loyalty" (p. 126). But she is a determined foe of the state, which she says "morally killed everything, territorially speaking, smaller than itself" (p. 122), and thereby illegitimately drained loyalty away from anything apart from the state (p. 121; cf. page 123). Hence for her, the state *per se*, rather than just particular instances of it, is "totalitarian" (p. 119). That is, she believed that common moral experience gives rise to such a thing as a genuine sense of *patrie*, and displaying loyalty and affection toward this *patrie* constitutes an authentic virtue. Such patriotism grows out of a love of the past, for "without history there can be no sense of patriotism" (p. 229). This suffices to expose internationalist ideologies as morally suspect (pp. 102 and 123), but it was equally her view that the nation-state as such is not a credible embodiment of this *patrie*.[17] The state puffs itself up with false ideas of worldly grandeur that are the very opposite of true (spiritual) grandeur (see page 235 on "the soul akin to holiness" as what defines true rather than false greatness).[18]

Viewed from the height of a "Platonic" social science, virtually everything in the social and political lives of modern societies caters to what

commitments of both of them were *chosen* rather than inherited: MacIntyre eventually converted to Catholicism, and Weil "converted" to her own mystically inflected version of Christianity. As the latter contrast implies, MacIntyre seems more receptive than Weil to institutionalized Christianity. To my knowledge, MacIntyre's only acknowledgment of Weil as a moral and political thinker is his brief discussion in "Moral Philosophy: What Next?" in *Revisions*, ed. Stanley Hauerwas and Alasdair MacIntyre (Notre Dame, IN: University of Notre Dame Press, 1983), pp. 12–13, where he rightly compares Weil and Iris Murdoch.

[17] Hence, on Weil's view there is, one could say, good patriotism and bad patriotism. (Admittedly, this is a pretty crude restatement of Weil's subtle and thoughtful historical account in the section of Part 2 devoted to "Uprootedness and Nationhood.") The notion of a normatively acceptable patriotism is captured in the following contrast: "A nation cannot be an object of charity. But a country can be one – as an environment bearing traditions [its particular language, ceremonies, customs, poetry] which are eternal" (*Gravity and Grace*, p. 169). Bad patriotism is of the kind "derived from Rome" (O'Brien, "Patriotism and *The Need for Roots*," p. 106); she calls it "patriotism in the Roman style" (*The Need for Roots*, p. 180; cf. page 140). But as we discuss elsewhere in this chapter, since it is her view that the modern state as such has completely sold out to the ideals of Rome (namely ambition, domination, and self-idolatry), any patriotism that takes the state as its focus automatically falls under the rubric of the bad, Rome-oriented variety.

[18] Even though Rousseau was a leading modern theorizer of the state, one often encounters a Platonic sensibility in his work quite similar to Weil's. One thinks, for instance, of his stirring denunciation, at the beginning of chapter 11 of *The Government of Poland*, of the main European powers seeking to bribe their citizens with "candy" (cf. *The Need for Roots*, p. 154). Accordingly, it is no surprise that Weil's references to Rousseau in *The Need for Roots* typically express high admiration.

is debased and materialistic rather than to what elevates and purifies the spirit. "Four obstacles above all separate us from a form of civilization likely to be worth something: our false conception of greatness; the degradation of the sentiment of justice; our idolization of money; and our lack of religious inspiration. We may use the first-person plural without any hesitation, for it is doubtful whether at the present moment there is a single human being on the surface of the globe who is free from that quadruple defect" (pp. 216–217). "History is a tissue of base and cruel acts in the midst of which a few drops of purity sparkle at long intervals" (p. 229). What fundamentally matters in human life is salvation of the individual soul, and Plato was right that "the collectivity ... hinders the soul's salvation" (p. 131). Weil's Platonism demands that we detach ourselves from the false idols set up by all modern societies (which *define* our false conception of civilization), and cultivate the kind of individual spiritual integrity (apprehension and love of the Good) needed to purify ourselves of the defilement necessarily entailed by participation in collectivities. Again, Conor Cruise O'Brien's insightful commentary on *The Need for Roots* does a good job of zeroing in on the essential issue:

Note [Weil's] trust in intelligence and distrust of friendship. What she says, though acute and interesting, and no doubt true for herself, is not necessarily true for other people. Does the love of good depend on the light of intelligence? It hardly seems so; we can all think of rather stupid people who are kind and honest, and of quite intelligent people who are mean and treacherous. Might not friendship conceivably be a more likely channel for the love of good than intelligence? And might not the impairment of friendship by the demands of intelligence be a greater evil than the impairment of the expression of intelligence by the demands of friendship?[19]

In the same context, O'Brien goes so far as to describe Weil as a rigorous "enemy of the first-person plural," pointing out that her fundamental objection to any "we" is that it posits "an illegitimate middle term between the soul and God."[20]

The question of loyalty or attachment is obviously a central one in the political philosophy of Weil. Naturally, in her view political loyalty to the state and its office-holders could only ever be "a limited and conditional

---

[19] O'Brien, "Patriotism and *The Need for Roots*," pp. 98–99. This is a response to page 27 of *The Need for Roots*.

[20] O'Brien, "Patriotism and *The Need for Roots*," p. 98. Cf. *Gravity and Grace*, p. 160: ancient Israel embodied the impossible project of a "supernatural social life." This was an impossible project because for Weil, the social and the supernatural are fundamentally at war with each other. In Weil's view, the pathologies of Israel were put right by Christianity's categorical emphasis on the individual soul, except insofar as Christianity itself was corrupted by the pathology of Israel.

loyalty" (p. 115). But this cannot help but raise the question of the proper scope of loyalty toward the more close-at-hand communities (including friendship) for which she had greater sympathy. And here her clear and powerful stance takes us to the heart of her thought: "a total, absolute and unconditional loyalty is owed [only] to the welfare of the soul, *or in other words to God*" (ibid.; my italics).[21]

If Plato is our best guide to a true social science by teaching us that it must seek to domesticate the great beast by understanding it in the light of "the idea of the supernatural," he was no less our supreme tutor on matters higher than mere social existence: "Eternal mathematics ... is the stuff of which the order of the world is woven.... Not only mathematics but the whole of science ... is a symbolical mirror of supernatural truths" (pp. 289–290). Weil's presumption that "spiritual science" takes truth more seriously than it is taken by modern science in a conventional sense is vividly conveyed in her startling suggestion (pp. 255–256) that the adoption of quantum theory owed more to fashion and caprice within (what she disparagingly calls) "the village of savants" than to a love for truth. She celebrates Greek science, "which was as scientific as our own, *if not more so*," since it proves the possibility of a form of science having "no trace of materialism about it" (p. 242; my italics).[22] Weil is deeply opposed to divorcing religion from science.[23] Nothing in the religious spirit should require the least sacrifice of "the virtue of intellectual probity" (p. 244): "one should be absolutely prepared to abandon one's religion, even if that should mean losing all motive for living, if it should turn out to be anything other than the truth" (p. 247). But she presupposes an idea of science pre-harmonized, so to speak, with her notions of the supernatural. On page 239, she explicitly declares herself to be "in radical opposition to" the science founded on the ideas of Galileo, Descartes, and Newton.[24] The modern science that these thinkers inaugurated exalts force and repudiates spirit, whereas the true need of the human

---

[21] The word that Wills translates as "welfare" is *salut*, which is better translated as "salvation." The context is a discussion of Richelieu, but that same discussion likely alludes to Machiavelli's doctrine of privileging the salvation of one's city over the salvation of one's soul.

[22] Cf. pp. 241–242: Greek science "equalled and even surpassed our own. It was more exact, precise, rigorous."

[23] See especially page 259.

[24] On page 237, she writes: "The Church in the thirteenth century had Christ; but it also had the Inquisition. Science in the twentieth century has no Inquisition; but neither has it Christ, nor anything equivalent to Christ." It would be hard to draw from this text any confidence that this tradeoff (losing the Inquisition, but at the cost of losing Christ) was one ultimately advantageous to the human race.

soul is to repudiate force and exalt spirit. True science is the mathematics-worship of Plato and the mysticism of St. John of the Cross,[25] which exposes the science of modernity as we know it as a spiritual fraud.

What Weil fundamentally offers is a radically democratized Platonism where every human being is presumed capable of exercising "the light of the intelligence" (p. 27) – especially in their working life – in a way that links them to something transcendent. That is, Weil's Platonism is a Platonism that extends to "the truth of physical labour" (p. 291).[26] Why is it especially within the world of labor that this light of the intelligence is to be exercised? As Robert Sparling nicely formulates it, labor – that is, labor as a possible site of liberty (which it rarely is in reality but *ought always to be*) – is central to Weil's concerns because for her "labor constitutes the bulk of our existence, and being intellectually engaged in the work, in the entire work, is what makes it satisfying. To locate liberty in some other realm of social interaction (such as one's speeches in the agora or one's artistic creations) is to locate liberty at the periphery of our lives."[27] For Weil, one might say, the capital desideratum for political philosophy is a fundamental rethinking of the meaning of labor and its place in a properly lived life.[28]

Here it is difficult not to think of Weil in critical juxtaposition to Hannah Arendt.[29] What one encounters in conceiving an Arendt-Weil dialogue is not only the striking contrast between Weil's Platonism and Arendt's

---

[25] See page 261: "The entire works of St. John of the Cross are nothing else but a strictly scientific study of supernatural mechanisms. Plato's philosophy also is nothing else than that."

[26] As Fred Rosen points out, this Platonism applied to the world of labor connects "what has been regarded for centuries as the lowest and highest of human activities," namely labor and contemplation; quoted in Lewis, "Consent to the Universe," p. 293. I am not sure that Weil ever really spells out the grounds of her view that concern with labor must be central to a proper science of the soul, so to speak; or at least she doesn't spell them out to the extent that Arendt, in *The Human Condition*, spells out an argument for the opposite view. In particular, one would like more elaboration of what Weil sees as the "Platonic" aspects of manual labor, namely its potential for giving human beings access to more clear-sighted apprehensions of what is truly real. For an interesting attempt to develop relevant lines of thought that were left unsupplied by Weil, see Matthew B. Crawford, *Shop Class as Soulcraft: An Inquiry into the Value of Work* (New York: Penguin Press, 2009). Crawford, though, is mainly focused on the virtues of working as an independent mechanic or artisan (hence he cites Arendt and MacIntyre as intellectual sources but not Weil); Weil, by contrast, is clearly more preoccupied by the spiritual signifi-cance of factory labor on a mass scale. Viewed through the prism of Arendt's distinction between work and labor, Crawford's concern with manual activity more aptly falls under the rubric of work than under that of labor. But of course this is a distinction that is relevant to Arendt's political philosophy, not Weil's.

[27] Robert Sparling, "Theory and Praxis: Simone Weil and Marx on the Dignity of Labor," *The Review of Politics*, Vol. 74 (2012), p. 97.

[28] As Sparling puts it, Weil's theorizing was more than anything intended to lay the groundwork for a future "philosophy of labor" ("Theory and Praxis," p. 87; cf. 107).

[29] Cf. Sparling, "Theory and Praxis," p. 88.

anti-Platonism, but also the stark difference in their respective accounts of labor within the broader ranking of human activities. There's paradox in the fact that for all of Arendt's philosophical reservations about ancient Greek political thought (because the Greek philosophers privileged thought over action, philosophy over politics), she reaffirms the Aristotelian view that labor contributes the least to the living of an excellent life; whereas Weil, much as she was intellectually infatuated with the Greeks,[30] radically repudiated that view. Interestingly, Arendt showers Weil with high praise for treating the labor question "without prejudice and sentimentality,"[31] yet Weil could never regard labor, as Arendt emphatically did, as purely "biological." For Weil, in sharpest possible relief to Arendt, one should never abstract from the potential *spirituality* of labor (notwithstanding the de facto oppressiveness of most labor under existing conditions).[32] Consider *The Need for Roots'* concluding sentences: "Immediately next in order after consent to suffer death, consent to the law which makes work indispensable for conserving life presents the most perfect act of obedience which it is given to Man to accomplish. It follows that all other human activities, command over men, technical planning, art, science, philosophy and so on, *are all inferior to physical labor in spiritual significance.* It is not difficult to define the place that physical labor should occupy in a well-ordered social life. It should be

---

[30] See Simone Weil, "The *Iliad* or The Poem of Force," trans. Mary McCarthy, in *Revisions*, ed. Hauerwas and MacIntyre, pp. 245–247: "The Gospels are the last marvelous expression of the Greek genius, as the *Iliad* is the first.... But the spirit that was transmitted from the *Iliad* to the Gospels by way of the tragic poets never jumped the borders of Greek civilization.... Throughout twenty centuries of Christianity, the Romans and the Hebrews have been admired, read, imitated, both in deed and word; their masterpieces have yielded an appropriate quotation every time anybody had a crime he wanted to justify." A collection of her writings bears the English title, *Intimations of Christianity among the Ancient Greeks* (London: Routledge and Kegan Paul, 1957), which captures an important Weilian theme. Weil's general line is that whereas Greek culture at its best led directly to Christianity, the Hebrews and the Romans were thuggish brutes; and although modern, Western civilization is *supposed* to be a Christian or post-Christian civilization, it in fact opted for the Hebrews and Romans over the Greeks. This is an interpretation that is sharply expressed in our quotation from Weil's essay on the *Iliad* but which also runs through Part 3 of *The Need for Roots*; see also *The Need for Roots*, p. 131, where she states that the mistake of losing the individual in a blind worship of collectivity is one "that we are continually committing ... ourselves, corrupted as we are by the dual Roman-Hebrew tradition." One does not have much trouble understanding why Susan Sontag, in the inaugural issue of *The New York Review of Books* (1963), p. 22, stated that she felt "offended" by Weil's insistence on tracing all human evil back to Rome and Israel.

[31] Hannah Arendt, *The Human Condition*, 2nd edition (Chicago: University of Chicago Press, 1998), p. 131, n. 83.

[32] See *The Need for Roots*, p. 98: "A civilization based upon the spirituality of work would give to Man the very strongest possible roots in the wide universe, and would consequently be the opposite of that state in which we find ourselves now, characterized by an almost total uprootedness." Also, page 97: "The contemporary form of true greatness lies in a civilization founded upon the spirituality of work."

its spiritual core" (p. 298; my italics).[33] Labor, like death, is (or should be) an act of self-transcendence. Weil, a few pages earlier, acknowledges that for the Greeks, "labour was held to be servile" (p. 293), but it is not clear that she owns up to how large a gulf is put between her and the ancient thinkers she most reveres when she includes philosophy among the human activities that she counts as less spiritual than physical labor. How can the Greeks be a guide to the properly spiritual life when they had no appreciation of the "spiritual core" of "a well-ordered social life"?

In this chapter and the one preceding it, we have examined two important "theocentric" political philosophies (namely a "Right-Platonist" political philosophy and a "Left-Platonist" political philosophy). Weil's conception of ancient Greece as an anticipation of Christianity[34] is highly reminiscent of Voegelin; so too is her suggestion that philosophy has not existed since the eclipse of ancient Greece because philosophy in the true sense means love of "divine Wisdom" (p. 254). And Weil's suggestion on page 91 that, "if children are brought up not to think about God, they will become Fascist or Communist for want of something to which to give themselves" shares a lot with a Voegelinian analysis of modern ideologies. One also detects something akin to a Voegelinian mode of thinking in her extreme idea that "the responsibility which savants and all who write about science have assumed in these days is such a heavy one that they ... are possibly guiltier of Hitler's crimes than Hitler himself" (p. 237), though it is hard to believe that Voegelin would go quite that far. However, there is virtually nothing in common between what each of them associates politically with Christianity. (Weil's Platonism yields a politics of love and solidarity; Voegelin's Platonism yields a politics of stiff-spined *Realpolitik* and scornful dismissal of utopian longings.) Weil could be speaking both for herself and for Eric Voegelin when she defines her intellectual program as follows: "The science of the soul and social science are alike impossible, if the idea of the supernatural is not rigorously defined and introduced into science on the basis of a scientific conception" (p. 291). Yet precisely with respect to this agreement between Weil and Voegelin, one would be tempted to say that these two

---

[33] Cf. page 295: modern civilization "is sick because it doesn't know exactly what place to give to physical labour and to those engaged in physical labour." When Weil writes on page 294 that "we very nearly had a Christian civilization," she evidently has in mind that a truly Christian civilization would instill a veneration for physical labor, and the civilization that we *consider* to be Christian civilization clearly fails to meet that standard.

[34] See note 30 above.

political philosophies merely have the effect of "cancelling each other out" if it didn't sound a little ridiculous to put it that way. For in suggesting that political philosophy must be founded on a conception of the rightly-ordered soul, as opposed to the corruptly-ordered soul (a view of political philosophy to which both of them display die-hard commitment), they show that such an understanding of the political-philosophic enterprise can yield absolutely different, even incommensurable, political visions. And since neither of them can offer much beyond their own sincerely-held intuitions about what defines the rightly-ordered soul, and what entailments follow from those intuitions for one's understanding of politics, juxtaposing the two of them can give one the impression of helping to discredit *both* of these political philosophies.

Weil, probably more than any of the other thinkers treated in this book, draws adherents on account of the unique force of her personality as we know it from the facts of her biography (saintly self-sacrifice; a willingness to subordinate intellectual labor to manual labor, however menial; a personal intensity that is present in her writing, to be sure, but clearly even more present in her life).[35] Yet a political philosophy must be judged by intellectual standards; it can vindicate itself only by the coherence and reasonableness of its argument, not by its personification in an exemplary or admirable life. At all the key points in Weil's philosophy, she presupposes the apprehension of spiritual truths to which we are given *experiential* and not merely *intellectual* access by her Platonic version of Christianity. (This again bears a strong resemblance to themes in Voegelin.) For her, the Gospels offer "a supernatural physics of the human soul. Like all scientific doctrine, this science only contains things which are clearly intelligible and experimentally verifiable" (p. 262) – a claim that is easy to assert but hard to "verify." Characteristically, she suggests that "a whole-hearted love of truth" is more reliably found in saints than in scientists (p. 263). In other words, embrace of a Weilian vision of the good seems to demand an experience of wisdom

---

[35] One should notice, for instance, how T.S. Eliot, in his preface to *The Need for Roots*, defends Weil against potential critics by privileging the force of her personality over the persuasiveness of her arguments. In this connection, one might also have a look at Jessica Stern's suggestive account, in the preface to her book, *Terror in the Name of God* (New York: HarperCollins, 2003), p. xvii, of the strong early impression made on her by her reading of Weil, and of how she acquired from Weil "a prejudice in favor of religion" from which she had to be weaned in the process of writing her book. That is, reading Weil in her youth, and thus encountering the indomitable personality disclosed in Weil's writings, gave Stern a predisposition to think of the religious soul as naturally oriented toward charity and devotion to others, whereas life in the post-9/11 world we all now inhabit taught Stern that the religious soul can also embody murderousness and hatred.

and holiness elevated far beyond what mere political philosophy is normally expected to supply. In this book, theorists are being celebrated insofar as they extend their reach with Platonic ambition – detaching themselves from the cave by pursuing a quest for transcendent standards (and in some cases, doing so while steadfastly refusing to acknowledge that that is what they are doing). Yet Weil may well be a case of going *too* far in that desirable direction – of taking too literally the aspiration to re-embrace Plato. (Quite telling, for me, is the fact that even a *fellow Platonist* can accuse Weil of "whitewashing Plato"![36]) That is, Weil's political philosophy seems to be a case of tasking the vocation of theorizing with a responsibility of spiritual insight (of seeing into the soul) that it cannot properly bear.

---

[36] Murdoch, "Knowing the Void," p. 160.

8

Hans-Georg Gadamer: Philosophy without Hubris

Hans-Georg Gadamer is a thinker who was schooled in uncompromising Heideggerian radicalism, but who wants to counterbalance that radicalism with a firm commitment to intellectual humility and moderation as well as a conservative appreciation of tradition. Heidegger embodied the kind of philosophical hubris that it takes to believe one has penetrated into the deepest mysteries of being, and plumbed the most abysmal errors of the dominant civilization. Gadamer's counter to Heidegger's hubris is an appeal to human finitude, and to an awareness of limits (including the limits of philosophy). The truth is: we need the kind of heroic hubris displayed by a Heidegger in order to maintain the vibrancy of the philosophical tradition. Philosophers in the epic mold need to believe that they have seized insights that have eluded all their predecessors; they need to believe that they have analyzed the problems of human existence at a deeper level than has yet been achieved. But against this, Gadamer insists on the wisdom that as human beings, we need humility as much as, and probably more than, we need hubris.

Radical assertions about civilizational crisis, and a deep tear in our relations to the past, are certainly not lacking in some of the thinkers canvassed in earlier chapters. Hannah Arendt, for instance, never ceased to insist that "the thread of tradition is broken, and ... we shall not be able to renew it."[1] In Strauss, too, there is an emphatic thesis about our time being characterized by a severe "crisis of modernity," made worse by the fact that the sharp rupture between moderns and ancients cuts us off from the classical wisdom we would need in order to deal adequately with this crisis. And the analysis

---

[1] Hannah Arendt, *Thinking* (New York: Harcourt Brace Jovanovich, 1978), p. 212. This was a constant refrain in Arendt's philosophical writings; for instance, it defines the central theme of her book *Between Past and Future*, but it is of course no less present in her other books. Cf. Alfred Kazin, *New York Jew* (New York: Alfred A. Knopf, 1978), pp. 196–197.

of crisis and rupture that we get in Voegelin is probably even more dire. No doubt, the crisis-sensibility exhibited by some of these thinkers, and the tone in which they express their analyses, owes something to the intellectual legacy of Heidegger.[2] (It must owe something as well to the sheer horrendousness of the middle of the twentieth century!) While Gadamer offers a thesis of his own concerning a kind of crisis of practical reason, and the civic challenges of living in a technology-intoxicated society, a central aspect of his intellectual project was to try to tone down these apprehensions of crisis and rupture, and reassert – against the post-Heideggerian hyperbole about being severed from all tradition – a sense that our relationship to the still-living philosophical tradition remains intact. Contrary to Arendt's exaggerated assertion, Gadamer's message is that "the thread of tradition" is basically *un*broken.[3]

One might say that the central problem of Gadamer's work is the problem of theory and practice. Modernity was intellectually driven by the idea that a perfection of theory, largely in the form of a rigorously scientific understanding of the world, could comprehensively guide human praxis. Adequate practice, according to the modern idea, is always an application of better and more scientifically disciplined theories. For Gadamer, there is a kind of misguided hubris in such notions, and it cannot help but have distorting and baleful social and civic consequences. Gadamer consistently appeals to Aristotle against this, in his view, modern self-misunderstanding about the nature of human practice, because the Aristotelian understanding of ethics and politics (as Gadamer interprets it) takes its bearings from an essentially dialogical reflection on human ends.[4] Human social life is itself a dialogue (or the embodiment of a dialogue) about how to be human,

---

[2] In a provocative series of studies, Richard Wolin argues that Arendt, Löwith, and others (including Gadamer) were intellectually contaminated by their personal proximity to Heidegger. See Wolin, *Heidegger's Children: Hannah Arendt, Karl Löwith, Hans Jonas, and Herbert Marcuse* (Princeton, NJ: Princeton University Press, 2001); as well as Wolin, "Untruth and Method," *The New Republic* (May 15, 2000), pp. 36–45, and Wolin, "Socratic Apology," *Bookforum*, (Summer 2003) (www.bookforum.com/archive/sum_03/wolin.html). I have challenged Wolin's interpretations in a book review of *Heidegger's Children: Bulletin of Science, Technology and Society*, Vol. 23, no. 6 (December 2003), pp. 486–487.

[3] "Gadamer on Strauss: An Interview," *Interpretation*, Vol. 12, no. 1 (Jan. 1984), p. 10: "for me the tradition remains a living tradition." Cf. Catherine H. Zuckert, *Postmodern Platos* (Chicago: University of Chicago Press, 1996), p. 270: for Gadamer, "there are [in principle] no unbridgeable rifts or differences." See also Gadamer's statement that "philosophy is a human experience that remains the same and that characterizes the human being as such.... There is no progress in it, but only participation" (cited in Zuckert, p. 71).

[4] To see the impact of this Gadamerian theme on the early Habermas, see the text entitled "The Classical Doctrine of Politics," in Habermas, *Theory and Practice*, trans. John Viertel (London: Heinemann, 1974), chapter 1; page 286, note 4 acknowledges his debt to Gadamer.

and no "science" or rule-governed intellectual mastery of the world will discharge us from the burden of coming to responsible judgments about our shared life. Building up and sustaining civic solidarity, creating laws and institutions, treating other members of our society, and members of other societies, as partners in a human dialogue – all of this is a matter of reflective judgment, hence we need ethical and dialogical resources that science, or theory in general, can never give us. These pillars of Gadamerian hermeneutics may well have the appearance of easy commonplaces, and maybe they are. But if so, Gadamer insists that we must be reminded of such commonplaces on account of what he again and again refers to as the "one-sidedness" of our scientific-technological civilization, which raises the pretensions of theory to unprecedented levels, and thereby slights the modest but indispensable contribution of ordinary lay (as opposed to expert) judgment and reflection.

The same problem of theory and practice, paradoxically enough, is posed by the unsettling figure of Heidegger. When a singular genius suddenly appears and claims to have penetrated the "original sin" of "the West" as a cultural totality (defined by the relentless "forgetfulness of Being" whose seed was originally planted by the Greeks but which comes to full blossoming in modernity), the ordinary capacities of human beings to reflect on their lives, to make ethical and political judgments, and to pursue dialogue with fellow citizens, come to seem beside the point. The relevance of these prosaic human capacities pales in comparison with the grand or heroic theory that depicts humanity's falling away from its own essence. So here again, in a very different way naturally, theory trumps or eclipses practice. And once again, Gadamer's philosophical mission is to reassert the humble dignity of ordinary practical judgment, and to vindicate it against hubristic or overweening theory.[5] With respect to political philosophy, what

---

[5] Cf. Roy Boyne, "Interview with Hans-Georg Gadamer," *Theory, Culture & Society*, Vol. 5 (1988), p. 26: Heidegger, like Nietzsche, "was an extremist. [However compelling was his demonstration of] how our technological era is the last consequence of the Greek beginning ... I am much less certain about Heidegger's vision of the complete forgetfulness of being, something which parallels the last man of Nietzsche.... Complete forgetfulness of being cannot be achieved; just as death will not be eliminated from human life, I'm almost sure that the industrial-technological revolution will not entirely transform the human condition." Cf. Gadamer, *Philosophical Apprenticeships*, trans. Robert R. Sullivan (Cambridge, MA: MIT Press, 1985), p. 170 (on Nietzsche and Heidegger's "radical recklessness of thinking"); as well as Gadamer, *Truth and Method*, 2nd rev. ed. (New York: Continuum, 1998), p. 539 ("the experimental extremism of Nietzsche"). See also the discussion transcribed in "Gadamer on Strauss." Ernest L. Fortin, in his conversation with Gadamer, repeatedly presses Gadamer to acknowledge that the hermeneutical problem of fusing horizons arises specifically in a crisis-situation characterized by "the shattering of all horizons" (p. 10). In response, Gadamer insists that human societies never confront an extremity of this kind: there are always implicit solidarities, disagreements undergirded

Gadamer offers is primarily a doctrine of prudence, and he relies mainly on Aristotle in developing and deploying this doctrine, which makes perfect sense in relation to the theme of theory and practice already discussed. Ethical life, in the Gadamerian view, is a "bottom-up," not a "top-down," construction, drawn from concrete experiences of social solidarity and dialogue about how to realize human ends, and, to the extent that the theory-infatuated character of modern experience suggests otherwise, return to the Greeks (especially Aristotle) can help remind us of the primacy of practice. Gadamer is hardly alone in making such points, but his hermeneutics is intended to provide us with a philosophical vocabulary – including making the word "hermeneutics" familiar and available to us – that helps us articulate what perhaps, at a deeper level, we all already know. Again, it may be that much of this is reducible to familiar commonplaces of human life, but it should be appreciated that Gadamer's appeals to the ordinary and the prosaic, mediated through Aristotelian conceptions like *ethos* (habituation) and *phronesis* (practical judgment), is very deliberate indeed and is intended as a corrective to what he sees as the various damaging forms of modern hubris – whether the hubris of modern scientism or the hubris of a philosopher-prophet like Heidegger.

As Gadamer writes in his essay, "The Heritage of Hegel," his appeal to the dialogical almost looks like "blind optimism" relative to the "eschatological pathos" of a Nietzsche or Heidegger. This "optimism," such as it is, flows directly from Gadamer's "profound skepticism regarding the role of 'intellectuals' and especially of philosophy in humanity's household of life."[6] This is a crucial theme in Gadamer's approach to theory, and we will come back to it repeatedly in this chapter. Philosophy, to be sure, is a central part of what secures the humanity of human beings; yet even philosophy doesn't displace from its primacy "the great equilibrium of what is living,

by a deeper foundation of agreement, efforts to orient one's judgment upheld by living and sustaining traditions. The depiction of a "cataclysmic" crisis of meaning (p. 9), whether by Nietzsche, by Heidegger, or by Leo Strauss, is in Gadamer's view in every case a matter of improperly underestimating what is constant and continuous in human experience. These are perennial Gadamerian themes (which may be of some relevance in explaining why Gadamer, in his chapter devoted to Karl Löwith in *Philosophical Apprenticeships*, repeatedly refers to himself as having "taken the same path" as Löwith). Putting so much emphasis on the idea of crisis is, for him, another instance of a pathological overweighting of theory in the balance between theory and practice. These issues get importantly debated between Gadamer and Strauss in their published correspondence, which Fortin refers to in his interview: see Leo Strauss and Hans-Georg Gadamer, "Correspondence Concerning *Wahrheit und Methode*," *Independent Journal of Philosophy*, Vol. 2 (1978), pp. 5–12.

6 Hans-Georg Gadamer, *Reason in the Age of Science*, trans. Frederick G. Lawrence (Cambridge, MA: MIT Press, 1981), p. 58. On Gadamerian "optimism," cf. our epigraph to the epilogue.

which sustains and permeates the individual in his privacy as well as in his social constitution and in his view of life."[7] The leading exemplars of Greek theory not unreasonably affirmed *theoria* as "the supreme form of human life," yet Greek wisdom "also knew that such theory is embedded within the practice of conditioned and lived life and is borne along by it."[8]

Gadamer did not invent the term *hermeneutics*, but he, more than any other theorist, gave the notion of hermeneutics renewed philosophical relevance (including its relevance for political philosophy). What does hermeneutics in its Gadamerian use mean? In trying to figure out how to orient ourselves within our present life-situation, we are not confined to the bare resources of our own selfhood (insofar as there is such a thing as the bare self). We put ourselves into dialogue with alien interlocutors in space and time – the traditions that form us, the forms of art and literature and philosophy that challenge our understandings of the world, the variety of unfamiliar cultures that again challenge the sufficiency of our own horizons – and allow all of these to alter the shape of our own self-understanding. For Gadamer, none of this is in any way restricted to cultural elites; on the contrary, *all* human beings are hermeneutical creatures struggling to make reasonable judgments concerning their concrete life-situation in the light of more open-horizoned reflection. This unfolds according to a circular process: we interpret alien horizons in the light of where we stand, and where we stand gets reinterpreted in the light of our exposure to these experiences of otherness.

We cannot pluck ourselves out of our own historicity; we have to start from where we start, with an experience of life pre-shaped by life in a particular society in a particular time and place. But starting where we start doesn't oblige us to end there. We open ourselves to horizons beyond those that are natural to us; self-alienation is an essential aspect of what makes us human. In Gadamer's famous phrase, we "fuse horizons" between what is familiar and what is strange, and allow each to challenge and be challenged by the other. Our horizons *expand* as we pursue the dialogical possibilities of historical existence. The need to engage hermeneutically with what is

---

[7] *Reason in the Age of Science*, p. 58.

[8] Ibid., p. 59. Cf. "Gadamer on Strauss," pp. 12–13: Aristotle understood that "we are mortals and not gods." We would perhaps be able to choose between the theoretical life and the practical life if we could be gods; as it is, "we have to take both lives into account." As mortals rather than gods, "we remain embedded in the social structures and the normative perspectives in which we were reared and must recognize that we are part of a development that always proceeds on the basis of some preshaped view." For Gadamer, that is a hermeneutical reality ("a fundamentally and inescapably hermeneutical situation") that cannot under any circumstances be conjured away.

foreign (ancient texts; problems of linguistic translation that are especially challenging; forms of poetry, music, or art that confound our usual expectations; the testing of our moral and political judgment in ways that seem to carry us into unexplored territory; and so on) is not a matter for specialists or scholars per se: it is a universal human task. Connecting ourselves to other cultures and other epochs is not effortless, it requires imaginative bridge-building and hermeneutical exertion, but without such hermeneutical exertion, our humanity is diminished.

The core of Gadamer's philosophy is a repudiation of the Hegelian aspiration to a *completion* of knowledge, to full *transparency* of self-understanding. This simply is not possible. Knowledge is always incomplete; self-understanding is always partially opaque. There are no techniques or short-cuts that guarantee either knowledge or self-knowledge. This leads to a teaching of radical finitude. We cannot extract ourselves from the history that we have lived and the social embodiedness that we are, but neither can we accept this history and cultural experience as dictating fixed boundaries. All human life is limitlessly open-ended as an adventure of unceasing interpretation and reinterpretation. Literary and philosophical texts of the past, cultural artifacts of the past, historical self-understanding developed over time – all of this is put in question by our very different historically-shaped horizons, but they in turn put in question our present historicity. We challenge the past and the past challenges us. In short, human life is itself a dialogical enterprise.

Are these new philosophical discoveries, or do they verge on banal truisms? For Gadamer, our civilization has moved in the direction of a one-sided worship of technology and a cult of expertise. One might think of this as a weakened or muted version of Heidegger's "forgetfulness of Being" thesis.[9] Gadamer thinks that in this context, it is essential that we remind ourselves of quite prosaic facts about human experience – the fact that we are shaped in our common human experience by a dialogue with the past; the fact that all of us have substantial ethical and cultural resources for the making of reasonable judgments, provided to us by the simple fact of having been socialized within a historically unfolded social environment; the fact that we always start within a given horizon, but that these are never rigidly

---

[9] Cf. "Correspondence Concerning *Wahrheit und Methode*," p. 8, referring to "the unreality of" Heidegger's assertion in regard to "the *complete forgetfulness of being*." Gadamer's view is that our fixation on the technical mastery of the natural and social world occludes quite a lot. But the self-occlusion is never carried so far that we cannot give ourselves salutary reminders of what we have forgotten, and hence claw ourselves back from the pure oblivion of Being.

fixed horizons – that they contract or expand depending on whether we exert ourselves in dialogue with otherness; the fact that *all* of human life and human experience elicits and demands interpretation and judgment; the fact that all truths are humanly appropriated truths, that all knowing depends on the deployment of our full human being.[10] What Gadamer is saying is that a more sober version of Heidegger's forgetfulness of being thesis is indeed true, but the appropriate response is neither Nietzschean hysteria and anti-rationalism nor Heideggerian extremism and prophetism, but simply a reaffirmation of common human reasonableness.

In the interview with Ernest Fortin, Gadamer pronounces himself to be a faithful "Platonist."[11] Of course, being a Platonist can mean radically different things depending on how one interprets Plato. For Hannah Arendt, Platonism means reducing politics in its authentic spontaneity to mere craftsmanship or techne. For Leo Strauss, it means esotericism, and the imperative to protect the shackled cave-dwellers from the subversive truths of the philosopher. For Eric Voegelin and Simone Weil, it means the promise of transcendence and hence a pagan anticipation of the truth of Christianity. What does being a Platonist mean for Gadamer?

The heart of a Platonic stance toward the social and political world, on Gadamer's construal, is "that there is no city in the world in which the ideal city is not present in some ultimate sense. [Recall] the famous statement about the gang of robbers whose members need some sense of justice in order to get along with one another. Well, that is indeed my perhaps overly conservative position."[12] If this is intended as a political philosophy, it would seem to set the bar exceptionally low with respect to its standard for judging human societies. Are we supposed to be *reassured*, in the midst of our current predicaments and of looming political challenges, to be told that even a band of criminals has its own proper solidarities, and therefore, that there is an intimation of the just city even in societies that are anything but just? I put exactly this challenge to Gadamer following a lecture entitled "Practical Philosophy Today" that he gave at Queen's University (Kingston,

---

[10] As Gadamer points out on page 137 of *Reason in the Age of Science*, the last of these hermeneutical insights corresponds to Aristotle's conception of politics as the "architectonic" science, in the sense of "embrac[ing] within itself all the sciences and arts of the ancient system," including, for instance, rhetoric as an essential human capacity. Hence: "the claim to universality on the part of hermeneutics consists of integrating all the sciences."

[11] "Gadamer on Strauss," p. 10.

[12] Ibid. For the text referred to by Gadamer, see *The Republic of Plato*, trans. Allan Bloom (New York: Basic Books, 1991), p. 30.

Ontario) on November 21, 1984 (in which he used many of the same lines that I have just quoted from the Fortin interview[13]). He responded[14] by saying that the fundamental context of Platonic-Aristotelian philosophy was the decline of the Greek polis. They did not have a philosophical solution to this decline, nor would it have been appropriate for them as philosophers to *presume* to have such a solution.[15] Like us, they lived in a society marked by ethical "corrosion." Yet it wasn't their job to offer prescriptions: Plato's *seeming* prescriptions in *The Republic* are transparently satirical. The byword of ancient political philosophy was *modesty*. This modesty was part of the Socratic legacy of both Plato and Aristotle. Aristotle's purpose was not to prescribe a remedy for the decline of the polis, but simply to remind people of what they were losing.[16]

We could perhaps brand this "Platonic minimalism": rather than taking our bearings from a utopian vision of justice and wisdom, we search out consoling traces of human fellowship even in societies where the expectations of civic solidarity are severely attenuated. Is there a political philosophy in all these counsels of humility? One could say that the core of Gadamerian political philosophy consists in the *critique of sophism* (which according to his reading is also the core of Socratic, Platonic, and Aristotelian political philosophy).[17] "The ideal of a political science that is not based on the lived experience of *phronesis* would be sophistic from Aristotle's point of view."[18]

---

[13] Similar lines also recur in the letter to Richard J. Bernstein appended to Bernstein's book, *Beyond Objectivism and Relativism* (Philadelphia: University of Pennsylvania Press, 1983). In particular, see page 264: "the displacement of human reality never even goes so far that no forms of solidarity exist any longer. Plato saw this very well: there is no city so corrupted that it does not realize something of the true city; that is what, in my opinion, is the basis for the possibility of practical philosophy." Quite clearly, this line of thought is in close proximity with Gadamer's repudiation of the radical Heideggerian specter of the oblivion of Being in consummately modern societies: the technicization of modern life may trump human solidarities up to a certain point, but this eclipse of the human way of being-together never goes so far that it isn't recuperable. Another way of putting the point is that (for Gadamer) Plato understood "the human realities" better than Heidegger did; Heidegger was so carried away by his vision of the abyss of modernity that he lost sight of certain basic verities that the Greeks, in their wisdom, never lost sight of.

[14] In what follows, I am drawing on the lecture notes I took during Gadamer's lecture.

[15] Cf. Chapter 6, note 30, quoting Voegelin to the effect that Plato and Aristotle knew the polis to be "doomed," and had no remedy to offer.

[16] This comes close to serving as an encapsulation of Gadamerian hermeneutics: the hermeneutical philosopher's primary mission is to remind people of the homely truths about ethical and cultural experience that are in danger of being eclipsed by a scientistic-technological society.

[17] Cf. Gadamer, *Philosophical Apprenticeships*, p. 181.

[18] "Gadamer on Strauss," p. 12. When Gadamer puts to Strauss the challenge that he fails to give sufficient weight to the classics' "absolute distinction between a politike techne and a politike phronesis" (*Truth and Method*, 2nd rev. ed., p. 541), he basically means that Strauss hopes to draw more of a positive doctrine out of Plato and Aristotle than they intended to supply.

For Gadamer, human beings ultimately have to make concrete practical choices, and being educated in a particular society nourished by whatever ethical resources that society is capable of supplying is really the only relevant consideration. The interpretation of texts is one hermeneutical skill among an endlessly extended range of ways of applying our human wisdom; hermeneutics in a vastly broader sense means being able to make the judgments that are called for *here* and *now*. To be sure, we presume that there is a long-term destiny of the human species (our eventual fate may well be that of extinction as suffered by other species), but it does not absolve us of our responsibility to make good judgments in the context at hand. As Gadamer interestingly puts it, "looking on a map of Germany [will not be helpful in trying to] decide where in my garden I should plant a particular flower." [19] The ethical and political challenges that really count are radically context-bound, [20] and an appeal to philosophical generalities as if they were capable of meeting our essential tasks as hermeneutical practitioners (including the hermeneutical praxis of simple citizenship) is always a form of sophism.

Philosophy is a perennial human pursuit, but even the philosopher is no less a human being – that is, a mortal creature joined with his or her fellows in the phronetic challenges of living a reasonable social life. [21] The fact that certain human beings are motivated to participate in the perennialness of philosophy is constitutive of our humanity, but no less constitutive of our humanity is our human obligation to exercise moral and political judgment in particular situations of choice ("where in my garden I should plant a particular flower") inescapably governed by circumstances I have not chosen. In Gadamer's view, *ethos* is what determines ethical life, and ethos can never be legislated by mere philosophers. To quote from the lecture I attended in 1984: "One cannot be convinced by argument to be virtuous. One must

[19] Boyne, "Interview with Hans-Georg Gadamer," p. 33.

[20] I once heard Stanley Rosen refer to Gadamer as a "trimmer" (that is, as someone who could, "fox"-like, manage to adapt to life under any regime that happened to be in power, whether fascist, or communist, or liberal). One has to wonder whether this is a natural effect of making phronesis (that is, context-governed practical judgment) the central category of one's political philosophy.

[21] Let me repeat a key a passage from the Fortin interview that goes to the heart of Gadamer's thought: "We are mortals not gods," a condition from which philosophers are in no way exempt. "We remain embedded in the social structures and the normative perspectives in which we were reared and must recognize that we [including we philosophers] are part of a development that always proceeds on the basis of some preshaped view" ("Gadamer on Strauss," pp. 12–13); cf. *Gadamer in Conversation: Reflections and Commentary*, ed. Richard E. Palmer (New Haven, CT: Yale University Press, 2001), p. 85. Philosophers are constantly tempted hubristically to forget this truth, but Greek wisdom, read correctly, brings it home to us again. A similar thought is expressed by MacIntyre: "in her or his practical life a moral philosopher is just one more type of plain person [i.e., non-philosopher]" (*The MacIntyre Reader*, ed. Kelvin Knight [Notre Dame, IN: University of Notre Dame Press, 1998], p. 147).

be 'solidarized' already. The simple man with a pure heart (as depicted by Rousseau and by Kant) has what is needed. It is pure arrogance to think that philosophy can supply it. Ethos is required — that is, the formation of normative standards."[22]

It is not that we lower our standards in judging human societies. It is just that we recognize that whatever ethical resources exist in a particular society derive from processes of moral habituation that are not subject to intellectual legislation[23]; and we learn from Plato and Aristotle as well as Rousseau and Kant that philosophers must avoid at all costs the arrogance of thinking that *they themselves* constitute society's moral anchor. Again, philosophical wisdom consists in the *negative* doctrine of eschewing hubris, rather than any positive prescriptions that will only have the effect of inflating philosophers' sense of their own importance. That is, one takes manifestations of human solidarity wherever one is able to find them, and doesn't delude oneself into according any special privilege to the practical wisdom of philosophers.[24]

Today, many theorists (postmodernists, for instance, or those influenced by Alasdair MacIntyre) assume that our time is one *uniquely* riven by incommensurable or near-incommensurable views of life. Gadamer insists that this isn't so — that the challenges of overcoming seeming incommensurabilities and the clash of putatively unbridgeable perspectives are in no way unique to our own culture. As he puts it in the letter to Bernstein: "The conflict of traditions we have today does not seem to me anything exceptional. Phronesis is *always* the process of distinguishing and choosing what one considers to be right [in the face of competing horizons]."[25] In the epilogue to this book, I cite a striking passage from the opening of the Fortin interview where Gadamer recalls how, in the wake of the German defeat in the Great War and the feelings of profound disorientation that it induced, thoughtful young students groped for some sense of an Archimedean point (perhaps to

---

[22] As before, I am relying on the lecture notes I took during Gadamer's lecture.

[23] Cf. "Gadamer on Strauss," p. 10: "As you know, we are formed between the ages of fourteen and eighteen. Academic teachers always come too late. In the best instance, they can train young scholars, but their function is not to build up character."

[24] Cf. *Reason in the Age of Science*, p. 112: Aristotle was right to view ethics as "only a theoretical enterprise"; "anything said by way of a theoretic description of the forms of right living can be at best of little help when it comes to the concrete application to the human experience of life." That is, the human responsibility to arrive at the judgments that are called for in concrete life-situations necessarily outstrips what theory can supply (hence Aristotle's crucial emphasis on the centrality of phronesis).

[25] *Beyond Objectivism and Relativism*, pp. 264–265; my italics. Similar points are made in Gadamer's critical response to MacIntyre. See Gadamer, "Gibt es auf Erden ein Maβ," *Philosophische Rundschau*, Vol. 32, no. 1/2½ (1985), pp. 1–7.

be found, they thought, in Weber or Von Gierke or Rabindranath Tagore).[26] Yet for the committed hermeneuticist, this is the human situation per se: we find ourselves at the intersection of not-easy-to-commensurate horizons, and we are obliged to help them speak to each other. We thereby give effect to our essentially dialogical nature.

One might say that Gadamer combines what is best in Habermas and what is best in Heidegger. What is best in Habermas is an acute appreciation of social-political life as a dialogical/communicative process. What is best in Heidegger is a powerful account of human finitude and historicity. Gadamer thinks Heidegger was right to place the emphasis on human finitude that he did, but Heidegger's way of doing philosophy (with its exaggerated pathos and its assumption of Hölderlinian poses) betrayed this insight. In short, Gadamer gives us Habermasian universalism *and* Heideggerian historicity. Let me conclude by trying to pose some critical questions about Gadamer's way of doing philosophy.[27] The question I want to raise is: *Is there something "post-philosophical" about Gadamer's philosophy?*[28] It is appropriate to wonder whether Gadamer makes available an actual political philosophy – a question we have already had occasion to ask at least once or twice in this chapter. (He often offers explicit disclaimers about his capacity to provide an ethics, and defends Heidegger's refusal to offer one.[29]) At various stages of my intellectual career, I have considered myself a Gadamerian political philosopher, so obviously in some sense I think that important and interesting things can be drawn out of Gadamer's philosophy that can speak to and instruct political philosophers. Nevertheless, one should take seriously the possibility that there is something to be said on behalf of Gadamer's self-understanding

---

[26] "Gadamer on Strauss," p. 1.

[27] A thoughtful Carleton University PhD thesis (entitled "Tradition and Dialogue in Hermeneutical Political Philosophy") by Devrim Sezer has been helpful to me in thinking through some of these questions.

[28] As commented on elsewhere in this book, virtually everyone doing philosophy today considers himself or herself to be anti-foundationalist, which it is possible to rephrase by saying: "We are all hermeneuticists today." But this in turn means that relative to the kind of epic theorizing celebrated in this book, in some basic sense there is something "post-philosophical" about philosophy as practiced by a broad range of contemporary philosophers. I don't find it surprising that the philosophical tradition is where it is, but I do think it poses a real problem for the continuing vitality of the theoretical enterprise. Similar thoughts were given memorable expression by Nietzsche in his acute depiction, in *On the Advantage and Disadvantage of History for Life*, of nineteenth-century historicists as men "born with gray hair," already consigned to the civilizational rocking-chair of an old people's home of the entire species, for whom human culture has lost any possibility of renewed youth or innocence.

[29] See, for instance, Gadamer, "On the Possibility of a Philosophical Ethics," in *Kant and Political Philosophy: The Contemporary Legacy*, ed. Ronald Beiner and William James Booth (New Haven, CT: Yale University Press, 1993), p. 362.

in this respect – namely, the self-understanding expressed in his disclaimers. Indeed, is it possible that there is more of a political philosophy in both Habermas on one side and Heidegger on the other side than there is in Gadamer? Heidegger is straightforwardly "Heideggerian" (admittedly, it sounds a bit bizarre to put it like this) and Habermas is straightforwardly Kantian or neo-Kantian. Gadamer, on the other hand, is committed to drawing the best from the entire history of philosophy, which in some sense means "hovering above it" – not committed to some particular position *within* the history of philosophy that doesn't get subsumed into a broader pan-philosophical synthesis. Precisely the *synthetic* character of Gadamer's philosophy (Platonic/Aristotelian/Hegelian/Heideggerian) makes it both more attractive politically *and* perhaps less interesting philosophically.

In the end, we come back to the issue with which we began. Gadamer's fundamental problem is to reconcile the critique of modernity that he shares with other post-Heideggerians with his intention to moderate Heideggerian radicalism. Quite telling for me is the following text: "Like many of my critics, Heidegger too would probably feel a lack of ultimate radicality in the conclusions I draw."[30] However, in implied criticism of Heidegger, Gadamer counters: "the role of prophet, of Cassandra, of preacher ... does not suit [the philosopher]. What man needs is not just the persistent posing of ultimate questions, but the sense of what is feasible, what is possible, what is correct, here and now."[31] Thus hermeneutics, rightly conceived, "limits the position of the philosopher in the modern world."[32] I certainly agree (agree emphatically!) with what Gadamer says here. But implicit in the alternatives he poses is a kind of turning away from philosophy. "What man needs" is *both* "the posing of ultimate questions" (philosophy practiced with Heideggerian radicality) and judgment about what makes sense practically (civic-minded prudence). The purpose of Gadamer's hermeneutics, in all its modesty and self-restraint, is to provide theoretical support for the latter. This is a kind of philosophy that very deliberately (and in some sense for *political* reasons) does not want to pose ultimate questions – namely, on account of the very real perils of Heideggerian philosophical radicalism.[33]

Such tensions show themselves not only in Gadamer's stance toward Heidegger and philosophy, but also in the substance of his own thought.

[30] *Truth and Method*, 2nd rev. ed., p. xxxvii (Foreword to the Second [German] Edition).
[31] Ibid., p. xxxviii.
[32] Ibid.
[33] Cf. our remarks concerning Isaiah Berlin in the first prologue.

For Gadamer, practical philosophy in the Aristotelian mode fundamentally means knowledge in the art of living. As we have seen, this is necessarily a *context-bound* form of knowledge (which runs counter to our general assumptions about what defines modern science). The decisive question in Gadamer's philosophy is: Is this a knowledge we still possess, or for which there is at least a good possibility of acquiring it? Both *yes* and *no* answers to this question exert a powerful gravitational pull on Gadamer. As regards the yes answer, we have already examined various texts – such as the correspondence with Leo Strauss, the letter to Richard Bernstein, and the interview with Ernest Fortin – in which he refers to the "unreality" of Heidegger's musings about a "night of Being" and so on, and insists that technical reason can never extend its empire sufficiently to "displace" the forms of human solidarity that are constitutive of our ethical life.[34] A darker, less confident tone can be heard in a text entitled "Hermeneutics and Social Science" presented at a symposium at Boston College in April, 1974:

The opinions which form the patterns of social life and constitute the normative conditions for solidarity are today dominated to a great extent by the technical and economic organisations within our civilization. Immediate and natural interaction in the course of daily life is no longer the unique source and the dominant mode for the elaboration of common convictions and normative ideas. That is why the alienation of the common citizen from public affairs is increasing and why the reaction against this precarious disintegrative power, i.e., against the "establishment," is so strong. How can we learn to recover our natural reason and our moral and political prudence? In other words, how can we reintegrate the tremendous power of our technique within a well-balanced order of the society and reconstitute a living solidarity?[35]

The question implicit in this text is: If "living solidarity" is not a given but something that must be "recovered" and "reconstituted" in the midst of a techne-dominated civilization, don't we need a mode of theorizing considerably more radical than the minimalist Platonism and conservative Aristotelianism sketched through most of this chapter?

---

[34] Cf. *Truth and Method*, 2nd rev. ed., p. xxxvii: the function of Gadamer's hermeneutics is to act as a "corrective" to the imagined specter of "science expand[ing] into a total technocracy," which (if it were true) could be plausibly interpreted as a realization of Nietzsche's prophecy of nihilism and Heidegger's heralding of "cosmic night."

[35] Gadamer, "Hermeneutics and Social Science," *Cultural Hermeneutics*, Vol. 2, no. 4 (January 1975), p. 314. This journal was later re-named *Philosophy and Social Criticism*.

9
Jürgen Habermas: Politics as Rational Discourse

Jürgen Habermas has had a long and fruitful intellectual career. One can distinguish different phases of his life's work, though running through all of these stages in the unfolding of his political philosophy are the twin themes of *the public sphere* and *communicative rationality*. He first came on the scene in 1962 with an interesting book on the history and sociology of the notions of publicity, public opinion, and the bourgeois public sphere, as these took shape in eighteenth-century European societies.[1] In 1968, he published an important work trying to establish the possibility of a form of knowledge constituted by a universal human interest in emancipation.[2] Habermas here takes psychoanalysis as his model of a type of knowledge serving an emancipatory human interest, where the analyst helps the patient throw off neuroses that inhibit or block his or her potentialities as a human being. However, Gadamer argues effectively against Habermas, in a famous debate between the two of them, that it would be more than a little worrisome for the society as a whole to put itself in the hands of "therapists," as the patient seeking help in being liberated from the grip of neuroses does, thus privileging the therapist's supposedly superior understanding over the self-understanding of the rest of us.[3]

Habermas then devoted a big chunk of his career to trying to draw a political philosophy out of the philosophy of language with his conception of an *ideal speech situation* as the standard by which we measure whether our

[1] English version: Jürgen Habermas, *The Structural Transformation of the Public Sphere: An Inquiry into a Category of Bourgeois Society*, trans. Thomas Burger (Cambridge, MA: MIT Press, 1989).
[2] English version: Habermas, *Knowledge and Human Interests*, trans. Jeremy J. Shapiro (Boston: Beacon Press, 1971).
[3] See, for instance, Hans-Georg Gadamer, *Philosophical Hermeneutics*, ed. David E. Linge (Berkeley: University of California Press, 1976), pp. 40–42. In support of Gadamer's side of the debate, consider the lampoon of psychoanalytic therapy in Philip Roth's *My Life as a Man*.

practice of politics is what it should be.[4] This is a conception that Habermas developed in a highly technical idiom, notwithstanding the simplicity of the basic idea. What is that basic idea? It is that no one would enter into a political debate (an exchange of presumed-to-be-valid reasons) unless they were already committed to the outcome reposing on the rational vindication of one set of reasons over its competitors, rather than non-rational considerations of whatever kind. It is supposed to follow from this that the normative ideal in play here is not simply conjured up by the theorist but is *immanent in political life itself*. To quote one of Habermas's own formulations: "discourse ethics puts forth [the thesis] that anyone who seriously undertakes to participate in argumentation implicitly accepts by that very undertaking general pragmatic presuppositions that have a normative content. The moral principle [disclosed by discourse ethics] can then be derived from the content of these presuppositions of argumentation if one knows at least what it means to justify a norm of action."[5] These "pragmatic presuppositions" are presumably robustly egalitarian, and hence Habermas's theoretical strategy is to establish a foothold for an egalitarian political vision on the basis of strictly "formalist and universalist assumptions" – formalist and universalist assumptions that, on Habermas's account, are taken on board by all communicative actors, willy-nilly, by virtue of *being* communicative actors.[6]

But of course, as Habermas knows, actual political existence never unfolds according to the ideal norms of communicative rationality, hence the decisive question is whether Habermasian political philosophy, as thus formulated, is fatally impugned by its utopianism, or whether philosophical elucidation of the always-presupposed norm of free and equal exchange of reasons

---

[4] For a text that is emblematic of this phase of Habermas's oeuvre, see, for instance, "Discourse Ethics: Notes on a Program of Philosophical Justification," in Habermas, *Moral Consciousness and Communicative Action*, trans. Christian Lenhardt and Shierry Weber Nicholsen (Cambridge, MA: MIT Press, 1990).

[5] Habermas, "Morality and Ethical Life: Does Hegel's Critique of Kant Apply to Discourse Ethics?" in *Kant and Political Philosophy*, ed. Ronald Beiner and William James Booth (New Haven: Yale University Press, 1993), p. 322.

[6] Ibid. It is clear that Habermas is firmly committed to what Charles Taylor has called a "procedural ethics." But Habermas's emphatic egalitarianism tells one that this proceduralism is presumed to yield a definite moral and political content. Hence there seems to be an element of having-your-cake-and-eating-it: that is, affirming a vigorously substantive moral and political philosophy while claiming that one's ethical theory is purely proceduralist. (One way of putting this would be to say: if everything really did rest on the outcome of an open-ended dialogue, one would imagine that it would be perfectly conceivable for conservatives to out-reason or out-argue liberals and radicals, yet Habermas seems to be assuming in advance that they won't.) My suspicion (supported by Taylor) is that what we get in Habermas – as is true of *all* forms of procedural ethics – is a case of moral content being smuggled in under the guise of proceduralism. See Taylor, "The Motivation behind a Procedural Ethics," in *Kant and Political Philosophy*, ed. Beiner and Booth.

provides helpful guidance in moving in the right direction. Throughout the writings in which Habermas develops these ideas, he insists that the metaphysical tradition is finished, and that therefore the appeal to reason can supply only the *formal* conditions of our communicative competence, not at all the substantive "worldviews" that philosophy in the past claimed to offer.[7] In one obvious sense, it is hard to imagine a less helpful theoretical construct than the ideal speech situation, for human communication can never be expected – certainly not in the constrained circumstances that we associate with political life – to live up to Habermas's transcendent standards of communicative equality and power-free discourse.[8] On the other hand, if one wants political philosophy to specify clear normative standards for judging why politics fails to satisfy the highest human ideals, the Habermasian ideal speech situation certainly does that.

In 1981, Habermas published a monumental two-volume treatise offering a systematic philosophical sociology intended to confront Weber's idea of Western rationalization on its own turf, but seeking to salvage normative possibilities that seem squeezed out by the Weberian "iron cage."[9] Habermas's fundamental ambition, as it culminates in *The Theory of Communicative Action*, is to synthesize sociology and normative theory in a way that both renders the sociology stronger and more normatively compelling and also renders the normative theory stronger and more sociologically compelling. The intellectual aspiration has been a high one, and Habermas's version of the

---

[7] See *Rationality To-day*, ed. Theodore F. Geraets (Ottawa: University of Ottawa Press, 1979), pp. 348–349, for a strong challenge by Gadamer to Habermas's project of a strictly formalist ethics. See also Gadamer, "Reply to My Critics," in *The Hermeneutic Tradition*, ed. G.L. Ormiston and A.D. Schrift (Albany, NY: SUNY Press, 1990), p. 293. I have very strong sympathy for Habermas's emphasis on truth, on reason, on free and equal communication, and on the idea of a robust public sphere. Still, Gadamer's challenges, which I have previously discussed in chapters 10 and 11 of Beiner, *Philosophy in a Time of Lost Spirit* (Toronto: University of Toronto Press, 1997), seem to me fundamentally right.

[8] What Habermas offers, arguably, is a politics for intellectuals. For a liberal-democratic critique of such a vision of politics, see Michael Walzer, *Politics and Passion* (New Haven, CT: Yale University Press, 2004), chapter 5; for a considerably harsher and tougher critique, see my discussion of James Fitzjames Stephen in relation to J.S. Mill in chapter 22 of *Civil Religion* (Cambridge: Cambridge University Press, 2011). At the beginning of Chapter 1, we cited Jeffrey C. Alexander's book, *The Performance of Politics*, with its endorsement of the Arendtian view that there is an essential performative dimension to politics. As Alexander's argument makes clear, Arendt's notion of politics as performance and Habermas's notion of politics as rational discourse are competing views, and as Alexander makes explicit on pages 11–12, it appears to follow from his account of the 2008 U.S. presidential election that Arendt's conception is closer than Habermas's conception to the reality of political life.

[9] English edition: Habermas, *The Theory of Communicative Action, Volume One: Reason and the Rationalization of Society*, trans. Thomas McCarthy (Boston: Beacon Press, 1984) and *Volume Two: Lifeworld and System: A Critique of Functionalist Reason*, trans. Thomas McCarthy (Boston: Beacon Press, 1987). For Weber's iron cage metaphor, see *The Protestant Ethic and the Spirit of Capitalism*, trans. Talcott Parsons (New York: Charles Scribner's Sons, 1958), pp. 181–182.

theory has been broadly influential. The question, of course, is whether the project has succeeded. The last of Habermas's large-scale treatises, *Between Facts and Norms* (originally published in German in 1992), offers a typically ambitious exploration of the relevance of communicative ethics for the constitutional norms of the kind of legal regime embodied in a modern liberal democracy.[10]

The work with which we are primarily concerned in this chapter, *The Philosophical Discourse of Modernity* (1985), is largely a dialogue with post-Nietzschean and post-Heideggerian tendencies in contemporary French thought that, if they were permitted to prevail philosophically, would defeat the fundamental purposes of Habermas's steadfast rationalism.[11] One of the key things that a modern political philosophy must deliver is a normative judgment on modernity. The thinkers canvassed in this book thus far are all in one way or another critics of modernity. (Some may consider Oakeshott an exception, although even in his case, his critique of "Rationalism," and his dire warnings about the "Tower of Babel" aspect of our civilization, may easily be construed as a critique of modernity.) Habermas is thus our first real *defender* of modernity (the other two being Rawls and Rorty),[12] and the plausibility of his political philosophy will hang fairly crucially on how compelling we find his vindication of modernity.

---

[10] English version: Habermas, *Between Facts and Norms: Contributions to a Discourse Theory of Law and Democracy*, trans. William Rehg (Cambridge, MA: MIT Press, 1996).

[11] English version: Habermas, *The Philosophical Discourse of Modernity: Twelve Lectures*, trans. Frederick G. Lawrence (Cambridge, MA: MIT Press, 1987); all parenthetical page references to come refer to this edition. It is possible to view what Habermas is doing in this work as a resumption of Lukács's critique of anti-rationalist philosophy in *The Destruction of Reason*. In fact, Habermas himself encourages such an understanding of his project (though the interview in which he made this suggestion predates *The Philosophical Discourse of Modernity*). See "The Dialectics of Rationalization: An Interview with Jürgen Habermas," *Telos*, no. 49 (1981), p. 12.

[12] MacIntyre's blanket rejection of modernity is uncontroversial. Of our twelve epic theorists, then, that leaves only Foucault, who, not untypically, goes out of his way to confound us. In "What is Enlightenment?" (*The Foucault Reader*, ed. Paul Rabinow [New York: Pantheon Books, 1984], pp. 32–50, esp. p. 39), Foucault, relying on Baudelaire, associates modernity with an "attitude" rather than an "epoch," and embraces it as a spur to aesthetic self-invention. The text is full of highly idiosyncratic gestures. In any case, we should not be fooled by this one rather bizarre essay into revising our judgment that Foucault's work delivers a truly severe indictment of modernity in the conventional sense.

There is a fairly direct correspondence between one's stance toward modernity and one's stance toward "liberalism" as a political philosophy. All the critics of modernity are (not by accident) critics of liberalism, and most defenders of modernity also defend liberalism (though of course Marx, for instance, is strongly committed to modernity while being equally strongly opposed to liberalism). Catherine Zuckert, in her recent edited volume, *Political Philosophy in the Twentieth Century*, places Habermas under the rubric of "Critiques of Liberalism." But notwithstanding his roots in the neo-Marxist tradition, Habermas is no less a liberal than John Rawls is. Cf. the telling point made by Perry Anderson that we cite in the first prologue, note 11.

At the risk of startling the reader, I want to begin the discussion of *The Philosophical Discourse of Modernity* with a comparison of Habermas and Leo Strauss. Habermas, no less than Strauss, sees our current situation in terms of a comprehensive challenge or set of challenges to philosophical reason and normative reason. However, this "crisis of reason," if we want to call it that, erupts not on account of the rise of modernity (Strauss's narrative), but precisely with the unfolding of a philosophical movement, or more precisely a set of overlapping but distinct philosophical movements, characterized by a fundamental embrace of *anti*-modernity. For Strauss, the crisis is a distancing from nature brought about by modernity's impulse to assert mastery over nature; for Habermas, the crisis is one of a backlash *against* modernity – which requires a restatement of the (still defensible) normative core of modernity by distinguishing what is normatively attractive from what is normatively problematic, and showing that modernity was a reasonable project with respect to its central aspirations.

The idea of communicative rationality is as central to Habermas's political philosophy as the idea of worldliness is to Arendt's political philosophy, or as the idea of power/knowledge is to Foucault's political philosophy, or as the idea of the common good is to MacIntyre's political philosophy. As far as *The Philosophical Discourse of Modernity* is concerned, the success or lack of success of Habermas's project really hangs on the last two chapters of the book (Lecture 11, on "Communicative versus Subject-Centered Reason," and Lecture 12, on "The Normative Content of Modernity"), so that is where we will focus our main discussion. But first, let's start with Lecture 1.

Habermas's starting-point is the idea that there is a kind of severance or detachment between "cultural modernity," on the one hand, and structures of economic or administrative "modernization" on the other (pp. 1–5).[13] In the language of *The Theory of Communicative Action*, this is a cleaving-apart of "lifeworld" and "system."[14] The cultural aspect of modernity is associated with the full ensemble of Enlightenment ideals:

---

[13] See in particular page 3, citing the views of Arnold Gehlen (which he associates with a "*neoconservative* leave-taking from modernity"): "a self-sufficiently advancing modernization of society has separated itself from the impulses of a cultural modernity that has seemingly become obsolete in the meantime; it only carries out the functional laws of economy and state, technology and science, which are supposed to have amalgamated into a system that cannot be influenced." The idea is that, according to this grim "neoconservative" depiction of modernity, "the husk of a cultural self-understanding of modernity" (p. 4) has been rendered basically irrelevant.

[14] Cf. page 12, on how "societal modernization tears apart [traditional] lifeworlds."

freedom, rationality, liberation from unreflective traditions, secularization. But the central preoccupation for Habermas is how these defining cultural ideals of modernity relate to the functionalist machinery of "modernization": in particular, "the capitalist enterprise" and "the bureaucratic state apparatus" as the twin pillars of "purposive-rational economic and administrative action" (pp. 1–2). This is the "system" side of modernity, and any attempted vindication of modernity in the face of both its neoconservative and its postmodern enemies[15] needs to address the fundamental question at the heart of post-Weberian sociology, namely, the problem of how the cultural or lifeworld side of modernity can be saved from reduction merely to the administrative, purposive-rational, or functionalist side of modernity. Is the sociological reality of modernity sufficiently and exhaustively defined by an account focusing on "modernization," or is there a cultural and normative dimension to modernity that is still intact and that surpasses its functionalist dimensions? Does modernity qua system swallow up or supersede modernity qua lifeworld? What is at stake here, obviously, is not just an adequate *sociological* account of modernity, but more importantly, the question of the appropriate *philosophical* judgment to be rendered upon modernity. Answering the questions that Habermas inherits from Weber requires not just debates between competing sociologies, but also debates between competing political philosophies (hence the choice of Hegel, Nietzsche, Heidegger, Adorno, Derrida, and Foucault as the key interlocutors).

Lecture 1 suggests that Habermas is preoccupied with the issue of modernity's relation to tradition. The issue of whether there is a meaningful cultural or normative core to modernity would be much more straightforward if modernity could draw its basic orientation toward the lifeworld from normative anchors in the past, but Habermas seems to be saying that it is somehow central to modernity's self-understanding that all such anchors are gone.[16]

[15] Habermas's suggestion is that the latter are (unintentionally) in league with the former; hence he speaks of neoconservative and postmodern thinkers as *together* "cloaking their complicity with the venerable tradition of counter-Enlightenment in the garb of post-Enlightenment" (p. 5). His famous characterization of Foucault as a "Young Conservative" ("Modernity versus Postmodernity," *New German Critique*, Vol. 22, no. 3 [1981], pp. 3–14) – i.e., aligning Foucault with leading German reactionaries of the post-World War I generation – carries the same implication. Habermas's primary target here is Foucault. But as should be obvious – given Habermas's intellectual roots in the Frankfurt School – the fact that Adorno's view of modernity was not any less unspeakably grim than Foucault's means that the Habermas-Foucault debate concerning modernity cannot help but directly engage Habermas's own intellectual identity, namely, as someone who inherited the mantle of the Frankfurt School and then undertook to liberalize this inheritance and reconcile it with modernity.

[16] There is some degree of family resemblance here with the Arendtian refrain that the thread of tradition is torn and unmendable. See note 1 of our Gadamer chapter.

Modernity as modernity *"has to create its normativity out of itself"* (p. 7; Habermas's italics); the problem of modernity per se consists in somehow "grounding modernity out of itself" (p. 8).[17] But how is it supposed to do that? The story more or less begins with Hegel because "Hegel was the first to raise to the level of a philosophical problem the process of detaching modernity from the suggestion of norms lying outside of itself in the past" (p. 16).

Hegel's problem is also Habermas's problem. But clearly, Hegel depends on a very large dose of metaphysics in order to conceive modernity as something capable of grounding itself. Equally clearly, this is not something that can be admitted by Habermas as a legitimate intellectual resource. "The metaphysical tradition" appealed to a "substantialist notion of reason" (p. 18), and since Kant, this is no longer available. Rather, post-Kantian reason is rigorously formalistic (pp. 18–19); Habermas takes all of this as a given, which is to say that whatever problem modernity sets for us will have to be solved by us on the basis of formal rather than substantive reason.[18] Whatever may have been the case with respect to the stage of modernity that Hegel confronted, *our* stage of modernity, Habermas insists, obliges us to be resolutely postmetaphysical. So having ruled out as impermissible any appeal to metaphysical conceptions, how does Habermas himself go about addressing Hegel's problem?

One might think that one very modest way to vindicate modernity would be simply to see if modern societies do a better job of providing for human welfare or meeting human needs (including needs for political freedom and personal autonomy) than premodern societies typically did. However, that kind of largely non-philosophical response would, so it seems, strike Habermas as altogether too prosaic. In other words, his way of stating the problem looks very much as if it is demanding a non-metaphysical answer to what has every appearance of being a metaphysical question.

Habermas has a long and complicated story to tell about why all the philosophical responses to modernity, from Hegel to Foucault, either fail to supply the normative "grounding" that is required, or are too anti-rationalist

---

[17] Cf. page 20, on modernity's need for "creating all that is normative out of itself" and page 21, on Hegel's project to locate an ultimate dialectical principle permitting modernity "to ground itself."

[18] See the important formulation on page xli of *Between Facts and Norms*: "modernity, now aware of its contingencies, depends all the more on a procedural reason, that is, on a reason that puts itself on trial. The [Kantian] critique of reason [follows from] the radically anti-Platonic insight that there is neither a higher nor a deeper reality to which we could appeal."

even to be interested in solving the problem. It would take far too long to review all the details of this story.[19] Our main concern, naturally, is with *Habermas's* political philosophy, and thus we need to jump ahead to Lectures 11 and 12 since, if he has a solution of his own to the problem that he poses, that is where we will find it.

As Habermas makes explicit on page 295, "the philosophical discourse of modernity [was] initiated by Kant." We need "to retrace the path [of this discourse] back to its [Kantian] starting point" (ibid.) in order to become aware of all the false byways and diversions that led modernity away from an adequate conceptualization of its own essence. In Hegel and Marx, for instance, modern thinking became captivated by a misleading vision of "ethical totality"; Hegelian-Marxist thought thereby strayed from "the [correct] model of unconstrained consensus formation in a communication community standing under cooperative constraints" (ibid.). Or again, Heidegger and Derrida offer further examples of how exaggerated philosophical fixations of various sorts somehow overshadow the primacy of "communicatively structured lifeworlds that reproduce themselves via the palpable medium of action oriented to mutual agreement" (ibid.). The "paradigm" privileged by Habermas is that "of mutual understanding between subjects capable of speech and action" (pp. 295–296), and all the post-Kantian currents of Western theory are criticized insofar as they privilege competing paradigms. In particular, critics of modernity write off Kantian rationalism too quickly because they fail to see how "the paradigm of the philosophy of consciousness" (or what Habermas also calls "the philosophy of the subject") can be rescued by "the paradigm of mutual understanding" (p. 296).[20]

---

[19] I think that the major motivation driving Habermas to trace the story all the way back to Hegel is his idea (a key motif of the book) that all the challenges that contemporary postmodernists seek to press against Kantian rationality can already be located in eighteenth- and nineteenth-century philosophical critics; hence these contemporary Derrideans and Foucaultians are never as philosophically original as they take themselves to be. See especially page 302: "The New Critique of Reason suppresses that almost 200-year-old counterdiscourse inherent in modernity itself" developed by Hegel, Schiller, and the German Romantics. Also, page 295: "The basic conceptual aporias of the philosophy of consciousness, so acutely diagnosed by Foucault ... were already analyzed by Schiller, Fichte, Schelling, and Hegel in a similar fashion."

[20] The basic idea, as I understand it, is that Kant presented his philosophy fundamentally as an account of the faculties of the human subject. Part of the problem with this aspect of how Kant conceived his own enterprise is that it divorced consciousness from history. The philosophical trajectory from Nietzsche and Heidegger to Derrida and Foucault seeks simply to toss this whole Kantian vindication of reason in the rubbish bin. By historicizing Kantian reason, and giving it more of a dialogical dimension than he thinks it has in Kant, Habermas hopes to salvage the distinctive philosophical discourse that Kant initiated – that is, to retrieve Kantian rationalism from the rubbish bin into which it has been consigned by anti-rationalist postmodernists. I think that is the overarching narrative, but Habermas's convoluted prose makes it exceedingly hard to get the story straight.

Unfortunately, these formulations are all oppressively abstract and hard to pin down. Habermas seems to be saying that a variety of intellectual mistakes diverted us from the possibility of an adequate political philosophy for modernity – for instance: Hegel and Marx's determination to conceive *Geist* as marching through History,[21] or Heidegger and Derrida's conception of philosophy as a grand struggle to break free of the metaphysical web conjured into existence by modern "humanism,"[22] or the commitment of the empirical social sciences to conceiving social life as a set of objective processes capable of being mastered from an objectifying standpoint. In each of these cases, one gets a type of theorizing that fails to appreciate modern social life as what it really is, a form of communicative agency. What defines social life is not an occult "macro-subject" to be wrestled with either metaphysically or by some manner of social-scientific objectification; rather, it is to be grasped as a dynamic drama of *inter*-subjectivity. Social life is *dialogical*. Theory needs "to treat communicative action as the medium through which the lifeworld as a whole is reproduced" (p. 299). That is, we need to conceive society as a living process of communicative agency where historical subjects try to understand each other and coordinate their shared historical existence through the attempt (successful or unsuccessful) to reach rational consensus. The fundamental reality of historical existence (especially in the context of self-conscious modernity) is the effort on the part of all members of a society to engage each other in an active dialogue about how to organize the social practices and institutions that they share – an insight into the nature of modern consciousness that has somehow eluded Hegel *and* Marx *and* the earlier Frankfurt School *and* a whole succession of post-Nietzschean and post-Heideggerian philosophers, as well as the vast contingent of social scientists committed to an objectifying depiction of social life. In short: Habermas's own communicative version of Kantianism is intended to present modern social reality as a dialogical quest for a mode of existence

[21] See pages 300–301, referring to "the conception of world history as a process of self-generation"; cf. page 342, on Marx's entanglement in "the totality thinking of Hegel" and the idea of "the subject-writ-large," and the discussion on page 357 of the eclipse of the idea of a self-knowing, self-determining "macrosubject." This obsolete conception of "a self-relating macrosubject" gets replaced by Habermas's own idea of an "intersubjectivity of public processes of opinion and consensus formation." See also *Between Facts and Norms*, p. 46: "Marx ... still held to a classical concept whose influence extends from Aristotle to Hegel, that of society as totality." One suspects that Habermas's emphasis on this theme partly reflects the impact of his debates with Niklas Luhmann, who directed the full force of his sociology against the idea of "society as totality."

[22] See page 301, referring to the idle yearning for "an impenetrable dispensation that makes the power of lost origins felt through the negativity of withdrawal and deprivation." Cf. page 307: "The potential for excitement stylized into the other of reason, becomes at once esoteric and pseudonymous; it comes up under different names – as Being, as the heterogeneous, as power."

capable of vindicating (communicatively) its own rational validity. It might seem pretty far-fetched to claim that any modern society actually lives up to this exalted conception of itself; it may be a more plausible version of Habermas's account of modernity to cast this as an ideal to which modern political communities are (knowingly or unknowingly) *aspiring* – allowing us to judge the imperfect realities of modern life relative to a philosophical ideal that (if the Habermasian thesis is right) is immanent in modern life itself.

Habermas advances the idea of a new kind of theory – a "reconstructive science," as he terms it, capable of excavating "the actually exercised rule-knowledge that is deposited in correctly generated utterances" (pp. 297–298). In this context, he offers the rather odd notion that this mode of reconstructing the presupposed conditions of competent speech allows us to get beyond "the ontological separation of the transcendental and the empirical" (p. 298), as if only his kind of pragmatics of communication suffices to free us philosophically from Kant's metaphysical dualism. Such a project of rational reconstruction relates "to the [formal-pragmatic] structures of the lifeworld in general, with a view to disclosing "the properties of communicatively structured lifeworlds *in general*" (p. 299). Somehow, Habermas has the idea that his own "formal-pragmatic concept of the lifeworld" (p. 300) will restore all that was attractive about the original Kantian philosophical enterprise, while evading the objections posed by subsequent German and French philosophy to the dualisms at the heart of Kantian critical philosophy. That is, the claim is that Habermas offers a version of transcendental (or quasi-transcendental) philosophy that has been suitably historicized (page 306: "a historically situated reason"), and hence purged of Kant's distinction between the transcendental and the empirical (or the noumenal and the phenomenal), thereby insulating Kantianism against the challenges raised by German Idealism against Kant's dualism (cf. page 322). One sees fairly clearly that Habermas wants neither the metaphysical baggage associated with Kant, nor the appeal to metaphysical "totality" or "comprehensive reason" (p. 305) invoked by Kant's critics, but the super-rapid jump to his preferred formal-pragmatic version of Kantianism gives us much too meager an account of why this particular philosophical construction delivers what Habermas promises and solves all the conundrums that Habermas is trying to avoid.[23] Now it may well be that Habermas's followers can make

---

[23] Needless to say, I am aware that Habermas has published many other books developing this project of his straddling philosophy and social theory. It is equally obvious that I would not be posing this challenge here if I thought that Habermas satisfactorily addressed it in one of his other books.

available a wide range of helpful reflections on how to reform contemporary politics in the direction of a more genuinely deliberative democracy; and it is certainly not my purpose to deny that such Habermas-inspired work is to be welcomed. But this will still leave us mightily puzzled as to why any of this requires a "reconstructive science" delving into formal-pragmatic conditions of communicative competence.[24]

The next important step in the argument comes with the claim that the anti-modern or postmodernist critique of reason "remains tied to the presuppositions of the philosophy of the subject from which it wanted to free itself" (p. 309). On the one side we have Kantian reason, indicted by its critics for being a "powerholder," excluding or marginalizing what is not itself. On the other side we have "the other of reason," whether in its Heideggerian or Derridean or Foucaultian versions, claiming to knock dominating reason from its citadel (ibid.). Reason is associated with "the paradigm of the philosophy of consciousness that was installed in the period from Descartes to Kant" (p. 310), and those who presume to challenge hegemonic reason, the enemies of Cartesian and Kantian rationality, want liberation from this supposedly oppressive "paradigm." However, what they offer is a phony liberation. In fact, the only genuine liberation from "the paradigm of self-consciousness" comes courtesy of Habermas's *new* paradigm, namely: "the paradigm of mutual understanding, that is, of the intersubjective relationship between individuals who are socialized through communication and reciprocally recognize one another" (ibid.). Rather than jettisoning rationality wholesale, one must reconceive it communicatively and intersubjectively. One must resituate reason in "the communicative practice of everyday life," and thus come to appreciate "intersubjective understanding as the telos inscribed into communication in ordinary language" (p. 311). Here again, one does not lack for suggestive metaphors and forceful polemics, but one might have had less heat and more light if Habermas were not so determined to whip up this squabble among intellectuals into a culture-clash of cosmic proportions (a war of paradigms). For sure, dialogical reason is better than monological reason; it's better to negotiate life in society through communication than through the exercise of raw power; and it's certainly better to relish reason than to trash it. But when we distance ourselves from the overheated polemics (a Habermasian trademark), the appeal to reason as communication seems an extremely modest basis for a political philosophy with such large ambitions.

[24] Cf. Beiner, *Philosophy in a Time of Lost Spirit*, p. 97.

One of Habermas's central ideas is that, provided that we interpret rationality according to the "communicative paradigm," and provided that the latter is developed in its full philosophical scope, the idea of reason will lead us to a conception of moral solidarity capable of providing modern social life with a normative foundation. When "we conceive of knowledge as communicatively mediated, rationality is assessed in terms of the capacity of responsible participants in interaction to orient themselves to validity claims geared to intersubjective recognition" (p. 314). This is a fairly convoluted way of saying that entering into a rational dialogue commits one to acknowledging one's interlocutor as an equal dialogue-partner; and if all members of a society can in principle be brought to recognize all other members of the society as dialogue-partners in this sense, then civic life as a whole will come to be informed by a kind of dialogical solidarity, so to speak.

To exchange reasons in what is conceived to be a rational dialogue of any kind is to acknowledge that it is the compellingness of those reasons that should determine the outcome, not any extraneous structures of power or authority, and *that* acknowledgment in turn commits all of the parties to the dialogue to the pursuit of a reason-based consensus (p. 315). If the decision making of the society is reconceived in this way, then all citizens will have good reason to embrace a solidaristic identity as civic interlocutors.[25] Admittedly, this latter conception seems very remote from life in society as we commonsensically experience it (to put it quite mildly), but presumably Habermas's hope is that, as we come to realize that commitment to such an ideal is already inscribed in the presuppositions of our own communicative praxis (in everyday situations), it will present itself as a normative vision to which we are (albeit unknowingly) pre-committed.

The focus of Lecture 12 is decidedly more sociological. The main question here, as it is in *The Theory of Communicative Action*, is to what extent Habermas's "communicative paradigm" can be given effect in modern societies that largely lend themselves to description in a Weberian idiom. If Habermas goes too far in emphasizing the possibility of portraying these societies as communicative communities, his theory will look implausibly utopian; if he concedes too much to Weber's dark reflection on our "fateful"

---

[25] Hence Habermas's claim on page 324 that his dialogical morality ultimately gives us a foundational insight into "the indivisibility of suffering," and into the fact that injustice "affects everyone equally." In short, buying into Habermas's idea of communicative rationality as a *universal* commitment will serve to abolish the age-old distinction between the few and the many.

times, on the other hand, the cause of post-Kantian reason will appear without hope. In short, the mission of Habermas's social theory consists in doing one's best to steer between utopia and despair.[26]

The core conception is anticipated in Lecture 11: "the communicative potential of reason [is embodied] in the patterns of modern lifeworlds," but this communicative potential gets overwhelmed by "the unfettered imperatives of the economic and administrative subsystems," which invade "the vulnerable practice of everyday life" and subordinate practical reason to a domination exercised by "cognitive-instrumental" aspects of the organization of society. As a result, Weberian modernity is characterized by the unhappy fact that the communicative potential of reason is "simultaneously developed and distorted in the course of capitalist modernization" (p. 315). A simpler way to put it is to say that the sociology of modern societies, as conceived by Habermas, is the site of a fundamental contest between communicative rationality and instrumental or "strategic" rationality, between lifeworld norms and system imperatives, where each side seeks to define the life of the society. The fact that "the economic and administrative subsystems" seem to have the upper hand – the fact that modern societies really don't *look* like open-ended dialogues about how to structure everyday praxis – is obviously the reason why Habermas's philosophical sociology (despite its determination to be clear-eyed about the realities) tends to have a conspicuously utopian appearance (which Habermas wouldn't – and needn't – necessarily apologize for). The key question for Habermas is whether modern society is pervasively defined by "steering mechanisms" (of money, power, administrative routines, the imperatives of the world of finance, and so on), or whether there continues to be a tangible living communicative praxis beyond the seemingly autonomous "subsystems" presided over by bankers, bureaucrats, and politicians. In principle, this is an open question for Habermas, but he is clearly committed to seeking out such "day-to-day communicative practice" (p. 325; cf. pages 323 and 353) wherever it may still be intact.[27] Habermas's vision of society as (potentially) a free intersubjective dialogue bears significant similarities to Hannah Arendt's vision of a republican political life shared by authentic citizens, but Arendt has the

---

[26] The idea of locating one's theorizing "between facts and norms" (as the English title of *Faktizität und Geltung* encapsulates Habermas's project) similarly suggests that one must somehow bridge the empirical realities of modernity and its normative aspirations.

[27] On page 325, Habermas speaks of "a communicative reason *at once claimed and denied.*" For Habermas, it is a question of *retrieving* dialogical possibilities that the sociology of modern existence is constantly suppressing, or at least putting on the defensive.

theoretical advantage, one might say, of projecting this utopian vision back onto a long-extinct Arendtian polis that may or may not have lived up to her ideal. She repudiates modernity wholesale and, hence, isn't obliged – as Habermas surely is – to hunt for traces of communicative praxis in the realities of a heavily "iron-cage"-inflected type of social existence.

There is a sense in which what Habermas offers is a much more modest and de-metaphysicalized version of Hegel's thesis that modernity is vindicated to the extent that it offers the prospect of synthesizing the universal and the particular. To assert a validity-claim in a way that is consonant with the philosophical discourse of modernity is necessarily to assert "*universal validity*" (p. 322). If something is right or morally sanctioned, it is *universally* right, but it is in the nature of these validity-claims to be deployed within "*context-bound* everyday practice" (ibid.). "The claim is always raised *here and now*, in specific contexts" (p. 323). Modernity as modernity appeals to a conception of reason that "bursts every provinciality asunder" (p. 322), but it does so without ceasing to be "incarnated in [particular] contexts of communicative action and in [particular] structures of the lifeworld" (ibid.). "[Lifeworld] identities always remain tied to the particularism of a special form of life," yet they have to assimilate the [universalistic] normative content of modernity ... that undermine[s] the force and concrete shape of any given particularity" (p. 365). Therefore, as Hegel articulated in a very different idiom, insight into the moral superiority of modernity requires a grasp of this indispensable dialectic of universalism and particularism. What we want are "*concrete* forms of life" that also satisfy the universalizing norms of life in modernity (p. 326). As regards specific political manifestations of such an aspired-to synthesis of the universal and the particular, Habermas tends to privilege the de-particularizing mode of political community taking shape in the European Union (pp. 366–367).

Does Habermas's epic project achieve the purposes that his theorizing is meant to accomplish? One can raise the same reservation in relation to Habermas's social theory as applies to his theory of rationality. It is expressed in such an uncompromisingly abstract theoretical language that it is hard to know how to go about weighing to what extent it's persuasive and to what extent it isn't. The theory might well have presented itself as more compelling if Habermas had allowed himself to convey his vision of politics in a narratively richer idiom. The idea of sixty million people watching Barack Obama and Mitt Romney pursuing a free debate in regard to competing visions of civic life may perhaps inspire the thought that this presents at least the intimation of a form of political life genuinely oriented toward "the logos" long venerated by Occidental tradition until contemporary critics of logocentrism undertook to expose it as a sham ideal (p. 311). More than that, it may prompt us to wish that much more of contemporary political life corresponded to such Habermasian aspirations. In any case, I am really not sure whether a theory as heavy on jargon and as light on narrative content can convince us that Habermas's dialogical ideal (as admirable as it is) is a realistic one.[28]

Habermas is certainly right that a "totalizing critique" of modernity carries little credibility. Modern (post-Reformation, post-Enlightenment, post-French Revolution) societies have made substantial progress in putting right the many social injustices that characterized premodern societies,[29] just as they have done much to render human beings far less exposed to the often capricious and destructive ravages of nature.[30] Thoroughgoing critics of modernity, such as the ones canvassed through much of this book, ought to be honest enough to spell out which premodern golden age they favor and why.[31] Whatever one's doubts or criticisms, Habermas has performed an important service in pushing back against these totalizing critics.

At the end of the day, my own judgment is that while Habermas's principles are undoubtedly attractive ones, the political philosophy articulated in *The Philosophical Discourse of Modernity* falls well short of putting us in possession of the "self-grounding of modernity" that Habermas seems to think is expected of a modern political philosophy as such. For instance, it is far from clear why Habermas puts as much emphasis as he does on the distinction between "subject-centered" reason and communicative reason. The idea

---

[28] Also, it seems telling that Barack Obama himself apparently viewed his televised debates with Romney as so contrived as to be almost fraudulent.

[29] See page 338: Heidegger, Adorno, Derrida, and Foucault "are all insensitive to the highly *ambivalent* content of cultural and social modernity. This leveling can also be seen [when one applies a] diachronic comparison of modern forms of life with pre-modern ones. The high price earlier exacted from the mass of the population (in the dimensions of bodily labor, material conditions, possibilities of individual choice, security of law and punishment, political participation, and schooling) is barely even noticed."

[30] As we all know, human beings are perfectly capable of inflicting calamities upon themselves quite apart from those bestowed by nature, and modern technology without question vastly increases the potency of these self-inflicted disasters. Yet none of this gives us the slightest reason to minimize the colossal achievements of modern science in treating heart disease or providing tsunami warnings. If it were one day discovered that a large asteroid were hurtling toward Earth, we would all owe an infinite debt to science and technology for (hopefully) intercepting it.

[31] Sometimes they do – as we have seen in earlier chapters. Leo Strauss tells Karl Löwith why he regrets the disappearance of the ancient polis. Alasdair MacIntyre waxes lyrical about the virtues of fishing villages and farming communities and of storytelling cultures in general – cultures that invariably succumb in the end to the bulldozer of modernity. The question is whether these accounts give a fair or balanced weighing-up of the strengths and shortcomings of modern life.

seems to be that subject-centered reason is monological – that Kant himself can in principle, through solitary reflection, figure out what the moral law, for instance, requires – whereas communicative reason is in essence dialogical; it requires discrete communicative subjects trading reasons back and forth between each other.[32] Still, one has to wonder why reconceiving Kantian reason according to this seemingly simple distinction suffices for a normative redemption of modernity, as Habermas appears to think that it does. Or, to pick another example: Habermas insists, again and again, on the "differentiation" of modern rationality, enforcing quite distinct ways of validating norms in the realms of science, morality, and art (see, for instance, pages 1, 313–315, 336, 339, and 365),[33] without offering much of an account of why this is unavoidable or why we should regard the notion of a unity of reason as irrecoverable.[34] Neither is it sufficiently clear why he thinks a theoretical conception as spare (and almost certainly utopian) as the idea of modern society as a partnership in public dialogue can suffice to redeem modernity in the face of its critics. Habermas can be an extremely penetrating critic of temptations toward irrationalism in rival theories (his critique of Foucault, for instance, is particularly powerful), but one often gets the sense that deficiencies in the persuasiveness of Habermas's own theoretical commitments are covered over by an over-reliance on jargon. It can readily be conceded to Habermas that the quality and robustness of public deliberation in modern societies – and the reasonableness of those deliberations – will always be an important measure of whether such societies can be considered normatively admirable. Whether such public deliberation can ever be robust enough or reasonable enough to constitute the kind of grand vindication of modernity that Habermas thinks is required seems quite a bit more questionable.

---

[32] "Habermas has remained mistrustful of the solipsistic implications of Kant's standpoint. He has forcefully argued that the individual subject's powers of moral reasoning need to be supplemented by a broader, communicative frame of reference. Discourse ethics holds that judgments of morality need to be redeemed by recourse to actual or hypothetical discourses with other people. In this way, moral reasoning ceases to be monological, as in Kant" (Richard Wolin, "Kant at Ground Zero," *The New Republic*, February 9, 2004). But – leaving aside the question of whether practical reason in Kant is really as monological as this suggests – if *hypothetical* discourses are sufficient to validate the claims of discourse ethics, one wonders whether it is unfair to say that this is still just monological reason posing as dialogical reason.

[33] Cf. *Between Facts and Norms*, p. xli.

[34] It is hardly obvious that notions of the unity of reason are obsolete; see, for instance, note 38 of our chapter on Strauss for an affirmation by Gadamer that reason is not differentiated but unitary. Indeed, it is plausible to see this doctrine of unity as central to Gadamer's overall philosophical project in *Truth and Method*. How so? What defines that project, in my view, is the attempt to argue – against Kant – that judgment concerning art, history, and morality is precisely *not* consigned to separate "value-spheres"; that understanding, insofar as it is obtainable, encompasses all of these domains; that wisdom is wisdom. Cf. Beiner, *Philosophy in a Time of Lost Spirit*, p. 188.

10

Michel Foucault's Carceral Society

It is hard to live in a society while thinking that the society, in virtually every aspect of its being, is a prison. The work of Michel Foucault shows that while it may be hard, it is not impossible. To be sure, this view is not unique to Foucault. Adorno, too, for instance, speaks of "the open-air prison which the world is becoming."[1] But Foucault surely went further than anyone else in building this conception into a full-fledged political philosophy.

The first thing to be said about *Discipline and Punish* (*Surveiller et Punir*) is that it is vastly more relevant to the world in which we are currently living (a post-9/11 world informed by ubiquitous concerns about security and surveillance) than the book was when first published (1975). When I stand in line at the cafeteria in the building where I have my university office, to pay for my lunch, a sign on the way to the cashier reads: "WARNING. YOU ARE UNDER SURVEILLANCE. THESE PREMISES ARE PROTECTED BY 24 HOUR VIDEO SURVEILLANCE." As the original French title rightly conveys,[2] although Foucault's book is a history of the modern prison, the idea of surveillance is conceptually prior to (or more primordial than) the notion of punishment. What preoccupies Foucault is not that modern societies punish delinquents, which of course premodern societies did as well, but the fact that they punish in a mode of penetrating surveillance, where in effect the gaze of the punishing apparatus is more dehumanizing than confinement or loss of liberty (or so at least

---

[1] Theodor W. Adorno, *Prisms*, trans. Samuel Weber and Shierry Weber (Cambridge, MA: MIT Press, 1981), p. 34.

[2] As is explained in a Translator's Note (Michel Foucault, *Discipline and Punish: The Birth of the Prison*, trans. Alan Sheridan [New York: Vintage Books, 1979], p. ix), Foucault himself was the source of the title for the English edition, even though it is quite different from the French title. All page references to follow refer to this edition. In certain cases (notably with respect to illustrations supplied by Foucault), we have also made use of the following French edition: *Surveiller et punir* (Paris: Gallimard, 1975).

Foucault's critical analysis seems to suggest). In a sense, Foucault's idea is that the surveillance that is part and parcel of modern punishment is *worse* than the punishment itself, or captures more fundamentally the basic nature of the "carceral society" in which we live. If that is so, then *all* of us, not just the delinquents and outcasts, are diminished or dehumanized by the omnipresent gaze of the authorities that monitor us, that track our movements and keep video records of our every step. Worst of all, from Foucault's standpoint, is that the kind of modern liberal society that deploys this sort of monitoring and tracking apparatus congratulates itself on its humanity and its liberality; Foucault's overriding mission is to expose this complacent self-image as a perverse ideology of modern "humanism":

The reduction in penal severity in the last 200 years is a phenomenon with which legal historians are well acquainted. But, for a long time, it has been regarded in an overall way as a quantitative phenomenon: less cruelty, less pain, more kindness, more respect, more "humanity." In fact, these changes are accompanied by a displacement in the very object of the punitive operation. (p. 16)

Foucault's *Discipline and Punish* presents itself as a work of history. Reading it, one can easily be fooled into thinking that Foucault, in this work, is not participating in the enterprise of political philosophy. My main purpose in this chapter is to tease out the subterranean political philosophy at work in this text, and "deconstruct" Foucault's persona (his "mask") as a mere historian. In order to see beyond this persona, it suffices to consider the scare quotes that Foucault places around the word *humanity* – for instance, in the text from *Discipline and Punish* that I just quoted.[3] Those quotation marks are themselves a "speech act": they communicate a kind of sneer about our liberal self-delusions, and this sneer is normatively motivated and normatively charged (as is true pervasively throughout Foucault's book and throughout his work).

There is an extensive literature on whether Foucault's theoretical enterprise does or doesn't commit him to a normative vision of a suitably desirable arrangement of human life.[4] Critics of Foucault tend to insist that

[3] Cf. "process of 'humanization'" (p. 7); as well as the repeated use of scare quotes around "humane" and "humanity" on pages 74–75; also page 226.

[4] See, for instance, Nancy Fraser's essays on Foucault in Fraser, *Unruly Practices* (Oxford: Polity, 1989); and Jürgen Habermas, *The Philosophical Discourse of Modernity* (Cambridge, MA: MIT Press, 1987), chapters 9 and 10. See also the important debate between Charles Taylor and William E. Connolly: Taylor, "Foucault on Freedom and Truth," *Political Theory*, Vol. 12, no. 2 (May 1984), pp. 152–183; Connolly, "Taylor, Foucault, and Otherness," *Political Theory*, Vol. 13, no. 3 (August 1985), pp. 365–376; Taylor, "Connolly, Foucault, and Truth," *Political Theory*, Vol. 13, no. 3 (August 1985), pp. 377–385. For a radical denial by Foucault of the relevance of normative concepts like justice and human fulfillment, see the famous 1971 TV debate between him and Chomsky: Noam Chomsky and Michel Foucault, *The*

this is unavoidable, whereas Foucault and his supporters tend to resist the idea that his enterprise is in any meaningful sense a normative one (which Foucault tends to assimilate to a project of "normalization"⁵ – a notion that itself certainly isn't lacking in normative resonance!). We should take all such disclaimers with a grain of salt. Foucault thinks we suffer from a very naïve view of what is involved in the deployment of power, what is involved in submitting human beings to this or that machinery of power, and in particular, very naïve about how power relates to knowledge, or at least institutional apparatuses of knowledge. Again, his mission is to emancipate us from this naivety. Foucault is indeed an analyst of structures of power and discipline, but he is no less committed to normative judgments about these structures of power and discipline, which presupposes a conception of human beings being entitled *not* to be subject to such a regime of normalization and control (as well as certainly being entitled to be free of the humiliating condition of deluding themselves about the character of the regime that normalizes and controls them).⁶

Chomsky-Foucault Debate: On Human Nature (New York: New Press, 2006), pp. 1–67. See, in particular, pages 54–55: "If you like, I will be a little bit Nietzschean about [whether, as Chomsky maintains, any sort of politics must make appeal to an ideal conception of justice]; in other words, it seems to me that the idea of justice in itself is an idea which in effect has been invented and put to work in different types of societies as an instrument of a certain political and economic power or as a weapon against that power. But it seems to me that, in any case, the notion of justice itself functions within a society of classes as a claim made by the oppressed class and as justification for it [that is, as an ideological weapon in a struggle between social classes, and nothing more than that]; and pages 57–58: "contrary to what you [Chomsky] think, you can't prevent me from believing that these notions of human nature, of justice, of the realization of the essence of human beings, are all notions and concepts which have been formed within our civilization, within our type of knowledge and our form of philosophy, and that as a result form part of our class system; and one can't, however regrettable it may be, put forward these notions to describe or justify a fight which should – and shall in principle – overthrow the very fundaments of our society." Chomsky, as one would expect, strongly (and rightly) objects to these formulations of Foucault's Marxified Nietzscheanism. Various video segments of the debate can easily be accessed on YouTube.

⁵ Cf. Beiner, *Philosophy in a Time of Lost Spirit* (Toronto: University of Toronto Press, 1997), pp. 65 and 67; and Fraser, *Unruly Practices*, p. 56 and p. 66, n. 1.

⁶ Relevant here is an interesting exchange I had with István Hont during a seminar of his in Cambridge that I had the pleasure of auditing in the fall of 2011. I started criticizing Foucault for failing to be upfront about his normative agenda. Hont replied on Foucault's behalf in more or less the following words: "Only misguided North Americans think that *normativity* counts for anything. Foucault's project (as articulated programmatically in his "What is Enlightenment?" essay) – to trace the genealogy of our entrapment in the modern welfare state, so that we can become self-reflexive about it – is the only one that matters. Defining normative ideals is just *dreaming* – it's pointless. If one is being tortured, the only relevant normative ideal is to stop being tortured. That's why Raymond Geuss – with his hyper-skepticism – teaches Foucault every year." I am not insensitive to the force of the line of thought expressed in Hont's rant (responding to my rant against Foucault), but let me respond with just a modest counter-challenge: If Foucault had not come to a normative judgment about the modern welfare state and its human deficiencies (presumably relative to a standard of something better – some generalized notion of a more attractive or less oppressive way to live life and organize social

I am going to suggest that Foucault's vision of modernity can be best encapsulated in the phrase, "the insidiousness of modern power."[7] And again, if this phrase accurately captures the core of Foucault's theoretical enterprise, it is not just an empirical description, but a description carrying a tremendous normative punch. It is a *critique* of modernity, not just a historical account of modernity's ruses and ideological self-concealment of those ruses.[8] Why is modern power insidious? Let's start with the unforgettable scene from eighteenth-century French history with which Foucault opens the book. Foucault reminds us of an epoch in the history of penal practices when it was considered an appropriate mode of punishment not just to have the body of the criminal drawn and quartered, but to have flesh systematically torn away, burned with sulphur, and "molten lead, boiling oil, burning resin, wax and sulphur melted together" poured onto it, and *then* to be drawn and quartered! (p. 3). One could only assume that after a description this graphic, modern penal practices could only appear in their aspect of humaneness, decency, gentleness, and so on. But of course this is not Foucault's intention at all. In fact, he obviously presents this scene of pre-Enlightenment brutality and torture as a way of heightening the deliberately paradoxical and provocative conception that modern penal practices are precisely *not* distinguished by their humanity, decency, liberal gentleness, and so on. Here is where the appeal to insidiousness comes in, and it plays a key role in explaining why liberal-modern-"enlightened" society has misconceived the real nature of its own practices, and the self-congratulatory self-understanding that envelops those practices.

A conventional account of the post-Enlightenment evolution in penal practices might applaud the diminished emphasis on "the body" as a legitimate object of penal discipline. Foucault regards this as a naïve interpretation.

existence), what would have impelled him to write its genealogy (and hence help debunk it)? One can also ask: If it is specifically benighted North Americans who suffer from an over-preoccupation with normativity, why is this issue so central to Habermas's critique of Foucault? During the seminar course, I was also struck by the fact that Hont's defense of Oakeshott was just as robust as his defense of Foucault. Hont attacked Perry Anderson's account of Oakeshott in his essay "The Intransigent Right" (cited in our Oakeshott chapter) as slanderously unfair, whereas I believe that Anderson gets Oakeshott brilliantly right and therefore I defended his essay against Hont. One can perhaps seize on this as an opportunity for reflecting on mutual affinities between Oakeshott's and Foucault's respective critiques of the "teleocratic" state.

[7] Cf. page 220: "a power that insidiously objectifies those on whom it is applied [un pouvoir qui objective insidieusement ceux à qui il s'applique]."

[8] Cf. Habermas, *The Philosophical Discourse of Modernity*, p. 246, referring to the "mercilessness" of Foucault's critique of modernity (focused as it is on "the internal kinship between humanism and terror"). As Habermas later puts it (pp. 276 and 282), Foucault's genealogical historiography is ineluctably drawn into being "cryptonormative."

He cites the Abbé de Mably to the effect that a desirable penal regime should be oriented away from the body and toward "the soul" (page 16: "The expiation that once rained down upon the body must be replaced by a punishment that acts in depth on the heart, the will, the inclinations"). That would involve a liberalization of punishment, right? Foucault disagrees: in "decorporalizing" punishment, one thereby "spiritualizes" it, hence expanding its reach and increasing its insidiousness:

> The old partners of the spectacle of punishment, the body and the blood, gave way. A new character came on the scene, masked. It was the end of a certain kind of tragedy; comedy began, with shadow play, faceless voices, impalpable entities. The apparatus of punitive justice must now bite into this bodiless reality. (pp. 16–17)

The shift from body to soul really represents the move from one regime of power/knowledge to another regime of power/knowledge, and it certainly should not be assumed, from Foucault's perspective, that a focus on the non-corporal is more liberal or more humane than a focus on the corporal. Rather, *both* serve merely as the articulations of "a certain type of power and ... a certain type of knowledge, the machinery by which the power relations give rise to a possible corpus of knowledge, and knowledge extends and reinforces the effects of this power" (p. 29). It would not be going too far to say that, for Foucault, "the historical reality of the soul" is in fact constituted by a particular constellation of "methods of punishment, supervision and constraint" (ibid.). The soul acquires reality insofar as it is conceived as an object of comprehensive scrutiny, and hence control and discipline:

> [The soul acquires] a reality ... by the functioning of a power that is exercised on those punished – and, in a more general way, on those one supervises, trains and corrects, over madmen, children at home and at school, the colonized, over those who are stuck at a machine and supervised for the rest of their lives. (ibid.)

Thus the emergence of the soul, Foucault more or less suggests, is itself the function of a new regime of surveillance and discipline (more insidious, and in that sense quite possibly less rather than more humane insofar as Foucault concedes a non-ideological meaning to "more humane," which he likely does not).

Another major theme of the book – perhaps *the* major theme – is "panopticism." This refers to Bentham's architectural scheme for a prison that would allow unlimited twenty-four-hour monitoring of the inmates by their warders.[9]

---

[9] Foucault's illustrations (thirty interesting plates in the French edition and a reduced selection of ten plates in the English edition) are very helpful in giving us representations of various versions

Each individual, in his place, is securely confined to a cell from which he is seen from the front by the supervisor; but the side walls prevent him from coming into contact with his companions. He is seen, but he does not see; he is an object of information, never a subject in communication. The arrangement of his room, opposite the central tower, imposes on him an axial visibility; but the divisions of the ring, those separated cells, imply a lateral invisibility. And this invisibility is a guarantee of order. (p. 200)

The Panopticon functions as a kind of laboratory of power. Thanks to its mechanisms of observation, it gains in efficiency and in the ability to penetrate into men's behaviour; knowledge follows the advances of power, discovering new objects of knowledge over all the surfaces on which power is exercised. (p. 204)

But if this is presented as a historical curiosity, why should some particular misguided brainchild of a rather peculiar late eighteenth-century social reformer be of great importance? In fact, this is not at all the spirit in which Foucault presents Bentham's Panopticon. It's as clear as daylight that his purpose is a normative one, namely to propagate panopticism as a defining image of all that is wrong with modern, post-Enlightenment society. This society is actually itself a giant Panopticon,[10] and therefore Bentham, in dreaming up his wild scheme of universal surveillance, does us a great clarifying service in permitting us to see our social arrangements in their true (sinister) light, thus cutting through the obfuscating delusion that social reform advances the cause of enlightenment. Foucault's account of Bentham's idea is preceded by a discussion (pp. 195–200) of early-modern schemes to cope with and contain plague and leprosy, and of how these early versions of the disciplinary society resulted in processes of "binary division and branding": "mad/sane; dangerous/harmless; normal/abnormal" (p. 199). These earlier versions of the disciplinary project were indeed precursors of

of the panoptical project. Plate 17 in the French edition (plate 3 in the English edition) reproduces Bentham's own plan for the Panopticon; and plate 26 in the French edition (plate 6 in the English edition) depicts a twentieth-century prison (Stateville Correctional Center in Crest Hill, Illinois) that allows us to see an actual penal institution furnishing a very close approximation to Bentham's vision. A Wikipedia article devoted to this penitentiary claims that the design was in fact deliberately inspired by Bentham's project. As noted elsewhere in this chapter, contemporary video technology obviously renders the architectural arrangements superfluous. But see also our discussion later, drawing on Nancy Fraser's persuasive commentary, to the effect that for Foucault, the prospect of internalized self-surveillance is much more ominous than actual surveillance, thus rendering the issue of technologies of surveillance (in the conventional sense of "technologies" rather than Foucault's expanded sense) ultimately redundant.

[10] Cf. page 216: What it means to live in a society that has become a disciplinary society is being rendered subject to "an indefinitely generalizable mechanism of 'panopticism.'" For sobering accounts of how online technologies are indeed turning Foucault's panoptical vision into a reality, see Ross Douthat, "Your Smartphone Is Watching You," *The New York Times*, June 9, 2013, p. SR11; and Ronald Deibert, "Metadata," *The Globe and Mail*, June 11, 2013, p. A11.

panopticism insofar as they too instituted regimes of social control where "inspection functions ceaselessly. The gaze is alert everywhere" (p. 195).[11] But one can say that panopticism itself is much worse, in the following sense: where surveillance and regulation of lepers or plague victims was primarily aimed at "the binary branding and exile" (p. 199) of the abnormal, the mad, or the dangerous (including lepers and potential spreaders of plague, but other outcasts as well), the panoptical regime submits *everyone*, undifferentiatedly, to a *uniform* regime of surveillance and regulation. The purpose now, one could say, is not inspection for the sake of spotting potential delinquents, but inspection for the sake of inspection.

Why is panopticism so important for Foucault in grasping the nature of modern power? We get some clues in a striking discussion on pages 184–189 of *Discipline and Punish* in which Foucault analyzes what we learn about modern power and discipline from shifting norms of "visibility." The immediate context is a commentary by Foucault on a new regime of "examination," illustrated by a variety of seventeenth- and eighteenth-century examples drawn from the history of schools, hospitals, and the military (in the case of hospitals: the "ritual" of a medical examination of patients; in the case of schools: examinations to test the knowledge of the pupils; in the case of armies: military reviews that inspect the orderly "geometry" of troops). These are all historical descriptions, but Foucault's analysis is (and is intended to be) of much broader relevance.

The examination combines the techniques of an observing hierarchy and those of a normalizing judgement. It is a normalizing gaze, a surveillance that makes it possible to qualify, to classify and to punish. It establishes over individuals a visibility through which one differentiates them and judges them. That is why, in all the mechanisms of discipline, the examination is highly ritualized. In it are combined the ceremony of power and the form of the experiment, the deployment of force and the establishment of truth.[12] At the heart of the procedures of discipline, it manifests the subjection of those who are perceived as objects and the objectification of those who are subjected. (pp. 184–185)

---

[11] On pages 199–200, Foucault claims that "all the mechanisms of power which, even today, are disposed around the abnormal individual, to brand him and to alter him," can ultimately be traced back to the two "disciplinary mechanisms" invented to deal with leprosy and the plague. Cf. page 144: "The medical supervision of diseases and contagions is inseparable from a whole series of other controls: the military control over deserters, fiscal control over commodities, administrative control over remedies, rations, disappearances, cures, deaths, simulations." On page 205, Foucault refers to civil measures deployed against the plague, on the one hand, and panoptical penal schemes, on the other, as "transformations of the disciplinary programme."

[12] This sentence expresses well a trademark Foucaultian theme: power and truth are not to be contrasted in the way that they conventionally are. Rather, they are *inseparable*, two sides of the same coin: a certain constellation of power enforces a particular regime of truth, and vice versa.

With respect to Foucault's military example (inspections of the troops of Louis XIV assembled into rigidly disciplined formations), Foucault claims that this serves to institute a radically new regime of visibility, so to speak. He highlights a commemorative medal marking the first such military review, in March of 1666. The medal (reproduced in plate 1 of the English edition and plate 2 of the French edition), according to Foucault, embodies the decisive moment when

the most brilliant figure of sovereign power [namely Louis XIV] is joined to the emergence of the rituals proper to disciplinary power. The scarcely sustainable visibility of the monarch is turned into the unavoidable visibility of the subjects. And it is this inversion in the visibility in the functioning of the disciplines that was to assure the exercise of power even in its lowest manifestations. We are entering the age of the infinite examination and of compulsory objectification. (p. 189)

There is a more general principle that is at play here, which Foucault refers to as "a whole [new] mechanism that linked to a certain type of the formation of knowledge a certain form of the exercise of power":

Traditionally, power was what was seen, what was shown and what was manifested....Those on whom it was exercised could remain in the shade; they received light only from that portion of power that was conceded to them, or from the reflection of it that for a moment they carried. Disciplinary power, on the other hand, is exercised through its invisibility; at the same time it imposes on those it subjects a principle of compulsory visibility. In discipline, it is the subjects who have to be seen. Their visibility assures the hold of the power that is being exercised over them. It is the fact of being constantly seen, of being able always to be seen, that maintains the disciplined individual in his subjection. And the examination is the technique by which power, instead of emitting the signs of its potency, instead of imposing its mark on its subjects, holds them in a mechanism of objectification. In this space of domination, *disciplinary power manifests its potency, essentially, by arranging objects*. The examination is, as it were, the ceremony of this objectification. (p. 187; my italics)

This text makes clear, in my view, that the fundamental enterprise is less one of telling a historical story, or a set of historical stories, than the articulation of a particular philosophy (less a *sociology* of power than a *metaphysics* of power, one might say). This philosophy comes across most clearly in the idea of disciplinary power as the arranging of objects. Of course, *we* are the objects being arranged – we are the entities being objectified in a novel regime of disciplinary power, and no historical description, but only a philosophical account of a particular kind, could carry us to this conclusion about our status in such a world. A particular constellation of power/knowledge is in fact a comprehensive organization of reality, and human beings are "objectified" in order to be surveyable, available for contemplation or cognition, according to the structuring of reality stipulated by this comprehensive dispensation. Human beings, according to the prevailing power/knowledge regime, are in effect entities that exist in order to be "beheld."[13]

The story that Foucault tells here, which is utterly consistent throughout the book, is obviously a story of "normalization." This is his master theme, and it forms the core of his theoretical vision.[14] However, one senses, in reading the passage we have quoted, that there is a more subtle dimension to Foucault's account. What does it mean to say that the kind of thorough subjection established by these rituals of uniform examination reposes on "a principle of compulsory visibility"? One thinks, perhaps, of butterflies in a butterfly collection (or moths in a moth collection? Or beetles?) arrayed in carefully laid-out rows for the obsessive contemplation of the collector. (I cannot help thinking of Darwin's astonishing beetle collection on display at the University Museum of Zoology in Cambridge.) *We* are these "objectified" beetles or moths – available to be beheld by those who have imposed the discipline in question, who have pinned us to the display board so we can be seen as they want us to be seen. Although Foucault does not quite spell this out, one gets an unmistakable impression that "objectification" in this sense of being arrayed in rows for the proud inspection of those whose gaze we are subject to is even more degrading than what is otherwise conveyed by the notion of normalization. I suspect that Foucault would resist the idea that regimes of power could be measured (normatively) according to whether they respect or insult our sense of our own humanity (power is power, he characteristically insists); still, I think that Foucault does intimate with this analysis that while normalization degrades us, or insults our humanity, deeper still is the degradation and insult to our humanity involved in being objectified so as to be available to power's gaze.

---

[13] As I doubt Foucault would deny, it's not hard to discern an echo of Heidegger in this analysis. What Heidegger would conceptualize as a constellation of Being, Foucault would conceptualize as a regime of power. I would be inclined to say that, philosophically speaking, these two conceptions are more similar than might be evident at first glance. See, for instance, Martin Heidegger, "The Age of the World Picture," in Heidegger, *The Question Concerning Technology and Other Essays*, trans. William Lovitt (New York: Harper and Row, 1977); as well as Foucault 's major philosophical work, *The Order of Things* [*Les Mots et les choses*] (London: Tavistock Publications, 1970). Again, I don't think it would be especially hard to get Foucault to acknowledge the Heideggerian overtones of his account of "compulsory objectification." We can add: Foucault's resistance to applying normative labels to his theorizing (even though it is normative through and through) is also a part of a (self-conscious) Heideggerian legacy in Foucault, Derrida, and others.

[14] See the discussion of normalization on pages 183–184. "Like surveillance and with it, normalization becomes one of the great instruments of power at the end of the classical age" (p. 184).

Let us offer one further important remark about Foucault's notion of "the gaze" as a mode of power. Nancy Fraser is surely right in suggesting that the ultimate Foucaultian nightmare is "a perfected disciplinary society in which normalizing power has become so omnipresent, so finely attuned, so penetrating, interiorized, and subjectified, and therefore so invisible, that there is no longer any need for confessors, psychoanalysts, wardens, and the like" – that is, a "fully 'panopticized' society [where] all would surveil and police themselves."[15] Hence the kind of surveillance by an invisible other depicted in films like Francis Ford Coppola's *The Conversation* and Florian Henckel von Donnersmarck's *The Lives of Others* does not represent the limit-point of Foucault's dystopian vision; self-surveillance (by something like a Freudian super-ego[16]) is in principle much worse.

Foucault, throughout his work, is obsessed by the idea of how knowledge and power are entangled with each other, and how regimes of knowledge always function in tandem with regimes of power. Knowledge is never liberating; it is always, so to speak, the manual being applied by the army of technicians or functionaries necessary for the functioning of a disciplinary society.

Historically, the process by which the bourgeoisie became in the course of the eighteenth century the politically dominant class was masked by the establishment of an explicit, coded and formally egalitarian juridical framework, made possible by the organization of a parliamentary, representative regime. But the development and generalization of disciplinary mechanisms constituted the other, dark side of these processes. The general juridical form that guaranteed a system of rights that were egalitarian in principle was supported by these tiny, everyday, physical mechanisms, by all those systems of micro-power that are essentially non-egalitarian and asymmetrical that we call the disciplines....The "Enlightenment," which discovered the liberties, also invented the disciplines. (p. 222)

Again, take note of how Foucault uses scare quotes (present in the French original) to signal his unmasking or debunking operation. The irony is almost too obvious to need pointing out: the Enlightenment took itself to be a gigantic enterprise of the unmasking of myths and prejudices, but for Foucault (as for Nietzsche and Adorno) it is itself in need of a more radical work of unmasking.[17] That is, liberal society, from its onset and consistently

---

[15] Fraser, *Unruly Practices*, p. 49.

[16] Recall that in the second prologue, I quoted Freud to the effect that with the creation of the super-ego, civilization disciplines the ego by "setting up an internal authority *to watch over him*, like a garrison in a conquered town." The proto-Foucaultian character of this text is obvious.

[17] Note the explicit language of "masking" [*s'est abrité derrière*: the rise of the bourgeoisie is sheltered/screened behind the corresponding juridical framework] in the passage that I have just quoted from

thereafter, has a Dr. Jekyll-and-Mr. Hyde character that it is the essential job of the genealogist to penetrate. This text supplies another key formula by which to encapsulate Foucault's broader vision of things: the disciplinary character of "*the disciplines.*" This play on words captures the intimate reciprocal entanglement of knowledge and power. As Foucault suggests on page 226, the natural sciences that arose in early modernity "had its operating model no doubt in the Inquisition," and "what this politico-juridical, administrative and criminal, religious and lay, investigation was to the sciences of nature, disciplinary analysis has been to the sciences of man."

Again, the notion that one cannot disengage power from truth or truth from power is one of Foucault's key ideas. In any society, they are locked together in a unified and inseparable nexus, in what he calls a power-right-truth "triangle": "truth isn't outside power.... Truth is a thing of this world; it is produced only by virtue of multiple forms of constraint.... Each society has its regime of truth, its 'general politics' of truth: that is, the types of discourse which it accepts and makes function as true."[18] A given regime of truth is constitutive of a given regime of power, and a regime of power is likewise constitutive of a regime of truth. Once again, this constellation of power-right-truth operates differently in different societies and different epochs, but in a "disciplinary" society like ours (in the dual sense of being geared to disciplining its subjects and using academic or intellectual knowledge-disciplines as crucial tools of its regimenting function), it is specifically the modern disciplines (psychiatry, economics, sociology, criminology, and so on) that provide the pivotal point of intersection joining power and truth.

This brings us to the last of the Foucaultian themes that I'm interested in sketching – namely, Foucault's profound and uncompromising skepticism that the main public services provided by modern society are really fundamentally geared toward the social purposes that they profess to be serving. Rather, Foucault-style genealogical analysis *sees through* these supposed purposes, and exposes them as being in fact driven by an urge toward society-wide supervision and control. In his discussion of Bentham's Panopticon, Foucault highlights the relation between Bentham's penal vision and the

---

page 222; the mask must be ripped off! Cf. the sentence from pages 16–17 quoted earlier: "A new character came on the scene, masked [*masqué*]." Habermas, in the title of chapter 9 of *The Philosophical Discourse of Modernity*, quite rightly characterizes Foucault's project as "an unmasking of the human sciences"; see also his reference on page 4 to the kind of totalizing critique that "pulls away the veil of reason from before the sheer will to power."

[18] Michel Foucault, *Power/Knowledge*, ed. Colin Gordon (New York: Pantheon Books, 1980), pp. 93, 131.

broad spectrum of other human purposes that are of concern to Bentham and that he thinks will be simultaneously advanced by "the panoptic mechanism" (discipline-cum-inspection): "Morals reformed – health preserved – industry invigorated – public burthens lightened – Economy seated, as it were, upon a rock" (p. 207, quoting page 39 of Volume IV of the 1843 edition of Bentham's *Works*). The broader aim, then, of "the panoptic schema" is "to strengthen the social forces – to increase production, to develop the economy, spread education, raise the level of public morality; to increase and multiply" (p. 208). By associating them with panopticism, that is, the goal of "a generalized surveillance" and of "a society penetrated through and through with disciplinary mechanisms" (p. 209), all of these public ends come to seem *utterly sinister*. Yet what kind of society can we have that *does not* minister to these kinds of social goods? Foucault never addresses this question. Foucault's job, as he sees it, is to trace the mechanisms, the technologies, by which "the disciplinary society" draws all of us into its "systems of micro-power," its "minute disciplines" (pp. 222, 223).[19] The point is that *all* the spheres of life within which standard human purposes are pursued have been colonized by this "subtle, calculated technology of subjection," by this "power that insidiously objectifies those on whom it is applied" (pp. 221, 220). The inevitable effect is not to focus on families as cultivators of the virtues of family life,[20] or schools as cultivators of learning, or hospitals as cultivators of healthiness and the curing of illnesses,[21] or places of employment as cultivators of decent livelihoods, but to focus on all of

---

[19] Cf. page 215: "'Discipline' may be identified neither with an institution nor with an apparatus; it is a type of power, a modality for its exercise, comprising a whole set of instruments, techniques, procedures, levels of application, targets; it is a 'physics' or an 'anatomy' of power, a technology." Also, page 225: panopticism represents "the abstract formula of a very real technology, that of individuals."

[20] As regards the family's complicity in modern society's conspiracy of discipline and micro-power, see pages 215–216: "intra-familial relations, essentially in the parents-children cell, have become 'disciplined,' absorbing since the classical age external schemata, first educational and military, then medical, psychiatric, psychological, which have made the family the privileged locus of emergence for the disciplinary question of the normal and the abnormal." In other words, the institution of the family serves as a kind of domestic police.

[21] One of the illustrations in the book (plate 10 in the English edition, plate 30 in the French edition) is for me of particular interest. It depicts a bent tree being forcibly straightened, plainly the reproduction of the frontispiece from an eighteenth-century manual on orthopedics. The implied suggestion is that orthopedics exists to advance a sinister project of "normalization" (as if there is something morally suspect about bent trees). Well, in fact a member of my family has had the orthopedic operation figuratively depicted in this illustration. Scoliosis, left untreated, has debilitating effects later in life, and it is one of the many miracles of modern medicine that corrective surgery is in fact possible. It seems questionable at best (and for victims of scoliosis, perhaps offensive) to suggest that orthopedic surgery of this kind is really geared toward *normalization* rather than toward the *medical purposes* such a science claims to be serving. (Needless to say, one could apply an analogous counter-analysis to all the other institutions stigmatized by Foucault.)

these social institutions as part of a universal network of pervasive power, as one stupendous "mechanism of discipline" (p. 223), enforcing submission by placing the subjects entangled in these institutions "under a gaze that supervises them" (p. 154). How can we come to view the different sub-spheres of our social life in this way without impugning the legitimacy of their putative purposes (health, education, public justice, a well-functioning economy, and so on)? And how can we impugn these purposes without rendering incoherent *any* conceivable vision of viable social life?[22] If the fundamental purposes of an organized modern society are, as Foucault thinks, a kind of "front" for "a society penetrated through and through with disciplinary mechanisms," it is hard to see how we avoid the normative outcome that all these social ends get thoroughly delegitimized. But if that happens, what *are* the genuine public purposes that a society can pursue without falling subject to Foucault's universal genealogical indictment? Taking Foucault's debunking account of schools, hospitals, factories, armies, prisons, and mental institutions with full seriousness thus induces a kind of intellectual vertigo. To be sure, no one living in the twenty-first century can fail to see that modern societies organize themselves in ways that are ludicrously complex and over-bureaucratized. Still, it is very important not to lose sight of the *social purposes* served by these hyper-bureaucratized routines – which is what happens when one regards them, à la Foucault, as surveillance for the sake of surveillance.

Our canvassing of themes in Foucault's book barely scratches the surface and gives only a mere glimpse of the richness of his historical vignettes and the rhetorical power of his theoretical analyses. Still, I think it suffices to allow us to see that there is a comprehensive vision here of what defines the modern social order, and why it is dehumanizing. It may be helpful to draw together the various strands of the Foucaultian mode of theorizing by way of a stylized contrast with Habermas, since they are in an important sense philosophical antipodes. To put the contrast fairly crudely, for Habermas, talk (deliberation, communication, the reaching of unforced consensus) is everything; the aim of politics is to allow talk to transcend power.[23]

---

[22] Cf. Habermas's references (*The Philosophical Discourse of Modernity*, p. 4) to "the anarchist farewell to modernity" and "the 'primordial' anarchism under whose sign postmodernity marches." Without question, Habermas would see Foucault as an exemplar of these theoretical tendencies – and in my view, rightly so.

[23] As Habermas puts it in *The Philosophical Discourse of Modernity*, p. 305, the self-understanding of the Enlightenment is that it confronts raw power with non-power or anti-power, "namely the unforced

For Foucault, by contrast, *power* is everything. It's not sufficient just to talk, we have to *fight back*. And fighting back requires us to comprehend (genealogically) just how manipulated and subjugated we are. The ideal of deliberation bewitches us into thinking power can be transcended.

As I have already observed, power sometimes takes on, in Foucault's writing, something approaching "metaphysical" status. Consider the following passage:

[The individual is] a reality fabricated by this specific technology of power that I have called "discipline." We must cease once and for all to describe the effects of power in negative terms: it "excludes," it "represses," it "censors," it "abstracts," it "masks," it "conceals." In fact, power produces; it produces reality; it produces domains of objects and rituals of truth. The individual and the knowledge that may be gained of him belong to this production. (p. 194)

These sentences strike me as shamelessly disingenuous. They represent Foucault's attempt to feign a normative neutrality that is completely contrary to the whole spirit of his book. The negative depiction of power, as objectifying, as manipulative, as dissembling and obfuscatory, and as a ceaseless insult to human dignity, is precisely how Foucault himself intends us to receive his critical analyses. *Discipline and Punish* is one long protest against our condition as slaves of modern power. Foucault's fundamental enterprise, as Habermas rightly suggests, is an *unmasking* of the human sciences, and as such, necessarily presents itself as *cryptonormative*.[24]

If there is one thing that will never cease to be rather baffling about Foucault as the political philosopher that he really is, it's the question of why he thinks fidelity to his intellectual enterprise requires him to disavow the normative power of his own theorizing. My project in this chapter has been to sketch some suggestions about how to draw a political philosophy out of *Discipline and Punish*. But of course it is not at all clear that Foucault himself would grant the legitimacy of such a project; on the contrary, we have good reason to think that he would resist our efforts to impute a normative vision to him. No doubt, Foucault's preferred self-image would not be that of a political philosopher but rather, that of a debunker of systems of power and of their supporting ideological mystifications. As he put it in his

force of a better insight" – in contrast to the dialectic of enlightenment thesis shared by Foucault and Adorno, which asserts that modern reason itself operates on behalf of raw power.

[24] See notes 8 and 17 above. In the passage just quoted from *Discipline and Punish*, p. 194, Foucault declares that "we must cease once and for all" conceptualizing power by applying to it pejorative notions of "masking" and "concealing" (as well as "excluding" and "repressing"). But as we have highlighted throughout this chapter, Foucault's own genealogical analysis makes no sense as soon as we subtract precisely these sorts of pejorative notions.

debate with Chomsky (cited in note 4), Nietzsche was right that normative ideals are merely ideological weapons in a struggle for power between those who *have* power and those who *seek* power. And Foucault self-consciously sides with the power-*seeking* side – those shut out of power and endeavoring to turn the tables on those who currently have the upper hand. That is, Foucault largely conceives his enterprise as a *political intervention* in a raw struggle for power – not primarily as an intellectual pursuit, or a quest for the truth.[25] In fact, the appeal to truth is, in his view, just as bogus and ideological as the appeal to justice, or the appeal to normatively elevated ideas about the proper fulfillment of human nature. Hence, vindicating the claim that Foucault belongs to the company of political philosophers articulating visions of how to realize our full humanity presumes that it is possible to rescue Foucault, or pry him loose from, his own resolute Nietzschean self-image. Can we do that without violating the whole spirit of his thought?[26]

Foucault would never deny that he is a committed critic of existing practices and institutions; the question then is whether root-and-branch social criticism can make sense except insofar as it is criticism in relation to a normative standard. If so, there has to be a political philosophy in Foucault whether he acknowledges it or not. Suppose Foucault, or someone defending Foucault, counters that his enterprise is that of a critically-minded historian, and that calling him a political philosopher imposes upon him an intellectual vocation that isn't his. So the claim would be that what Foucault offers is strictly a historical account of the rise of modern society. However, this does not prove that Foucault's narrative isn't informed by normative commitments or that his work as a historian is normatively innocent. On the contrary, it may be possible to draw from Foucault's theorizing a better appreciation of the *reciprocal interaction* between empirical claims and normative claims than is granted in many quarters (including by Foucault). That is, to the extent that what Foucault presents as the history of modernity is a true history, his normative commitments gain rational credibility;

---

[25] It would not be entirely off the mark to suggest that Foucault himself sees his books as the intellectual equivalent of anarchists at an anti-globalization riot throwing rocks at the police.

[26] Aristotle's claim in the opening sentences of the *Nicomachean Ethics*, that human beings cannot help being animated by some conception – presumed to be true, but always capable of being off the mark – of what the appropriate ends of human life (whether power or pleasure or wealth or virtue or wisdom) are, seems incontestably right. Political philosophy is in that sense simply the extension, pursued by concerted intellectual exertion, of a desire for grasp of the right ends that is inscribed in all human life. If Foucault is right then Aristotle is wrong, and vice versa. No reader of this book can be in any doubt about my own position: that Aristotle's view possesses a philosophical coherence that Foucault's view lacks.

conversely, the more it's true that what concerns him normatively really is worthy of the intellectual energy he invests in those concerns, the more likely it is that his exertions as a historian of our modern social universe will attend to features of our historical experience that truly need to be intellectually brought to light. In other words, empirical claims and normative theorizing gain compellingness (or lose compellingness) in tandem. And the same thing would apply in the case of the other thinkers considered in this book.[27]

Overall, Foucault's rhetoric relentlessly pounds into us the idea that all our supposed freedoms are just masks of oppression; that all the agencies of modern social life that supposedly serve human welfare (schools, clinics, mental hospitals, social welfare organizations, armies, places of employment) constitute the thousand tentacles that strangle us in every aspect of our being; and that all the science and modes of knowledge by which we supposedly enlighten ourselves are really just an extension of the Inquisition.[28] In short, it is all just an enormous prison, or worse, a panopticon that imprisons us and then humiliates us by exposing us to omnipresent inspection and manipulation. And as I mentioned at the start of this chapter, the video cameras that record our every movement in twenty-first-century cities would no doubt be seen by Foucault (and perhaps rightly so) as fully confirming and vindicating his identification of panopticism as a key organizing principle of

[27] Admittedly, the idea of an easy harmony between the enterprise of historiography and the enterprise of political philosophy is not free of puzzles. For instance, Leo Strauss, in *The City and Man*, presents Thucydides as a political philosopher alongside Plato and Aristotle; and I have long wondered whether this is really possible. To the extent that one is principally exerting oneself to get the facts of history right, as Thucydides insists that he is, it seems that one loses the freedom to fashion a normative vision. Consider the relation between speeches in Thucydides' *History* and speeches in Plato's dialogues: with the former, one is constrained to seek correspondence with what actually transpired in the past, something that doesn't apply to the latter. That is, if Thucydides truly is committed to historiography, the Thucydidean speeches convey (or seek to convey) what the historical protagonists did in fact say, and hence cannot convey the writer's normative vision. Of course, one may think that history itself, narrated veridically, conveys essential insights or truths about the right way for human beings to live a good life (think of Hobbes's *Behemoth* or Hume's *History of England*); Hobbes obviously translated Thucydides' *History* into English for just that reason. Yet this seems like a somewhat different enterprise than the crafting of, say, a Thucydidean political philosophy. (Positivism, perhaps, derives from a radicalization of this line of thought.) In any case, all of this is surely less of a problem for Foucault, since, as we have noted, he indicates again and again that he regards "truth," no less than justice, merely as an ideological weapon in the struggle for power.

[28] Of course, the self-image of the Enlightenment is that it represents a triumph over the Inquisition because it stands for uncoerced liberty of philosophical reflection (for instance, with respect to Galileo's right to see what he saw through his telescope and to think freely the thoughts that followed from what he saw). See Hobbes, *Leviathan*, ed. Richard Tuck, rev. student edition (Cambridge: Cambridge University Press, 1996), pp. 471 and 480. Foucault's deliberately paradoxical counter-claim is that the Enlightenment, no less than the Inquisition, was in fact an instrument of social control, hence of unfreedom.

contemporary social life. The dream of knowledge and freedom turns out to be the worst nightmare, but the characterization of social reality as a nightmare is no less a normative vision than the characterization of it as a dream. No one would disqualify Plato as a political philosopher if it turned out that he really was no purveyor of a utopia (which in fact he probably wasn't); that is, if it turned out that the only purpose of his theorizing was to shatter or puncture the false pretensions of the various debased regimes dominating the political life of his time (and arguably all times). And the same applies to Foucault. To unleash a critique, however harsh and however unbounded in its scope, is still, ineluctably, to deliver a normative judgment.

One can easily see the line of thought prompting Foucault's hostility to the normative enterprise as he conceives it – namely, the idea that every time a set of exalted ideals gets proclaimed, whether those of liberalism, Marxism, or any other grand ideal, it serves merely (Foucault thinks) to erect another prison, and he is determined to avoid that.[29] However, if Foucault is right that the liberal state and liberal society's agencies of health, education, sanitation, penal justice, and so on, are not really in the service of the human needs they claim to serve, but rather, constitute merely the thousand tentacles of unfreedom, then this idea, willy-nilly, conjures up a vision of unstrangled human possibilities no less than the ruling ideas he is resolved to debunk. Life isn't livable without the articulation of views of what life should be, and despite Foucault's emphatic disclaimers (prompted by his "Nietzschean" commitment to stick to the task of unmasking spurious grand ideals[30]), he too has a view of life outside the prison.

---

[29] For Foucault, there is no doctrine of liberation because all such doctrines presuppose the possibility of identifying one key source of illegitimate power (for instance, in the case of Marxism: a capitalist-run economy; in the case of anarchism: state coercion; in the case of ideologies of sexual liberation: sexual repression; and so on), so that the way to achieve liberation is to overthrow that particular locus of oppressive power. But Foucault is committed to the doctrine that power is *everywhere* – encapsulated in the key Foucaultian conception of the "capillary" nature of modern power. (Cf. the social theory of Niklas Luhmann as encapsulated by Habermas on pages 357–358 of *The Philosophical Discourse of Modernity*.) And if power is everywhere, then overturning one type of power will merely erect another, opposing regime of power. This is why Foucault, in his debate with Chomsky, refuses to recognize a regime-independent idea of justice: every regime proclaims its own version of justice, hence one has to simply throw in one's lot with one or another side in the ubiquitous struggle for power. Ancient political philosophy, helpfully enough, gives us a name for this specific doctrine – sophism.

[30] Foucault's enterprise is intended to be Nietzschean in the sense that Foucault conceives "genealogy" (the unmasking or debunking of mendacious ideals) as exhausting the business of theory. But Nietzsche unquestionably had a very clear idea of what constituted human nobility, and championed this ideal very robustly. So Foucault's intellectual project is Nietzschean only with respect to the negative or critical side of Nietzsche's theorizing, not at all the positive side. For further discussion of decisive contrasts between Foucault and Nietzsche, see Beiner, *Philosophy in a Time of Lost Spirit*, pp. 65–67.

II

Alasdair MacIntyre: Fragmentation and Wholeness

Alasdair MacIntyre is a thinker who belongs on any list of the leading critics of modernity of the last half-century. In previous chapters, we have canvassed several of the other thinkers who belong on such a list, but MacIntyre's critique is significantly different from theirs and it is important to understand what distinguishes him as a critic of modernity and see what themes are characteristic of his distinctive mode of theorizing. As between Arendt's emphasis on freedom and Strauss's emphasis on virtue, MacIntyre clearly sides with Strauss, but he would have no interest in or patience with Strauss's esotericist (i.e., Averroist) view of religion,[1] and while MacIntyre does not favor egalitarianism over hierarchy in all respects (he is after all a committed Catholic), hierarchy, for him, is so to speak hierarchy in the service of egalitarianism, which is not at all the case for Strauss. Like both Arendt and Strauss (Voegelin too), MacIntyre offers a very ambitious historical meta-narrative, leading from virtuous antiquity to corrupt modernity (or in Arendt's case, I guess, leading from *free* antiquity to *slavish* modernity). Much of the force of MacIntyre's theorizing flows from the actual details of his meta-narrative, which (like Strauss's and Voegelin's) largely consists in powerful interpretations of great thinkers in the history of philosophy; as for Strauss, the history of our moral decline is traceable principally via a story of decline etched in the sequence of epic thinkers from Plato and Aristotle onward. For MacIntyre, Aristotelian ethical theory is more or less perfected in Aquinas, and the moral theories spawned during the Enlightenment, which for us tend to be seen as intellectually and morally authoritative, MacIntyre sees as a mere battleground of moral conflict and moral

---

[1] I attempt to elaborate aspects of MacIntyre's unspoken stance toward Strauss in a discussion at the end of this chapter.

incoherence.[2] We don't have the space to work our way through all the details of this tale of ethical unraveling (mediated by the history of philosophy); a summary of and brief critical engagement with MacIntyre's version of neo-Aristotelianism will have to suffice.

The first thing that we need to do in reading MacIntyre is to think seriously about the title of *After Virtue*. What does "after virtue" mean? It means, fundamentally, that there was an era when the practice of virtue, as a coherent human practice, was a genuine human possibility, and that is not the era in which we now live. It has to be "coherent" in the sense of fitting into some larger ensemble of social practices and social understandings and self-understandings, and those conditions of coherence have somehow been erased or have lapsed or been hollowed out. (One can use different metaphors here, and of course, something will inevitably hang on the kind of metaphors that are deployed.) Obviously, a fairly large narrative (including a historical narrative) is required in order to clarify what these conditions of moral coherence are and how they might disappear or cease to be present, and the main onus resting on MacIntyre is to supply this narrative; that is what his book is intended to do.

If ethical Aristotelianism means anything, it first of all has to mean that it is meaningful to reflect on something like a notion of the human telos, a notion of human flourishing capable in the best circumstances of being fully consummated by human animals.[3] Plants flourish when they receive

---

[2] As Brian Barry not unjustly observes, for MacIntyre, Thomism is sufficiently vindicated by its improvements in the coherence of traditions of moral discourse inherited from Aristotelianism and Augustinianism. "But this scarcely seems good enough. We should surely begin by asking whether it makes any sense to suggest that modern societies should be reconstructed on a model that would entail rolling back not only the Enlightenment but the Reformation." See "The Light that Failed?" *Ethics*, Vol. 100, no. 1 (October, 1989), pp. 160–168, at p. 168. MacIntyre never straightforwardly asserts that the Reformation and the Enlightenment were colossal mistakes, but such a claim does seem implied by the general thrust of his meta-narrative. MacIntyre's ubiquitous theme that the Enlightenment fails to redeem its promise of a universal and rational morality seems an indirect way of impugning the Enlightenment without actually repudiating it explicitly. (I come back to MacIntyre's attitude toward the Enlightenment at the end of this chapter.) To be sure, MacIntyre might regard Barry's challenge as an instance of what Foucault, in a famous phrase, called "the blackmail of the Enlightenment" (*The Foucault Reader*, ed. Paul Rabinow [New York: Pantheon Books, 1984], pp. 42–45) – that is, the counterclaim that it is a question too complex to admit of a straightforward yes or no answer (yes the Enlightenment benefited humanity or no it didn't). Foucault had very definite reasons for resisting such questions, bound up with his unique (and often perverse) conception of theory. However, pace Foucault, in principle it seems to me perfectly reasonable to ask whether human beings are better off overall by virtue of living in a post-Enlightenment rather than pre-Enlightenment world.

[3] As we note elsewhere in this book, it is not exactly easy to reconcile a teleological account of ethical life with what modern science has established as a non-teleological account of the universe. We see this, for instance, in Leo Strauss's acknowledgement, in the introduction to *Natural Right and History*,

the right amount of sunlight and the right amount of water; animals flourish when they are fed and exercised in certain ways; humans flourish when they receive cultural and intellectual stimulation of the right sort, and when they are educated in ways that bring out their highest potential. Hence with MacIntyre (unlike other thinkers treated in this book), there is no attempt to obscure, or elide, or hedge on, the fact that moral philosophy, no less than moral reflection, is necessarily implicated in conceptions of the good (nor is he the least bit agnostic about these conceptions themselves).[4] Of course, it is much easier to say that there is a human telos of some description yet to be specified than to spell out in detail exactly what its content is.[5] Aristotle went pretty far in sketching the content of a flourishing life, and while MacIntyre's depiction is not always as determinate, it is fair to say that he does give us clear enough hints about forms of human life that move in the direction of a consummated human telos, and forms of human life that move away from such a telos. It is obviously not an accident that the forms of human life that move away from the human telos as sketched by MacIntyre are invariably aligned with contemporary social life as we know it.

Like Habermas (as we will see in a later chapter), MacIntyre wants to bring the insights of sociology to bear upon moral philosophy, but the lessons that he draws from this fusion of sociology and philosophy are radically different from those drawn by Habermas. Unlike Habermas, MacIntyre's

---

that no clear solution to "this basic problem" presents itself (which seems correct). In "Bernstein's Distorting Mirrors" (*Soundings*, Vol. 67, no. 1 [1984], p. 39), MacIntyre offers the following interesting suggestion:"if we find compelling reasons for accepting a particular view of the virtues and the human telos, that in itself will place constraints on what kind of theory of human nature *and what kind of cosmology* are rationally acceptable"; my italics. But how exactly is this supposed to work? Is MacIntyre saying that the philosophical plausibility of an Aristotelian interpretation of ethical teleology gives us reasons to reconsider modern science's rejection of Aristotelian cosmology?

4 Notwithstanding perfectionist versions of liberalism (that of Joseph Raz, for instance), of which MacIntyre is clearly aware, MacIntyre's anti-liberal polemics often give the impression that a demonstration that appeals to conceptions of the good are unavoidable suffices as a refutation of liberalism, which in turn presumes that liberalism presupposes neutrality. However, as Brian Barry convincingly argues in the review essay cited in note 2 ("The Light that Failed?" pp. 167 and 168), this is a mistake because more coherent versions of liberalism are non-neutralist. For a fuller elaboration of Barry's *liberal* critique of liberal neutrality, see "How Not to Defend Liberal Institutions," in *Liberalism and the Good*, ed. R.B. Douglass, G.M. Mara, and H.S. Richardson (New York: Routledge, 1990), pp. 44–58. Barry's challenge to MacIntyre is one that could also be deployed against my book, *What's the Matter with Liberalism?* (Berkeley: University of California Press, 1992).

5 MacIntyre famously declared that "the good life for man is the life spent in seeking for the good life for man" (Alasdair MacIntyre, *After Virtue*, 3rd ed. [Notre Dame, IN: University of Notre Dame Press, 2007], p. 219; subsequent references to the book will be to this edition). It would be hard to argue with someone who protested that arriving at this conclusion is much too easy an answer to the question of the human telos.

insistence upon the relevance of history and sociology to moral philosophy yields a deep dissatisfaction with modernity, as well as a deep dissatisfaction with liberalism as the, so to speak, official philosophical articulation of modernity.

For MacIntyre, human beings are first and foremost storytelling animals. We cannot be properly socialized, nor can we acquire ethical identities (shaped by an understanding of virtues and vices), without thick narratives told to us by our cultures. The purpose of a culture is precisely to teach us what it is to be virtuous and what it is to be vicious, and these ethical teachings cannot be conveyed in an abstract fashion; they have to be embodied in stories about what a particular society expects of us as human beings – that is, what it means to be a human being in the context of such a society. As MacIntyre develops in chapter 15 of *After Virtue*, a human life enacts a particular story, narratable once the life has completed its full trajectory, and we live our lives, implicitly if not self-consciously, with a view to the narrative coherence of the persons we're trying to be.[6] But social life is no less an exercise in narrativity – our existence in common becomes meaningful insofar as it generates stories that build up a thick shared identity or a robust collective self-understanding.

---

[6] See *After Virtue*, 3rd ed., p. 205, where MacIntyre avows his commitment to the "concept of a self whose unity resides in the unity of a narrative which links birth to death as narrative beginning to middle to end." As a point of contrast to MacIntyre's narrativist view of moral selfhood, consider Julian Barnes, *Nothing to be Frightened of* (London: Jonathan Cape, 2008), pp. 189–190: "if, as we approach death and look back on our lives and 'we understand our narrative' and stamp a final meaning upon it, I suspect we are doing little more than confabulating: processing strange, incomprehensible, contradictory input into some kind of believable story – but believable mainly to ourselves.... Doctors, priests and novelists conspire to present human life [misleadingly] as a story progressing towards a meaningful conclusion." Barnes hits on the crux of the issue when he writes: A book written by my mother about her life "might have contained anecdotes, scenelets, character portraits, satire, even levity; but this would not add up to a narrative. [In our lives we get] one damn thing after another ... rather than a story. Or ... there is no proper announcement of theme, followed by development, variation, recapitulation, coda, and crunching resolution. There is an occasional heart-lifting aria, much prosaic recitative, but little through-composition." That is, *real* narratives possess a narrative coherence (corresponding to the coherence of musical compositions – development, variation, recapitulation, coda, resolution) that human lives as such do not possess. However, one can put the counter-challenge back to Barnes: but then why is Barnes himself, as a novelist committed to narrative "through-composition," telling his *own* life-story in the very book from which I have drawn these passages? (It should be noted that on page 249, Barnes *readmits* the possibility – by which he is either "tempted" or "deceived" – "that a human life is after all a narrative, and contains the proper satisfactions of a decent novel.") For a philosophically more fleshed-out – and even more radical – challenge to the kind of narrativist view one gets in MacIntyre, see Galen Strawson, "Against Narrativity," in *Real Materialism and Other Essays* (Oxford: Clarendon Press, 2008). As is clear from Barnes's book, he and Strawson are friends, and therefore he may well have developed the thoughts I have quoted as a way of reflecting on, or trying to come to terms with, Strawson's militantly anti-narrativist position. Barnes follows this up with some good reflections on what is at stake between narrativism (a là MacIntyre) and anti-narrativism (a là Galen Strawson) in his brilliant essay on Lucian Freud, "Heart-Squasher," in the December 5 issue of *London Review of Books*.

Although he never exactly puts it like this, one way of formulating MacIntyre's critique of liberal modernity is to say that modern liberal culture falls short as a begetter of normatively meaningful stories; it is not thick enough as a culture to generate the kinds of stories we require in order to be properly socialized, to be instructed in how to be a virtuous human being rather than a vicious human being. Roughly put, MacIntyre's thesis is that ethical resources in modern liberal societies have atrophied because the storytelling capacities of such societies have atrophied.[7] Modern liberal culture, to too great an extent, leaves us free to compose our own individual narratives out of the ethical resources we construct for ourselves. That is to say, the ethical resources available to us are in a state of intolerable atrophy even before we receive them, and this has dire consequences for the prospect of living an ethical life, for reasoning and deliberating with each other as social and political beings, and even for living lives that are individually meaningful. This sounds like an extremely unhappy cultural dispensation in which to find oneself situated, and MacIntyre fully intends it to sound grim. MacIntyre perceives modern life as merely a shell of what a properly flourishing human life should look like, and his descriptions consistently fit this perception of modernity as thoroughly dismal. As MacIntyre puts it in the closing sentences of the prologue to the third edition of *After Virtue*, "the dominant social, economic, and political order of advanced modernity" calls for resolute resistance – albeit a just, temperate, and prudent resistance.[8]

One response to the MacIntyrean characterization of the empty-shell-like character of modern life would be to say that we do not need descriptions of what is wrong but rather *prescriptions* of what would render modernity better. This MacIntyre is resistant to offering. Given his heavy emphasis on the historical and the sociological as central to moral reflection, he is naturally very skeptical that we can lift ourselves out of the history we are currently living. One is reminded of Rousseau's critique of modernity; just as Rousseau had little to offer *prescriptively* in the face of Europe's headlong plunge into modernity other than nostalgic evocations of the

---

[7] "History suggests that in those periods when the social order becomes uneasy and even alarmed about the weakening of its moral bonds and the poverty of its moral inheritance and turns for aid to the moral philosopher and theologian, it may not find those disciplines flourishing in such a way as to be able to make available the kind of moral reflection and theory which the culture actually needs." *Revisions*, ed. Stanley Hauerwas and Alasdair MacIntyre (Notre Dame, IN: University of Notre Dame Press, 1983), p. vii; this text is from a short preface to the book co-written by MacIntyre and Hauerwas. The phrase "poverty of its moral inheritance" nicely sums up MacIntyre's whole critique of liberal thought and liberal practice.

[8] *After Virtue*, 3rd ed., p. xvi.

traces of residual premodernity glimpsable in rural Switzerland, Poland, and Corsica, so one tends to get the same in MacIntyre. He evokes premodern ways of life (farming, fishing, craft economies) that are barely hanging on at the margins of modern Western societies, and he insists that they, and they alone, preserve a reminder of what an ethically integrated, ethically coherent culture looks like.[9] What modernity offers is just the opposite of what these premodern cultures supplied by way of ethical socialization and narrativity. If one makes the point to MacIntyre that we cannot now go back to a craft economy, or a way of life founded on everyone in the society fishing together in the same fishing boats or mining together in the same mines, he will not hesitate to agree. That, he will say, is precisely the problem; without fishing in the same fishing boats or mining in the same mines, our storytelling capacities will atrophy, and as our storytelling capacities atrophy, so too will our ethical capacities. That's the modern predicament!

An example of normatively meaningful storytelling from *After Virtue* can perhaps illustrate what he thinks is missing from (in his view) narratively atrophied, or what we can call "narratively challenged," modern culture. What particularly needs to be grasped here is, for MacIntyre, the essential relation between narrative and morality, because for him the two are inseparable. In chapter 9 of *After Virtue* (pp. 111–113), MacIntyre gives us an account of the Polynesian taboo against men and women eating together. This moral practice was obviously not a free-standing moral rule; it was an integral aspect of, for instance, Polynesian cosmology, which told the Polynesians a story of the universe as well as their relation to it. That is, these taboo rules were meaningful to them because they inhabited *a real culture*; it provided all-encompassing structures of intelligibility, and the taboo was meaningful as long as – and *only* as long as – the broader cultural package maintained its coherence (which it eventually lost).[10] It is the *history*

---

[9] As I discuss in chapter 15 of *Philosophy in a Time of Lost Spirit* (Toronto: University of Toronto Press, 1997), such themes (e.g., the eclipse of craft economies) also figure prominently in the work of Christopher Lasch. MacIntyre is interested in "oases" of communitarian existence within the liberal desert that (for him) vindicate the continuing possibility of stubborn "holdouts" against the overwhelmingly dominant economic and social order. For instance, in an interesting paper entitled "Practical Rationality and Irrationality and their Social Settings," MacIntyre examines the Thorupstrand Guild of coastal fishermen, a Danish fishing co-op in Northern Jutland. MacIntyre fully recognizes that such holdouts will eventually succumb to the dominant structures of money and power. Still, he sees their perseverance, however doomed, as (perhaps indispensable) hedges against total despair.

[10] MacIntyre would certainly be uncomfortable being positioned alongside Nietzsche, but it is undeniable that there are significant analogies between their conceptions of modernity. See, for instance, Friedrich Nietzsche, *On the Advantage and Disadvantage of History for Life*, trans. Peter Preuss (Indianapolis: Hackett, 1980), p. 24: "Our modern culture ... is no real culture at all."

of a particular culture that governs the transition from a state where "a set of taboo rules and practices [are] in good order" to one where "a set of such rules and practices ... have been fragmented and thrown into disorder" (p. 113), and this historical logic of intelligibility or unintelligibility applies with as much force to advanced modernity as it did to eighteenth-century Polynesia. As was true of the Polynesians, our modern moral concepts once meant something; today, they exist merely "as a survival from some previous more elaborate cultural background" (pp. 112–113). Because moral practices such as these depend fundamentally on a particular cultural history, there is no guarantee that they will last indefinitely. In the case of the Polynesian taboo, it was legislated out of existence in 1819, and this clearly came about, according to MacIntyre's interpretation, because the constitutive cultural background had ebbed away. On MacIntyre's account, that is the situation of *all* modern moralities: we may fool ourselves into thinking that they are still functioning "in good order"; in reality, they are just the residual fragments of a decayed moral culture that has lost its core, that is no longer whole in the way that real cultures need to be. Today we are *all* in the situation of post-1819 Polynesia, with moral practices that have lost much of their intelligibility – because we are too deracinated to take seriously the cultural narratives that once gave these moralities their point.

From *After Virtue* onward, MacIntyre is very consistent in the articulation of the key themes that concern him; and these key themes fit together into an integral package. We have already devoted some discussion to one of these master-themes – namely, MacIntyre's emphasis on the importance of narrativity, both for making sense of individual lives and for the understanding and judgment of whole cultures. Let us follow this up with sketches of six additional trademark MacIntyrean themes. The following brief survey of key conceptions in MacIntyre's philosophy is obviously incomplete, but it is sufficient for purposes of suggesting the contours of the broader intellectual package.

[1] We can start with *practical reasoning*. If the Aristotelian theme of *phronesis* and practical rationality is crucially important for Gadamer, it is no less important for MacIntyre. If we are to flourish as human beings, we need to exercise our capacities as practical reasoners, deliberating on how to realize the human good within the specificity of a concrete life.

[2] However, in order to bring about full flourishing, this cannot be merely individual reflection on one's own good. Rather, it ought to be *communal*

reflection on a *common good* ("a common mind arrived at through wide-spread shared deliberation governed by norms of rational enquiry," to cite one of his formulations[11]). Hence common good, its possibility and its status as a binding normative standard, is another key MacIntyrean theme.

[3] In order to exercise the moral capacities that are of concern to MacIntyre, we need (as already discussed) thick rather than thin ethical resources. In particular, we must be able to draw upon traditions of discourse, both intellectual and moral (and probably religious-theological as well[12]). The Enlightenment project, for MacIntyre, was misguided because it was focused on *universal* rationality – a mode of reasoning that would be authoritative for all human beings as human beings[13] – and hence slighted the importance (crucial for MacIntyre) of immersion in specific traditions of thinking and deliberating. So tradition is another key notion for MacIntyre. If we are to reason *together* on an appropriate *communal* embodiment of the good, we need to do so on the basis of thick traditions of shared rationality, founded on shared premises.[14] For MacIntyre, this explains why science is a successful cognitive enterprise that actually makes progress. MacIntyre is preoccupied with the question of why philosophy comes up short relative to the standard

[11] MacIntyre, *Dependent Rational Animals: Why Human Beings Need the Virtues* (Chicago: Open Court, 1999), p. 131; cf. 129. See also *The MacIntyre Reader*, ed. Kelvin Knight (Notre Dame, IN: University of Notre Dame, 1998), p. 239.

[12] Cf. MacIntyre, *Three Rival Versions of Moral Enquiry* (Notre Dame, IN: University of Notre Dame Press, 1990), p. 223: the kind of "homogeneity in fundamental belief" required in order for a community of inquirers to participate in productive rational dialogue encompasses not only intellectual and moral dimensions but "often enough moral-cum-theological dimensions" as well. See also *The MacIntyre Reader*, p. 152: Giving a coherent account of moral life requires the notion of progressing toward ultimate ends. However, an account of moral life in terms of ultimate ends makes sense "if and only if the universe itself is teleologically ordered, and the only type of teleologically ordered universe in which we have good reason to believe is a theistic universe"; cf. page 267. It follows that the intelligibility of morality depends on theology. Unless one presupposes the truth of theism, a teleological view of the world is out of reach, which in turn makes nonsense of morality (at least on a MacIntyrean view of ethical life). As he himself puts the point: the individual's "moral progress ... towards her or his ultimate good is always a matter of more than morality" (p. 152) – meaning: no morality without theology.

[13] Of course, since MacIntyre is committed to the search for universally valid conceptions of the good grounded in a universal doctrine of the human telos, he is no less interested in the pursuit of what's philosophically authoritative for human beings as human beings than the philosophers of the Enlightenment were. The difference is that he thinks we can only arrive at these universally valid teachings via thicker, more particularistic (more parochial) tradition-sustained communities of inquiry. His quarrel with what he takes to be the Enlightenment project concerns the *route* to the philosophical destination (truth), not the destination itself.

[14] For a good discussion, see MacIntyre, *Three Rival Versions of Moral Enquiry*, chapter 10. Consider, in particular, the appeal to "a high degree of homogeneity in fundamental belief" as a precondition of fruitful inquiry on page 223.

of cognitive progress set by science.[15] MacIntyre's standard line is that contemporary philosophy, and perhaps philosophy in general, is severely impugned by the failure of philosophers to overcome their disagreements (which he tends to see partly as cause, partly as effect, of the moral failures of *post-Enlightenment liberal societies*). MacIntyre may be the only philosopher (I am not aware of any others) who regards the mere fact of disagreement as a severe indictment of a particular field of inquiry (especially when one is speaking of a field of inquiry as stubbornly resistant to consensus as philosophy) – to say nothing of the fact that our lack of convergence on moral and intellectual questions certainly does not date from the onset of modernity but is coeval with our humanity. MacIntyre consistently holds it to be a fatal flaw of post-Enlightenment thought that the most prominent varieties of liberal political philosophy – deontological, consequentialist, contractarian, and so on – depart from incompatible premises, and therefore will never reach a rational convergence. They are stuck in radical disagreement, and always will be. But of course it is no less true that MacIntyre disagrees fundamentally with these Enlightenment philosophies, and proponents of those philosophies disagree fundamentally with him. Hence, it is hard to grasp why this does not this implicate *him* in the same philosophical impasse. Why is he (or Thomist Aristotelianism) *exempt* from the impasse that in his view condemns Enlightenment-inspired theorizing? Why should there be some special privilege associated with committing oneself to a premodern form of philosophy (as if it were elevated above the disagreements endemic to modernity)?

[4] Next, the MacIntyrean idea of a *practice*. This is another very important theme throughout his work, and is certainly central to the argument of *After Virtue* (chapter 14 of which is devoted to its explication). In his own words: "By a 'practice' I am going to mean any coherent and complex form of socially established cooperative human activity through which goods internal to that form of activity are realized in the course of trying to achieve those standards of excellence which are appropriate to, and partially definitive of, that form of activity, with the result

---

[15] I discuss this issue in "The Parochial and the Universal: MacIntyre's Idea of the University," *Revue internationale de philosophie*, no. 264 (2013), pp. 169–182. As I point out in that essay (p. 169, n. 1), MacIntyre, right from the very first page of *After Virtue*, presents science as setting a standard of rational consensus that moral philosophy must aspire to match. See also MacIntyre's important account of the nature of scientific progress in "Epistemological Crises, Dramatic Narrative, and the Philosophy of Science," in MacIntyre, *The Tasks of Philosophy* [Selected Essays, Vol. 1] (Cambridge: Cambridge University Press, 2006) pp. 3–23.

that human powers to achieve excellence, and human conceptions of the ends and goods involved, are systematically extended."[16] More economical is the following definition: practices refer to "cooperative forms of activity [string quartets, fishing crews, the collaborative interaction of architects and construction workers] whose participants jointly pursue the goods internal to those forms of activity and jointly value excellence in achieving those goods."[17]

[5] There is another key theme in MacIntyre whose importance is flagged in the title of this chapter: the need of human beings for a dimension of social life that gives them an experience of life *as integrated rather than fragmented*, as a coherent whole rather than an isolated part. One of the things that MacIntyre is very unhappy with in modern liberal society as he perceives it is that it is a society "deformed by compartmentalization."[18] MacIntyre thinks that Erving Goffman's sociology of role-playing captures something essential about modern existence as we live it.[19] Functionaries reflect on their purposes according to the perspective of what is expected of them as functionaries; people

---

[16] *After Virtue*, 3rd ed., p. 187. Immediately after this text, MacIntyre commits the non-trivial blunder of claiming that bricklaying does not constitute a practice. It suffices to read chapter 2 of *Hannah's Child: A Theologian's Memoir* (Grand Rapids, MI: William B. Eerdmans, 2010) by MacIntyre's (ex-bricklayer) friend, Stanley Hauerwas, to see the pitfalls of presuming to judge from the outside what is or is not a practice in MacIntyre's sense. The questionableness of MacIntyre's exclusion of bricklaying from his conception of a practice is also noted by James Bernard Murphy (though he doesn't go so far as to call it a blunder) in "The Teacher as the Forlorn Hope of Modernity," *Revue internationale de philosophie*, No. 264 (2013), p. 187.

[17] *The MacIntyre Reader*, ed. Knight, p. 140. One of the things I admire about Philip Roth's novels is Roth's gift for capturing what defines a particular practice as the practice that it is – for instance, the practice of leatherwork in *American Pastoral*, or the practice of digging a grave in *Everyman*. For a powerful account of how a craft culture based on one such practice (stonemasonry) gets extinguished by modernity, see Seamus Murphy, *Stone Mad* (London: Routledge and Kegan Paul, 1966). If one conjures up an image of, say, a hundred such cultural worlds being similarly obliterated, one gets a very good picture of the meaning of modernity as conceived by MacIntyre!

[18] *The MacIntyre Reader*, ed. Knight, p. 249; cf. page 243.

[19] See *After Virtue*, 3rd ed., pp. 32, 115–117, and 204–205. This theme is forcefully encapsulated in a lecture by MacIntyre entitled "A Culture of Choice and Compartmentalization"; the lecture can be viewed at the following website: http://ethicscenter.nd.edu/video/fall-conference-videos/a-culture-of-death-videos. It is significant that in the sketch of "the societies of advanced Western modernity" offered in "Politics, Philosophy and the Common Good" (*The MacIntyre Reader*, ed. Knight, pp. 235–252), the "central feature of those societies" with which MacIntyre commences his account "is the exceptional degree of compartmentalization imposed by their structures, so that the norms governing activities in any one area are specific to that area....A compartmentalized society imposes a fragmented ethics" (pp. 235–236). For a good discussion of the theme of compartmentalization in MacIntyre, see Murphy, "The Teacher as the Forlorn Hope of Modernity," pp. 185 and 189–197. In his "Replies," *Revue internationale de philosophie*, No. 264 (2013), pp. 210–211, MacIntyre both reasserts his thesis that "compartmentalization and fragmentation" are part and parcel of the sociology of modernity and claims that "movements of resistance" at "the margins of modern societies" are sometimes effective in combatting these disfiguring features of modernity as such.

holding managerial positions according to the perspective of what is expected of them as managers; and so on.[20] Social existence is too compartmentalized for individuals to reflect on what accords with the broader purposes of human life in general. Everyone is too immersed in their discrete role-playing to stand back and ask how it all fits together into a coherent whole (or to be able to pose critical questions about why coherence is lacking). This may look like an unduly harsh judgment on the denizens of liberal modernity, and perhaps it is. But it is important to note that insofar as MacIntyre's analysis does get at something about life lived within characteristically modern liberal horizons, his chief intended target is the shortcomings in the social structures of life within these horizons, not necessarily failings in these individuals as individuals.

It is easy to see the philosophical anthropology developed in Aristotle's ethics or politics as offering a counter-model to what MacIntyre sees as deficient in liberal modernity. Ethics and politics conceived in an Aristotelian mode are an exercise not only in obtaining this or that particular good, pursuing this or that particular purpose; what is at stake is a way of reflecting on how to instantiate the human good in general (as an all-encompassing good).[21] "We look for the universal in the particular."[22] Where in contemporary life, one might reasonably ask, does one find the moral space, so to speak, for overarching reflection of this kind? Ethics and politics as Aristotle presents them aim at an architectonic or all-encompassing good (namely, an experience of the human telos).[23] MacIntyre's thesis is that, judged relative to the Aristotelian standard, modernity per se entails the compartmentalization of contemporary existence, and hence stymies Aristotelian-style overarching reflection on the human good in general (what MacIntyre calls: "the nature of

[20] Relevant here is MacIntyre's famous depiction, in chapter 3 of *After Virtue*, of the therapist, the corporate manager, and the aesthete as defining "characters in the cultural dramas of modernity"; cf. page xv (prologue to the third edition), where MacIntyre adds the self-righteous conservative moralist as a fourth notable character type.

[21] As MacIntyre puts it, Aristotelian moral reflection aims at relating the various goods that are on offer within human life to the question "of how these goods are to be ordered, of which part each is to play within the structures of a whole life" (*The MacIntyre Reader*, ed. Knight, p. 141). Put otherwise: every human life, interpreted in an Aristotelian way, is a quest for narrative unity – except when distorted by the dominant practices of modernity, and distorted even further by the non-Aristotelian philosophies spawned by modernity.

[22] Ibid.

[23] Cf. Charles Taylor, "The Motivation behind a Procedural Ethics," in *Kant and Political Philosophy*, ed. Ronald Beiner and William James Booth (New Haven: Yale University Press, 1993), p. 355: MacIntyre "gives his own sense to Aristotle's notion of an 'architectonic' good."

the supreme good"[24]). No doubt, one can challenge this sociology of modern life and the moral psychology that accompanies it, but there can be no denying its central place among the concerns that animate MacIntyre's theorizing.

As we discussed earlier in connection with the Polynesian taboo, for MacIntyre it is crucial that a culture keep itself whole, for once its cultural unity begins to unravel, it is not just the culture that loses its coherence and unity and starts to dissolve into fragments; the moral self, too, loses *its* unity and it too becomes intolerably fragmented.[25] Does MacIntyre actually approve of, or sympathize with, the Polynesian segregation of men and women? Since he prides himself on his egalitarianism, it is unlikely that he does.[26] Then why lament the collapse of the taboo? Presumably, he would have to give some kind of answer along the following lines: human beings cannot realize their proper telos, cannot flourish as human beings, without being socialized into the kind of thick cultural narrative that renders moral practices intelligible in general. All such cultural narratives will be questionable or dubious in certain respects, but the dubious aspects of a given culture are *secondary* in relation to our *primary* need for a comprehensively enwrapping culture robust enough to generate a coherent morality.[27]

[6] We come, finally, to the last, and most "political," of MacIntyre's key notions: *local community*. If we are to reason practically, through communal deliberation (the exchange of reasons and counter-reasons), with a view to instantiating the common good in a particular time and place, emplanted in particular circumstances and on the basis of cognitive resources supplied by a shared tradition, then clearly there has to be an institutional setting within which this whole process of collective reasoning and judgment unfolds. That is, if we are to have something corresponding to what Aristotle depicted in the *Ethics* and *Politics*, then we are in need of some counterpart to the Greek polis. And for MacIntyre, the modern state, with its anonymous bureaucrats, its intimidating scale,

---

[24] *The MacIntyre Reader*, ed. Knight, p. 141.

[25] Cf. ibid., p. 147: "The standard modern anti-Aristotelian self will be a particular kind of divided self."

[26] For a forceful feminist critique of MacIntyre, see Susan Moller Okin, *Justice, Gender, and the Family* (New York: Basic Books, 1989), chapter 3. As we have just flagged, there is no question that MacIntyre *wishes* to align himself with feminism; the problem, though, is how this can be made to fit or cohere with broader philosophical positions adopted by him.

[27] We see something similar in his argument concerning the university in chapter 10 of *Three Rival Versions of Moral Enquiry*: the pre-liberal university, on his account, falls far short of acceptable standards of justice, yet that does not prevent MacIntyre from expressing considerable nostalgia for it relative to its modern liberal counterpart.

and (perhaps worst of all) its complicity in the capitalist organization of social and economic life, certainly doesn't fit the bill. We have to know our fellow-citizens and share a robust way of life with them in order to participate in communal practical reasoning aimed at securing and sharing "thick" common goods (no less thick than, for instance, the reciprocal solidarity of those inhabiting a mining community, or the love for music animating those who perform together in an orchestra). The radicalism of MacIntyre's view is encapsulated well in his categorical judgment that "contemporary liberal political societies have no citizens."[28] Hence, MacIntyre insists that Aristotelian politics, whether in the ancient world or today, *must* be a politics of *local* community. This carries us to the threshold of MacIntyre's political philosophy.

Naturally, one cannot help wondering what implications MacIntyre's story about storytelling, virtue, and culture has with respect to *political* philosophy. Let me add some further remarks with respect to this last installment of the story. One of the key questions that a self-professed Aristotelian must answer is what kind of political community allows human beings to fulfill their nature as political animals. MacIntyre realizes that, as an Aristotelian, he must have an answer to this question, but it is not clear that he has a response that actually meets the desideratum. There is no lack of clarity about the *negative* part of his doctrine; that is, it is clear that he regards the modern state as a human disaster, and sees it as a non-starter with respect to providing an institutional setting within which to realize the ethical and political ideals his philosophy is intended to articulate. As we have already sketched to some extent, his substitute candidate for the polis we don't possess is "local community" – but since all local communities (with the exception, perhaps, of city-states like Monaco or Singapore) are embedded within much larger political entities – states on the modern scale, and often trans-state political and legal institutions as well – it is difficult to see how they could, even in theory, serve the "architectonic" or all-encompassing or overarching ends that Aristotle associated with the polis. Municipalities by definition are subject to the more encompassing authority of larger political structures (and still more so is this the case with the mobilization of solidarities within churches, clinics, or schools); therefore their claim to being

---

[28] MacIntyre, "Replies," p. 220; cf. pages 202–203, on how the citizenship of "most ordinary citizens" is "in practice nullified" by pervasive inequality in the modern liberal state. See also the MacIntyre epigraph on page 99 of Beiner, *What's the Matter with Liberalism?*

plausible successors to the type of ultimate locus of political identity that the polis was for Aristotle appears weak.

The objections to MacIntyre's political vision seem fairly obvious, which is why he presents it not as a *prescription* (a "nostrum"[29]) but strictly as a critique of life as it currently exists. Because of his insistence on confronting historical and sociological realities, MacIntyre isn't interested in constructing a utopia, but if his appeal to a form of ethical, social, and political existence that no longer exists (except in isolated pockets of the modern world) is not a utopia, what is it? One should be clear, we're not going back to the world of the Lancashire loom-weaver.[30] And in the meantime we have some real political problems to sort out in the political world that we do inhabit. MacIntyre doesn't himself believe that the world of the Lancashire loom-weaver is coming back, but that doesn't stop him from using it as a normative mallet with which to beat the moral and political world we're actually stuck with, and that doesn't seem the most helpful way of appealing to, for instance, the vocabulary of common goods. What we need is a conception of *civic* common goods, where "civic" refers to the community of citizens associated with states as they are currently constituted.

I allow that MacIntyre's critique of the modern state has considerable force to it.[31] To be sure, it is very difficult to have meaningful collective deliberation about the provision for shared needs, given both the scale of modern political communities and the oligarchical power relations that dominate life in liberal democracies (two issues very effectively highlighted by MacIntyre), and, one could add, also given the staggering technological complexities of problems with which contemporary societies must wrestle. These are not trivial impediments to a meaningful political existence. However, it's not clear to me that MacIntyre's "politics of local community" is fully or appropriately "political." Politics as theorized from Aristotle onward has to mean taking responsibility in an encompassing way for the collective problems that a given society must confront, making the decisions that have to be made and exercising the authority that has to be exercised adequate for addressing the fundamental problems of shared civic life. In the case of contemporary society, that must include things such as structuring economic life in a way

---

[29] See MacIntyre, "An Interview with Giovanna Borradori," in *The MacIntyre Reader*, ed. Knight, p. 265.
[30] See *The MacIntyre Reader*, ed. Knight, pp. 231–232.
[31] For further discussion, see chapter 5 of my book, *Liberalism, Nationalism, Citizenship: Essays on the Problem of Political Community* (Vancouver: University of British Columbia Press, 2003). For two good statements of his views, see *Dependent Rational Animals*, chapter 11; and "Politics, Philosophy and the Common Good," in *The MacIntyre Reader*, ed. Knight.

that provides decent employment and protects citizens against widespread poverty; guaranteeing the civil rights and liberties of all citizens; dealing with issues of war and peace, including protecting the security of citizens of a given state against terrorist threats; and trying to ensure our very survival in the face of the perils of climate change. As I say, it is not at all clear that a politics of local community has the appropriate scope or authority even to address these issues, let alone solve them.[32] Modern states may or may not be doing a good job in tackling such problems. However, in principle I think they do have the appropriate scope and authority, whereas local communities – especially those founded on solidaristic ways of life that no longer exist! – fall short of the appropriate scope and authority.

MacIntyre comprehensively rejects the institutions of the capitalist market; fair enough! And a large part of his critique of the modern state – not the whole of that critique but a large part of it – is that the state is fatally implicated in the market at its worst, so that any claim to shared common goods on the part of the state is morally compromised by the injustice of the market.[33] But what is the alternative? We cannot go back to a premodern craft economy, and MacIntyre knows that we cannot go back to that. My question is this: if MacIntyre's central idea of common goods yields a normatively more attractive account of social and political life than the categories that define the currently dominant political philosophies, shouldn't it be applicable to the social and political world we *do* inhabit: a world of states and markets and a scale of economic and political interaction that far exceeds the local?

What MacIntyre offers us at the end of the day is an intriguing, provocative, and also problematic blend of conservatism and radicalism. With

---

[32] At a seminar given by MacIntyre that I attended on May 24, 2012, he stated that in principle a politics of local community would be possible in a city the size of Chicago, and in a country the size of Iceland, even more so. So MacIntyrean politics isn't necessarily a matter of isolated villages. But leaving aside Chicago, he is otherwise emphatic that this kind of politics is possible only on the basis of some solidaristic mode of existence generally tied to a premodern form of economic life. Hence the question of scale obviously is not the only relevant consideration.

[33] MacIntyre seems to assume that questions of economic power and economic justice are the only ones relevant to judging the modern state as a (just or unjust) form of political community. Those issues are undoubtedly of huge importance, but it is not clear that they exhaust the relevant political judgments. I remember as a child driving with my parents through certain southern states of the U.S. and seeing racially segregated toilet facilities. Today the United States has a black president. That means that during my lifetime that particular modern state has gone through at least one defining political transformation of immense proportions. That is certainly not an instance of political change that could have occurred local community to local community. It seems obvious that a politics of local community will not be adequate to other questions of large consequence, such as whether the earth will remain livable much beyond the present generation.

respect to his radicalism, MacIntyre's moral rejection of capitalism remains as uncompromising as ever: he may have jettisoned his early faith that Marxism offers *answers* to our current dissatisfactions, but his fidelity to Marxism as a moral diagnosis of the injustice of a capitalist economy and society is undiminished. As regards his conservatism, his conception of what he regards as a coherent social order seems somewhat akin to that of a stereotypical village priest. (Not fortuitously, Ernest Gellner was already calling him "Father MacIntyre" a full decade before *After Virtue* was published.[34]) Communities of farmers or fishermen live coherent moral lives, in MacIntyre's view, because they inhabit thick cultures that transmit the kind of stories of virtue and vice that human beings require in order to meet correct standards of Aristotelian or Thomist flourishing. But we moderns, with our heterogeneous moral experience and our deracinating individualism, have an experience of social life that can only be condemned as a form of moral chaos or moral anarchy masquerading as a viable culture. If our only philosophical purpose is to impugn liberalism of any stripe as a false philosophy, then this amalgam of Marxism and Thomism[35] seems to supply what one seeks, but if one is looking for a political philosophy that articulates, in a more positive fashion, what is true and what is dubious in contemporary experience, then MacIntyre's synthesis of conservatism and radicalism looks quite a bit more questionable.

What I have offered in this chapter is no more than a very compressed sketch of MacIntyre's philosophical concerns, but there is one further important issue I would like to engage before leaving MacIntyre. The issue I have in mind is how philosophy relates to religion and the implications this has for the relationship between philosophers and non-philosophers. On May 24, 2012, MacIntyre gave a seminar at London Metropolitan University, which I attended. During the question period, I asked him to elaborate on his idea of the "plain person" – a term MacIntyre sometimes uses to connote an individual who is more or less innocent of philosophy.[36] He responded

---

[34] Ernest Gellner, *The Devil in Modern Philosophy*, ed. Ian C. Jarvie and Joseph Agassi (London: Routledge and Kegan Paul, 1974), p. 197. Gellner's book review was first published in 1971.

[35] In the summer of 2008, I attended a gathering of the International Society for MacIntyrean Enquiry (held at a monastery in St. Meinrad, Indiana), and couldn't help noticing that the majority of the participants (not me) were either Thomists or Marxists. It was very striking how these two constituencies reflected the two sides of MacIntyre's intellectual personality.

[36] See, for instance, "Plain Persons and Moral Philosophy: Rules, Virtues and Goods," in *The MacIntyre Reader*, ed. Knight. In his exchange with me at London Met, MacIntyre credited Pope John Paul II as the source of his reflection on how plain persons relate to philosophers. MacIntyre, *The Tasks of Philosophy*, p. 180, cites passages from *Fides et Ratio* that relate to this MacIntyrean theme, but *Fides et*

by saying that religion tells plain persons (i.e., non-philosophers) how to live their lives. Plain persons are given *answers* by their religions: where they come from, what is expected of them, how they respond to death, etc. Then the philosophers come along and ask more systematic questions about truth, rational justification, and meaning. A reflective plain person, he said, is different from a philosopher. The question about how to have a dialogue between plain persons and philosophers is one that we must continually ponder; and he concluded by lamenting the fact that, instead of the dialogue between philosophers and non-philosophers that *ought* to exist, what we have at the moment is "absolute non-dialogue."

I was surprised by how far this account went (or at least seemed to) with respect to the potential subversion, by philosophers, of the plain person's view of life. So I was keen to continue the discussion via e-mail. Wasn't there something in the account he gave at the seminar, I asked MacIntyre in my follow-up e-mail, that was reminiscent of the Straussian problem of the natural antagonism (as Strauss and his followers saw it) between the philosopher and the non-philosopher? As I put it in my e-mail, the philosophers' desire for a logos can put in an unforgiving light the cognitive credentials of the beliefs of non-philosophers, which potentially puts philosophers and non-philosophers at odds with each other. (How well will the Polynesian cosmology of the eighteenth century stand up to philosophical scrutiny? Aren't there countless beliefs held by people living in the twenty-first century that will fare no better in the face of philosophical interrogation than the beliefs of the Polynesians?) As MacIntyre himself pointed out, philosophers are distinguished by their being driven to inquire more systematically into problems of meaning, rational justification, and especially truth; non-philosophers, by implication, can settle for less in determining how to live their lives (although the more awareness they have of what concerns philosophers, the more difficult this may become). I pointed out that Strauss and the Straussians thought they knew the solution to this problem: philosophers qua philosophers need to communicate with each other in a secret code that allows them to both avoid persecution *and* avoid disturbing the tissue of non-philosophical belief that isn't designed to survive rigorous philosophical scrutiny. I told MacIntyre that I was quite sure that he had no sympathy for that "solution" (nor did I). The idea of philosophers

---

Ratio (1998) was published six years after the original publication of the essay cited at the start of this note. In fact, MacIntyre's use of the idiom of "plain persons" can be traced all the way back to 1983: see MacIntyre, "Moral Arguments and Social Contexts," *Journal of Philosophy*, Vol. 80, no. 10 (Oct. 1983), p. 590.

dissembling their real views in a post-Enlightenment situation where they can declare those views without fear of persecution seems grossly anti-philosophical. And in any case, once Strauss starts broadcasting the theme of esotericism to all and sundry, esotericism is by that very fact no longer possible as a philosophical practice.[37] I concluded that I myself don't see a problem in a reciprocal dialogue between the philosopher and the non-philosopher, where each disturbs the other's complacency with respect to their core beliefs. But there is a glaring asymmetry in this reciprocal dialogue: philosophers tend to thrive (MacIntyre himself is a wonderful exemplar of this) when presented with doubts, objections, and rational challenges to their intellectual commitments. The case may be otherwise when it's a matter of challenging the rational credentials of views of life held by non-philosophers. Hence the Strauss-like question of what happens when the constitutive beliefs of non-philosophers are exposed to the Socratic insistence on truth and when they are confronted with the high bar for rational justification set by philosophers. In my view, the Enlightenment redefined this relationship between philosophers and non-philosophers for the better, and it was the deliberate intention of Enlightenment philosophers to do just that. But Strauss disagrees: he writes either as if the Enlightenment never happened with respect to the need for and desirability of esotericism, or as if the Enlightenment initiative, in trying to recast the relation between philosophers and non-philosophers, has been purely destructive.

MacIntyre wasn't inclined to take up my questions concerning Strauss and the Enlightenment (he merely referred to Strauss's "unfortunate mistakes" – without specifying what those mistakes were – and said that, as regards the Enlightenment, he and I "disagree too deeply for any short statement to be useful").[38] However, he gave a very interesting and generous

---

[37] For further elaboration of these challenges to Strauss, see my essay, "Gadamer's Philosophy of Dialogue and Its Relation to the Postmodernism of Nietzsche, Heidegger, Derrida, and Strauss," in *Gadamer's Repercussions: Reconsidering Philosophical Hermeneutics*, ed. Bruce Krajewski (Berkeley: University of California Press, 2004), pp. 145–157; as well as chapter 16 of *Civil Religion* (Cambridge: University of Cambridge Press, 2011).

[38] MacIntyre gestures toward his radical philosophical disagreements with Strauss in "Replies," page 207. His remarks there are directly relevant to his e-mail exchange with me. As for the Enlightenment, consider MacIntyre's suggestion on page 92 of *After Virtue* that it be viewed as "a peculiar kind of darkness." (My thanks to David Sayer for reminding me of this text.) Robert Wokler, in "Projecting the Enlightenment," in *After MacIntyre*, ed. John Horton and Susan Mendus (Notre Dame, IN: University of Notre Dame Press, 1994), pp. 108–126, attempts to draw MacIntyre into a broader dialogue about the moral and civic virtues of the Enlightenment. In his response (p. 299), MacIntyre steadfastly refuses to take up Wokler's challenge. Instead, he sticks to his standard line: that different Enlightenment philosophies depart from incommensurable premises, and therefore cannot deliver on philosophy's promise of eventual consensus.

response to the question of plain persons and how philosophers and plain persons relate to each other:

Plain persons generally – always? – share in some culture and, in so doing, share a set of only partially explicit presuppositions about the order of things, their place in it, and how, given that place, they should live. Plain persons are always potentially and often actually practically rational agents and they may be more or less reflective about what they believe and what they do. They value understanding, something evidenced by their responses when accused of failing to understand or when suspicious of having been misled. They vary enormously in their degree of cultural and intellectual sophistication. They include Spartans and Andaman Islanders, Cleopatra and Mark Anthony, the Gaelic speaking farmers and fishing crews of my youth, the coal miners I knew in Yorkshire, some Vice-Chancellors whom I have known, and my aunts. All philosophers start as plain people and in an important way remain plain people in many aspects of their lives. So every philosopher begins from within some particular culture, posing questions that elicit and put in question an explicit statement of some shared beliefs of that culture. The questions that philosophers initially – see both the Greeks and the Chinese – ask about the order of things, our place in it, and how we should live turn out to be questions to which plain persons have already given answers in the myths that they tell, the rituals that they enact, and the laws that they recognize. So philosophical enquiry and philosophical conversation become an important part of certain cultures. What philosophy brings to those cultures is an awareness of the concepts of truth, meaning, and rational justification and of their importance, thus transforming those cultures. Here, if I were writing at adequate length, I would have to discuss the different courses that such conversation may take and has taken. As I am not, let me say only that on my view a central task of philosophy is to enable plain persons to become adequately reflective as practically rational agents and by so doing to avoid being misled and confused by the dominant modes of thought and judgment of their culture. The academicization of contemporary philosophy and its transformation into an increasingly narrow set of subdisciplines has resulted in a failure to engage with this task, so that plain persons now take philosophy to be irrelevant to their concerns and are often happily and disastrously unreflective, while professional philosophers are too often unaware of their own frequent ineptitude as practically rational agents. There has thus emerged a very different contrast between the philosopher and the plain person, one according to which either the plain person congratulates her or himself on her or his superior grasp of practical affairs or the academic philosopher congratulates her or himself on her or his superior intellectual sophistication. It goes without saying, I hope, that this is not at all what is implied by my contrast.

A few observations are in order. First of all, it should be noted that the potentially subversive implications with respect to common beliefs that I perceived in his remarks at the London seminar are no longer present in this elaboration of his views. In effect, the question that I had put to MacIntyre was: How can philosophers do what philosophy is supposed to do without *subverting* the self-understanding of non-philosophers? Addressing that question head-on would require MacIntyre to acknowledge that the Enlightenment is in continuity with what philosophy has been about from the very outset – would require him to acknowledge that the spirit of Socrates is alive in the Enlightenment. In this respect, MacIntyre and Strauss are on the same side, since both are determined to resist this acknowledgment of the properly Socratic spirit behind the Enlightenment.[39] MacIntyre himself avows that the job of philosophy is to *transform* the various received cultures by highlighting issues of meaning, justification, and truth. Again, in London, MacIntyre phrased this in a way that gave it a subversive or at least potentially subversive complexion, whereas his e-mailed follow-up (I think deliberately) retracts this suggestion of philosophy having any kind of a subversive edge vis-à-vis non-philosophical cultural narratives.[40] For MacIntyre, philosophy at its best is meant to help free non-philosophers from being "misled and confused." He makes the further claim that it is on account of the resolute specialization of philosophy, its transformation into a hyper-technical academic discipline, that contemporary philosophers fail to make good on this public responsibility. However, it is not their received myths and stories (e.g., Biblical religion) that mislead and confuse non-philosophers; rather, it's *deracinated liberal elites* that mislead and confuse them, and the deracinating Enlightenment works hand-in-hand with these liberal elites. Hence, it might be said that Spinoza, for instance, is not a symbol of liberation but rather a symbol of oppression, the reason being that if philosophy serves to alienate plain persons from their received cultural narratives, it renders them more, not less, vulnerable to manipulation by the elites that oppress them. Such a line of thinking would require MacIntyre to be careful (more careful than he was in London) to deny any suggestion about philosophy being subversive of religion-based common cultures. For MacIntyre, moral life is ultimately constituted by cultural

---

[39] Or at least this is Strauss's *exoteric* stance toward the Enlightenment. There are hints here and there (some of which I have cited elsewhere) that esoterically, he may have had more sympathy or sense of solidarity with Enlightenment philosophers qua philosophers than he is willing to avow exoterically.

[40] It is possible, of course, that I discerned more of a suggestion of philosophy's possible subversiveness in MacIntyre's original statement than he intended. (In a powerful lecture entitled "Catholic Instead of What?", available on YouTube, MacIntyre spells out very clearly that his beliefs as a philosophical Catholic are in no way different from those of Catholic "plain persons.") But the problem that I was trying to draw out of his own formulation is conspicuously present in the history of philosophy in any case. As I have already suggested, the tension in life-horizons between philosophers and non-philosophers that I was trying to highlight by invoking Strauss did not begin with the Enlightenment; it goes back to the Socratic origins of philosophy.

solidarities, and all is lost if philosophy is permitted to imperil or put in question this basis of moral solidarity (as is typically the case according to an Enlightenment understanding of philosophy) – as opposed to (as MacIntyre prefers) providing the "plain" narratives with better intellectual grounding, clearer self-consciousness, or (most importantly) better insulation against the deracinating sallies of liberal elites. Hence his unwillingness (on my interpretation) to take up a discussion of the Enlightenment or Strauss.

Finally, it's hard to resist the temptation to do a bit of further unpacking of MacIntyre's intriguing line about "Spartans and Andaman Islanders, Cleopatra and Mark Anthony, the Gaelic speaking farmers and fishing crews of my youth, the coal miners I knew in Yorkshire, some Vice-Chancellors whom I have known, and my aunts." The implication seems to be that the archetypal plain person is premodern, or non-modern, or in some way in tension with liberal modernity. This has to be of some significance in interpreting what MacIntyre is up to in using this term. The suggestion, surely, is that the average denizen of liberal-bourgeois societies is *not* a plain person. On the surface it *appears* that the human race divides up, in a binary way, into philosophers and plain persons, but my hunch is that his *real* view (left unspoken in his e-mail to me) is that there is actually a *three-way* divide: philosophers, plain persons, and "barbarians." We have the misfortune (in his view) to live in an epoch when hardly anyone is either a philosopher or a plain person, and almost everyone is a barbarian (hence the famous last paragraph of *After Virtue*). That is, according to the interpretation that is being suggested here, MacIntyre's notion of the plain person doesn't demarcate an *empirical* concept of the non-philosopher. On the contrary, it is a normative conception – a marker for what the non-philosopher *can and ought to be* in a society that is narratively coherent, and where philosophers are a source of guidance for the culture because they are capable of making intellectual progress within their own ranks. But in actual fact, our situation is one where the society is morally disordered and culturally hollow, and philosophy is a Babel of incommensurable voices; hence, plain persons don't really exist (or exist only in very exceptional cases).

12

Short Excursus on the Rise and Decline of Communitarianism as a Political Philosophy

If political philosophy is about confronting radical alternatives with respect to possible visions of human life, the theoretical debate between liberalism and communitarianism ought to reach down to the philosophical foundations. One could, for instance, contrast the highly individualized life typical in Western societies with the intensely communal life monks experience living in, say, a Tibetan Buddhist monastery. Such a contrast would indeed open up truly far-reaching philosophical issues. Suppose it really is true that in order for human beings to flourish fully, they require a much thicker constitution of memory, identity, and communal purpose than contemporary liberal societies make available. What if life in a cloistered monastery more nearly approaches what is required to meet the essential needs of human beings than life in our own high-paced, high-mobility society? What sort of judgment would be cast upon the highly pluralized and highly individualistic societies of the West if a quiet, static, and rigidly communalized monastic life really defined the standard of judgment for a fully human life? Ought we to assume so complacently that our society constitutes the defining norm – a kind of society where millions of people live in deracinated and soulless suburbs, where individuals decide what kind of car to buy and where to drive it, decide who to marry or whether to reproduce, where consumer choices loom larger than loyalty to a way of life, where a regime of individual rights is fundamental and social obligations are secondary?

We know what the standard liberal-pluralist rejoinder would be to the hyper-communitarian vision of life associated with life in a Buddhist monastery. Why legislate this issue, as important as it is, for all human beings? Let individuals choose. Let those who are attracted to the virtues of the monastic life choose that life. And let those who prefer lives characterized by more variety and more risk choose those very different lives. Issue settled! But of course the liberal-pluralist solution begs the very issue posed by the communitarian challenge in its purest form. For if the contest between individual liberty and communal identity is rendered contingent on individual choice, then the balance is already tilted toward the individualist side, and a form of community life that is *more* than a construction of individual choices is surreptitiously removed as a real possibility. Casting the issue as a matter of individual choice (which *seems* to leave open the option of choosing an intensely communitarian existence) really implies that liberal-pluralist society is best, since it is precisely the kind of society that guarantees the availability of these choices. So the suggestion that liberal pluralism is neutral or does not prejudice the choice of individualist versus communitarian ways of life turns out to be a mirage.

Communitarianism as a theoretical movement promised to pursue such radical lines of thought, and, of course, in part it delivered what it promised. However, communitarianism seems to have run out of gas within mainstream political philosophy, and an important reason for this, I believe, is a failure to follow through on the promised radicalism of its questions and challenges. Today, communitarianism is in large measure a spent force, in part because its insights were too easily accommodated by the liberal-individualist theories it meant to challenge, and in part because the theoretical energies it released were diverted in other directions (such as multiculturalism and other forms of identity politics). In this excursus I will look briefly at five prominent theorists of community – namely, Michael Sandel, Michael Walzer, Charles Taylor, Alasdair MacIntyre, and Christopher Lasch – in order to trace the ways in which communitarianism partly, but only partly, realized its full potential as a form of radical social criticism vis-à-vis life in a liberal-individualist society (a discussion premised in turn on the idea that communitarianism does or does not have intellectual force as a political philosophy in proportion as it makes good on its promise to deliver a bold vision of the good).[1]

Sandel, Walzer, and Taylor all composed important theoretical critiques of contemporary liberal theory.[2] While none of them was keen to embrace

---

[1] For an account of these five thinkers that complements the one offered in this excursus, see my essay "The Way We Live," *The Responsive Community*, Vol. 11, Issue 1 (Winter 2000/2001), pp. 34–40. As I point out in that essay, there is an important sense in which communitarianism's radicalism consists in, or is inseparable from, its conservatism; hence the telling fact that MacIntyre and Lasch are simultaneously more conservative and more radical than Taylor, Walzer, and Sandel.

[2] I think I can rightfully claim some credit as a midwife at the birth of communitarian political philosophy. The key event in the coming-to-be of communitarianism as a movement within contemporary political philosophy was the encounter between Taylor and Sandel in Oxford in the late 1970s. (Sandel

the communitarian label, what was common to the theoretical challenge
to individualist liberalism developed by each of them was an insistence on
what we can call the "pre-constitution" of individual identity by shared
social self-understanding. For instance, Walzer, in his terrific book *Spheres
of Justice*,[3] argued that, contrary to what is assumed by liberal theorists of
justice like John Rawls, a normative social theory should not be addressed
primarily to the question of how to distribute goods fairly on the basis of
the ends that individuals choose for themselves, for these ends are constituted by shared understandings of what the relevant goods are on the part
of the whole society. That is, what appear to be individual ends are actually
constituted at a deeper level by shared conceptions of what is humanly
meaningful and important; for instance, it is only within a certain social and
historical context that civic membership is generally considered to be an
essential human good, and it is on the basis of this shared understanding of
what is good that one then attempts to determine a just allocation of this
good. Sandel and Taylor each developed their own forceful versions of this
thesis, and during the 1980s, at least, the combined effect of Walzer/Sandel/
Taylor evidenced some success in putting liberal theorists on the defensive.

Subsequently, two things happened. First, theoretical defenders of liberalism were quick to emphasize that they had no quarrel with the social-
constitution thesis, and in fact some of them began to argue that liberalism
as a shared public philosophy furnishes the basis for a constitutive moral-
historical community of precisely the kind that communitarians seemed to
be demanding. And indeed, if Sandel, Taylor, and Walzer were right to claim
that individual selfhood is more deeply constituted by social identities than
liberal theorists were willing to acknowledge, merely making this acknowledgment, it would seem, suffices to disarm the communitarian challenge. If
the communitarians are right that members of existing societies, including
liberal societies, are constituted in their selfhood by deep shared understandings, and are simply unaware that this is so, how does this yield an
ambitious critical standard? Walzer perhaps summed up best the relationship between liberalism and the kind of communitarianism represented by
Taylor, Sandel, and himself when he suggested that the purpose of this sort

had already been a student of MacIntyre's at Brandeis in the early 1970s.) As it happens, I was the one
who introduced Taylor to Sandel early in the Michaelmas term of 1976, soon after Taylor arrived at All
Souls to take up his position as Chichele Professor of Social and Political Theory. (Taylor had been my
teacher at McGill; I met Sandel halfway across the Atlantic, on a sailing of the Queen Elizabeth II from
New York to Southampton.) And as the saying goes, the rest is history. But this excursus is concerned
more with the eclipse of communitarian theory than with its genesis.
[3] Michael Walzer, *Spheres of Justice* (New York: Basic Books, 1983).

of communitarian theory was merely to provide a corrective to one-sidedly individualistic self-understandings within liberal theory, not to attempt to propose a radically alternative political vision to the liberal vision, and that communitarianism was basically a more community-oriented version *of* liberalism, not a counter-doctrine *to* liberalism.[4]

Second, theorists who were more critical of liberalism began to argue that if individuals are importantly constituted by group identity, what follows is a theoretical grounding for a kind of politics that privileges the identity of marginalized minorities – i.e., multiculturalism. Thereby, communitarianism evolved or mutated from a critique of individualism in the society as a whole into a theoretical justification of a political program for empowering particular groups. That is, multiculturalism absorbed or appropriated the critical force of communitarianism. The defense of multiculturalism may be politically helpful in various ways; after all, if people have strong cultural identities, they can be drawn into a sense of shared citizenship only if they are assured that common citizenship will not require forgoing these identities. (The Quebec government's proposed Charter of Quebec Values offers a vivid example: saying to Islamic citizens, as the proposed law says to them, "We welcome you as citizens, but only if you are not visibly Islamic" is really a case of saying that in fact you are *not* welcome.) But putting the theory enterprise in the service of multicultural politics is philosophically unambitious; if this is what defines the central agenda for political philosophy, this in itself may constitute a defeat for political philosophy.

While there are things that can reasonably be said in support of (some versions of) multiculturalist politics, there is a definite downside as well. Communitarianism conceived as a diagnosis of moral and cultural debilities that ail the society as a whole, which must be addressed by the society in common, gives way to a political doctrine that encourages social groups within the society to turn inward, to look out for their own interests, and to subordinate society-wide concerns to the group's own preoccupations. The

---

[4] See Michael Walzer, "The Communitarian Critique of Liberalism," *Political Theory*, Vol. 18, no. 1 (1990), pp. 6–23; and "Comment," in Charles Taylor, *Multiculturalism: Examining the Politics of Recognition*, ed. Amy Gutmann (Princeton, NJ: Princeton University Press, 1994), pp. 99–103. My own somewhat pessimistic view (which I hope will be received as in a spirit of realism, not cynicism) is that in the tug of war between individuality and community, it is quite hard for human cultures to get the balance right: what we tend to get are the vices of hyper-individuality, or the vices of hyper-community, or sometimes the worst of both worlds. We rarely get the best of both worlds. Let me just make a few additional quick points. First, I don't think my overall stance is as pessimistic as this makes it sound. Second, I think theorists have a quasi-obligation not to lose hope. Third, I think my emphasis on the importance of citizenship aims this duty of hopefulness at a dimension of social life where it is likely to have best effect.

result is a kind of politics that may weaken inter-group solidarities, whereas the kind of highly pluralistic societies in which we now live need *greater* solidarity and shared civic consciousness among the culturally diverse groups that compose the society. On the one hand, a co-opting of communitarian insights by liberal theorists; on the other hand, a diversion of communitarian concerns into a potentially more ghettoized, less civic-minded kind of politics. This exhaustion, failure of nerve, or displacement of communitarian thinking[5] perhaps tells us something important about how difficult it is, philosophically, to challenge in a fundamental way the shape of our mode of life as it currently exists, or how difficult it is, as a political project, to conceive radical revisions of our social practices and the institutional structures of our existing way of life.

There is no lack of radicalism in Alasdair MacIntyre (as we have seen in the previous chapter). He is even more forceful and explicit than the others in disowning the communitarian label, but in important ways he comes much closer to a purer (i.e., less liberal) communitarian vision.[6] One reason that MacIntyre has for wanting to disassociate himself from other fellow-communitarians (or so-called communitarians) is that he sees the others as investing more confidence in the modern state and its characteristic institutions than he can himself summon up. In fact, there is a powerful anti-statist dimension to MacIntyre's social thought, and no doubt he would see it as an entailment of his deep philosophical reservations about modernity as such. Also, MacIntyre insists that the focus of his theoretical concern is not community as such, for "communities are always open to corruption by narrowness, by complacency, by prejudice against outsiders and by a whole range of other deformities."[7] Rather, he is interested in local and close-knit communities as possible (and privileged) sites for humanly valuable virtues and moral practices (as opposed to those forms of social life that are more centrally reflective of characteristically modern

---

[5] Has the same thing now happened to theoretical versions of multiculturalism? Have they too gone through a process of rise and decline? If so, it provides support for the case I am trying to make in this book, which is that the only thing in the political philosophy world with significant staying-power is the work of epic theorists.

[6] MacIntyre clearly came to the view that he was the "odd man out" in relation to the other three leading communitarians (Walzer, Taylor, Sandel). Either they were real communitarians and he was not, or he was a real communitarian and they were not. MacIntyre very emphatically opted for letting Walzer, Taylor, and Sandel have the communitarian label (whether they wanted it or not), but a strong case can be made that if any of these four thinkers deserves this label, it is MacIntyre.

[7] Alasdair MacIntyre, *Dependent Rational Animals: Why Human Beings Need the Virtues* (Chicago: Open Court, 1999), p. 142.

norms, and are therefore, in his view, incapable of sustaining coherent moral experience). MacIntyre is right to reject community as an end-in-itself, but this does not distinguish him from other communitarians since they very clearly disavow "community as such" as their normative foundation no less than he does.[8]

There is a third reason as well: MacIntyre sees contemporary communitarians as subscribing to a particular political program, which implies that the social and moral predicaments we face can in principle be put right, and therefore liberal modernity can be redeemed. This seems to him too optimistic a view, underestimating how profound a transformation of our current ways of living is required. Hence he writes: "I do not believe in ideals or forms of community as a nostrum for contemporary social ills. I give my political loyalty to no program."[9] This is not entirely true, for (while it would perhaps be unfair to call it a "nostrum") MacIntyre *does* have a clear vision of what ideal political arrangements would look like, and what kind of fundamental reworking of social life and social practices would approximate his ideal. As we discussed in the previous chapter, MacIntyre is committed to something he calls "the politics of local community," which involves structuring polis-like rational deliberation in settings such as fishing villages or rural farming communities where people share a close-knit way of life and strongly identify with common purposes.[10] Coherent moral and political life is possible in something like a Tibetan Buddhist monastic community (the example we cited at the very start of this excursus), but is *not* possible within the basic structures of modern society as we know it. In insisting that he offers no nostrums and adheres to no political program, MacIntyre is really saying that the kind of compromises required in order for his social and political views to be squared with the basic structures of modern life are not compromises that he is willing to accept (in other words, he is loyal to no political program *relevant to the world of the modern state*). So we are left with a choice between types of communitarian thought that in the end offer too-easily-accommodated challenges to the liberal-individualist vision of life, or more bracing challenges that turn out to be

---

[8] See, for instance, Sandel's "Preface to the Second Edition," in Michael Sandel, *Liberalism and the Limits of Justice*, 2nd ed. (Cambridge: Cambridge University Press, 1998), pp. ix–xvi.

[9] "An Interview with Giovanna Borradori," in *The MacIntyre Reader*, ed. Kelvin Knight (Notre Dame, IN: University of Notre Dame Press, 1998), p. 265.

[10] See "Politics, Philosophy and the Common Good," in *MacIntyre Reader*, ed. Knight.

(and know themselves to be) much too remote from our current social universe to constitute a meaningful alternative.

In common with each of the other thinkers canvassed previously,
Christopher Lasch is loath to call himself a communitarian, and tends to
associate communitarianism with a form of social nostalgia that he thinks
we must firmly resist.[11] However, Lasch's social criticism offers a very good
example of the richer kind of theoretical reflection opened up when one
gives a central place to communitarian concerns such as the problem of
sustaining civic virtue. Philosophical liberals tend to be very disdainful of
this sort of virtue-talk, as is graphically illustrated in the following two
quotations. Richard Rorty, in a review of Lasch's book, *The Revolt of the
Elites*, declares: "People start writing books about spiritual plight only when
they have pretty much given up on politics – when they can no longer
figure out what concrete practical measures might help. Then they say that
only moral regeneration, or a return to religion, or a revolution in philosophy can do any good."[12] Stephen Holmes is similarly dismissive when
he writes: "As diagnosticians of liberal self-deceit, [communitarians] claim
to be the midwives of our spiritual rebirth."[13] These anti-communitarian
polemics seem to me to go much too far, for of course politics involves,
must involve, attempts to address the moral health of one's society. Can any
society – including liberal society – afford to be indifferent as to whether
its citizens dutifully pay their taxes or seek to evade them? Work hard at
their jobs or slack off? Read books and watch films that are thoughtful
and sophisticated rather than mindless and vulgarizing? Are generous rather
than mean-spirited toward fellow-citizens less fortunate than themselves?
Are civic-minded or completely focused only on their own narrow selves?
Take a serious interest in public affairs or let it all slide over them uncar-
ingly? Conceive a self-understanding where citizenship really means something versus one where politics is strictly reduced to the interests of one's
own pocketbook? Such matters may seem too commonplace to be properly
treated under the grand-sounding rubric of "soul-craft," but it strikes me
that the language of civic virtue is entirely the right language to use in such

---

[11] See Christopher Lasch, *The True and Only Heaven: Progress and Its Critics* (New York: W.W. Norton, 1991), pp. 16, 119, 166–167, 172, 303, 328; and Lasch, *The Revolt of the Elites and the Betrayal of Democracy* (New York: W.W. Norton, 1995), chapter 5.

[12] Richard Rorty, "Two Cheers for Elitism," *The New Yorker*, January 30, 1995, p. 87.

[13] Stephen Holmes, *The Anatomy of Antiliberalism* (Cambridge, MA: Harvard University Press, 1993), p. 182.

contexts.[14] Arguably, there is even a kind of modest soul-craft at stake in something as prosaic as the expectation that people will take pride in basic civic amenities such as well-groomed parks and public spaces that are not vandalized or strewn with litter. In any case, what follows is a fairly typical Laschian catalogue of contemporary ills:

Having defeated its totalitarian adversaries, liberalism is crumbling from within.... The [first] Gulf War provided a momentary distraction, but ... it will be impossible, in the long run, to avoid the day of reckoning. Already the signs of impending breakdown are unmistakable. Drugs, crime, and gang wars are making our cities uninhabitable. Our school system is in collapse. Our parties are unable to enlist the masses of potential voters into the political process. The global circulation of commodities, information, and populations, far from making everyone affluent (as theorists of modernization used to predict so confidently), has widened the gap between rich and poor nations and generated a huge migration to the West and to the United States in particular, where the newcomers swell the vast army of the homeless, unemployed, illiterate, drug-ridden, derelict, and effectively disenfranchised. Their presence strains existing resources to the breaking point. Medical and educational facilities, law-enforcement agencies, and the available supply of goods – not to mention the supply of racial good will, never abundant to begin with – all appear inadequate to the enormous task of assimilating what is essentially a surplus population.

Even the children of privilege are no longer assimilated into the culture of liberalism. One survey after another shows that college students no longer command even a rudimentary knowledge of Western history, literature, or philosophy. A kind of deculturation has clearly been going on for some time.... The modernization of the world, as it was conceived when liberals were running the show, implied the creation not only of a global market but of a global culture in which liberal values – individual freedom, open inquiry, religious tolerance, human dignity – would be universally respected. We have a global culture all right, but it is the culture of Hollywood, rock and roll, and Madison Avenue – not a liberal culture but a culture of hedonism, cruelty, contempt, and cynicism.[15]

---

[14] Richard Flathman gave a name – "virtue liberalism – to post-Rawlsian versions of liberalism that sought to make greater allowance for such concerns. But the liberals treated in this book – Oakeshott, Habermas, Rawls, Rorty – would tend to see virtue liberalism as conceding too much to communitarianism. For further discussion, see chapters 2–4 of Ronald Beiner, *Liberalism, Nationalism, Citizenship: Essays on the Problem of Political Community* (Vancouver: UBC Press, 2003).

[15] Christopher Lasch, "The Age of Limits," in *History and the Idea of Progress*, ed. Arthur M. Melzer, Jerry Weinberger, and M. Richard Zinman (Ithaca: Cornell University Press, 1995), pp. 228–229. For a fuller account of Lasch's contribution, see my discussion in chapter 15 of *Philosophy in a Time of Lost Spirit* (Toronto: University of Toronto Press, 1997). For a more recent example of the sort of potent cultural criticism that Lasch exemplified, see Matthew B. Crawford, *Shop Class as Soulcraft* (New York: Penguin Press, 2009). (My thanks to Kimberly Carter for alerting me to Crawford's excellent book.) To be sure, it would be wrong to think that only works of high theory can supply the kind of trenchant culture-critique that we need. In principle, a good novel or good film can perform the same function.

In my view, communitarianism at its best yields social criticism with just this kind of bite, and it is not clear to me that communitarian theory that merely places itself in the service of multiculturalism and other forms of groupist politics has the same kind of critical bite.[16]

---

[16] In the case of Taylor – inveterate political animal that he is – one sometimes gets the impression that his mode of theorizing is aimed more at putting together a political coalition, so to speak, than at articulating unshakeable normative standards. This, not surprisingly, detracts from the radicalism of his intellectual enterprise. One could make a similar judgment about John Rawls, and for similar reasons – namely, because for both Rawls and Taylor their theorizing seems dominated by the concern with promoting good or better citizenship. I have explored this unlikely affinity between Taylor and Rawls in a forthcoming essay entitled "Taylor, Rawls, and Secularism."

13
John Rawls and the Death
of Political Philosophy

John Rawls wrote two very famous books. In what follows, I'll discuss the
second of these two books (the one first published in 1993 rather than the
one first published in 1971) because in my view that is the one that has
far-reaching consequences for what political philosophy as a field of intellectual endeavor is supposed to be, and that potentially puts out of business
the conception of political philosophy I have sought to defend throughout
this book.[1] It seems outrageous to discuss the work of Rawls under the
rubric of "the death of political philosophy." My objective in this chapter
is to defend my choice of this provocative rubric, and explain *both* why the
key philosophical move that Rawls initiates with *Political Liberalism* (and the
essays leading up to it) makes sense from within his own intellectual framework, *and* why it has quite damaging consequences for the conception of
theorizing defended in this book.

Any discussion of Rawls must begin with his theory of justice, so that is
where we'll start. I don't have the space to go into the technical details
of Rawls's theorizing, which are often quite intricate, and some of which
Rawls repeatedly revised. Rather, I'll content myself with trying to map out
the broader vision that shapes both the content of Rawls's political philosophy and his conception of what political philosophy is.

The basic idea of Rawlsian justice is easy to grasp. Human beings are
subject to what Philip Roth has called "the tyranny of contingency."[2] That

---

[1] John Rawls, *Political Liberalism*, paperback ed. (New York: Columbia University Press, 1996); the paperback edition includes an introduction that the hardbound edition lacks. All parenthetical page references to follow refer to this work.
[2] Philip Roth, *Nemesis* (Toronto: Hamish Hamilton Canada, 2010), p. 243. There are obviously limits
to what political communities can do to ameliorate contingency's tyranny. People will get sick and
die according to the arbitrary dictates of fortune regardless of the constitutional order in which they
live. (Just consider the scale of cosmic injustice involved in the fact that some people happen to be

is, life prospects are meted out in ways that are often patently unfair. The world is not just: some are born to wealthy parents, others born into harsh poverty; some are born with natural talents or superior endowments, others are not; some are born healthy, others are born disabled or fated to suffer incapacitating illness. The human condition is a lottery. Yet even if life is unfair, *social* life can be organized in ways that, at least in some measure, provide remedies for this unfairness. As human beings, we take responsibility for constructing basic social and political institutions that are not necessarily compelled to take the world's injustice as a given. Even if the world is unjust, we can – as partners in the construction of a shared civic existence – create a reasonably just structure of social cooperation if we are determined to erect the framework of our interaction on a principled basis. Citizenship, according to Rawls's account, means participation in a shared enterprise of offsetting, to the extent that we can do this through civic exertion, the basic unfairness in the distribution of life prospects.

Life in society, rightly organized, can compensate for life's inequitable distribution of its goods, but how do we know what constitutes fairness? Rawls's fundamental idea is that life in political society involves implied submission to fair principles of social cooperation, and that it would be a mistake to attempt to draw these principles from *nature*, or immanent structures of *historical development*, or conceptions of an essential *human nature*, or a theological conception of the universe and its Creator, or anything else that transcends the mundane purposes of individual citizens agreeing to participate in the society as a scheme of cooperative life. Basing one's conception of justice on any of these rival philosophical foundations would be wrong because it would be unacceptably *controversial*, and hence impossible to obtain as a basis of agreed principle among free and equal citizens.[3] That is, the basis of principled civic life must rely on the citizens themselves – on what *they* would agree to in a (hypothetical) situation of primal choice of principles (or at least, what it would be *reasonable* for these primal

born blind – an injustice that no reform of social institutions will ever be able to undo.) Rawls's idea, quite clearly, is not that justice will *emancipate* us from the tyrannical sway of contingency, but merely that it will mitigate its social effects to the extent that a certain structuring of political institutions can.

[3] The unfairness of relying on these particular "conceptions of the good" in order to define the charter of shared civic existence – unfair, from Rawls's point of view, because no such conception is universally shared among all citizens, and therefore would have to be imposed by those who subscribe to it upon those who don't subscribe to it – mandates Rawls's doctrine of "the priority of the right to the good." This is a doctrine that straddles *A Theory of Justice* and *Political Liberalism*; for the version developed in the latter work, see *Political Liberalism*, Lecture 5.

contracting citizens to agree to).[4] This is Rawls's contractualism, or what he also calls a "constructivist" rendering of Kantian political morality.[5] As Rawls puts it: "As a device of representation the idea of the original position serves as a means of public reflection and self-clarification. It helps us work out what we now think, once we are able to take a clear and uncluttered view of what justice requires when society is conceived as a scheme of cooperation between free and equal citizens" (p. 26).

In justice as fairness the institutions of the basic structure [i.e., the major social institutions as an integral system[6]] are just provided they satisfy the principles that free and equal moral persons, in a situation that is fair between them, would adopt for the purpose of regulating that structure. (p. 271)

That is, justice refers to principles of fair civic coexistence that *would be* chosen by those who will be subject to these principles in a (contractual) situation of choice *that is itself fair.* We cannot expect just principles if these principles are determined by people other than those who are subject to them within the basic structure; nor can we expect just principles if one has a skewing of fundamental equality within the boundaries of the contractual situation where the principles are to be chosen (say, by giving some of the

---

[4] The implied question here – whether Rawls's postulated hypothetical "dialogue" between deliberating parties in the original position is genuinely dialogical, or whether it is just a monological account by the Rawlsian theorist artificially projected back upon a community of contractors who don't actually exist – is an important theme of Michael Sandel, *Liberalism and the Limits of Justice* (Cambridge: Cambridge University Press, 1982); see chapter 3 of Sandel's book. We encountered more or less the same problem in Habermas's theory in our chapter devoted to Habermas (despite the fact that Habermas insists that he affirms dialogical rather than monological reason); in both cases, these are theories that supposedly rely on "procedural ethics" (to use Taylor's label) to generate valid outcomes, yet at the same time the philosophers who deploy these theories feel equipped to *anticipate* what those dialogically-generated outcomes will turn out to be.

[5] Rawls explains the meaning of Kantian moral constructivism by distinguishing it from "rational intuitionism," in which "first principles, as statements about good reasons, are regarded as true or false in virtue of a moral order of values that is prior to and independent of our conceptions of persons and society, and of the public social role of moral doctrines" ("Themes in Kant's Moral Philosophy," in *Kant and Political Philosophy,* ed. Ronald Beiner and William James Booth [New Haven, CT: Yale University Press, 1993], p. 303). "This prior moral order is already given, as it were, by the nature of things and is known by rational intuition (or in some views by moral sense)." However, from a Kantian perspective (as Rawls reconstructs it), rational intuitionism's appeal to an independent moral order, rationally apprehended, is *heteronomous* because it violates or fails to respect "our conception of ourselves as reasonable and rational persons (as possessing the powers of practical reason), and of the public role of moral principles in a society of such persons" (p. 304). Of course, a Kantian approach to moral and political philosophy insists upon a respect for rational autonomy. "Thus an essential feature of Kant's moral constructivism is that the first principles of right and justice are seen as specified by a procedure of construction … the form and structure of which mirrors our free moral personality as both reasonable and rational." Cf. the Habermas text contrasting Kant and Plato quoted by Rawls on page 377 of *Political Liberalism.*

[6] See *Political Liberalism,* p. 258: "the political constitution, the legally recognized forms of property, and the organization of the economy, and the nature of the family, all belong to the basic structure."

contractors two votes and others one[7]). Rawls's conception of the original position is meant to preclude either kind of basic unfairness.

So, what principles of justice are affirmed once we have gone through that whole exercise in reflection and self-clarification? The resulting vision of justice is maintained consistently by Rawls throughout his political philosophy (that is, it remains constant notwithstanding other important transformations in his thought in the move from *A Theory of Justice* to *Political Liberalism*). Here is Rawls's theory as stated in the passage we were just quoting from page 271 of *Political Liberalism* (cf. page 291):

> The main two principles read as follows: a) Each person has an equal right to the most extensive scheme of equal basic liberties compatible with a similar scheme of liberties for all. b) Social and economic inequalities are permissible provided that they are i) to the greatest expected benefit of the least advantaged; and ii) attached to positions and offices open to all under conditions of fair equality of opportunity.[8]

The principles are pretty clear: civil rights of the standard liberal kind come first, then promotion of a moderate egalitarianism. A Rawlsian liberal cannot be indifferent to the plight of the disadvantaged, and must be prepared to accept state intervention in economic life (within limits)[9] in order to render the distribution of life prospects among fellow citizens less unfair.

As we noted at the start, Rawls penned two grand statements of his political philosophy, which in some respects overlap and in other respects are in significant tension. The second of these, namely *Political Liberalism*, is in important ways subversive of the conception of political philosophy defended in this book. It is important to see why Rawls tilts the enterprise of political philosophy in the direction that he does, and what is at stake in transforming that enterprise in ways that withdraw foundationalist claims (including

---

[7] But of course, as is true in Rousseau's *Social Contract*, the parties to the original contract do not vote (which obviously they cannot do anyway because they're merely *hypothetical* deliberators). The idea is that the principles will strike everyone as fair to everyone and, hence, will command unanimous assent. (For Rawls as for Rousseau, one resorts to voting only once this primeval contract has made it possible to erect the fundamental social and political institutions that define the society as a whole.) Rawls's claim is that his principles will strike everyone as fair, but since this hypothesis is never tested in an actual contractual situation, one may harbor doubts that the Rawlsian vision of justice will command the moral unanimity that he asserts on its behalf.

[8] The wording is slightly different from that offered in Rawls, *A Theory of Justice* (Oxford: Oxford University Press, 1978), p. 60, but the substance of the two principles seems identical. As Rawls highlights on page 291 of *Political Liberalism*, even the most seemingly minor differences in wording carry great weight for Rawls himself.

[9] Cf. *Political Liberalism*, p. lix.

claims to truth) and put it in the service of civic consensus (or what Rawls imagines to be civic consensus).

Rawls does not make it his purpose as a political philosopher to pass judgment on the decisions of individuals about what to do with their lives. Rather, the purpose of political philosophy, in his view, is to reflect on what is required, in the formation of basic social and political institutions, in order to give individuals a fair shot at *realizing* their individual conceptions of a good life, whatever those individual conceptions turn out to be.[10] However, the liberal determination not to dictate to people how to live their lives generates a problem that Rawls takes up in a more radical way in *Political Liberalism*, as compared with *A Theory of Justice*. In what sense is *Political Liberalism*'s approach "more radical," and what is the problem common to the two works that elicits this more radical *démarche*? We can call it the problem of neutralism (as an obligatory aspect of Rawlsian justice). Rawls's original idea was to conceive a framework of civic cooperation that would be fair to individuals adhering to a diversity of conceptions of the good, whatever those conceptions of the good happened to be (provided they were consistent with liberal justice). In *A Theory of Justice*, this gave rise to the doctrine of the priority of the right to the good. But still, this reflection on principles of fairness was supposed to generate a comprehensive doctrine on which all could agree, and justice as fairness was supposed to be that comprehensive doctrine. *Political Liberalism* was sparked by the idea that *no* comprehensive doctrine (including justice as fairness) could in principle trump "the fact of reasonable pluralism." Hence we must allow for existential pluralism (a multiplicity of legitimate conceptions of the good, none of which is privileged) not just on the "input" side of our philosophy of justice, so to speak, but on the "output" side as well. The result is the new political philosophy articulated in *Political Liberalism*, which is intended to offer a more *thoroughgoing* priority of the right to the good, a more thoroughgoing neutralism.

The heart of *Political Liberalism* is the idea of a form of liberal political philosophy that is not founded on a "comprehensive doctrine." A moral conception, according to Rawls,

is comprehensive when it includes conceptions of what is of value in human life and ideals of personal character, as well as ideals of friendship and of familial and

---

[10] Liberals are not obliged to be neutralist liberals: see Brian Barry, "How Not to Defend Liberal Institutions," in *Liberalism and the Good*, ed. R.B. Douglass, G.M. Mara, and H.S. Richardson (New York: Routledge, 1990). But *Rawlsian* liberals are more or less bound to swallow a large dose of liberal neutralism.

associational relationships, and much else that is to inform our conduct, and in the limit to our life as a whole. A conception is fully comprehensive if it covers all recognized values and virtues within one rather precisely articulated system. (p. 13)[11]

A "*political* conception of justice," by contrast, is (merely) political because it provides a civic meeting-ground for citizens who are adherents of *differing* comprehensive doctrines. If we are citizens of a communist regime or a theocratic regime, the expectation is that all citizens qua citizens affirm the *same* system of beliefs and views about the living of a properly human life, but what is distinctive of a *liberal* regime (as theorized by Rawls) is that it allows citizens to differ in their visions of the truth about how to live life, and yet agree on a set of "basic" institutions and on a set of civic principles that define the character of those institutions. What is decisive is segregating one's vision of a citizen from one's vision of a comprehensive understanding of what renders human life fully human. If these two things can successfully be kept insulated from each other, with respect to basic principles, then it will be possible for individuals who *differ* substantially in their views of life (e.g., on whether there is a Creator, on whether the universe is or is not providential, on whether individuals can achieve salvation and if so, on how to achieve that salvation) nonetheless to *agree* on how to share a common political community.

In a sense, Rawls's key idea in *Political Liberalism* is that one arrives at a political philosophy not by going out on a limb with a normative vision that articulates a contestable or controversial ranking of human ends. Rather, liberal political philosophy, so to speak, "falls into one's lap," because it so happens that the generality of one's fellow citizens are liberals, or historically socialized to liberalism, which happily spares the political philosopher the dubious task of invoking reason on behalf of a philosophy of life that might differ from what various individuals composing the society might invoke on their own behalf. The *reasonableness* of members of a liberal political community renders this unnecessary.[12] Here are some important

---

[11] Cf. John Rawls, *Collected Papers*, ed. Samuel Freeman (Cambridge, MA: Harvard University Press, 1999), p. 617.

[12] See the important discussion of Rawls's distinction between the reasonable and the rational: *Political Liberalism*, pp. 48–54. But Rawls seems to put far more of a burden on the appeal to reasonableness than it can plausibly bear. Consider, for instance, the following quite devastating challenge posed by Brian Leiter: the Rawls of *Political Liberalism* "thinks that a 'liberal' state cannot respect its citizens if it does not justify itself in terms that all 'reasonable' citizens with differing comprehensive views can nonetheless accept. Since there are no views acceptable to all 'reasonable' citizens – unless one denominates as unreasonable anyone who isn't a political liberal in basically the Rawlsian mode – it would seem that the kind of 'respect' Rawls imagines isn't a live option in the real world"; *Why Tolerate Religion?* (Princeton, NJ: Princeton University Press, 2013), p. 135n. The enormous paradox lying at

texts in which Rawls develops this self-abnegating conception of political philosophy:

> The aim of justice as fairness ... is practical: it presents itself as a conception of justice that may be shared by citizens as a basis of a reasoned, informed, and willing political agreement. It expresses their shared and public political reason. But to attain such a shared reason, the conception of justice should be, as far as possible, independent of the opposing and conflicting philosophical and religious doctrines that citizens affirm. In formulating such a conception, *political liberalism applies the principle of toleration to philosophy itself.* The religious doctrines that in previous centuries were the professed basis of society have gradually given way to principles of constitutional government that all citizens, whatever their religious view, can endorse. Comprehensive philosophical and moral doctrines likewise cannot be endorsed by citizens generally, and they also no longer can, if they ever could be, serve as the professed basis of society. (pp. 9–10; my italics)[13]

> To apply the principles of toleration to philosophy itself is to leave [it] to citizens themselves to settle the questions of religion, philosophy, and morals in accordance with views they freely affirm. (p. 154)

Again, the concern is not to *dictate* to ordinary citizens what they should think about the totality of things that really matter, and philosophy as philosophy (preoccupation with "the whole truth") inescapably represents a yearning to achieve an Archimedean point from which one will precisely be in a position to dictate such things to non-philosophers.[14]

> By avoiding comprehensive doctrines we try to bypass religion and philosophy's profoundest controversies so as to have some hope of uncovering a basis of a stable overlapping consensus. (p. 152)

> The only alternative to a principle of toleration is the autocratic use of state power. Thus, *justice as fairness deliberately stays on the surface, philosophically speaking....* Philosophy as the search for truth about an independent metaphysical and moral

---

the heart of Rawls's political philosophy is that while Rawls offers a version of liberalism intended to honor reasonable pluralism more than other versions of liberalism do, he presumes far more convergence between citizens about what a reasonable politics requires than actually exists.

[13] On the notion of applying the principle of toleration to philosophy itself, cf. *Collected Papers*, ed. Freeman, pp. 388 and 395.

[14] This is also a theme in at least two of the other thinkers in this book, namely Arendt and Rorty. For discussion of Arendt's version of the theme, see my essay "Rereading 'Truth and Politics'," *Philosophy and Social Criticism*, Vol. 34, nos. 1–2 (2008), pp. 123–136. For Rorty's version of the theme, see "The Priority of Democracy to Philosophy," in Richard Rorty, *Objectivity, Relativism, and Truth* (Cambridge: Cambridge University Press, 1991), pp. 175–196. It is also possible to see it as an issue in Oakeshott, insofar as Oakeshott is anxious to liberate the practice of politics from what he sees as the tyranny of "Rationalism." In the case of Arendt, it is clear that she is prompted to move in this direction by the idea that the two thinkers who for her most consummately embody what it means to be a philosopher, namely Plato and Heidegger, both had notions of realizing their philosophies via tyranny. But this kind of account obviously does not work for Rawls or Rorty.

order cannot, I believe, provide a workable and shared basis for a political conception of justice in a democratic society.[15]

And I consider the following to be a particularly important statement of
the underlying assumptions that define political liberalism as a way of doing
political philosophy:

> A continuing shared understanding on one comprehensive religious, philosophical,
> or moral doctrine can be maintained only by the oppressive use of state power. If
> we think of political society as a community united in affirming one and the same
> comprehensive doctrine, then the oppressive use of state power is necessary for
> political community ...The Inquisition was not an accident; its suppression of her-
> esy was needed to preserve that shared religious belief.The same holds, I believe, for
> any reasonable comprehensive philosophical and moral doctrine, whether religious
> or nonreligious. A society united on a reasonable form of utilitarianism, or on the
> reasonable liberalisms of Kant or Mill, [or, by implication, the doctrine of justice
> as fairness interpreted as a comprehensive version of liberalism,] would likewise
> require the sanctions of state power to remain so. (p. 37)[16]

Rawls wants to apply "the principle of toleration to philosophy itself" (p. 10).
Yet how are we supposed to do *that* without *disavowing* philosophy?[17] In fact,

---

[15] *Collected Papers*, ed. Freeman, pp. 394–395 (my italics); cf. page 395: "we try to avoid the problem of
truth," and *Political Liberalism*, p. 242: public discourse conceived in a Rawlsian manner "can seem
shallow" by virtue of disavowing concern with "the whole truth." See also Richard Rorty, "Posties,"
London Review of Books, September 3, 1987, "When it comes to the communal self-reassurance of the
modern democratic societies, most of the work gets done not by deep thinkers (e.g., people attracted
by Plato and Kant) but by superficial dreamers."
  As regards political philosophy's renunciation of concern with an "independent metaphysical and
moral order," see the discussion in note 5 of Rawls's rejection of the notion – associated with rational
intuitionism as the alternative to moral constructivism – of philosophy's capacity to make available
the apprehension of an independent "moral order of values." Ultimately, Rawls wants to appeal to
the (convergent) civic judgments of rational and reasonable citizens, *rather than appealing to some metaphysical principle* (and to somehow do that without philosophically privileging autonomy as a moral
ideal). One can find a similar theme in the thought of Habermas: part of what is driving Habermas's
emphasis on sociology is a desire to have less emphasis put on metaphysics (including "metaphysical"
accounts of human nature).
[16] In a footnote attached to this text (n. 39), Rawls acknowledges the paradox involved in conjuring
up the prospect of a theocratic autocracy founded on the teachings of Kant or Mill. It would not be
wholly off the mark to say that Rawls is driven here by a quasi-Nietzschean or quasi-Foucaultian
view of philosophy – that is, an idea of philosophy as animated not by truth for its own sake but
willy-nilly by a kind of lust to rule, an implicit desire to be a *philosopher-king*. What I mean by this
is that philosophers like Kant or Mill – that is, these thinkers in their role as philosophers qua philosophers – did not articulate their teachings as a prelude to imposing these teachings on the whole
society; they articulated them in the context of an intellectual *search for the truth*. Therefore, while it
is indeed a paradox to treat canonical liberals as potential sources of state autocracy, the much deeper
paradox is treating *any* philosopher in abstraction from the strictly intellectual-cognitive purpose that
defines philosophy as philosophy.
[17] Hence Rawls's worries, expressed on pp. 42–43, of the civic consequences of "a zeal for the whole
truth." If civic responsibility mandates an attenuation of this zeal, where does this leave the possibility
of such a thing as philosophy?

it is difficult to know how to interpret the texts we have quoted other than as pursuing a determinedly anti-philosophic agenda. Rawls's formulation in the "Reply to Habermas" (*Political Liberalism*, p. 375) is that political liberalism "leaves philosophy as it is" – "it leaves untouched all kinds of doctrines" received from the history of philosophy. Somewhat oddly, Rawls still refers to his politics-oriented rather than truth-oriented version of liberalism as *political philosophy*, but it is clearly a form of political philosophy that refuses to allow itself to participate in anything properly philosophical. One starts to wonder whether we might be letting Rawls off too easily when we say that this entails the death of political philosophy; suicide of political philosophy seems closer to the mark. Philosophy practiced in the way that it has always been practiced – with a view to the intellectual vindication of truth claims – is, Rawls declares quite unmistakably, *anti-civic* in effect if not by intention. Basically, Rawls is saying that it isn't necessary to erect his political philosophy by appealing to an independent philosophical standard – whether reason, nature, or history – because his fellow citizens have been civically virtuous enough to have already embraced the right political philosophy (namely, a political philosophy of tolerant reasonableness, and concern for justice). However (and it's a gigantic however), Rawls provides no evidence to convince us that his fellow citizens are as Rawlsian as he is.[18] A blunt way of putting this would be to say that Rawls wants to emasculate political philosophy in the grand sense, and since the "politically liberal" consensus is less assured than Rawls assumes it to be, this renunciation of concern with philosophical truth and the articulation of a foundationalist liberal vision likely has the consequence that Rawls ends up emasculating (at least to some extent) his own version of liberalism.[19]

Ultimately, Rawls's idea is that *liberals must not be hypocrites*. If they require religionists of various stripes to subordinate their larger conceptions of life (of what is required for salvation, of the meaning of death, of the Creator's purpose in fashioning the universe, including human inhabitants of the universe, and so on) to the imperatives of shared civic coexistence, then secular liberals are obliged to bracket their own visions of life in deference to the same imperatives of coexistence with those who don't share those visions of life. The duties of citizenship must be reciprocal, so if Christian, Muslim, and Jewish believers are expected to shelve their ultimate beliefs (not, of course,

---

[18] Cf. notes 12 and 24.
[19] For a full elaboration of this critique, see Beiner, *Civil Religion* (Cambridge: Cambridge University Press, 2011), chapter 23. One might say that the theory is intended as a *principled* self-emasculation.

in how they live their non-political lives, but strictly in the political domain, for purposes of civic coexistence, so all can live together as citizens), then fairness requires that non-believers ought to do the same thing. Moreover, if there can be Christian liberals and Muslim liberals and Jewish liberals and agnostic liberals and atheist liberals, that suggests that there is an independent basis for commitment to political liberalism that *transcends* what is specific to the belief systems of Christians, Muslims, Jews, agnostics, and atheists. This civic commitment independent of what individuals believe in in their non-political existence is what commands civic loyalty with respect to the "overlapping consensus" that undergirds political liberalism. What answer can be given to this line of argument?

The essential question is whether a conception of the good life is not implicit in (or surreptitiously smuggled into) Rawls's theory of liberal justice. Rawls insists that this isn't so; critics of Rawls have had their doubts. Of course, as an individual living his own life, Rawls is not obliged to be any more agnostic about the ends of life than any other human being, and probably couldn't be agnostic about this even if he wanted to be. But his line is that such views about what makes for a good life do not play any role in his political philosophy, and in fact it would violate the civic principles of a self-consistent liberal political order if such conceptions of the good *were* privileged in relation to rival conceptions of the good (provided that both sets of conceptions adhere to the civic requirements articulated in the idea of political liberalism). Here is a good statement of his view: "Given the conflicting comprehensive conceptions of the good, how is it possible to reach ... a political understanding of what are to count as appropriate claims? The difficulty is that the government can no more act to maximize the fulfillment of citizens' rational preferences, or wants (as in utilitarianism), or to advance human excellence, or the values of perfection (as in perfectionism), than it can act to advance Catholicism or Protestantism, or any other religion. None of these views of the meaning, value, and purpose of human life, as specified by the corresponding comprehensive religious or philosophical doctrines, is affirmed by citizens generally, and so the pursuit of any one of them through basic institutions gives political society a sectarian character" (pp. 179–180). This text expresses the philosophical core of Rawls's definitive political philosophy; it goes to the heart of what is driving him to articulate liberal principles as "political" liberalism.

As this text implies, giving civic privilege to a particular comprehensive doctrine – whether it be a religious-theological view or a liberal-secular view – would amount to a kind of theocracy. The whole idea of *Political*

Liberalism revolves, quasi-obsessively, around this theoretical preoccupation. The question for Rawls is: If Catholics can't legitimately found the state on a Catholic view of life (because its laws and policies will also apply to Protestant co-citizens), and if Protestants can't found the state on a Protestant view of life (because its laws and policies will apply to Catholic co-citizens), then how could it possibly be legitimate to found the state on a liberal-secular philosophy of life (because – again – those who do not subscribe to this philosophy of life will be bound by its laws and policies)? If Catholic theocracy is prohibited by liberalism, and Protestant theocracy is prohibited, then surely "liberal-secular theocracy," so to speak, is no less prohibited by the same moral logic. This problem is what thoroughly preoccupies Rawls in devising the revised theory that takes form in *Political Liberalism*, and he thinks that political liberalism, and only political liberalism, is capable of solving it. Any version of comprehensive liberalism counts as a "sectarian" doctrine among other sectarian doctrines, and if other sectarian doctrines are barred from turning the state into a theocratic instrument of their own hegemony, comprehensive versions of liberalism have to be bound by the same strictures. Insofar as Kantians want to promote liberal autonomy for all citizens, or liberal utilitarians want all citizens to embrace a consequentialist vision of aggregate welfare, they are making the same mistake about subordinating the state to a sectarian philosophy of life as is committed by, say, evangelical theocrats. Hence (despite the paradox), it is illegitimate in Rawls's view to appeal to a liberal philosophy of life in founding a liberal polity.

But does political liberalism actually succeed in abstaining from founding its vision of politics on a liberal philosophy of life? Can any political philosophy be agnostic with respect to alternative conceptions of attractive or less attractive visions of life? Even if Rawls distances himself from the philosophical endorsement of, say, individual autonomy as a privileged vision of life, is he not committed to *citizenship in a pluralistic society* as a normatively sanctioned existential (and not merely "political") ideal? If we imagine a few cases of types of non-liberal or anti-liberal political reflection that would be hostile to *Political Liberalism*'s conception of liberal-justice-centered citizenship, it is fairly easy to see that this presumed agnosticism starts to look quite suspect. For starters, how would one go about persuading either Nietzsche or Marx that Rawlsian liberalism involves no philosophically controversial existential commitments? Suppose one has a view like Eric Voegelin's, according to which liberalism per se is a Gnostic ideology – that is, a doctrine that allows a Gnostic civilization to justify itself to itself. Or suppose one has a view like Michael Oakeshott's, according to which every individual human life ought to be conceived "as an adventure in personal self-enactment," fearlessly staking its existence on "the chancy and intermittent satisfactions of chosen actions," and disdainful of the idea that the state needs to offer itself as "an association of invalids," providing remedial assistance for the unlucky and exerting itself to mitigate the perilousness of life for all of its citizens.[20] Relative to this intrepid Oakeshottian vision of what individuality should be and how the modern state is at war with that, a Rawlsian conception of justice looks like a celebration of cowardice and servility.[21] And it would look very much like the same thing even relative to more pedestrian versions of libertarian politics.

Is there anything existentially agnostic about the vision of life presupposed in *Political Liberalism* as seen from the very different vantage point occupied by Alasdair MacIntyre? For MacIntyre, the modern state is part and parcel of a morally compromised way of life (a way of life that promotes deracinated individualism, deficient acculturation, and exploitative market relations), hence it's hopeless to propose the liberal state, as Rawls does, as a legitimate vehicle of morally sufficient conceptions of justice. On what basis could one say that it is metaphysically agnostic to opt for Rawls's vision of life over MacIntyre's? Or metaphysically agnostic to say that political participation is optional, to be embraced or not embraced at the discretion of individuals (*Political Liberalism*, pp. 205–206), over against Hannah Arendt's claims that alienation from the public world is necessarily dehumanizing? Or metaphysically agnostic in relation to Michel Foucault's nightmare vision of a social world where the modern welfare state caters to the needs of its citizens merely as a pretext for keeping them more minutely supervised and normalized? Only for someone already inhabiting a liberal vision of life – a liberal metaphysical horizon – do liberal justice, liberal citizenship, and the liberal state look like reasonable and natural ways to organize a society. When one starts to reflect in this broader dimension, existential

---

[20] Michael Oakeshott, *On Human Conduct* (Oxford: Clarendon Press, 1975), pp. 241, 236, 308.
[21] F.A. Hayek once asserted (fairly astonishingly) that there is no fundamental difference between his political-philosophic principles and those of Rawls: see Hayek, *Law, Legislation and Liberty, Volume 2: The Mirage of Social Justice* (Chicago: University of Chicago Press, 1978), p. 100 (although *The Fatal Conceit*, ed. W.W. Bartley III [Chicago: University of Chicago Press, 1989], p. 74, seems to suggest the opposite). Rawls himself made the same kind of startling assertion in relation to Oakeshott's political philosophy: see *Political Liberalism*, p. 42, note 44. If it were really true that there were no difference between Rawlsian politics on the one hand and Hayekian or Oakeshottian politics on the other, one would be tempted to ask, a little despairingly: what's the point of bothering with political philosophy at all?

"sectarianism" starts to look inescapable – an unavoidable accompaniment of living and endorsing a particular way of life, structured by social and political institutions that will necessarily reflect a particular vision of a normatively legitimate way to live. As Jeremy Waldron has nicely put the point, "it is impossible to avoid commitment in political theory. If we try too hard to be non-sectarian, we will end up saying nothing."[22] As suggested earlier, the Rawlsian vision of living as a tolerant citizen amidst a moral diversity of other citizens, all respectful of each other, in a condition of reciprocal civic partnership, seems no less a view of how to live a normatively attractive human life than Oakeshott's vision of living as a "self-enacting" risk-taking adventurer; or MacIntyre's vision of living a life of close-knit solidarity; or Simone Weil's vision of living in a society whose moral touchstone is proper respect for the dignity of labor; or Arendt's vision of living as a citizen for whom the moments of most intense political experience are the only ones that render life meaningful. In that sense, a certain aspect of comprehensive liberalism is embedded within Rawlsian political liberalism whether he wants it to be or not.

Neutralism – or the *profession* of neutralism, a neutralism that Rawls cannot possibly make good on – is the Achilles heel of Rawlsian liberalism. We conceded earlier that the fact that there are Christian liberals and Muslim liberals and secular-humanist liberals does seem to lend support to something like a Rawlsian overlapping consensus. Yet this does not rule out that liberalism nonetheless presents itself as a discrete experience of life vis-à-vis rival experiences of life. If so, it is not existentially-metaphysically agnostic in the way that Rawls's conception of political philosophy requires. That is: Rawlsian political philosophy *privileges* a particular way of being human, even if it is a way of being human that can be agreed upon by Christian, Muslim, and secular-humanist inhabitants of a liberal society. The idea that one could affirm a vision of politics without endorsing any particular conception of ultimate human flourishing strikes me as chimerical. A society centered on liberal-egalitarian ideas of decency and mutual respect is obviously very different from societies fundamentally geared toward warrior honor, or Sparta-like republican virtue, or piety, or contemplative communing with nature, or other non-liberal views of the human good. So non-neutral conceptions of the good are inscribed in the liberal experience of life, whether Rawls wants to acknowledge this or not. I have argued elsewhere

---

[22] Jeremy Waldron, *God, Locke, and Equality* (Cambridge: Cambridge University Press, 2002), p. 239. Cf. Waldron's comment on Sandel, quoted in our first prologue, note 19.

that there is indeed an implied comprehensive doctrine in Rawls – namely an ideal of ecumenical citizenship.[23] That is, anyone for whom principled commitment to citizenship in a morally diverse and justice-seeking society is *not* a privileged conception of how to live life would find Rawls's political philosophy to be an existentially controversial ideal of life of precisely the kind that Rawls himself insists he wants to avoid.

I suppose Rawls would or could assert that he isn't required to provide a full-blown philosophical defense of this conception of how to be human because it has already been tacitly (that is, knowingly or unknowingly) embraced by all, or virtually all, members of a liberal society qua participants in the already-evolved overlapping consensus. However, the fact that, say, the existing reality of the United States as a political community contains many millions of citizens (probably a majority[24]) who are *not* Rawlsian liberals tells us that this overlapping consensus remains a philosophical ideal, not an achieved reality; and this puts the burden *back* on Rawls of giving a (philosophically controversial and therefore "sectarian") account of why his ideal of justice-oriented civic existence is a desirable model of what it is to be human. That is, it puts him back in the sphere of contestable comprehensive doctrines (the sphere of political philosophy interpreted along pre-*Political Liberalism* lines).[25]

---

[23] I have made this suggestion in various recent essays, but see especially Beiner, *Civil Religion*, chapter 23.

[24] What we need to do here is add up the vast number of Americans for whom owning a gun, or attending church, or displaying patriotism, or upholding traditional ideas of the family, is more central to the proper purposes of a human life than a civic commitment to using the state to compensate disadvantaged co-citizens for the unfairness of life. The number of Americans who opposed "Obamacare" (let alone a health care system closer to satisfying Rawlsian justice! – cf. *Political Liberalism*, p. lix), as compared with those who supported it, provides quite a good index of just how far removed the American political community is from being a genuinely Rawlsian public culture. Cf. Brian Barry, "The Light that Failed?" *Ethics*, Vol. 100, no. 1 (October 1989), p. 167: Rawls "is excessively optimistic in supposing that his premises are shared so widely in his own society."

[25] Here is an example of how political liberalism easily hobbles itself, relative to the philosophically more robust comprehensive liberalisms that the Rawls of *Political Liberalism* rejects. If a liberal civic community takes its stand on the principle of full civic equality, it is hard to see how it can permanently resist the claim to equality instantiated in gay marriage. Abiding by Rawlsian strictures, we declare that this change in civic norms is "philosophically neutral," related neither to a religious vision of life nor to a non-religious vision of life; it is metaphysically and existentially agnostic. It is simply the playing-out of the free-standing *political* commitments of citizens of a liberal polity. But how would, say, an evangelical Christian (or a hard-core Catholic like Rick Santorum) react to this claim of neutrality? And wouldn't the evangelical Christian be right to react with incredulity? Surely there's *some* vision of life at play in affirming a robust conception of gays as citizens among citizens. And a political philosophy that acknowledges this is likely to do better in fending off opposing views than a political philosophy that refuses to acknowledge its own existential non-neutrality. In that sense, it is to Rawls's *advantage* to drop political liberalism and re-embrace comprehensive liberalism – or rather, it is to the advantage of the civic ideals to which Rawls is committed. (On page 170 of *Political Liberalism*, Rawls tellingly

Elsewhere in this book, we have offered suggestions about the appeal to moral and philosophical pluralism as defeating political philosophy conceived as the quest for "the one big idea," which on our account is precisely what serves to define it as an intellectual enterprise with epic aspirations. We will conclude this chapter by applying such a line of thought to Rawls.

Political Liberalism is intended as a response to "the fact of reasonable pluralism" (pp. 36–37 and 58–66).²⁶ Rawls's purpose is to found political philosophy on an acknowledgment that reason does not dictate a single view of how to live but encompasses a plurality of reasonable views, and then to provide normative directions for a stable framework within which this plurality of views can coexist and in fact flourish civically in each other's presence. (Of course, implicit here is the awareness that not all views of life are *reasonable* ones; the aim of Rawlsian liberalism is to secure stable coexistence and cooperation among the *reasonable* [i.e., liberal] views, not to negotiate a truce between the reasonable and the unreasonable. As Locke and Rousseau put it, tolerating the intolerant is not an option.) This means that Rawls is no less committed to the idea of moral pluralism than Isaiah Berlin is.²⁷ There may indeed be a view of how to be human that possesses ultimate validity, but it is not the job of the political philosopher to locate and vindicate that view, since devoting intellectual energy to *that* task will draw energy away from the *true* task, which is to promote stable coexistence and civic cooperation among citizens who will naturally divide themselves into an unavoidable diversity of views about how to live life rightly.

All versions of liberalism will articulate some variant of the doctrine just stated, and liberalism possesses the philosophical attractiveness that it does because such a doctrine of reasonable pluralism captures not just an essential truth about modern societies but an essential aspect of the *human* truth. However, liberalism itself will be impoverished (as, in my view, Rawlsian liberalism is impoverished) if it draws the entailment that the philosophical dialogue among competing visions of human existence (including illiberal visions of

---

acknowledges that it may be a case of him being unduly "optimistic" in assuming that "all the main historical religions" can be readily harmonized with his tolerationist liberalism.)

²⁶ On page 614 of *Collected Papers*, Rawls states that *A Theory of Justice* had presented justice as fairness "as a comprehensive liberal doctrine ... in which all the members of its well-ordered society affirm that same doctrine." By virtue of taking on board the fact of reasonable pluralism (i.e., the misguidedness of trying to base a liberal society on a shared comprehensive doctrine), "*Political Liberalism* regards [the kind of society conjured up by *A Theory of Justice*] as impossible."

²⁷ See *Political Liberalism*, p. 197, n. 32 (cf. pages 57 and 303–304), where Rawls both cites and endorses the tragic vision of Berlin according to which "there is no social world without loss," from which it therefore follows that no liberal society, however expansive in the space it opens up for diverse conceptions of life, will accommodate all possible reasonable visions of human existence.

human existence) is something that, civically speaking, we can no longer afford. The harshest formulation of this Rawlsian entailment is his suggestion that if the public sphere becomes the forum for debating grand visions of life, death, and salvation, then we are on the slippery slope to a sixteenth- or seventeenth-century-style war of religions. (Of course, Hobbes had the same thought when he urged that a ban be put on teachings about a supposed *summum bonum!*[28]) There is much that is morally and civically attractive about political liberalism as Rawls elaborates it, but liberalism ought not to have the intellectual consequence that human beings no longer exchange conceptions, fleshed out in philosophically ambitious ways, about life in its totality. Moreover, as pointed out elsewhere in this book, if there is to be a continuing dialogue about the nature of the good (and how can we be human if such a dialogue is brought to a halt?), then political philosophers must remain committed to articulating particular (i.e., non-pluralistic) visions of what that human good is.

Having initiated a comparison between Rawls and Berlin, it might be appropriate to close by reflecting on one further aspect of the Rawls-Berlin relationship, namely, the sense in which the vision of political philosophy as a contest between competing conceptions of the ends of life remains intact in Berlin in a way that it doesn't in Rawls. The relevant contrast is sharply drawn in a recent essay by Alan Ryan. Ryan's account begins with the revelation that Berlin found Rawls's theoretical preoccupations "profoundly boring," and then gives the following interesting elaboration of what distinguishes Berlin's own preoccupations as a political theorist from the signature Rawlsian concerns:

> [The center of Berlin's interests was] the core values that a liberal must defend against all comers. And the comers against whom he was concerned to defend them were for the most part philosophers with large visions: Hegel, Maistre, Saint-Simon and the like. The enemy are the great simplifiers or the cloudy visionaries with their vast historical schemes rather than incompetent civil servants incapable of designing a taxation system that might curb the greedy and the exploitative. Berlin really thought that human beings were readily swept away by visions of one sort and another; some of these visions were profoundly liberticidal, and his fight was with those.[29]

Another way of formulating the contrast is to say that Berlin's view is that a robust dialogue with anti-liberal comprehensive doctrines is precisely *not*

---

[28] On the Rawls-Hobbes parallel, cf. Beiner, *Civil Religion*, p. 298. See *Collected Papers*, ed. Freeman, p. 620, for Rawls's suggestion that political liberalism, on the one hand, and "fighting it out," sixteenth-century-style, on the other hand, are the only two alternatives.

[29] Alan Ryan, "Isaiah Berlin: The History of Ideas as Psychodrama," *European Journal of Political Theory*, Vol. 12, no. 1 (January 2013), pp. 70, 71. See Ramin Jahanbegloo, *Conversations with Isaiah Berlin* (London: Peter Halban, 1992), p. 46, for an affirmation by Berlin that political philosophy is best defined in terms

philosophically dispensable, whereas Rawls's whole mature project is to presume that such a dialogue *is* dispensable. I'm not inclined to retract my inclusion of Rawls in this survey of epic theorists of the twentieth century, but the question of what is lost in preferring a liberalism like Rawls's to a liberalism like Berlin's (that is, a view that, unlike the former, sees a grand dialogue between liberalism and anti-liberalism as still relevant) continues to be worth thinking about.

Finally, what of Rawls's worry that a liberal state that endorses a particular philosophy of life will prove itself to be sectarian — show itself to be, at the level of principle, no better than, or no less illegitimate than, non-liberal varieties of theocracy? Ultimately, the response has to be that *life* demands sectarianism in the sense that it gives us no choice but to opt for some definite view of how to live and to privilege some such view in a particular constellation of social life. Clearly, this does not mean that the liberal state commits itself to arm-twisting every individual to adopt a particular set of doctrines, as is the case with genuinely theocratic or authoritarian regimes. Still, the adjective "liberal," if taken seriously, tells us that the liberal state would not be the liberal state unless it favored or privileged a particular horizon of life, a particular interpretation of what matters or what counts in the living of life, whether liberal philosophers acknowledge this or not.[30]

---

of reflection on the ends of life. Precisely this Berlinian conception has recently been polemically targeted by Jeremy Waldron: see, for instance, "How Politics are Haunted by the Past," *The New York Review of Books*, February 21, 2013, pp. 40–41. The complaint is that this way of conceiving the enterprise of theory puts far too much weight on strictly normative concerns and not enough weight on institutional questions, and Waldron explicitly views Rawls (or the style of theorizing inspired by Rawls) as subject to the same criticism. Pace Waldron, my own very different view is that Rawls actually falls considerably short of the Berlinian conception of theory as defined by broad reflection on the ends of life — or at least that Rawls *thinks* that one can reflect on justice without simultaneously reflecting on the nature of the ends that define a proper human life. Admittedly, Berlin's conception (as he elaborates it in the conversation with Jahanbegloo) is more a matter of debunking misguided visions of the ends of life than of championing one of his own (as we discussed in the first prologue). Still, Berlin's openness to ambitious dialogue with philosophies well outside the liberal horizon gives us strong reason to resist Waldron's assimilation of Berlin and Rawls.

[30] Consider Rawls's doctrine of public reason. The idea of public reason mandates that, with respect to constitutional essentials, citizens address one another in a non-sectarian (philosophically agnostic) language of public discourse. Clearly, this would not fly in a country like Egypt, whose public culture is predominantly Islamic. But then, relative to Egypt, public reason itself *is* sectarian, in the sense that it presumes the possibility of a kind of civic discourse that abstracts from religious identity — something that most Egyptians would deem not only controversial but unacceptable. In other words, public reason in Rawls's sense is viable only in a society in which citizens subscribe to a shared philosophy of life more or less corresponding to liberalism (which is probably the most plausible way of interpreting Rawls's claim that his political philosophy is founded on a preexisting overlapping consensus).

14
Richard Rorty: Knocking Philosophy off Its Pedestal, or the Death of Political Philosophy Postmodernized

As we saw in the previous chapter, John Rawls put on the agenda (tried out as an experiment, so to speak) the possibility of a mode of political philosophy that would dispense with appeal to the idea of truth, and, as we have seen elsewhere in this book, the same line of thinking was anticipated by other thinkers, such as Arendt and Foucault. But Richard Rorty went the furthest in putting this non-truth-based reconception of political philosophy at the center of his philosophizing. Hence, anyone concerned with the future of political philosophy as an intellectual discipline must confront Rorty, and, one hopes, repel his idea of detaching philosophy from truth.[1] Rorty had a talent for forging syntheses among philosophical views that one would otherwise assume to be utterly incombinable: Dewey and Heidegger, Derrida and Rawls, and so on. The sense of paradox associated with some of these unlikely combinations helped a lot, I believe, to win Rorty a large readership, although he also should not go without credit for generating novel insights by means of this often bold mixing-and-matching. As regards political philosophy, what Rorty offers is an amalgam of Rawlsian and Shklarian liberalism, rendered distinctive via a postmodernish radicalization of *Political Liberalism*'s move away from the age-old notion that it is the job of political philosophy to articulate and defend truth-claims. There is nothing perceptibly postmodern about how this conception is presented by Rawls, but it *becomes* postmodern in the hands of Rorty. Rorty's core agenda for political philosophy is captured

---

[1] For a particularly blunt statement of this project, see Richard Rorty, "The Priority of Democracy to Philosophy," in Rorty, *Objectivity, Relativism, and Truth* (Cambridge: Cambridge University Press, 1991), p. 177: "For pragmatist social theory ... truth is simply irrelevant." See also Richard Rorty, *Contingency, Irony, and Solidarity* (Cambridge: Cambridge University Press, 1989), p. xiii: Historicism "has helped us substitute Freedom for Truth as the goal of thinking and of social progress"; all parenthetical page references in this chapter are to this book.

well in the three banners that figure in the title of his book: irony, solidarity, and contingency. Each of these themes will figure to some extent in the discussion that follows, but it is chiefly the emphasis on irony that makes Rorty a postmodern liberal, rather than a liberal of the standard Rawlsian sort, and the coherence or incoherence of Rorty's political philosophy will ultimately hang on whether an appeal to irony makes for a coherent version of liberalism (or any other political philosophy).

It is hard not to suspect that Rorty evolved into the maverick "post-philosophical" thinker he eventually became in reaction against his original training and early career as a conventional analytical philosopher.[2] According to the intellectual identity he started with, the purpose of philosophy is to secure a veridical representation of "the way the world really is," or "the way the mind or the self really is," and to locate a set of valid propositions about the world that would map onto this "in-itselfness" of the world, so to speak. However, as Rorty came to doubt that this intellectual ambition is in fact a realizable one, he faced the unavoidable question: if philosophy *isn't* the pursuit of a valid representation of the way the world really is, *what is it?* The work for which Rorty is most famous (including the book that concerns us in this chapter) is intended to answer that question.

Rorty's master-idea is that the vocabularies by which we describe the world, which different cultures at different historical moments obviously do in very different ways, cannot be a matter of approximating to a truer, or deeper, or more authentic match with the world as it really is – for the simple reason that we have no vocabulary-independent (or "vocabulary-neutral") access to the world as it really is, and hence no possibility of measuring the degree of fit between our categories or descriptions and the world that those categories are meant to describe.[3] The idea of vocabularies that do not depict, do not hook onto, and do not even represent

---

[2] For a short but helpful intellectual biography of Rorty, see Michael Bacon, "Richard Rorty: Liberalism, Irony, and Social Hope," in *Political Philosophy in the Twentieth Century*, ed. Catherine H. Zuckert (Cambridge: Cambridge University Press, 2011).

[3] One can perhaps illustrate this notion with the idea of so-called wave-particle duality in quantum mechanics. It can be useful for certain purposes to use the vocabulary of waves and useful for certain other purposes to use the vocabulary of particles, but it makes no sense to privilege one or the other of these vocabularies according to the idea that the entities of physical nature "really are" waves or "really are" particles. In that sense, the vocabularies of contemporary physics refer to these elusive entities *as if* the vocabularies being deployed allowed one to penetrate to the fundamental reality of nature, which in truth they do not. Still, it seems obvious that quantum mechanics wouldn't exist at all without the notion of trying to come up with theoretical conceptions that fit the reality of nature better than previously available theoretical conceptions (e.g., the ability of Heisenberg's physics to correspond to the world in a way that surpasses that of Newton's physics).

progressively closer approximations to realities beyond those vocabularies can easily be experienced as debilitating or demoralizing; Rorty means for us to experience this idea not as the source of a feeling of vertigo, but rather, as liberating, even exhilarating. Part of Rorty's endeavor here is to get us to feel comfortable with a forthrightly historicist self-understanding: "There is no standpoint outside the particular historically conditioned and temporary vocabulary we are presently using from which to judge this vocabulary" (p. 48). The worry here, of course, would be that this locks us into a vocabulary we just happen to share with some particular group of human beings with whom we contingently share a culture – just a throw of the historical dice, nothing more. How do we take our moral and cognitive commitments seriously if they don't assert claims to having won a superior purchase on the way we are and the way the world is?[4] Naturally, we want these beliefs and commitments to have some firmer metaphysical status than merely the contingent fact that we have these vocabularies. Rorty would say that reacting in this fashion just shows that we are still too hung up on the old preoccupations – the fixation on "grounding" our beliefs, rather than being open to a plurality of modes of "self-creation" and seeing this as liberating. The answer for Rorty is simply to try out more vocabularies and drop the metaphysical hang-ups. Having *more* poems and *more* novels in the world makes the world a better place; why shouldn't the proliferation of vocabularies similarly make the world a better place?

The Rortyan project, as he expresses it on page 44, is to see whether "the institutions and culture of liberal society would be better served by a vocabulary of moral and political reflection [that] revolves around notions of metaphor and self-creation rather than around notions of truth, rationality, and moral obligation." Carrying these ideas to the limit (and Rorty seems to have little inhibition about carrying them as far as they will go) would appear to have revolutionary implications with respect to how we understand ourselves and our relation to the world. All science and all morality, as

---

[4] Rorty writes: "The fundamental premise of [*Contingency, Irony, and Solidarity*] is that a belief can still regulate action, can still be thought worth dying for, among people who are quite aware that this belief is caused by nothing deeper than contingent historical circumstance" (p. 189). I can see the theoretical interest of exploring whether this is true or not, but the premise itself seems far from convincing. Why *would* people die for beliefs and commitments that were seen as no truer, no more rational, no more normatively binding, than beliefs and commitments on the opposing side? Or putting the same question in slightly different terms: Why wouldn't pervasive irony applied to people's beliefs and commitments attenuate the moral power associated with those beliefs and commitments, as experienced by those who held them? If there were satisfying answers to these questions, Rorty would surely have persuaded more of his readers (or at least more of his fellow philosophers) than seems to be the case.

we generally think of them, presuppose that our vocabularies refer to something beyond themselves; therefore, living in a Rortyan universe requires, at a minimum, reconceiving science and morality such that they still make some sense in a situation where "truth is simply irrelevant." Again, if that involves plunging into a whole new cultural paradigm, Rorty is only too eager to take that plunge. But he thinks that the consequences for our vision of politics are fairly modest. This is because good politics are a matter of cultivating compassion and a sense of justice, and this depends much more on imagination than on reason; more on novels and poetry than on theory or philosophy. So if we have to settle for a conception of our world-describing vocabularies that drops appeals to their being truer, deeper, more real than rival vocabularies, the reduced authority of reason and truth is something we can live with. More than that, Rorty believes that a conception of liberalism oriented more toward imagination and less toward reason and argument is a positive gain, provided that we can adjust to the new, more playful stance toward our existential commitments.

We need a redescription of liberalism as the hope that culture as a whole can be "poeticized" rather than as the Enlightenment hope that it can be "rationalized" or "scientized." ... [Doing this would serve the purpose] of providing contemporary liberal culture with a vocabulary which is all its own, cleansing it of the residues of a vocabulary which was suited to the needs of former days. (pp. 53, 55)

It is a question of seeing ourselves as enriched by taking ourselves and our conceptions of the world less seriously. After all, poets, when they compose a new poem, are not compelled to see this poem in a kind of competition for rational authority vis-à-vis other poems. A new poem is a new poem, and it expands the imaginative resources available to us: why can't we think of our relation to our political and intellectual commitments in a similar way? This is where the idea of irony comes in. An "ironist" on Rorty's account is someone who "has radical and continuing doubts about the final vocabulary she currently uses" (p. 73). Here, an irony-inflected "final vocabulary" means more or less: an authoritative vocabulary that (paradoxically) has been divested of its authority, one that is "final" only in the sense that it is chronologically the most recent, but awaits its demise since it may be dropped at any moment as we try out and experiment with alternative vocabularies with equally dubious authority. "Metaphysicians believe that there are, out there in the world, real essences which it is our duty to discover and which are disposed to assist in their own discovery" (p. 75). But no one is obliged to be a metaphysician in this sense. We can generate descriptions and re-descriptions in the way that poets generate new poems, as a kind of reveling in the open-endedness of the world and our possible relations to it.[5]

Notwithstanding Rorty's very real debt to the "political not metaphysical" phase of Rawlsian liberalism, it is interesting to ask whether the agnosticism toward comprehensive doctrines insisted upon by Rawls is also to be found in Rorty. Consider the following important passage in *Contingency, Irony, and Solidarity*:

In its ideal form, the culture of liberalism would be one which was enlightened, secular, through and through. It would be one in which no trace of divinity remained, either in the form of a divinized world or a divinized self. Such a culture would have no room for the notion that there are nonhuman forces to which human beings should be responsible. It would drop, or drastically reinterpret, not only the idea of holiness but those of "devotion to truth" and of "fulfillment of the deepest needs of the spirit." The process of de-divinization ... would, ideally, culminate in our no longer being able to see any use for the notion that finite, mortal, contingently existing human beings might derive the meanings of their lives from anything except other finite, mortal, contingently existing human beings. (p. 45)

This text makes fairly clear that an important aspect of what is driving Rorty's emphasis on contingency is the wish to align himself with the Enlightenment's revolt again Christian theism. However, somewhat strangely, he wants the Enlightenment's assertion of human autonomy without the Enlightenment's appeal to rationality and truth (see page 57). It is hard to imagine who would be interested in contesting a vision of human beings as "finite" and "mortal"; and only those not yet prepared to defer to the truth of Darwinian evolution could challenge the idea that there is something fundamentally contingent about the fact that human beings exist at all. Less clear is why a thinker as supportive of the Enlightenment as Rorty is would want to drop truth into the same rubbish bin as holiness, or why he thinks reflection on "the deepest needs of the spirit" is now redundant. Leaving aside all those difficult questions, let's note that there is certainly no abstention from comprehensive doctrines in this text. Rawls believes that one can do political philosophy without taking sides in the controversy, unavoidable in Western culture since the seventeenth century, about whether theism is

---

[5] Cf. "The Priority of Democracy to Philosophy," p. 189: Liberation from metaphysics consists in being "able to see moral progress as a history of making rather than finding." Poetry is superior to reason insofar as reason merely "unveils" (or claims to unveil) what is already there. And since we lack vocabulary-independent access to the reality supposedly being unveiled, appeal to what reason claims to unveil – whether moral principles, or universal rights, or other ideas to which one imputes some special normative authority – is (Rorty repeatedly suggests) directly analogous to theology's appeal to a non-existent God.

true or false; Rorty *does* take sides in that controversy, and wants the culture of liberalism as a whole to be on the side he is on.

Rorty's vindication of liberalism seems to me a little too easy. Liberalism, as defined by Rorty, is a vision of life devoted to the hope of arranging human institutions in ways that render them less cruel than they currently are: "hope that suffering will be diminished, that the humiliation of human beings by other human beings may cease" (p. xv). In Rorty's view, this political project loses nothing by abandoning political philosophy's aspiration to anchor its vision of political good in appeal to a deeper reality, a more fundamental truth, because literature, which does not assert truth claims but rather pushes the boundaries of human imagination, can do a better job of sensitizing lay readers to the desirability of justice, and hence can do more to serve the cause of liberal hope than philosophy can. Rorty may well be right about the efficacy of great literature in expanding moral sensibilities in comparison with that of philosophy. Still, one has to wonder whether he is right that nothing is lost, humanly speaking, in abandoning the aspiration to out-argue (and therefore engage in reciprocal argument) those committed to opposing visions of life. His point seems to be that if liberals are people who share a commitment to reducing needless cruelty and suffering, arguing with those who *believe that cruelty and suffering are okay* (obtuse and demented as those potential interlocutors must be) will be a complete waste of time.[6] However, part of the problem here, arguably, is defining liberalism in a way that leaves no non-liberal interlocutors worthy of engagement. Suppose we conceive this potential interlocutor as someone who rejects the liberal view of life because it doesn't take seriously the centrality of piety and obedience to a well-lived human life. Or even saintliness. No doubt, there are liberal "re-descriptions" that would cast such views as merely a pretext for cruelty and suffering. Yet it seems an unwarrantedly short-circuited intellectual move to put all such alternatives to the liberal horizon of life under the rubric of infliction of suffering right off the bat. Presenting liberalism as the natural philosophy for all those repelled by the cruelty human beings do to each other hardly seems to do justice to any morally serious rival conception of life. Nor is it obvious that tacit truth claims concerning the self and the world aren't lurking, unacknowledged, in this account of liberalism. How do we even appeal to the idea of liberal progress, the hope of advancing to a more humane and more just organization of social life, without judgments about how things stand with respect

---

[6] See, in particular, "The Priority of Democracy to Philosophy," pp. 187–188.

to a vocabulary-independent reality? Wouldn't liberalism itself as a political vision be strengthened by equipping it to envision those who see life according to non-liberal standards as intellectually respectable interlocutors rather than as morally blind lovers of cruelty?

As with Rawls, the appeal to a post-philosophical liberal "we" seems to be doing most or all of the work in Rorty's theory. To be sure, if such a "we" reliably exists, then the articulation of a political philosophy of the traditional sort starts to look redundant. But here it may be worth asking a question that Rorty never really asks, which is why pre-Rawlsian or pre-Rortyan political philosophers troubled themselves to erect intellectual foundations in the first place (appealing to essences, or an essential self, or metaphysically privileged vocabularies, or whatever)?[7] The answer, very clearly (almost self-evidently), is that the social worlds in which human beings find themselves have always been riven by profound disagreements about the right way to conceive the ends of life; and philosophy represents (represented in the past, and continues to represent, for those who do not share Rawls's and Rorty's liberal complacency) an effort to draw people over to the theorist's side of a particular existential or metaphysical controversy by appeal to *something* that seems to have special force.[8] (Even the original position postulated by the early Rawls had this character – namely, the ambition to give non-liberals some special reason to start seeing the moral world in a liberal way, which is precisely why *A Theory of Justice* looks too philosophically ambitious from the perspective of the Rawls of *Political Liberalism*.) If "we liberals" all agree on the appropriate horizon for living a satisfactory human life, then appeal to a final vocabulary of this kind indeed looks beside the point. But if Rawls and Rorty have prematurely announced the consolidation of a stable liberal consensus, then mere "contingency" and "solidarity" seem insufficient to

---

[7] Cf. Beiner, *Civil Religion* (Cambridge: Cambridge University Press, 2011), pp. 291–292, where I distinguish between projective or forward-looking versions of liberalism, which have to appeal to the rational or philosophical superiority of liberal principles because they are trying to win whole societies over to a culture of liberalism that doesn't yet exist, and retrospective or "owl of Minerva" versions of liberalism (like those of Rawls and Rorty), for which such foundationalist exertions appear redundant because they take the victory of liberalism to be a historical given. It would seem that the latter tacitly assume a metaphysical faith in the progressivity of history, for otherwise, how do we know that liberal principles, insofar as they are culturally entrenched today, won't get rolled back or revoked fifty or a hundred years from now?

[8] Consider the telling formulation on page 194: "[Although] 'reason' ... was very useful in creating modern democratic societies, it can now be dispensed with.... The democracies are now in a position to throw away some of the ladders used in their own construction." The clear suggestion is that a post-Enlightenment society is a fully secure achievement, rather than one that continues to be fundamentally contested. One wonders if Rorty would have been able to write complacent sentences like this if *Contingency, Irony, and Solidarity* had been composed subsequent to the rise of jihadist Islam.

221

give us the guidance we seek, and philosophical foundationalism of various descriptions may once more reaquire its rationale.[9]

What does it mean to make irony central to one's political philosophy? Clearly, it is a kind of rhetoric – one founded on the judgment that political philosophy would benefit by loosening up on the insistence that the philosopher's preferred "vocabulary is closer to reality than others, that it is in touch with a power not herself" (p. 73). As Rorty puts it on page 82 (referring back to page 44), distinctions between absolutism and relativism, between rationality and irrationality, and between morality and expediency "have become impediments to the culture of liberalism." Again, we need to become more poetic, more playful, less fixated on rationally "grounding" our commitments. In this respect, Rorty's work naturally provokes a reflection on the range of rhetorics available to political philosophy.

Rorty and Voegelin may seem like an unlikely juxtaposition, but I think that considering them together yields an interesting study in contrasting rhetorics. The Voegelinian rhetoric depicts the West as sliding headlong into the abyss. Our souls are corrupted, and we have the kind of morally and intellectually compromised social order that one would expect of a body politic distinguished mainly by its spiritual degeneracy. Rortyan rhetoric is at the opposite pole: take a Valium! There's no crisis. Pragmatic-minded social democrats indeed have political work to do (and always will), but depth-plumbing foundational reflection on cosmic realities, spiritual realities, or the ultimate ground of human nature and of our nature as political beings will contribute nothing to the civic exertions that are needed in the face of contemporary challenges. If modern liberal societies – and the souls that compose them – are bland and shallow, we shouldn't gnash our teeth over this but at worst see it as a small price to pay for living in "a society that cherishes individual liberty."[10] Certainly, no one can accuse Rorty of setting himself up as a "guru." If anything, the problem with his conception of theorizing lies at the other extreme: if a theorist like Voegelin runs the risk of excessively ratcheting up the pathos

---

[9] Cf. Roger Scruton, "Richard Rorty's Legacy": "Rorty was paramount among those thinkers who advance their own opinion as immune to criticism, by pretending that it is not truth but consensus that counts, while defining the consensus in terms of people like themselves" (http://www.opendemocracy.net/democracy_power/people/richard_rorty_legacy). Scruton would surely apply the same judgment to Rawls (as would I).

[10] "The Priority of Democracy to Philosophy," p. 190.

of philosophy, Rorty runs the contrary risk of (deliberately) banalizing it.[11] If this is something that worried or bothered Rorty, he obviously wouldn't have chosen to write in the philosophical style that he does in the first place. But it does worry and does bother us because – making some allowance for its prophylactic effect as a corrective to the hubris of philosophy – if this becomes the universal style in which philosophers henceforth philosophize, philosophy will have fallen so far from the pedestal it previously occupied that it will likely cease to make any claims whatsoever on human culture or human interests.[12]

Rorty owes a substantial intellectual debt to three of the thinkers addressed earlier in this book, namely Oakeshott, Gadamer, and Rawls.[13] From Oakeshott and Gadamer he gets the idea that human reason has been made to carry a much heavier burden with respect to the understanding of moral and political life than it can really bear. Philosophy is merely a part of a broader human conversation, and it would be a mistake (a mistake that has defined much of the history of Western philosophy) to elevate it to a privileged status beyond its proper station as a humble conversational partner. From Rawls, Rorty gets the related idea that one can commit oneself to liberalism *politically* without presuming that political philosophy can endow liberalism with anything as grand as "rational foundations." A common thread among the sources selected by Rorty – whether Oakeshott and Gadamer or Wittgenstein and Dewey – is that all of them emphasize the need for a rebalancing in the theory/practice relation that gives significantly more weight to practice.[14]

In my own work, I have tried to develop the idea that it is a mistake to want either to subordinate theory to practice or to subordinate practice to theory. A better conception is what I tend to think of as a robustly *"dualistic"*

---

[11] In "The Priority of Democracy to Philosophy," p. 193, Rorty acknowledges "the air of light-minded aestheticism" that characterizes his philosophical writing, but he adds, "there is a moral purpose behind this light-mindedness. The encouragement of light-mindedness about traditional philosophical topics serves the same purposes as does the encouragement of light-mindedness about traditional theological topics. Like the rise of large market economies, the increase in literacy, the proliferation of artistic genres, and the insouciant pluralism of contemporary culture, such philosophical superficiality and light-mindedness helps along the disenchantment of the world. It helps make the world's inhabitants more pragmatic, more tolerant, more liberal, more receptive to the appeal of instrumental rationality."

[12] The reader should not take this as suggesting that I consider this a real possibility, or even a highly remote possibility. I think it is impossible, for reasons articulated elsewhere in this book.

[13] For the debt to Gadamer and Oakeshott, see Richard Rorty, *Philosophy and the Mirror of Nature* (Princeton, NJ: Princeton University Press, 1979), chapter 8; for the debt to Rawls, see "The Priority of Democracy to Philosophy."

[14] But as regards Oakeshott and Rorty, see note 14 of our Oakeshott chapter.

view.[15] That is, philosophy and citizenship are defined by radically distinct purposes: the job of philosophy is to strive unconditionally for truth, and the job of citizenship is to strive for good and prudent judgment about the common purposes of civic life, and each should focus strictly on fulfilling its own appointed end without worrying too much about the other. As is well-captured in the title that Mark Lilla gave to his book *The Reckless Mind*,[16] great theorists are commonly *not* good models of civic responsibility. Thankfully, countless of our fellow-citizens in liberal democracy have much sounder judgment and a much better grip on the demands of responsible practice than a Martin Heidegger or a Michel Foucault. But those prudent citizens cannot give us what Heidegger or Foucault gives us: the capacity in their texts to explode our accustomed categories of experience and thus enable us to see the world afresh. Being faithful to the theory tradition in all its radicalism requires, in my view, a steady appreciation of the fundamental chasm between what we (*as citizens*) need in the world of practice and what we (*as human beings*) need from the world of theory. (Recall that very similar issues arose in our discussion of Gadamer in Chapter 8.) From this perspective, Rawls and others are wrongly tempted to clip the wings of philosophy in order to make it more serviceable to good citizenship.

It is undeniable that coming to a deeper appreciation of the primacy of practice over theory can be quite salutary, especially when one considers the forms of hubris often displayed in the philosophical tradition (as discussed in our Gadamer chapter). And one also has to admit that there is something distinctly attractive (because self-effacing) about a leading philosopher like Rorty putting so much effort into trying to downplay the cultural importance of philosophy and play up the cultural importance of literature. Still, it becomes a bit worrisome when this rebalancing gets carried so far that many of the leading political philosophers of our time see fit to distance themselves from truth as the central defining desideratum of the philosophical vocation. Is Rorty's pragmatization of philosophy the swan song of the philosophical tradition?[17]

---

[15] There are various articulations of this dualistic conception in my book *Philosophy in a Time of Lost Spirit* (Toronto: University of Toronto Press, 1997), starting with the preface. As I discuss in chapter 8 of that book, one can find elements of this dualistic conception in Rorty's work, insofar as he insists that the purposes of politics, namely pursuing justice and solidarity, are quite separate from those of philosophy; however, a key difference is that unlike Rorty, I don't associate philosophy as a private, non-political pursuit with the business of self-creation or poetry. Clearly, I remain committed to a much more traditional understanding of philosophy as cognitive and truth-oriented.

[16] Mark Lilla, *The Reckless Mind* (New York: New York Review Books, 2001).

[17] Leaving aside the pragmatists celebrated by Rorty, Leo Strauss was speaking for the philosophical tradition as a whole when he wrote: "Utility and truth are two entirely different things" (*Natural Right*

Western intellectuals seem to have gone a little too far with their anti-foundationalism, or so I'd propose. As human beings, we need to know where we stand normatively, and that means giving a rational account of the ground on which we stand. Understandably, contemporary intellectuals want to privilege dialogue and pluralism, and that seems to point toward the disavowal of foundationalist (or "monist") ambitions. But if the interlocutors in this dialogue (meaning all of us) are chiefly driven by the desire to be respectful of fellow interlocutors, how will they come up with views robust enough or interesting enough or intellectually compelling enough to sustain the dialogue on the things that matter most to us as human beings? (What modes of life are worth living? What constitutes a satisfying organization of social and civic existence? Under what conditions do human beings flourish or fail to flourish? And so on.)

If philosophical acknowledgment of the bankruptcy of the search for foundations means that we are always floating in mid-air to some extent, is that an image of our condition that we can really live with?[18] In other discussions at various points in this book, we have suggested that all political philosophers of the epic variety, qua political philosophers, offer some kind of Archimedean point, that is, some privileged conception that provides a point of ultimate intellectual leverage for thinking about the things that human beings as human beings need to think about.[19] What is Rorty's Archimedean point? Paradoxically, his Archimedean point is not having an

and History [Chicago: University of Chicago Press, 1974], p. 6) – although, somewhat paradoxically, Straussian hermeneutics generally interprets the great texts of the theory canon as being attuned at least as much to utility as to truth, if not more so. In any case, if the truth/utility distinction is itself true and not merely useful, then it stands as the refutation of all pragmatism in philosophy, including Rorty's. Cf. David Runciman, "Where's Hobbes?" *Times Literary Supplement* (27 February 2013), quoting Noel Malcolm: "it is hard to escape the conclusion that [Hobbes] wrote as he did for one compelling reason above all: he believed that what he wrote was true."

[18] Interesting in this context is the powerful set of exchanges between Hans Jonas and Hannah Arendt quoted on pages 114–116 of my edition of Hannah Arendt, *Lectures on Kant's Political Philosophy* (Chicago: University of Chicago Press, 1982). Jonas suggests that in a post-twentieth-century world where human beings have the unprecedented power to utterly reshape their conditions of life in irreversible ways – in ways that "affect the total condition of things on earth and the total future condition of man" – we shouldn't necessarily be sanguine about renouncing "that which has by unanimous consensus ... been declared dead and done with – namely, metaphysics." Jonas asks: however weak our confidence in the Western metaphysical tradition may have become, *particularly in a world where what we do engages absolute stakes*, can we really dispense with an appeal to metaphysical ultimates? As I point out in my commentary, Jonas largely concedes the ensuing argument to Arendt, but I think Jonas's challenge has quite a lot more force than Arendt appreciates.

[19] This claim is illustrated well by Foucault. Foucault presents himself as a resolute Nietzschean, much more interested in the contingent realities of power than in universal truth. However, as we argued in our Foucault chapter, a quasi-metaphysics is nonetheless present in his work that decisively shapes his political philosophy. Correspondingly, there is in Foucault, just as there is in Nietzsche, a grand metanarrative at least as ambitious as those offered by standard-bearers of traditional Western rationalism.

Archimedean point. (Or, to put it in Lyotardian terms: the meta-narrative is not having a meta-narrative.) Is this coherent? Without the desire for rational foundations, no one would ever write so much as a single sentence. It's unavoidable. Hence the postmodern impulse to eschew or disavow foundations is an impossible project. Just as Aristotle claimed that the experience of wonder is an intrinsic part of human nature, so the same thing is true of our aspiration to provide rational grounding to our experience of life – we are both wonder-experiencing animals and foundation-seeking animals. It's telling, in this context, that Rorty's means of urging liberal culture to be more poetic, or to render poetry more central to the intellectual identity of this culture, isn't to write a poem; he proceeds by weighing arguments available both within the history of philosophy and within contemporary philosophy, and by marshaling what he clearly takes to be his own superior, more compelling arguments. Isn't there already a form of "foundationalism" implicit in this priority accorded by Rorty himself to philosophical argument over poetry? If these things are not adjudicated in the medium of argumentative rationality (where the appeal to rationality is not just a way of fooling ourselves about a particular kind of rhetoric), what's the point of Rorty trying to win over his readers with arguments he presumably considers compelling? (Or is he saying that his arguments *are* just a type of rhetoric?) Following Oakeshott and others, Rorty is strongly partial to the notion of philosophy as contributing to a "conversation" rather than as argumentative (producing some manner of intellectual trump card); yet he, no less than his philosophical interlocutors, tends to present his conceptualizations and analyses as ways of dispelling intellectual confusion, drawing entailments that have been overlooked or inadequately drawn, and generally bringing greater clarity and coherence to the intellectual landscape. That is, he offers his vocabulary not just as a *new* vocabulary but also as a *better* vocabulary; he wants the various aspects of his story to be received not merely as "conversational" (as attractive as that image is) but as rationally persuasive.

At the end of the day, one has to ask oneself: What would prompt an intellectual to divest himself or herself of meta-narratives, or Archimedean points or even attempts at an Archimedean point, of appeals to universal reason, ending with the jettisoning of the idea of truth itself? Doesn't the intellectual put himself or herself out of business once all of this has been cast aside? The answer in Rorty's case – as in the case of some of the other thinkers canvassed in this book – is that the commitment to truth (which makes no sense unless it claims some singular privilege for itself) is in some fundamental way antithetical to the demands of good citizenship; that is, Rorty thinks that a poetic, boundaries-expanding, pluralistic culture will do more to cultivate the citizens that modern democratic society needs than one oriented toward scientific and moral realism. It would of course be going too far to say that there exists a consensus among our twelve chosen thinkers that philosophy must lower its sights. Yet it is surely a little alarming when one surveys just how many of them seem to want to see philosophy knocked off its pedestal. The following selection of texts can serve as a reminder of how broad the chorus of such thinkers has become:

ARENDT: What Mercier de la Rivière once remarked about mathematical truth applies to all kinds of truth: "Euclide est un véritable despote; et les verities géométriques qu'il nous a transmises, sont des lois véritablement despotiques." ... Seen from the viewpoint of politics, truth has a despotic character.... It peremptorily claims to be acknowledged and precludes debate.... The modes of thought and communication that deal with truth, if seen from the political perspective, are necessarily domineering."[20]

GADAMER: "[The hermeneutical universalism that I have championed] limits the position of the philosopher in the modern world.... What man needs is not just the persistent posing of ultimate questions, but the sense of what is feasible, what is possible, what is correct, here and now. The philosopher, of all people, must, I think, be aware of the tension between what he claims to achieve and the reality in which he finds himself. The hermeneutical consciousness, which must be awakened and kept awake, recognizes that in the age of science philosophy's claim of superiority has something chimerical and unreal about it."[21]

FOUCAULT: "Truth isn't outside power, or lacking in power: contrary to a myth whose history and functions would repay further study, truth isn't the reward of free spirits, the child of protracted solitude, nor the privilege of those who have succeeded in liberating themselves. Truth is a thing of this world: it is produced only by virtue of multiple forms of constraint. And it induces regular effects of power. Each society has its régime of truth, its 'general politics' of truth: that is, the types of discourse which it accepts and makes function as true."[22]

RAWLS: "Political liberalism moves within the category of the political and leaves philosophy as it is. It leaves untouched all kinds of doctrines – religious, metaphysical, and moral – with their long traditions of development and interpretation.... For in presenting a freestanding political conception and not going beyond that, it is left entirely open to citizens and associations to formulate their own ways of going beyond, or of going deeper, so as to make that political conception congruent with their comprehensive doctrines. Political liberalism never denies or questions these doctrines in any way, so long as they are

---

[20] Hannah Arendt, *Between Past and Future* (New York: Penguin Books, 1993), pp. 240–241.
[21] Hans-Georg Gadamer, *Truth and Method*, 2nd rev. ed. (New York: Continuum, 1998), p. xxxviii.
[22] Michel Foucault, *Power/Knowledge*, ed. Colin Gordon (New York: Pantheon Books, 1980), p. 131.

politically reasonable.... Political liberalism views [the] idea of the reasonable as sufficient. The use of the concept of truth is not rejected or questioned, but left to the comprehensive doctrines to use or deny, or use some other idea instead."[23]

RORTY: "About two hundred years ago, the idea that truth was made rather than found began to take hold of the imagination of Europe.... The German idealists, the French revolutionaries, and the Romantic poets had in common a dim sense that human beings whose language changed so that they no longer spoke of themselves as responsible to nonhuman powers would thereby become a new kind of human beings. The difficulty faced by a philosopher who, like myself, is sympathetic to this suggestion – one who thinks of himself as auxiliary to the poet rather than to the physicist – is to avoid hinting that this suggestion gets something right, that my sort of philosophy corresponds to the way things really are. For this talk of correspondence brings back just the idea my sort of philosopher wants to get rid of, the idea that the world or the self has an intrinsic nature." (pp. 3 and 7–8)

If the postmodern sensibility is to be associated with the apprehension that aspiring to something as grand as truth is likely to produce more harm than benefit, then all of the theorists just quoted, as different as they are, share in that sensibility.[24]

Taken together, the non-philosophical (or even anti-philosophical[25]) reconception of political philosophy by Rawls and the anti-foundationalist pragmatism of Rorty as well as the endeavor on the part of postmodernists to debunk reason and truth certainly seem to present us with a rather deflating or anticlimactic conclusion to the grand tradition set in motion by Socrates and Plato. But of course the key question is whether it is appropriate to speak in this context of a "conclusion" to the theory tradition.[26] More likely, it is an *interlude*, and – one hopes – a short one.

---

[23] John Rawls, *Political Liberalism* (New York: Columbia University Press, 1996), pp. 375, 377–378, and 395.

[24] Let me quote Scruton again, since he very nicely captures my own view: "I believe that the concept of truth is fundamental to human discourse, that it is the precondition of any genuine dialogue, and that *real* respect for other people requires an even greater respect for truth" ("Richard Rorty's Legacy").

[25] Rawls himself certainly does not present his theory as anti-philosophical, but it is hard to avoid this entailment when one considers his suggestion (for instance, on page 37 of *Political Liberalism*) that even paragons of liberalism within the philosophical tradition such as Kant or Mill are implicitly anti-liberal or anti-civic insofar as they remain preoccupied with a quest for truth in the context of a properly philosophical contest among comprehensive doctrines, rather than (like Rawls) merely looking for common ground among reasonable views.

[26] Rorty writes: "My hunch is that Western social and political thought may have had the last *conceptual* revolution it needs" (p. 63; cf. the rhetoric of "we latecomers" on page 55). When one encounters that kind of Hegel-like suggestion, one naturally thinks of the "end of history" thesis promulgated by Francis Fukuyama around 1989 (the same year that Rorty published *Contingency, Irony, and Solidarity*). In that case too, the story was supposed to be over, but who today takes seriously the suggestion that history ended in 1989?

Epilogue: On Not Throwing in the Towel

GADAMER: I am very skeptical of every kind of pessimism. I find in all pessimism a certain lack of sincerity.

CARSTEN DUTT: Why?

GADAMER: Because no one can live without hope.[1]

Our topic in this book has been twentieth-century political philosophy. Twenty-first-century political philosophy doesn't yet exist. It is impossible to imagine that the twenty-first century *won't* generate political philosophy, but it has not yet taken shape, and therefore it is anyone's guess what it will be. In my early career as a theorist, my thinking moved within a zone of theorizing largely delimited by about half a dozen important thinkers: Arendt, Habermas, Gadamer, Strauss, MacIntyre, and Charles Taylor. My life as a theorist has been in large part a continuing dialogue with these thinkers, and an effort to put them in a dialogue with each other. As I hope this book evidences, this dialogue, or set of dialogues, is still in progress. Naturally, the longer one reflects on these thinkers, the more attentive one becomes to the philosophical weaknesses in each of them.[2] I am certainly no longer the Arendtian or Habermasian or Gadamerian or Straussian or communitarian that I may have been at earlier stages of my intellectual journey.[3] But in

---

[1] *Gadamer in Conversation: Reflections and Commentary*, ed. Richard E. Palmer (New Haven, CT: Yale University Press, 2001), p. 83.

[2] In the course of my life as a theorist I have been able to witness six of the dozen thinkers highlighted in this book (Oakeshott, Gadamer, Habermas, MacIntyre, Rawls, and Rorty) in dialogue with a roomful of skeptical interlocutors. In no case did I see any of them offer such a compelling account of their philosophical views that they succeeded in silencing or winning over their critics. Being an exemplary theorist certainly does not mean winning every argument. I have made clear that in my view we (we theorists and we human beings) cannot relinquish our pursuit of an Archimedean point. But if anti-foundationalism means that no theorist has yet come up with a particular set of arguments that trumps all rival arguments, then of course I too am an anti-foundationalist.

[3] The reader will notice that being a Rawlsian has never formed part of my intellectual identity. The fact is, my view of how to be a citizen is probably closer to Rawls than to any of the theorists who *have* left an imprint on my intellectual identity. But the point here is that one's stance as a citizen and

229

good Hegelian fashion, these earlier stages of theorizing do not get simply discarded or jettisoned as one obtains better insight into the limits of these philosophical sources (again, they *all* have their limitations and weak spots). Restating some of the things I learned from these thinkers cannot help but be an exercise in criticism (and self-criticism), but focusing just on the criticism does not do justice to the philosophical education supplied by such a dialogue. If we have succeeded in our task in this book, we have shown that it is possible to show respect for these thinkers as interlocutors in a critical dialogue without bowing down to them as gurus.[4] That is, we have sought to treat them as deserving of gratitude for serving as exemplars of the practice of political philosophy in its most ambitious versions without absolving them of tough intellectual challenges.

I began this book with an account of Isaiah Berlin's philosophy of moral pluralism as an Anglicized, less *Angst*-ridden version of Max Weber's notion of human beings as divided in their allegiance among a diversity of gods. However, if this Weberian-Berlinian conception of human beings as being unavoidably and untranscendably subject to competing ideals is true – if the human condition is defined not by "the Human Good" but by plural and irreconcilable goods – what is the point of political philosophy as a quest for an overarching idea of the ultimate standard, the ultimate Human Good? So after our survey of a set of leading twentieth-century contenders for the mantle of an authoritative political philosophy, we come back to the question with which we started: If none of the considered rivals for the crown can intellectually vanquish their competitors, why does political philosophy as such not succumb to the skeptical anti-metaphysics of Weber and Berlin? Can political philosophy be vindicated, or does it make more sense clear-sightedly to reject it, as Weber and Berlin seem to do? If all of the contending political philosophies capture *some* of the truth about the normative foundations of human experience but none of them captures all of it, would not that prove Berlin right in his view that political philosophy fails to redeem its intellectual promises and that normative pluralism is the ultimate truth? In short, is belief in the possibility of political philosophy tantamount to a kind of (implausible) religious faith?

---

the formation of one's intellectual identity are (in my view) two different things, and it is a mistake to see one as a necessary or natural entailment from the other. If this strikes some readers as paradoxical, so be it.

4 In the view of Brian Barry, as we saw in our first prologue, epic theorists such as Arendt, Strauss, Voegelin, and Oakeshott offer nothing intellectually "chewable"; disciples swallow their doctrines whole whereas non-disciples find nothing worth engaging with and hence spit them out. As should

Among our authors, this theme of philosophy needing to be able to redeem its promises is particularly emphasized by MacIntyre. As I put it in a recent article, trying to encapsulate MacIntyre's view:

Why should one pursue philosophy as a way of life at all unless one has a viable hope of achieving *the truth* (i.e., true philosophical views concerning topics that philosophers have spent centuries arguing about)? (To borrow [MacIntyre's standard analogy with natural science]: would one devote a whole lifetime to a career as a cancer researcher if one thought that solving the mysteries of cancer were in principle out of reach?)[5]

One can certainly see the force of this challenge. However, as I argued in the first prologue, normative pluralism makes little sense unless "monist" thinkers have already articulated in a robust way the diverse philosophical ideals that define this pluralism. As I put it in that discussion, philosophical pluralism is in that sense *parasitic upon* philosophical "monism." We need to know what the normative alternatives are even if we are not in a position to declare that one of these alternatives has consolidated its authority in relation to the others.

Two of our twelve theorists (namely MacIntyre and Habermas) emphasize the theme that philosophy should henceforth be a collaborative enterprise – that it should be far less focused on singular epic thinkers than it has been historically.[6] This book is built on the opposite premise, that

---

be obvious, that is not at all my view. There is a huge difference between offering arguments that are weak or questionable in various ways, and offering (as Barry thinks) *no* arguments.

[5] Ronald Beiner, "The Parochial and the Universal: MacIntyre's Idea of the University," *Revue internationale de philosophie*, no. 264 (2013), pp. 169–182, at pp. 170–171.

[6] See, for instance, the view of philosophy attributed to Adolf Reinach (and implicitly endorsed by MacIntyre) in MacIntyre, *Edith Stein: A Philosophical Prologue 1913–1922* (Lanham, MD: Rowman and Littlefield, 2006), pp. 57–58 ("Philosophy ... is to become a cooperative project, just as physics or astronomy is, rather than an arena of conflicting standpoints"). Cf. pages 139–141; as well as MacIntyre, *God, Philosophy, Universities* (London: Continuum, 2009), p. 17. For discussion, see my essay, "The Parochial and the Universal," cited in the previous note. In "Replies," *Revue internationale de philosophie*, no. 264 (2013), pp. 201–220 at p. 212, MacIntyre surprisingly disputes my claim that he "endorses" Reinach's view. As regards Habermas, see, for instance, "Does Philosophy Still Have a Purpose?" (in Habermas, *Philosophical-Political Profiles*, trans. Frederick G. Lawrence [London: Heinemann, 1983]), in which Habermas heralds the end of a "style of thought bound to individual erudition and personal testimony" (p. 2), and welcomes a mode of post-philosophical critical thought that "would no longer have any need of the organizational form of a doctrine embodied in individual philosophers" (p. 17). See also "The Dialectics of Rationalization: An Interview with Jürgen Habermas," *Telos*, no. 49 (1981), p. 30: "The thinker as life-style, as vision, as expressive self-portrait is no longer possible." Habermas adds: "I am not a producer of a *Weltanschauung*," which sounds somewhat reminiscent of Brian Barry urging us to beware of philosophical gurus. See also Michel Foucault, *Power/Knowledge*, ed. Colin Gordon (New York: Pantheon Books, 1980), pp. 126–131, for Foucault's discussion of the eclipse of "the 'universal' intellectual" ("the rhapsodist of the eternal" [p. 129], capable of delivering "a new

philosophy (or at least political philosophy) thrives when it is a contest of grand visions articulated by grand thinkers. Things are in something less than a thriving state when, as is largely true in our current theoretical situation, arguments get traded back and forth between third- or fourth- or fifth-generation Arendtians and Straussians and Habermasians and Foucaultians and Rawlsians, reflecting larger philosophical visions that originated in the 1950s or 1960s or 1970s. We are still largely drawing upon the intellectual capital of earlier decades. This overstates the case somewhat. But it is close enough to the truth to challenge the MacIntyre-Habermas view that we ought to shift from theory associated with epic theorists to theory as a collaborative enterprise. If the story told in this book is persuasive, MacIntyre and Habermas are *themselves* twentieth-century epic theorists, and hence, to some extent, their own contributions and their own stature refute their aspirations for the theory enterprise.

Is it a coincidence that political philosophy seems to flourish when the stakes are supremely high? We need to ask: Why was the mid-twentieth century (according to our depiction) a "golden age" for political philosophy? Why was the mid-seventeenth century a golden age for political philosophy? Why is the present *not* a golden age? What was driving these theorists, and why could their purposes be fulfilled only through epic theory? Consider the scope of what some of our twelve thinkers undertook to do with their theorizing: Arendt wanted to reassert the idea of human dignity that had been so viciously battered by the Nazis, and hence tried to re-establish the tradition of republican political thought from the ground up, so to speak. (To me it seems fairly clear that central to what was animating Arendt was the idea of responding to the twentieth century's revelation of politics at its very worst by appealing to a counter-image of politics as supremely lofty, ennobling, and even redemptive, drawing inspiration from the civic-republican tradition but equipping it with an entirely novel philosophical framework of her own design.) Gadamer wanted to offer a more humble conception of the philosophical life, as an alternative to the prophetic hubris of Heidegger, as well as trying to restore an appreciation of the innate hermeneutical resources of ethical life. Löwith offered the radical idea (seemingly hopeless as it might be) of re-enfolding ourselves in a sense

world-view" [p. 130]): "we are at present experiencing the disappearance of the figure of the 'great writer'" (p. 129). Needless to say, the irony here is that the desire on the part of MacIntyre, Habermas, and Foucault to move beyond a conception of philosophy focused on individual epic theorists is, in each of these cases, gainsaid by their *own* status as epic theorists.

of nature that is "one and whole" (an experience of the cosmos as *das Eine und Ganze*).[7] Strauss and Voegelin gave us, in each case, an epic engagement with the entire Western philosophical tradition, in order to trace where (in their respective accounts) things began to slip, where the rot set in. And so on.[8] As the stakes get diminished (with Rawls and Rorty), philosophy gets banalized (deliberately banalized?).

We began this book by quoting Brian Barry's philosophical verdict on Arendt, Oakeshott, Strauss, Voegelin, and probably a few others included in these chapters. My enterprise, quite explicitly, has been to respond to Barry's slander against epic theory. Hence, our purpose has been to explain why Brian Barry's story about the "revival" of political philosophy is the wrong story. That is, we have tried to show how one can be *respectful* of the leading political philosophers – and regard them as doing something that is in fact more important than what we get from theorists who are not gurus – while not falling for their mistakes or yielding to their sometimes ridiculous conceits (as distinguished from Arendtian or Straussian or Voegelinian disciples who *do* fall for these conceits). One can go so far as to say that Barry's view is the opposite of the correct one – political philosophers who are not "gurus" (that is, who are not reflecting in the grandest possible way on the ends of life) *are not fulfilling their job description!*

If I am right in claiming that the "golden age" of political philosophy occurred in the immediate post-war period, and Brian Barry is wrong in

---

[7] Karl Löwith, *Der Weltbegriff der neuzeitlichen Philosophie* (Heidelberg: Carl Winter Universitätsverlag, 1960), pp. 7, 19, 20, and 23; Löwith, *Nature, History, and Existentialism*, trans. Arnold Levison (Evanston, IL: Northwestern University Press, 1966), pp. 139 and 140; Löwith, *My Life in Germany Before and After 1933*, trans. Elizabeth King (London: The Athlone Press, 1994), pp. 166 and 167. Concerning the broad intellectual tradition to which Löwith is likely alluding in all these texts, see Jan Assman, *Moses the Egyptian* (Cambridge, MA: Harvard University Press, 1998), pp. 139–143. As Hans Blumenberg puts it in *The Legitimacy of the Modern World*, trans. Robert M. Wallace (Cambridge, MA: MIT Press, 1985), p. 28, Löwith's critique of historicism is presented in anticipation, so to speak, of "the recurrence of unhistory" – without Löwith giving any indication of exactly how we are supposed to resurrect the experience of cosmos that we have lost. On the lack of a solution in Löwith, cf. *The Collected Works of Eric Voegelin, Volume 11: Published Essays 1953–1965*, ed. Ellis Sandoz (Columbia, MO: University of Missouri Press, 2000), p. 237.

[8] To be sure, one is not obliged to respond to the catastrophes of the mid-twentieth century by formulating critiques of modernity. Habermas was nearly sixteen years old at the time of the defeat of Hitler's Germany, so surely the totalitarian madness left no less of an imprint on him than it did on the others. (For a discussion by Habermas of the impact of this formative experience on his subsequent intellectual career, see his address on receipt of the 2004 Kyoto Prize, "Public Space and Political Public Sphere: The Biographical Roots of Two Motifs in My Thought": http://www.inamori-f.or.jp/laureates/k20_c_jurgen/img/lct_e.pdf.) Yet his philosophical response was not to participate in trashing modernity but to try to re-articulate the normative aspirations that, if they could be redeemed, would render modernity worthy of affirmation.

claiming that it occurred in 1971, then this may prompt a broader reflection on what gives rise to epic theorizing. Think of what these thinkers (Barry's "gurus") lived through: a titanic war of ideologies; genocide on an absolutely unprecedented scale; the world upturned and made to suffer vehement convulsions. I do not want to suggest that large issues of war and justice were not also in play in the years leading up to 1971, but they are not quite comparable in terms of what was at stake. Nor does one want to be too quick to say that the world should go to hell just so that theory will raise its ambitions. Still, there does seem to be a relation, perhaps an essential relation, between living in a world where the grandest alternatives are on display, and what motivates thinkers to embrace truly grand theory.[9]

One encounters an abundance of personal and professional connections among the particular constellation of thinkers treated in this book, which prompts reflection on whether the flourishing of political philosophy is a *generational* phenomenon. (Obviously, similar reflection is elicited by other notable "axial" moments in the history of political philosophy: Socrates, Xenophon, Plato, and Aristotle, of course; or Hobbes, Harrington, and Locke; or Schiller, Hölderlin, and Hegel.) Arendt, Strauss, Gadamer, and Löwith (as well as Hans Jonas) all knew each other going back to the early 1920s, and it is possible that all of them were in the same seminar room when Plato's *Sophist* or Aristotle's *Ethics* was being interpreted by Martin Heidegger. Strauss, Löwith, Arendt, and Habermas all taught at the New School for Social Research at various points. Arendt and Strauss were (mutually hostile) colleagues at the University of Chicago, where Strauss's classes were attended by Rorty. According to Arendt's biographer, the young Leo Strauss had unrequited romantic designs on the young Hannah Arendt![10] Löwith was recruited to Heidelberg by Gadamer, and then Habermas in turn was recruited to Heidelberg by Gadamer and Löwith together. Arendt,

---

[9] Consider Gadamer's poignant account of the philosophical searching after authoritative worldviews on the part of young scholars in Germany in the wake of the Great War: "The general feeling was one of disorientation. One day ... a number of us got together and asked: 'What should we do?' 'How can the world be reconstructed?' The answers were very different. Some thought we ought to follow Max Weber; others, Otto von Gierke; others still, Rabindranath Tagore." "Gadamer on Strauss: An Interview," *Interpretation*, Vol. 12, no. 1 (Jan. 1984), p. 1. For two other versions of the same story, see Gadamer, *Philosophical Apprenticeships*, trans. Robert R. Sullivan (Cambridge, MA: MIT Press, 1985), pp. 14–15; and *Gadamer in Conversation*, ed. Palmer, p. 103. Again and again, human affairs give us the sense of everything being utterly turned upside down, which is not a trivial motivation to return to the search for philosophical ultimates.

[10] Elisabeth Young-Bruehl, *Hannah Arendt: For Love of the World* (New Haven, CT: Yale University Press, 1982), p. 98.

when she made trips to Germany after the war, paid social visits to Löwith in Heidelberg and to Voegelin in Munich.[11] Strauss, Gadamer, and Löwith sent each other their books, and they exchanged arguments back and forth concerning the philosophical validity of those books. Famous debates took place (mainly in print, but sometimes also in person) between Arendt and Voegelin; Strauss and Voegelin; Gadamer and Habermas; MacIntyre and Rorty; Rorty and Habermas; Habermas and Foucault; and Habermas and Rawls. Is all of this merely contingent, and irrelevant to political philosophy as political philosophy? I tend to think it is relevant.

I remain an unreserved and undeflateable optimist on the question of whether political philosophy in the epic mode has a future. Political philosophizing of the epic sort is an ineliminable aspect of the human condition. So if it is currently dormant, the proper question, I believe, is not whether it will return but when. Will it be twenty years? Or fifty? Or one hundred? It is impossible to say. (It is a bit like Heidegger's waiting-for-a-new-god.) But if it is a question of waiting for the return of epic political philosophy, we should, in the meantime, clarify for ourselves what it is and why it is necessary. That way, we will at least be able to recognize it when it returns.

---

[11] *Within Four Walls: The Correspondence between Hannah Arendt and Heinrich Blücher,* ed. Lotte Kohler (New York: Harcourt, 2000), pp. 205, 208, 294, 378. Consider also the following quite memorable story of the first encounter between Arendt and Habermas, related by Peter L. Berger: "There is a sort of apostolic succession in [the] tradition of revolutionary dreams, from Weimar to Paris to New York – and back again. It is an ambiguous tradition and, in my opinion, a harmful one. Yet it has nobility, and Arendt represented that nobility with honor. I will take the liberty of [offering] a personal episode. It occurred in New York in that fateful year 1968. Several of us were gathered in the apartment of Aron Gurwitsch, a philosopher who knew Arendt from Paris. The main purpose of the gathering was to introduce Arendt to Jürgen Habermas, who had recently emerged as one of the luminaries of the German New Left and who was in America on a visiting professorship. Arendt arrived late and was introduced to Habermas, who got up and greeted her very deferentially. They sat down facing each other. Arendt said nothing for a moment, looked steadily at Habermas with an expression of enormous pleasure, then exclaimed: 'Jürgen Habermas!' The ambiguous torch had been handed on." "A Woman of This Century," *New York Times,* April 25, 1982.

Index

action
  Arendt and, 20–24, 20n23
  belief and (Rorty), 217n4
  free (Arendt), 20n23
  generating narrative-worthy events (Arendt),
    16n21
  generating something new (Arendt), 23
  traits of genuine (Arendt), 20n24
Adorno, Theodor, xiv, 140, 151, 160
adventurers versus pilgrims (Oakeshott), 26
After Virtue (MacIntyre, 1981), x, 171,
    172, 174
Agamben, Giorgio, xv
agency, 21
aggression,
  innate (Freud), xxxix
Alexander, Jeffrey C., 137n8
Anaxagoras, 46
anti-foundationalism, 225
  defined, xxvii
Aquinas, Thomas, 168
Arendt, Hannah (1906–75), 1–24, 51, 77, 92, 95,
    113, 122, 147, 215, 232, 234
  compared to Oakeshott, 37–40
  Heidegger and, 6n8, 7n11
  Strauss and, 39n33
  Voegelin and, 105n36
Aristotelianism, ethical, 169
  Aquinas and, 168
Aristotle, 24, 46, 49, 50, 60, 65, 81, 123
association
  civil (Oakeshott), 28–29, 31, 38
  dramatic and intelligent versus organic
    (Oakeshott), 26
  enterprise (Oakeshott), 27–28, 32
  freedom of (Weil), 111
  practice-based (Oakeshott), 28
  purposive (Oakeshott), 30, 32
  workers' (Weil), 112

atheism, lii n26
  orthodox (Strauss), 24n27
Autobiographical Reflections (Voegelin), 93
autonomy, 27, 54, 141, 208, 219
  of practical experience, (Oakeshott), 27n5, 32,
    33n14, 36n25
Averroes, 46
Averroism, 43n7
Avicenna, 46

Bacon, Francis, 50, 61, 88
Badiou, Alain, xv
Barnes, Julian, 171n6
Barry, Brian, xi, 39, 107, 170n4, 233
Bayle, Pierre, 46
Benjamin, Walter, xiv
Bentham, Jeremy, xii, 162
Berlin, Isaiah, 24, 212–214, 212n27, 230
Bernstein, Richard, 131, 134
Between Facts and Norms (Habermas), 138
Bin Laden, Osama, lv
Bloom, Allan, 42, 77
Bohr, Niels, 61
Bosanquet, Bernard, xi
Brahe, Tycho, 67
Brudner, Alan, 54n24
Burckhardt, Jacob, 71n19, 89n18
bureaucratic state apparatus (Habermas), 140

Camus, Albert, xv
capitalism, 98
  MacIntyre and, 183
capitalist enterprise (Habermas), 140
Carens, Joseph, xviii
cave, fable of (Plato), 49, 50
censorship, 110
  Freud and, 42
charisma (Weber), li
Chomsky, Noam, 152n4, 165

Index

Index

Index

Index

politics (*cont.*)
  localization of (MacIntyre), 180
  as meaning-conferring (Arendt), 2
  multicultural, 190
  as noble and vexatious (Ignatieff), ln25
  as a pact with satanic powers (Weber), liv, lii
  of philosophy, 42
  as rational discourse (Habermas), 135–50
  of the soul (Weil), 108–21
  of truth (Foucault), 161, 227
  pathological nature of modern
    (Voegelin), 103
  performativity of (Arendt), 1–24, 12n16
  Platonic-Aristotelian, 81
  premeditated ideology and (Oakeshott), 34
  privileged status of (Arendt), 1
  rationalist, 33
  revolutionary (from Cromwell on), 74
  Science as a Vocation (Weber) and, xliii
  as second-rate human activity (Oakeshott), 38
  ultimate meaning of (Arendt), 9
Politics, The (Aristotle), xvi, 60
Politics as a Vocation (Weber), l–lv
Polybius, 74
polytheism (Weber), liiin28
Popper, Karl, xii
positivism, 166n27
power-right-truth triangle (Foucault), 161
practice (MacIntyre), 176
praxis (action), 16n20
primordial drives (Freud), xxxv
proceduralism (Habermas), 136n6
progress, 74
  liberal, 220
  secular philosophies of, 97
  Weber and, xlv
property, xxxvi
Protagoras, 46
psyche, 100
  defined (Voegelin), 100n24
  fundamental forces in, xxxviii
psychoanalysis, xxiv
  Habermas and, 135
public sphere (Habermas), 135
punishment, xxxix
Puritanism (Voegelin), 93
purposive-rational action (Habermas), 140

Rancière, Jacques, xv
rationalism (Oakeshott), 33n17, 34n20
Rationalism in Politics (Oakeshott), 34
rationality
  communicative (Habermas), 135, 139–46,
    146n25
  universal, 175
rationalization (Weber), 78n44

Rawls, John (1921–2002), 84, 191, 198–214,
    215, 233
  Berlin and, 212n27, 213, 214n29
  Foucault and, 205n16
  Habermas and, 205n15, 206
  Nietzsche and, 205n16
  Taylor and, 197n16
reality
  as a manifestation of the divine (Voegelin), 92,
    94
  principle (Freud), xxxiii
reason, xxvi
  communicative potential of (Habermas), 147
  crisis of (Strauss), 139
  dialogical, 105, 145
  and fairness, 204
  Freud and, xlii
  hegemonic, 145
  Kantian, versus Heideggerian/Derridean/
    Foucaultian, 145
  modern/postmodern critique of, 145
  monological self-centered versus dialogical
    communicative (Habermas), 149
  moral solidarity and (Habermas), 146
  natural, 134
  noetic (Voegelin), 105
  political, 35
  post-Kantian formalistic, 141, 147
  practical, 147
  procedural, 141n18
  public (Rawls), 214n30
  revelation and (Veogelin), 96n12
  secular, 104, 106
  subject-centered (Habermas), 149
  unitary (Gadamer), 150n34
Reason in the Age of Science (Gadamer, 1981), x
reasonableness (Rawls), 203n12
reasoning
  moral (Habermas), 150n32
  practical, 174
    communal, 180
    universal rationality and, 175
Reckless Mind, The (Lilla), 224
reflection
  communal, on common good
    (MacIntyre), 175
  moral (MacIntyre), 172, 178n21
Reformation, the, 49n15, 93
  MacIntyre and, 169n2
religion
  eschatological, 91
  as a form of cowardice (Freud), xxxiv
  Freud and, xxxiii
  philosophy and, 43, 183
  problem of theodicy and, liv
  Rolland and, xxxi

244

Index

Wolin, Sheldon, 22n25
women's rights, 35
work
    Arendt and, 17–19
    instrumentality and (Arendt), 19
world-alienation (Arendt), 9, 67n9, 209
    Löwith and, 9n14
worldlessness (Arendt), 9

worldliness (Arendt), 9, 17

Xenophon, 46

Young, Iris, xi

Žižek, Slovoj, xv
Zweig, Stefan, xxxvii

CPSIA information can be obtained
at www.ICGtesting.com
Printed in the USA
FFOW02n2051090118
44459504-44252FF